Snow White with the Red Hair

Sorata Akiduki

15

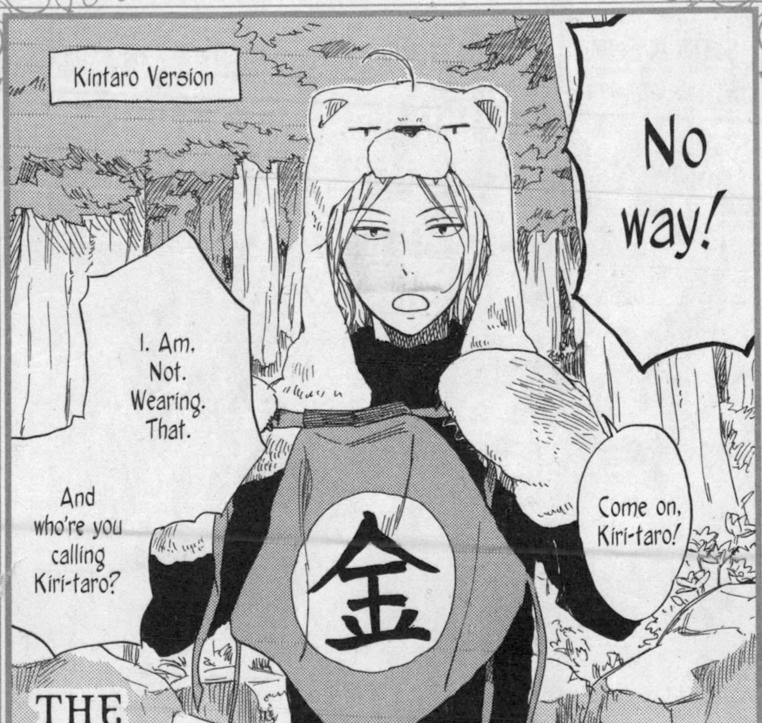
Kintaro Version
No way!
I. Am. Not. Wearing. That.
Come on, Kiri-taro!
And who're you calling Kiri-taro?
THE END

THE STORY

Shirayuki was born with beautiful hair as red as apples, but when her rare hair earns her unwanted attention from the notorious prince Raj, she's forced to flee her home. A young man named Zen helps her in the forest of the neighboring kingdom, Clarines, and it turns out he is that kingdom's second prince! Shirayuki decides to accompany Zen back to Wistal, the capital city of Clarines.

Shirayuki has met all manner of people since becoming a court herbalist, and her relationship with Zen continues to grow, as the two have finally made their feelings known to each other.

SHIRAYUKI
"They say that red is the color of destiny."
PRINCE ZEN
The second prince of the kingdom of Clarines.
Working as a court herbalist. Has feelings for Zen—feelings that he shares.
RYU
MITSUHIDE & KIKI
OBI

Shirayuki's boss. A brainy kid who became a court herbalist at a young age.

Zen's aides. They're good friends who share a strong bond.

Former assassin. Currently, Zen's underling. Served as Shirayuki's bodyguard for part of her stay in Lilias.

After becoming a full-fledged court herbalist, Shirayuki takes a work trip to the northern city of Lilias with her boss, Ryu. When a mysterious illness starts spreading, they put their skills to use and figure out what's causing it.

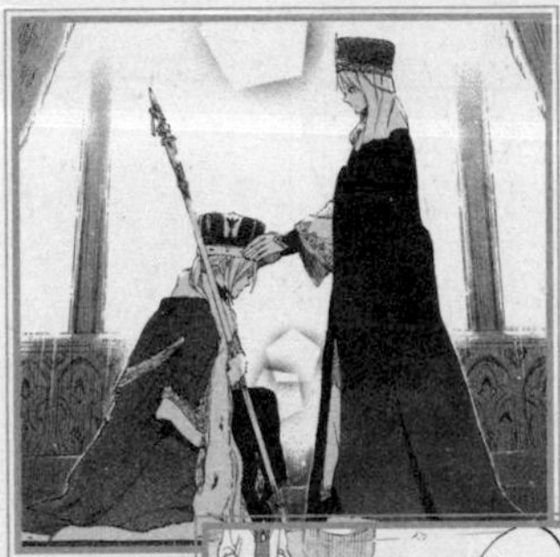

Once back in Wistal, the newly crowned king Izana orders Shirayuki and Ryu to return to Lilias. But this time, it's no mere business trip—it's a personnel transfer for two whole years. Still, Shirayuki finds the resolve to do what she must to advance her career. Zen also dispatches Obi to Lilias, where the capital trio begin their new lives.

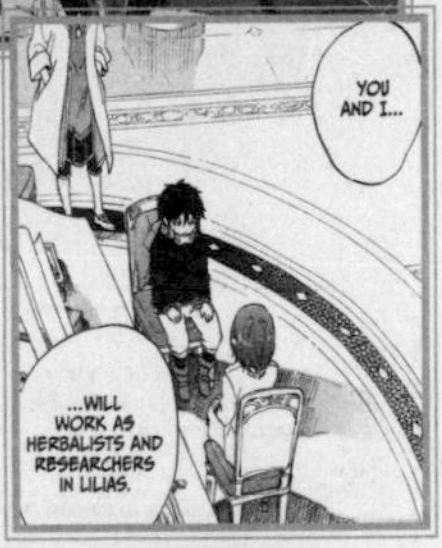
YOU AND I...
...WILL WORK AS HERBALISTS AND RESEARCHERS IN LILIAS.

Shirayuki starts researching how to neutralize the toxin of the glowing orimmallys—the same plant that caused the earlier outbreak. With help from colleagues in the City of Academics, the research progresses well enough, but they can't figure out how to retain the glowing properties of the seeds once the toxin is removed.

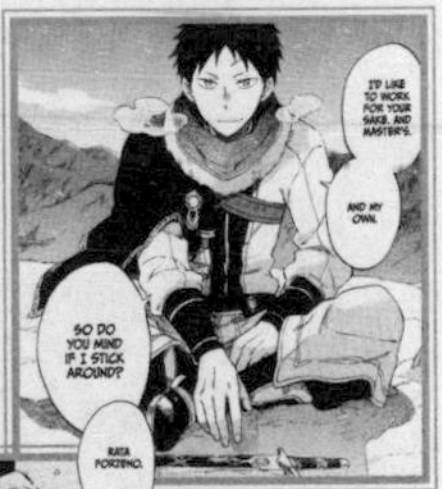
I'D LIKE TO WORK FOR YOUR SAKE, AND MASTER'S.
AND MY OWN.
SO DO YOU MIND IF I STICK AROUND?

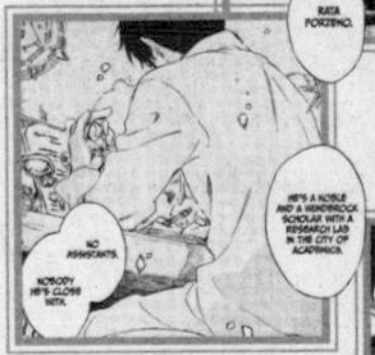
RATA FORZENO.
HE'S A NOBLE AND A WUNDEROCK SCHOLAR WITH A RESEARCH LAB IN THE CITY OF ACADEMICS.
NO ASSISTANTS.
NOBODY HE'S CLOSE WITH.

The search for scholars who deal with light and heat leads the group to a noble named Rata Forzeno, who studies wunderocks and other glowing stones. The slippery noble keeps evading Shirayuki's grasp, however, so as a final resort, she manages to get him invited to a royal soiree at the palace!

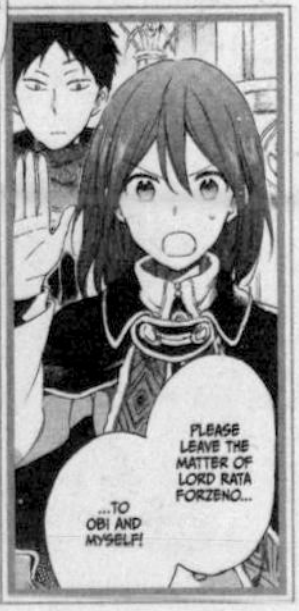
PLEASE LEAVE THE MATTER OF LORD RATA FORZENO...
...TO OBI AND MYSELF!

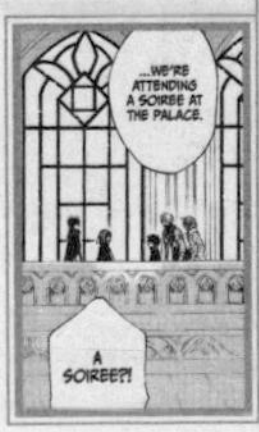
...WE'RE ATTENDING A SOIREE AT THE PALACE.
A SOIREE?!

VOLUME 15
TABLE *of* CONTENTS

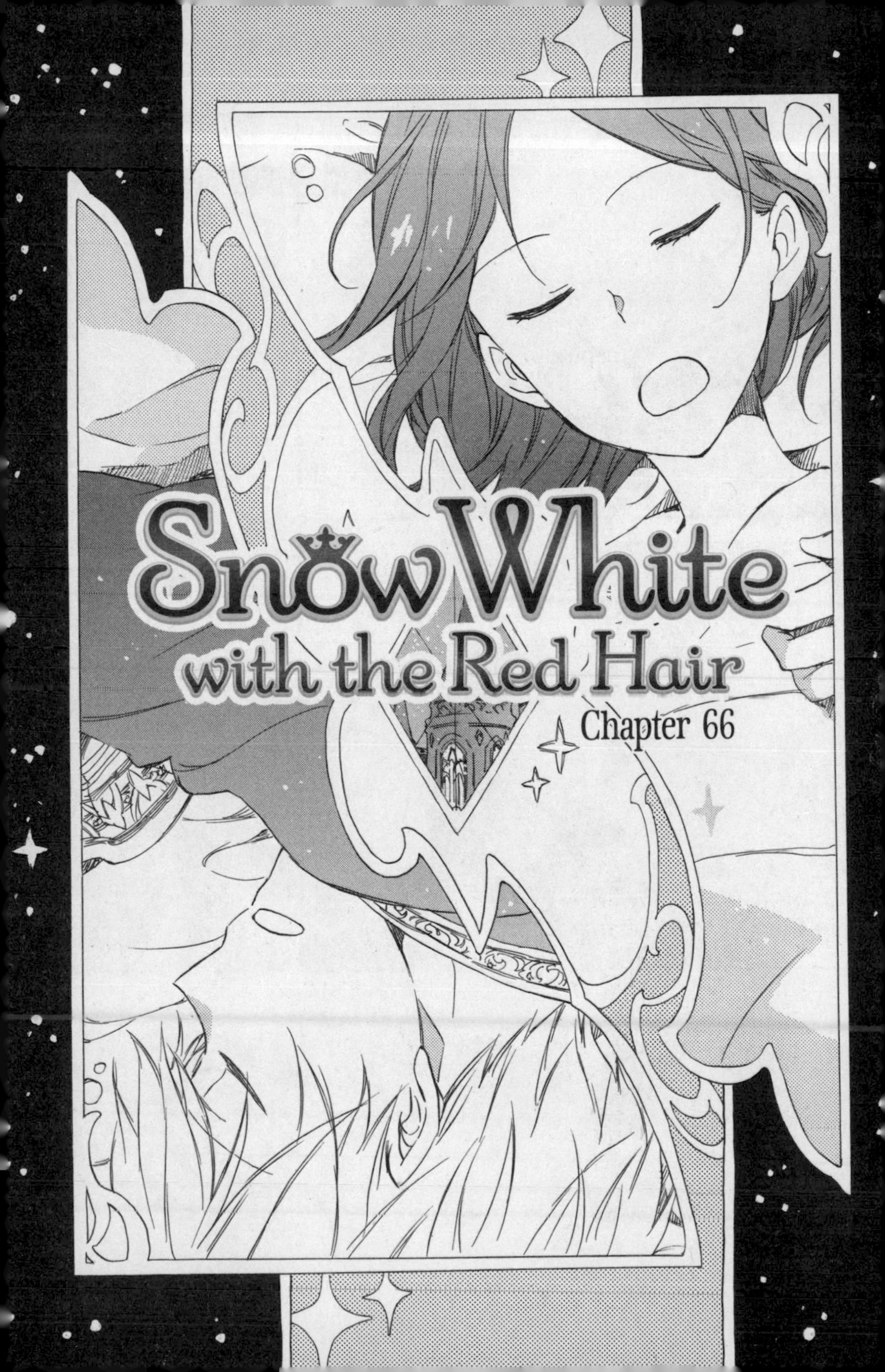
Snow White
with the Red Hair
Chapter 66

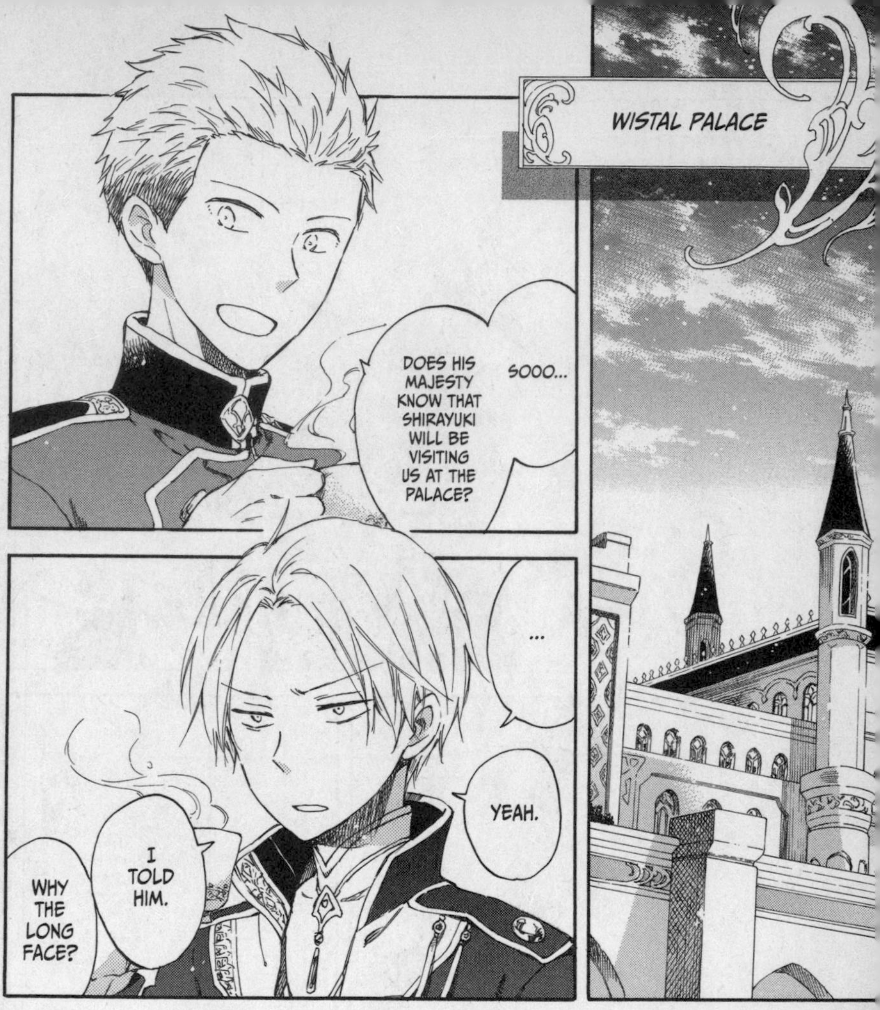
WISTAL PALACE
SOOO...
DOES HIS MAJESTY KNOW THAT SHIRAYUKI WILL BE VISITING US AT THE PALACE?
...
YEAH.
I TOLD HIM.
WHY THE LONG FACE?

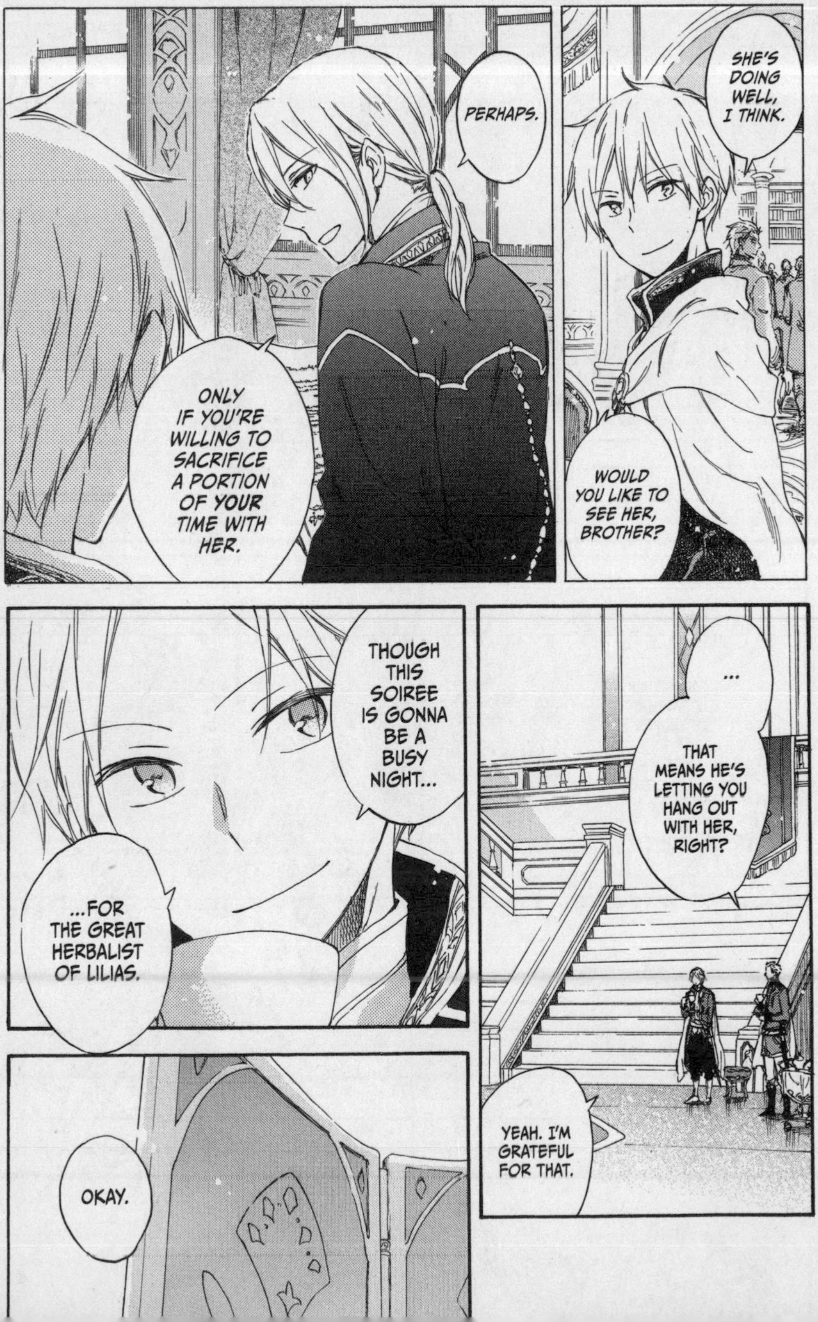
SHE'S DOING WELL, I THINK.
WOULD YOU LIKE TO SEE HER, BROTHER?
PERHAPS.
ONLY IF YOU'RE WILLING TO SACRIFICE A PORTION OF YOUR TIME WITH HER.
...
THAT MEANS HE'S LETTING YOU HANG OUT WITH HER, RIGHT?
YEAH. I'M GRATEFUL FOR THAT.
THOUGH THIS SOIREE IS GONNA BE A BUSY NIGHT...
...FOR THE GREAT HERBALIST OF LILIAS.
OKAY.

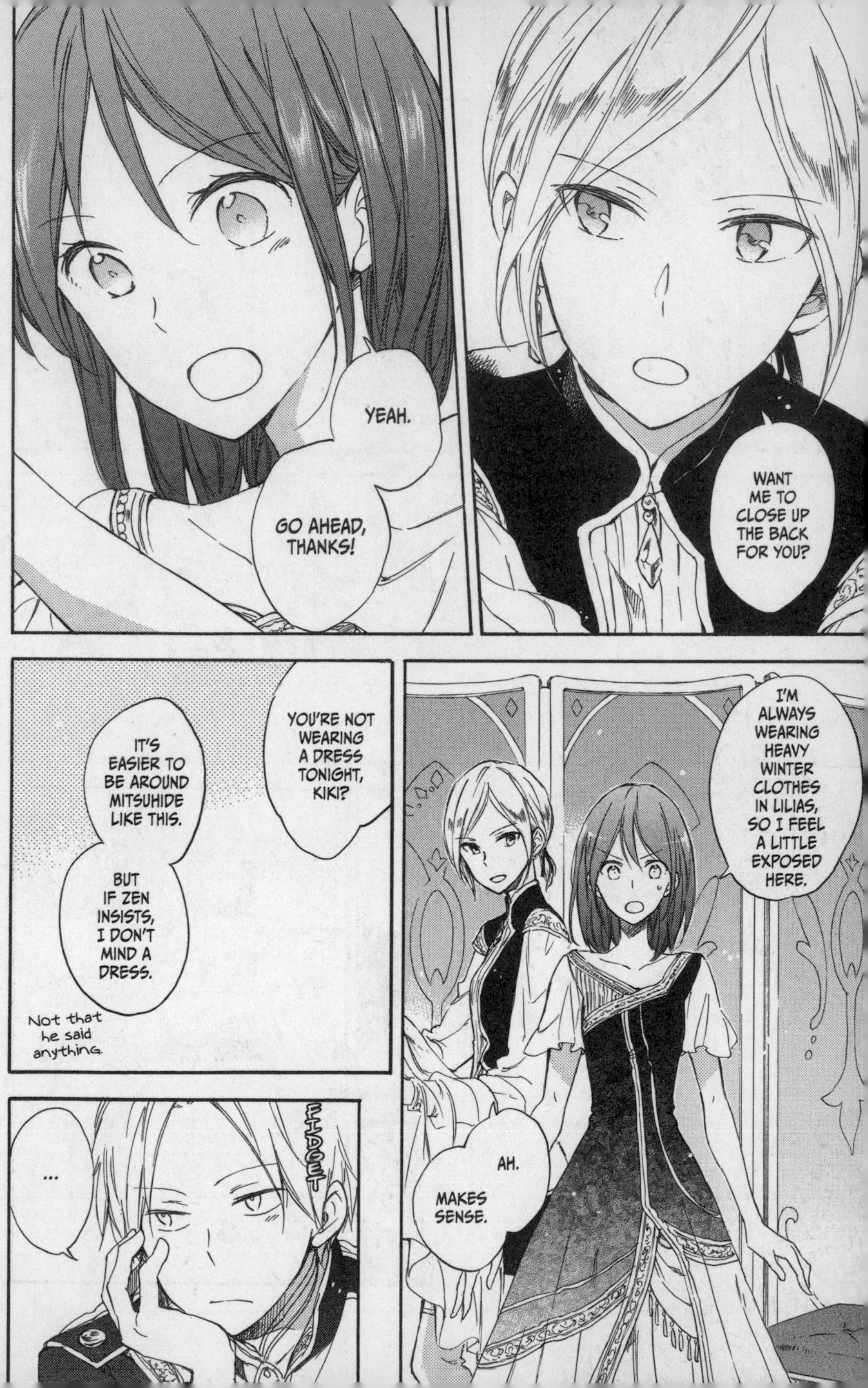
WANT ME TO CLOSE UP THE BACK FOR YOU?
YEAH.
GO AHEAD, THANKS!
I'M ALWAYS WEARING HEAVY WINTER CLOTHES IN LILIAS, SO I FEEL A LITTLE EXPOSED HERE.
AH.
MAKES SENSE.
YOU'RE NOT WEARING A DRESS TONIGHT, KIKI?
IT'S EASIER TO BE AROUND MITSUHIDE LIKE THIS.
BUT IF ZEN INSISTS, I DON'T MIND A DRESS.
Not that he said anything.
FIDGET
...

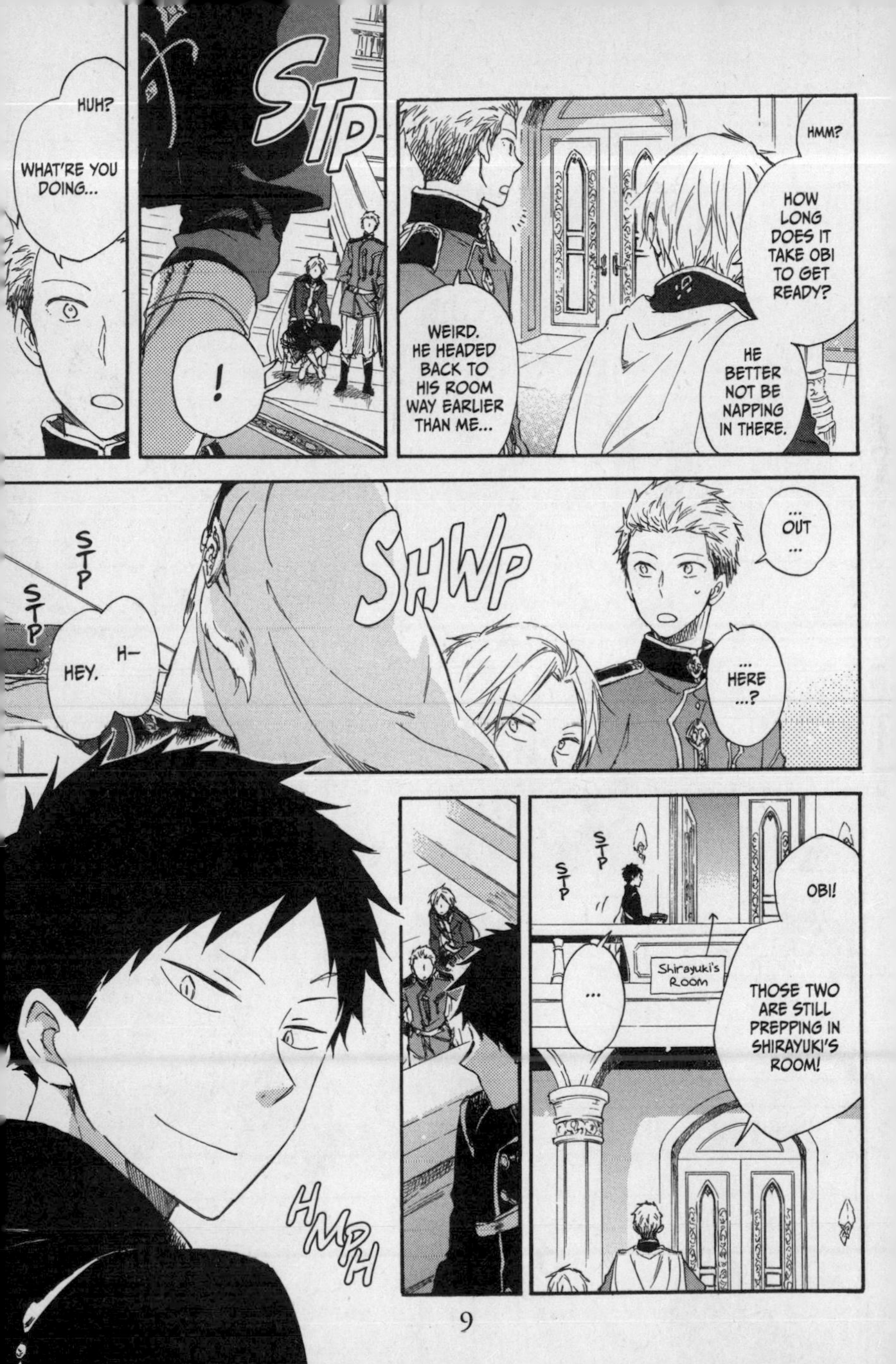
HMM?
HOW LONG DOES IT TAKE OBI TO GET READY?
HE BETTER NOT BE NAPPING IN THERE.
WEIRD. HE HEADED BACK TO HIS ROOM WAY EARLIER THAN ME...
STP
!
HUH?
WHAT'RE YOU DOING...
... OUT ...
... HERE ...?
SHWP
STP
STP
H—
HEY.
OBI!
THOSE TWO ARE STILL PREPPING IN SHIRAYUKI'S ROOM!
STP
STP
Shirayuki's Room
...
HMPH

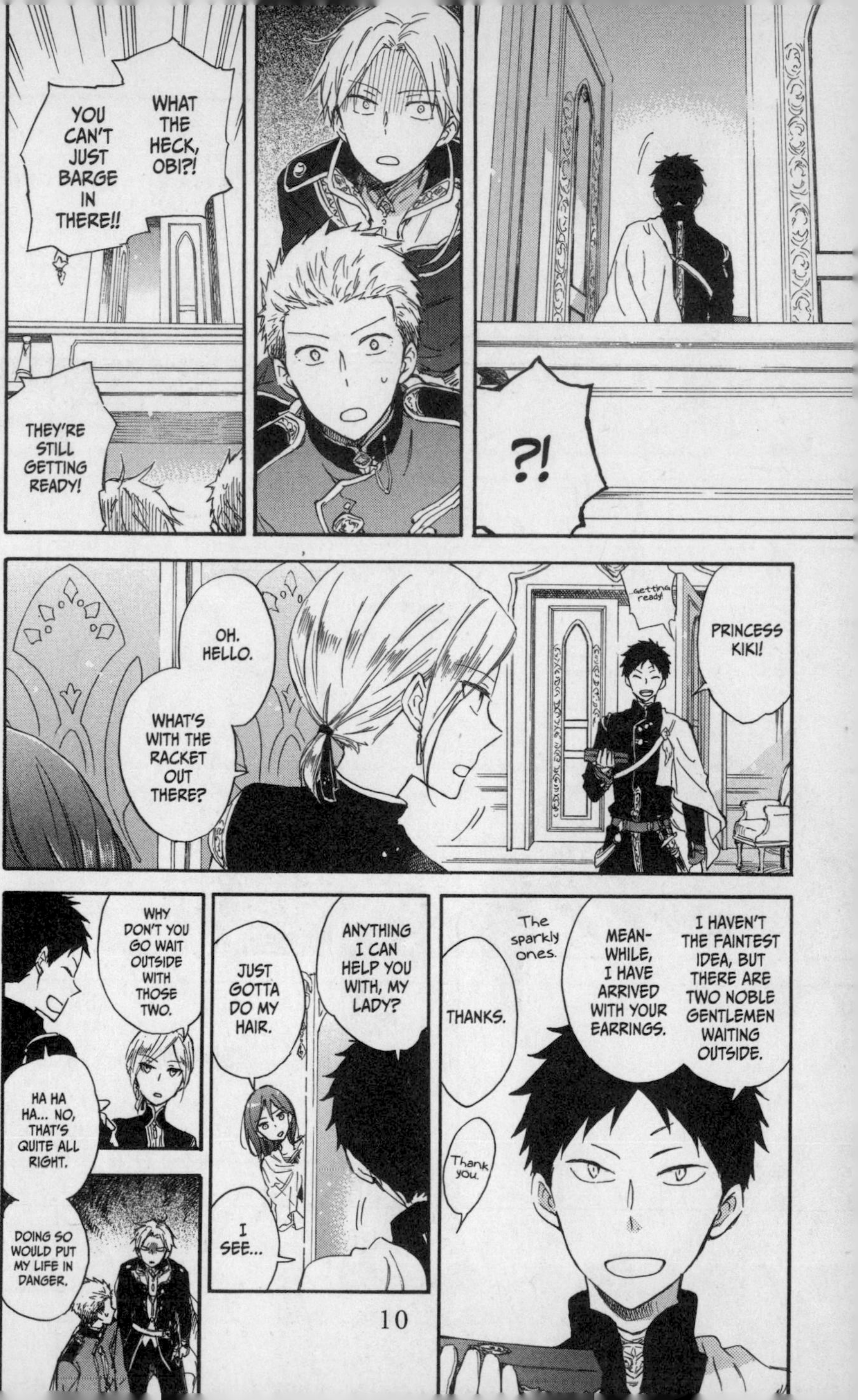
?!
WHAT THE HECK, OBI?!
YOU CAN'T JUST BARGE IN THERE!!
THEY'RE STILL GETTING READY!
PRINCESS KIKI!
Getting ready!
OH. HELLO.
WHAT'S WITH THE RACKET OUT THERE?
I HAVEN'T THE FAINTEST IDEA, BUT THERE ARE TWO NOBLE GENTLEMEN WAITING OUTSIDE.
MEAN-WHILE, I HAVE ARRIVED WITH YOUR EARRINGS.
The sparkly ones.
THANKS.
Thank you.
ANYTHING I CAN HELP YOU WITH, MY LADY?
JUST GOTTA DO MY HAIR.
I SEE...
WHY DON'T YOU GO WAIT OUTSIDE WITH THOSE TWO.
HA HA HA... NO, THAT'S QUITE ALL RIGHT.
DOING SO WOULD PUT MY LIFE IN DANGER.

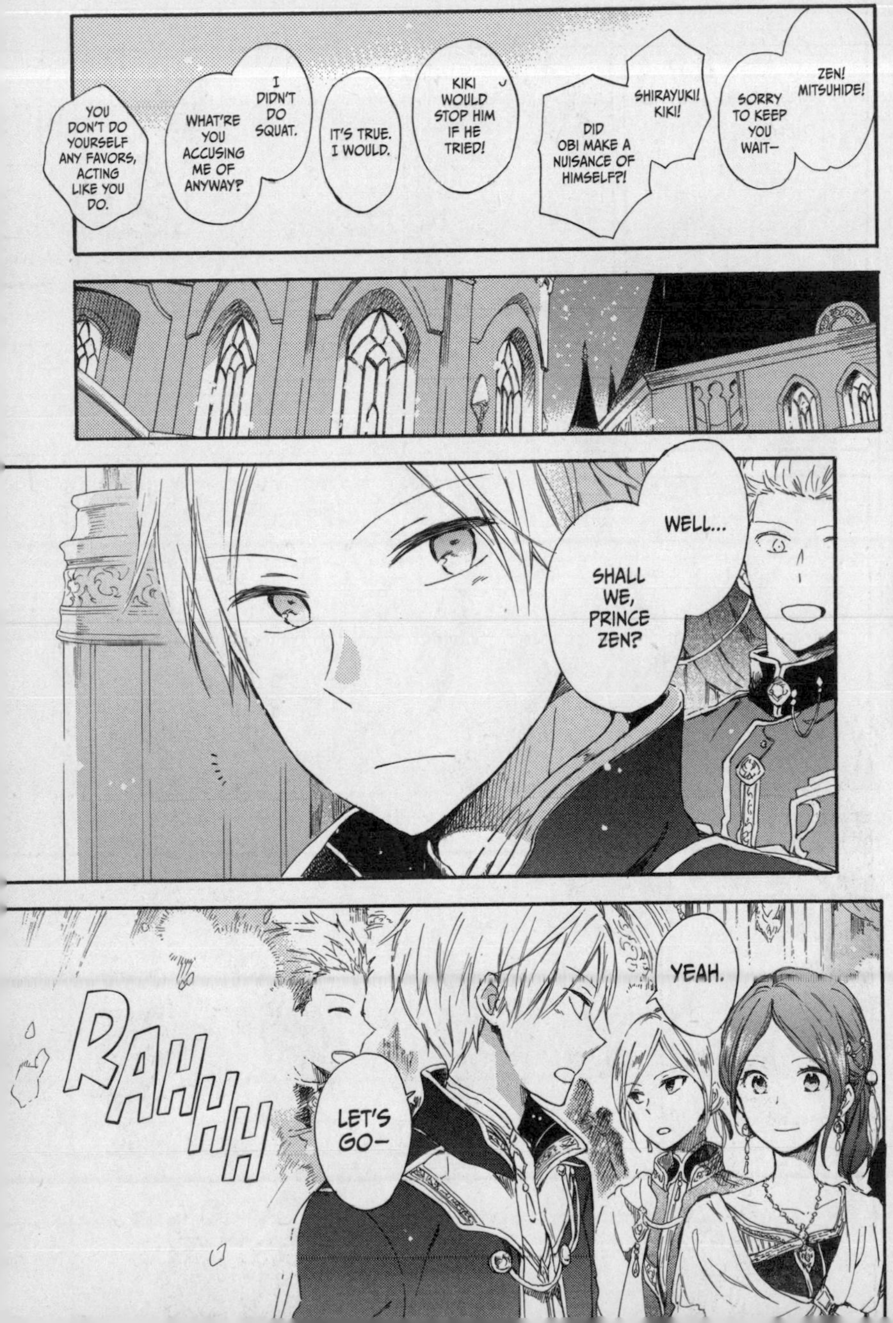
ZEN! MITSUHIDE!
SORRY TO KEEP YOU WAIT—
SHIRAYUKI! KIKI!
DID OBI MAKE A NUISANCE OF HIMSELF?!
KIKI WOULD STOP HIM IF HE TRIED!
IT'S TRUE. I WOULD.
I DIDN'T DO SQUAT.
WHAT'RE YOU ACCUSING ME OF ANYWAY?
YOU DON'T DO YOURSELF ANY FAVORS, ACTING LIKE YOU DO.
WELL...
SHALL WE, PRINCE ZEN?
YEAH.
LET'S GO—
RAHHHH

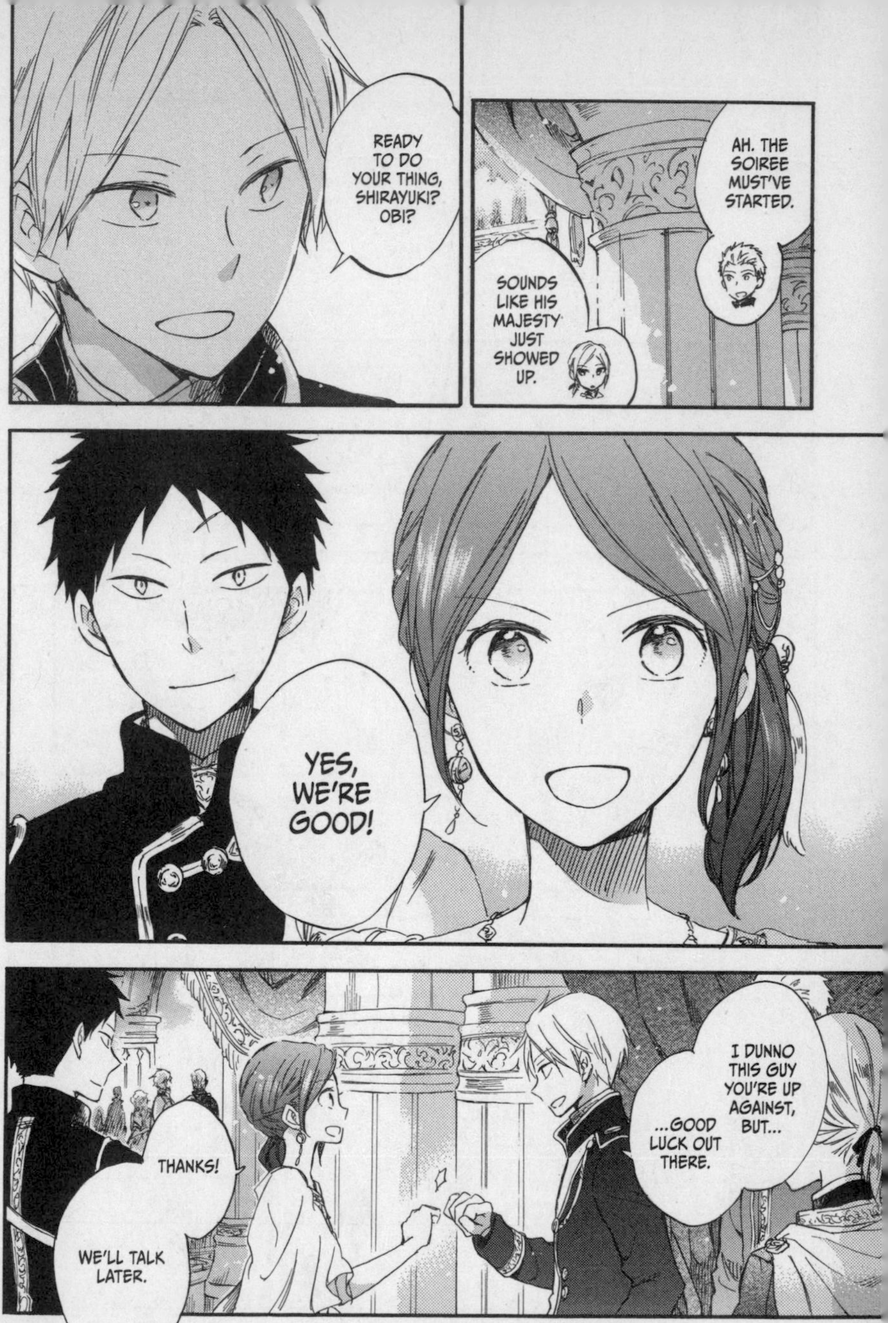
AH. THE SOIREE MUST'VE STARTED.
SOUNDS LIKE HIS MAJESTY JUST SHOWED UP.
READY TO DO YOUR THING, SHIRAYUKI? OBI?
YES, WE'RE GOOD!
I DUNNO THIS GUY YOU'RE UP AGAINST, BUT...
...GOOD LUCK OUT THERE.
THANKS!
WE'LL TALK LATER.

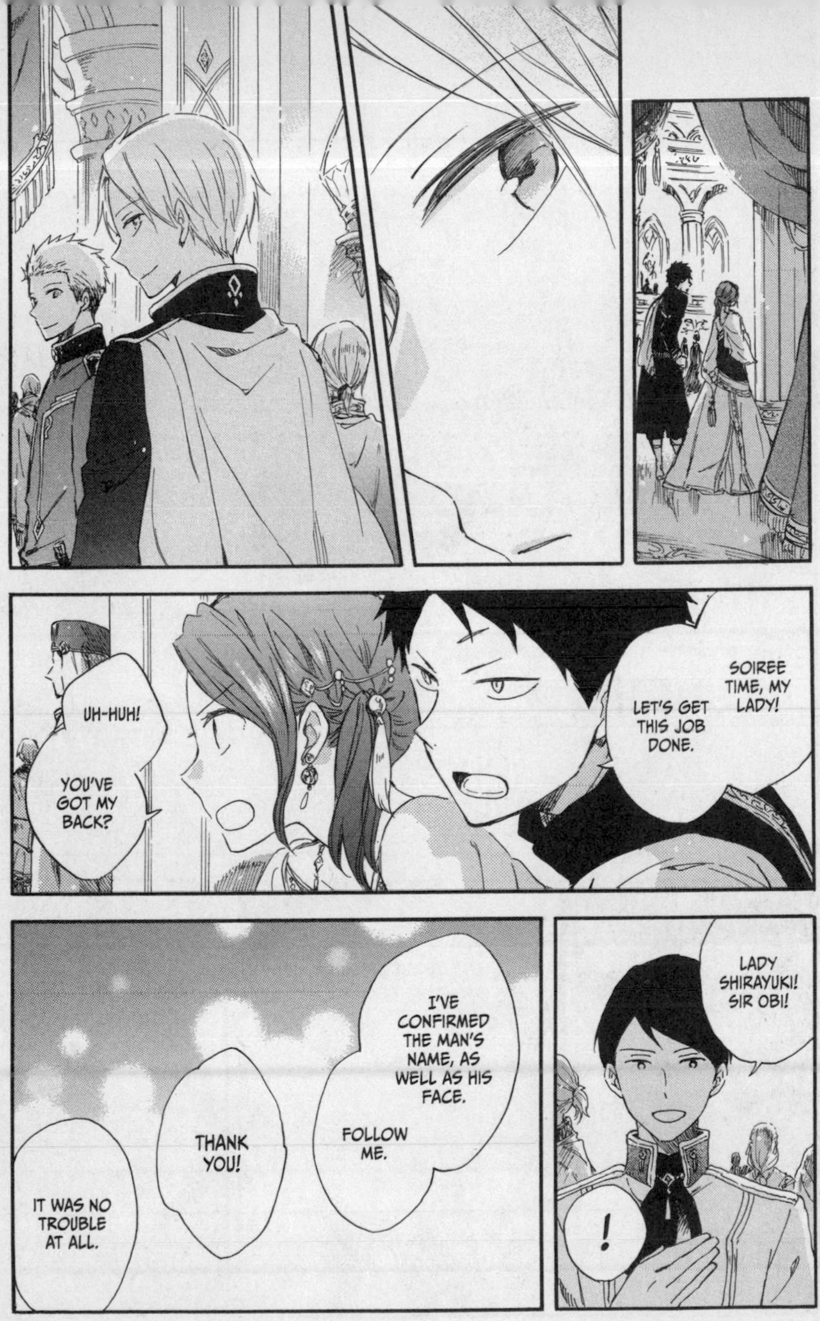
SOIREE TIME, MY LADY!
LET'S GET THIS JOB DONE.
UH-HUH!
YOU'VE GOT MY BACK?
LADY SHIRAYUKI! SIR OBI!
!
I'VE CONFIRMED THE MAN'S NAME, AS WELL AS HIS FACE.
FOLLOW ME.
THANK YOU!
IT WAS NO TROUBLE AT ALL.

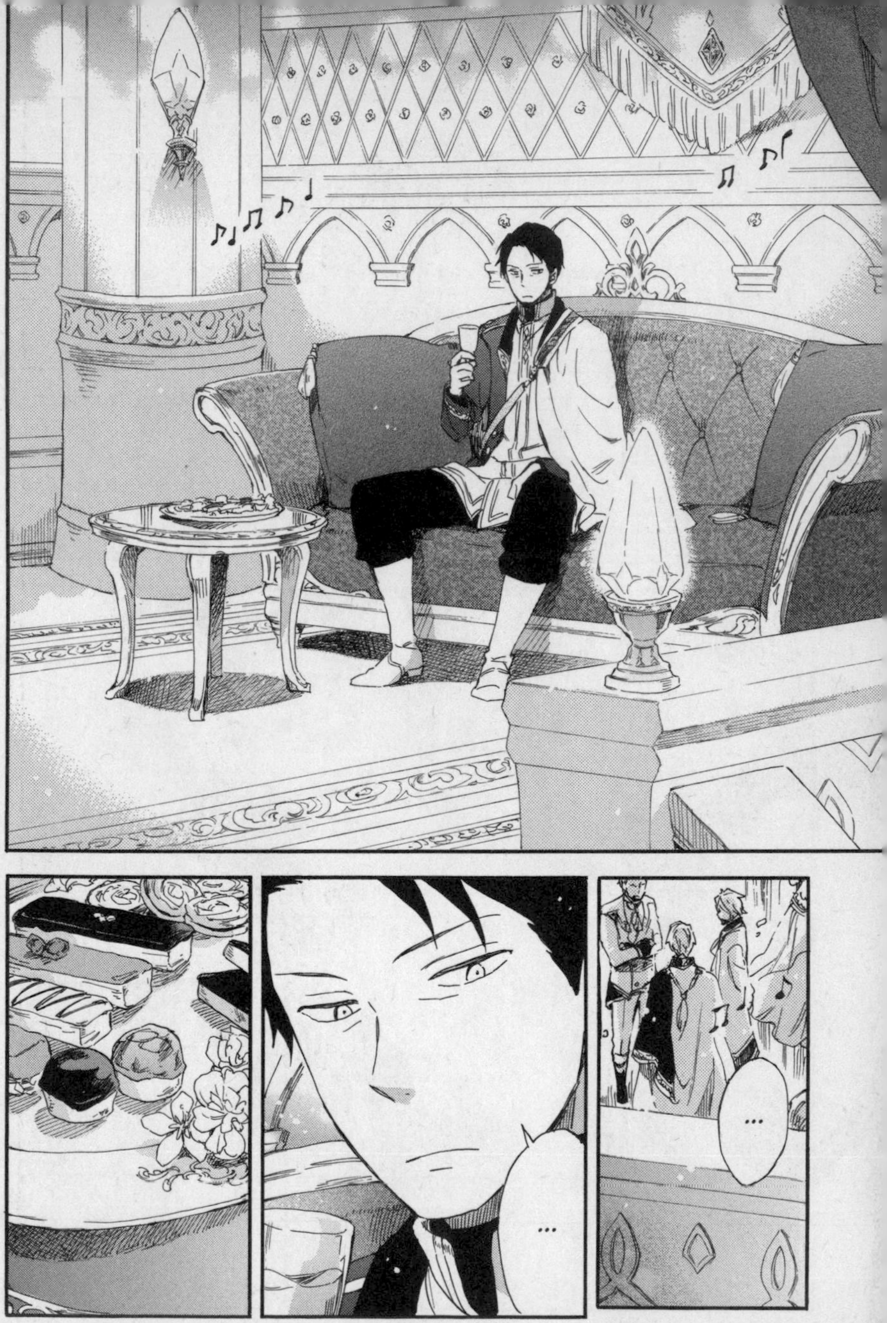
...
...

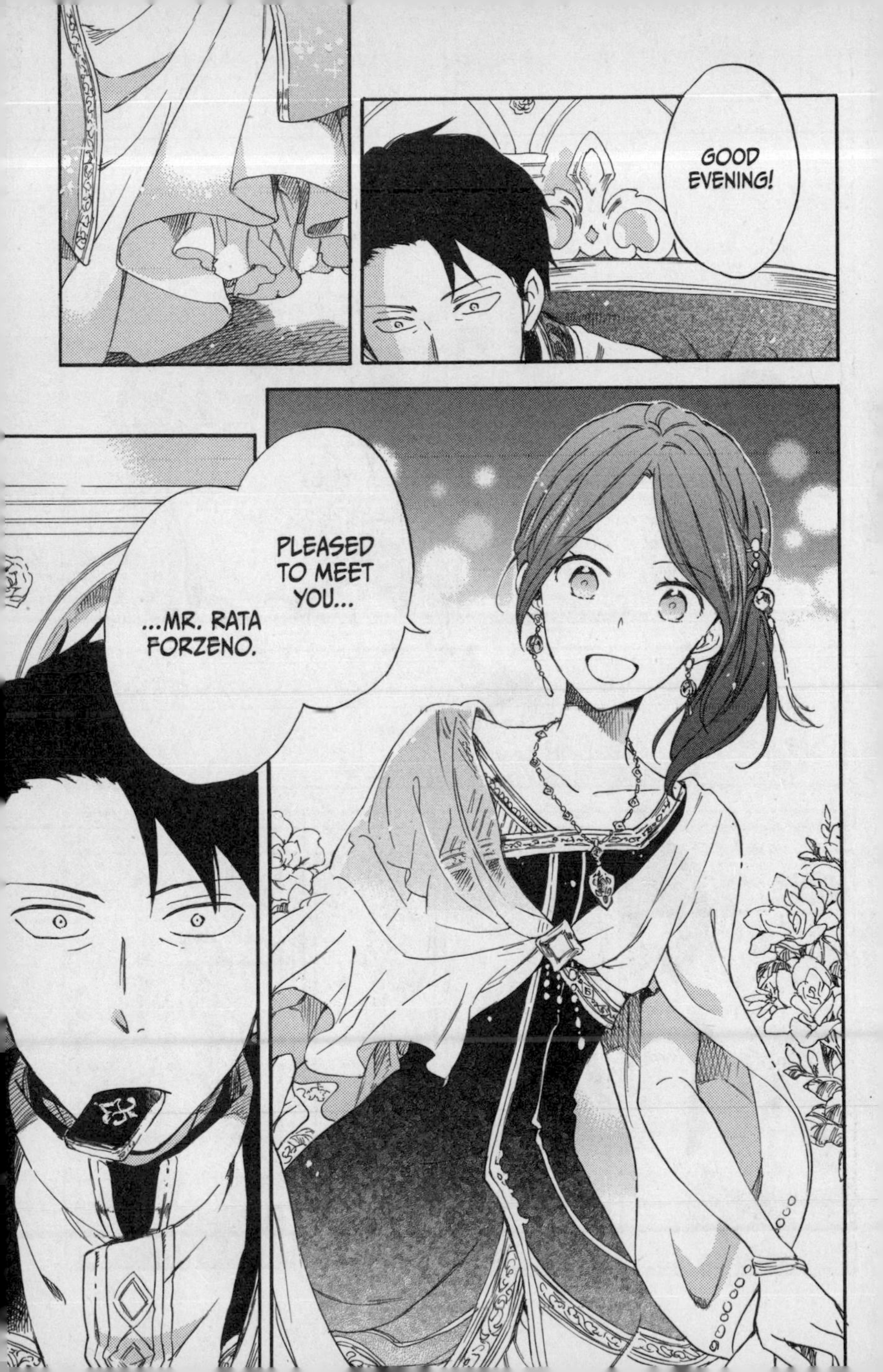
GOOD EVENING!
PLEASED TO MEET YOU...
...MR. RATA FORZENO.

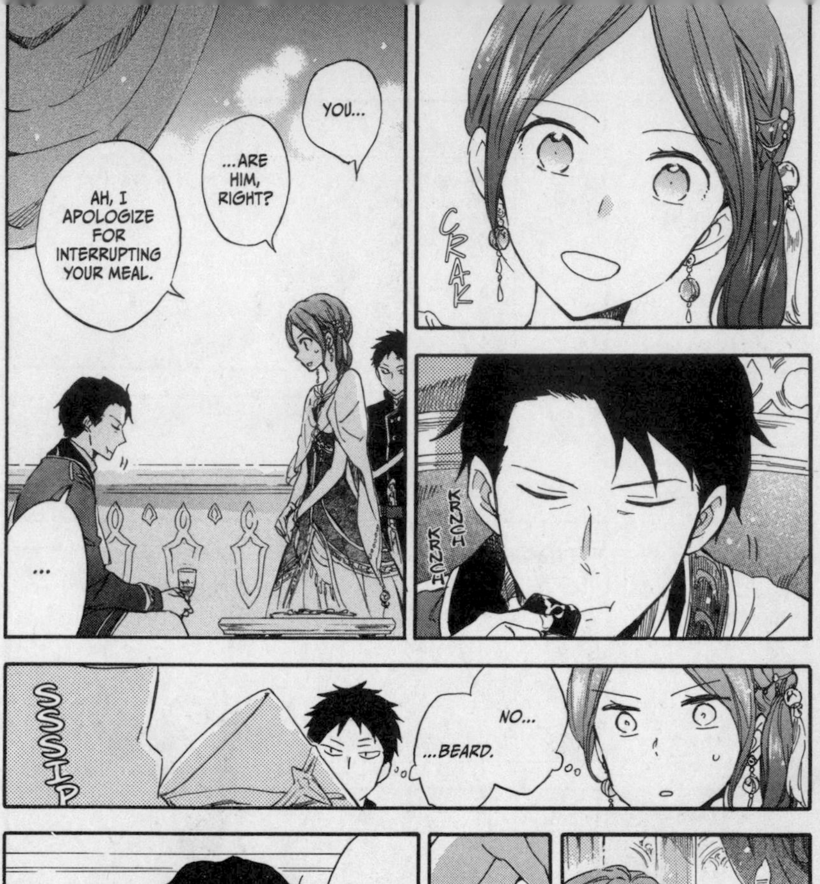
CRAK
KRNCH
KRNCH
YOU...
...ARE HIM, RIGHT?
AH, I APOLOGIZE FOR INTERRUPTING YOUR MEAL.
...
NO...
...BEARD.
SSSIP
GAB
GAB
KLNK
COME, LET'S GO DOWN-STAIRS.
!

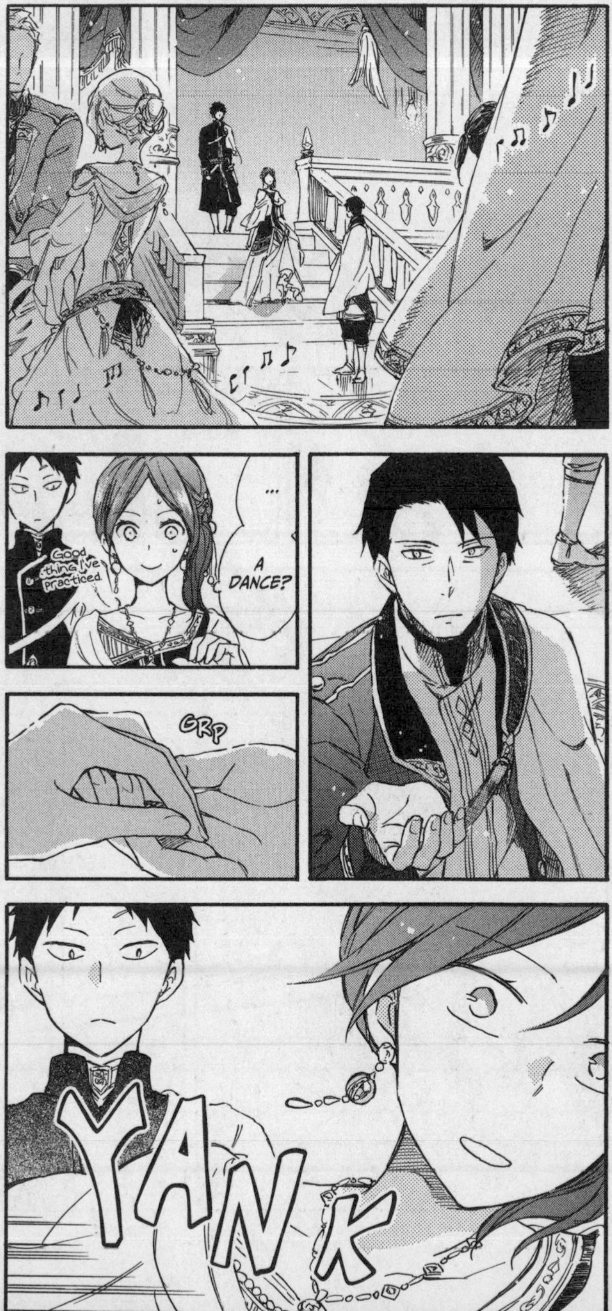
...
A DANCE?
Good thing I've practiced
GRP
YANK

1

GREETINGS

Hello, all!
This is Akiduki.
Thank you for purchasing volume 15 of Snow White with the Red Hair!!

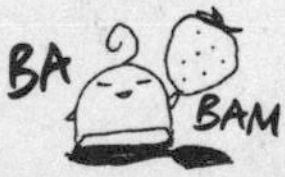
BA
BAM

This volume's cover features the boys. Bet you didn't see that coming!

I'd love to have all five main characters grace the cover in a group shot at some point, but they'd probably end up too squished together. Someday... Someday! Just gotta make sure they have enough elbow room.

I do have a general idea of who's going to appear on which volume cover. But often, the chapters included in a given volume end up being slightly different than planned, which can throw a wrench in those earlier cover design choices.

Anyway, it's volume 15! Onward ho!

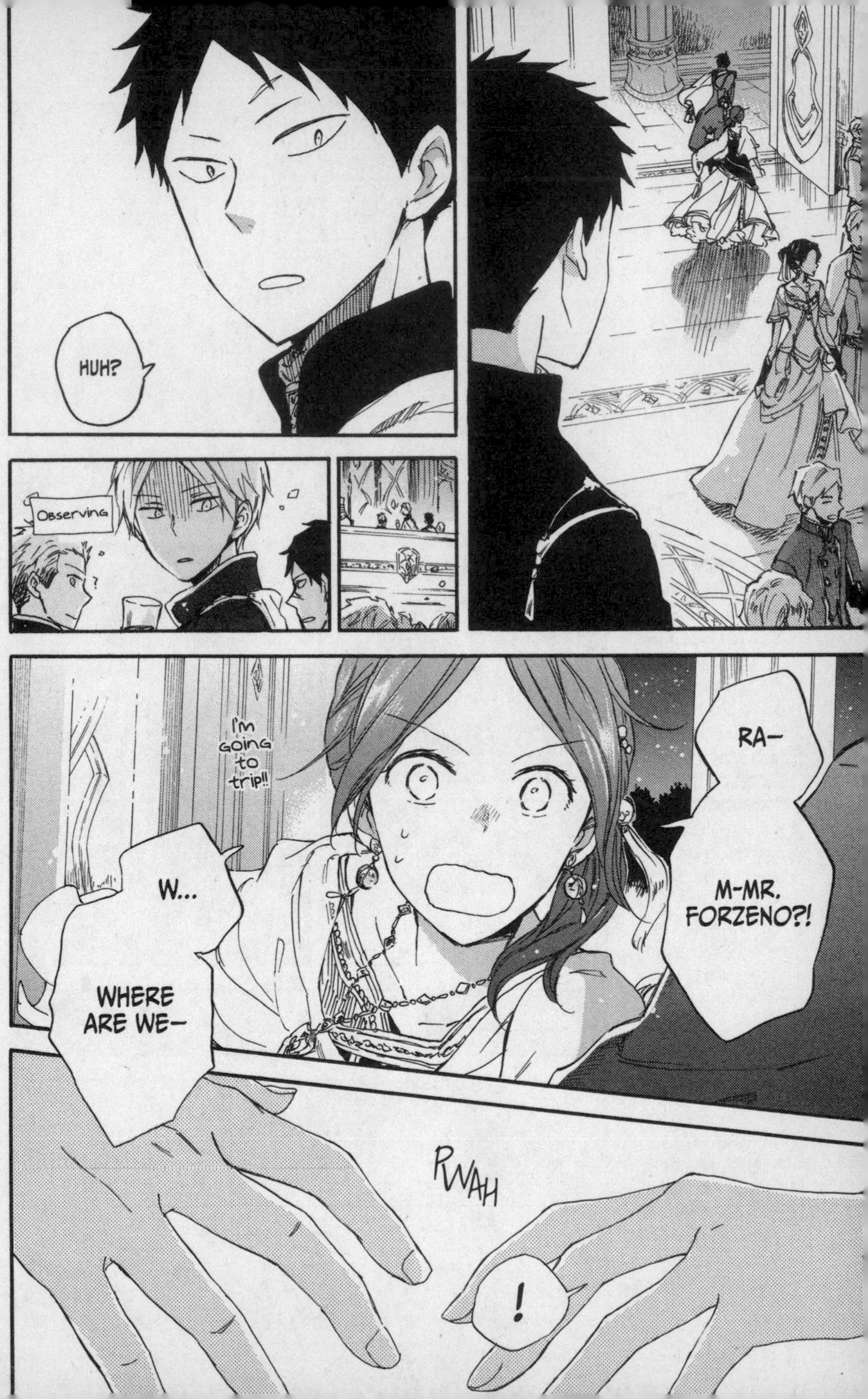
HUH?
Observing
RA-
M-MR. FORZENO?!
I'm going to trip!!
W...
WHERE ARE WE-
PWAH
!

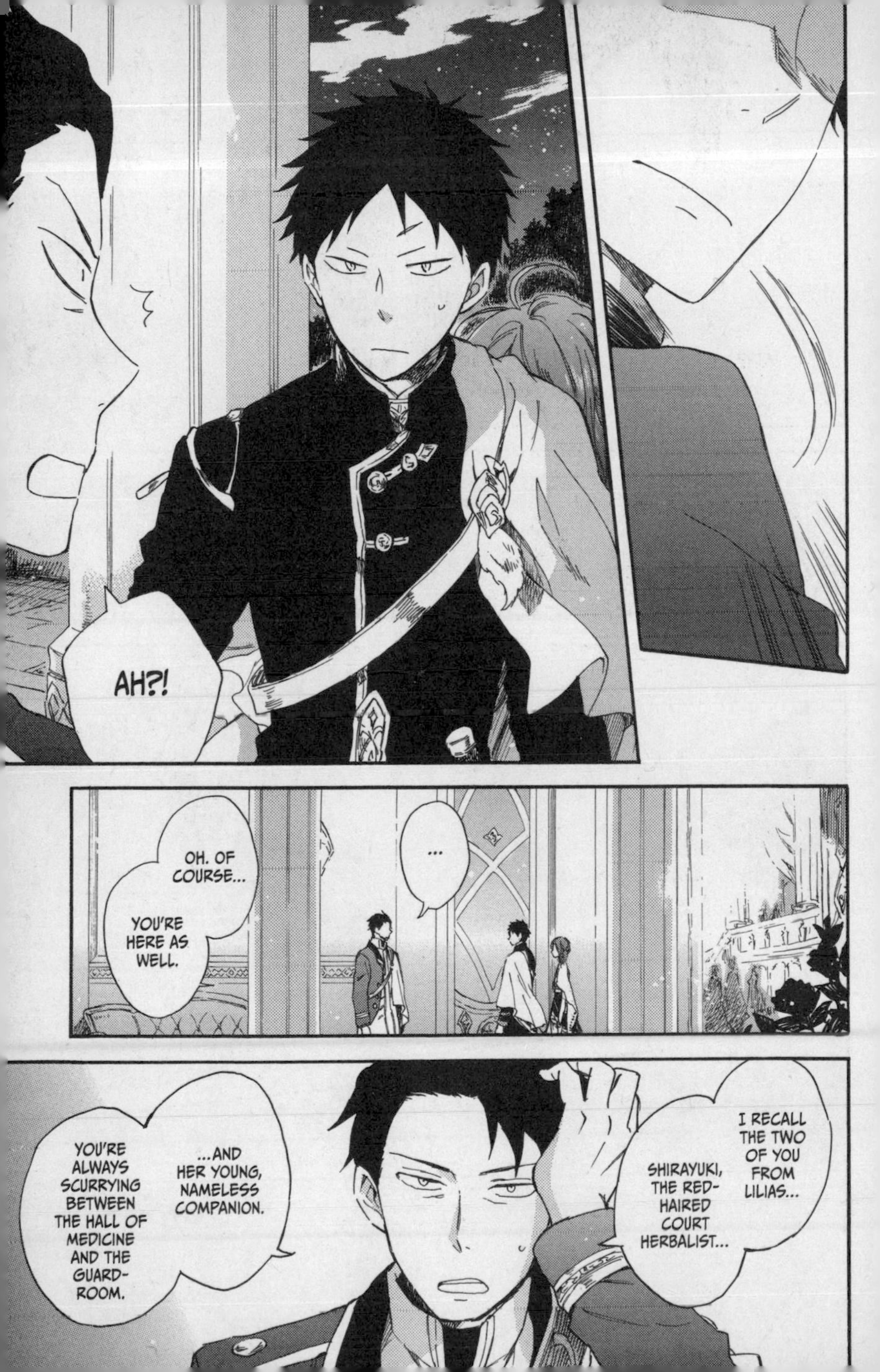
AH?!
...
OH. OF COURSE...
YOU'RE HERE AS WELL.
I RECALL THE TWO OF YOU FROM LILIAS...
SHIRAYUKI, THE RED-HAIRED COURT HERBALIST...
...AND HER YOUNG, NAMELESS COMPANION.
YOU'RE ALWAYS SCURRYING BETWEEN THE HALL OF MEDICINE AND THE GUARD-ROOM.

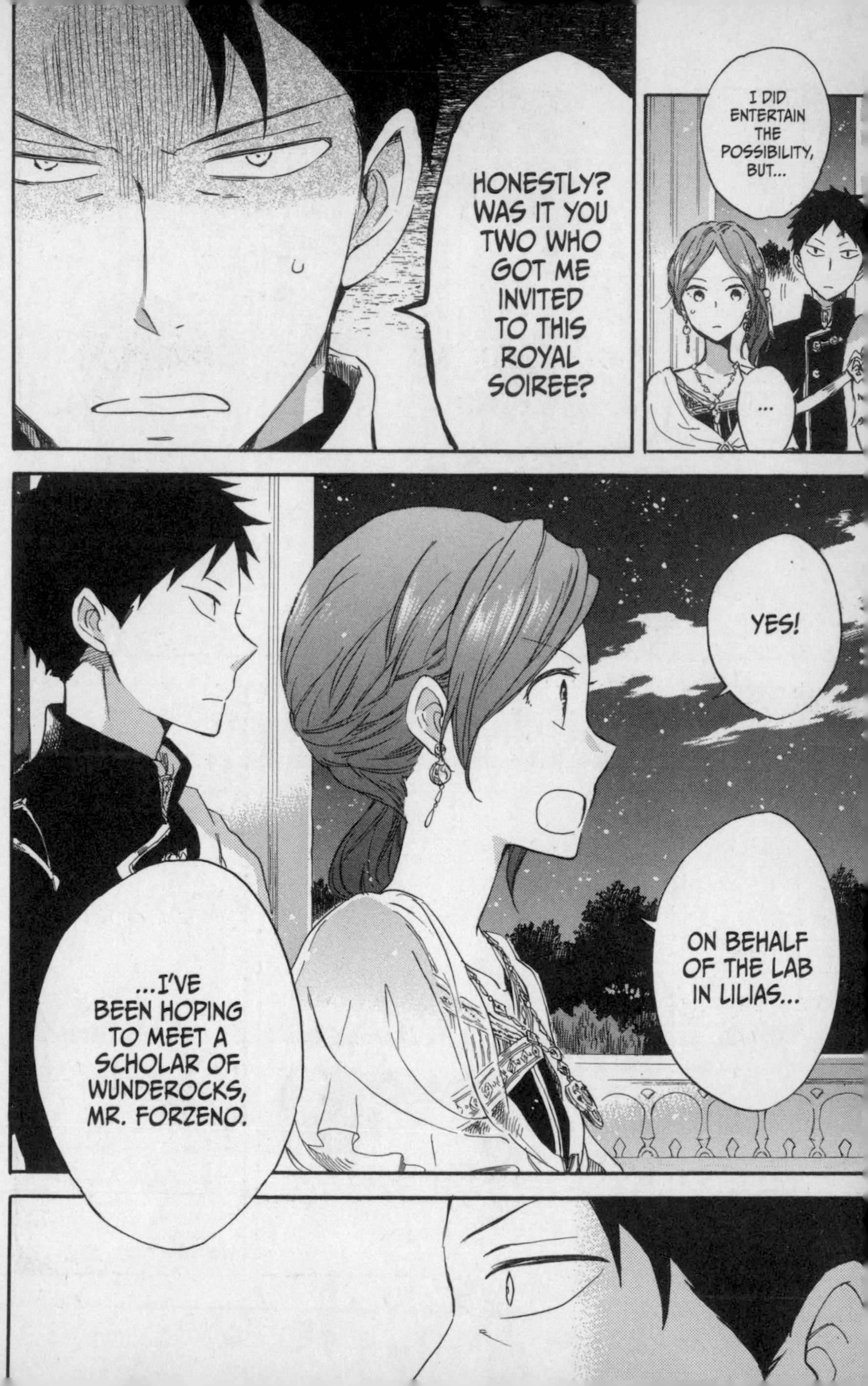
I DID ENTERTAIN THE POSSIBILITY, BUT...
...
HONESTLY? WAS IT YOU TWO WHO GOT ME INVITED TO THIS ROYAL SOIREE?
YES!
ON BEHALF OF THE LAB IN LILIAS...
...I'VE BEEN HOPING TO MEET A SCHOLAR OF WUNDEROCKS, MR. FORZENO.

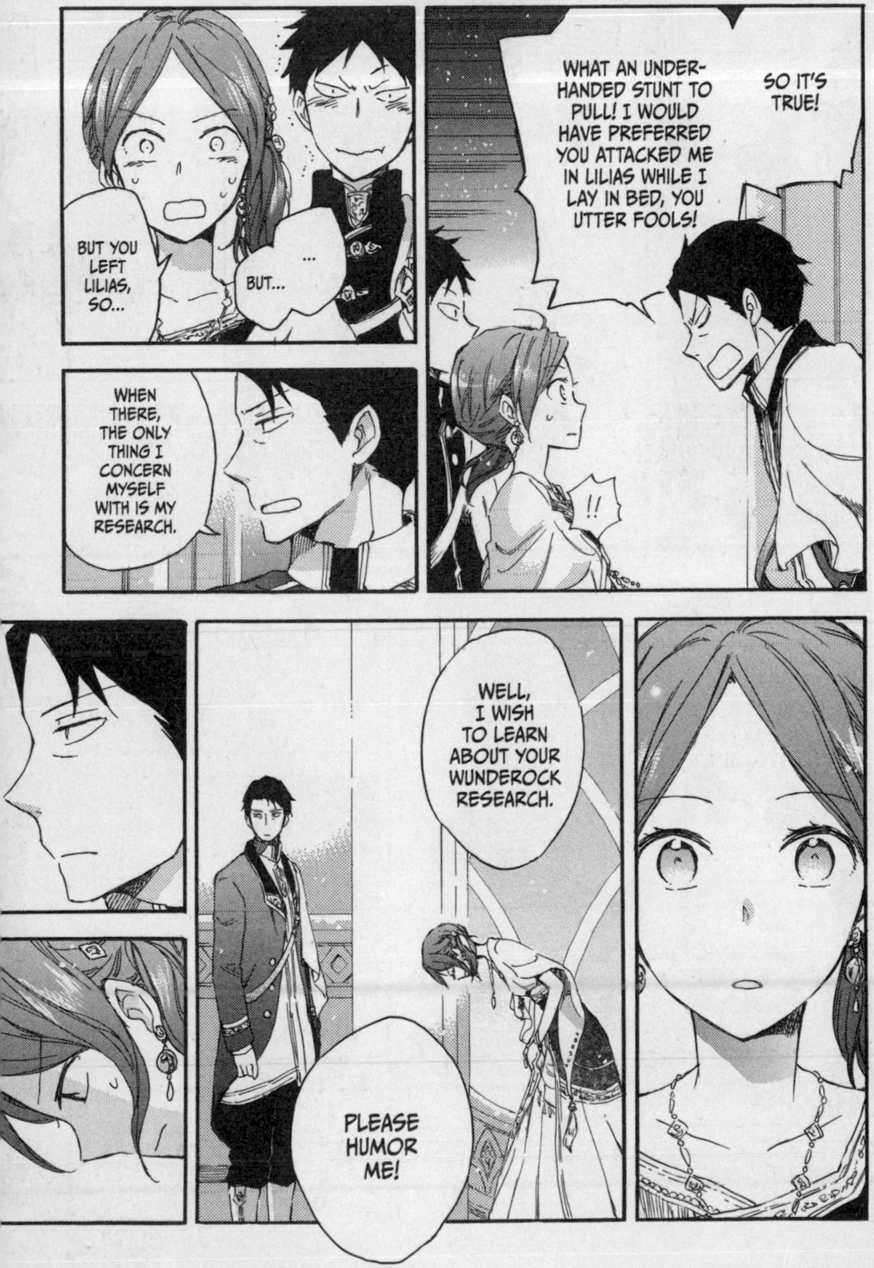
SO IT'S TRUE!
WHAT AN UNDER-HANDED STUNT TO PULL! I WOULD HAVE PREFERRED YOU ATTACKED ME IN LILIAS WHILE I LAY IN BED, YOU UTTER FOOLS!
!!
...
BUT...
BUT YOU LEFT LILIAS, SO...
WHEN THERE, THE ONLY THING I CONCERN MYSELF WITH IS MY RESEARCH.
WELL, I WISH TO LEARN ABOUT YOUR WUNDEROCK RESEARCH.
PLEASE HUMOR ME!

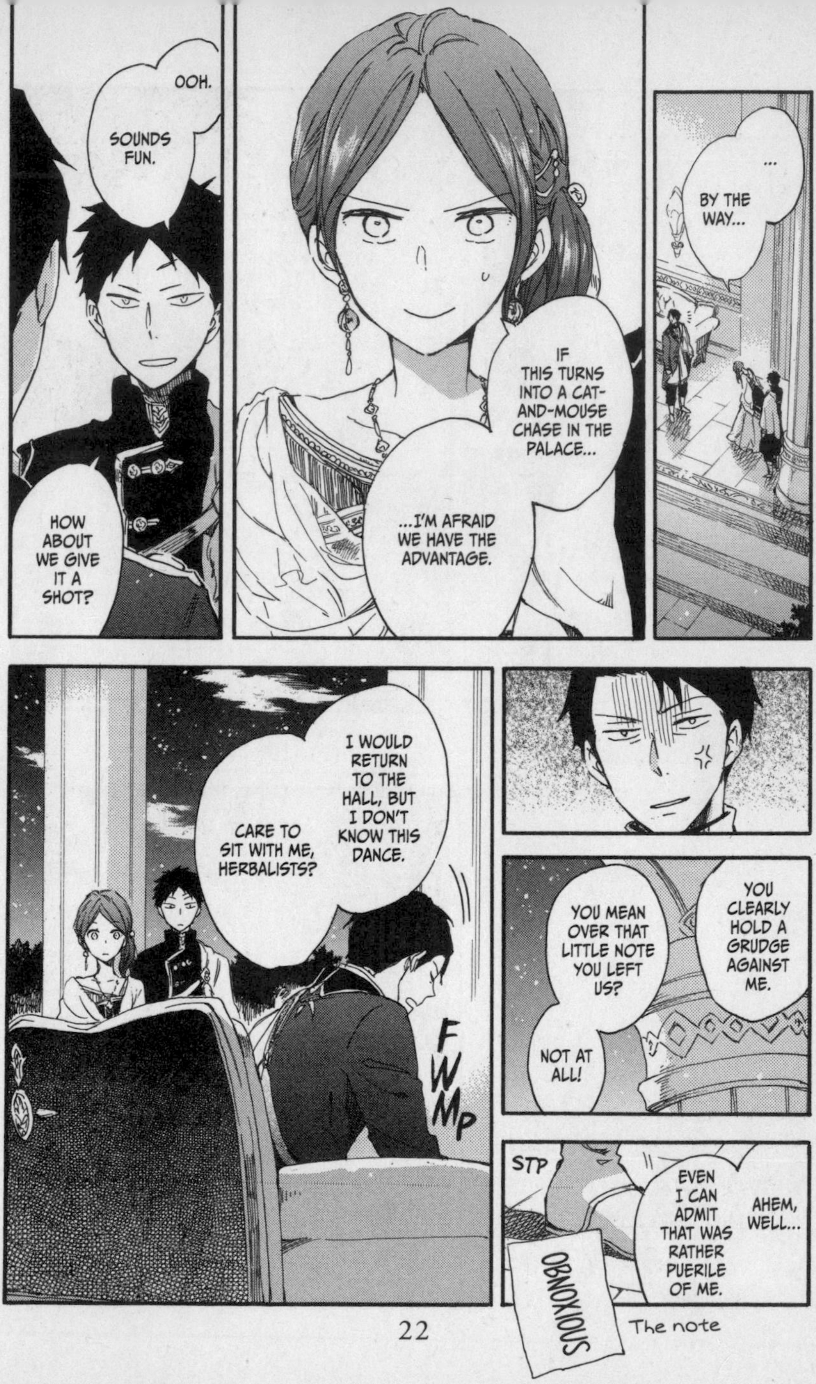
...
BY THE WAY...
IF THIS TURNS INTO A CAT-AND-MOUSE CHASE IN THE PALACE...
...I'M AFRAID WE HAVE THE ADVANTAGE.
OOH.
SOUNDS FUN.
HOW ABOUT WE GIVE IT A SHOT?
YOU CLEARLY HOLD A GRUDGE AGAINST ME.
YOU MEAN OVER THAT LITTLE NOTE YOU LEFT US?
NOT AT ALL!
AHEM, WELL...
EVEN I CAN ADMIT THAT WAS RATHER PUERILE OF ME.
STP
OBNOXIOUS
The note
FWMP
I WOULD RETURN TO THE HALL, BUT I DON'T KNOW THIS DANCE.
CARE TO SIT WITH ME, HERBALISTS?

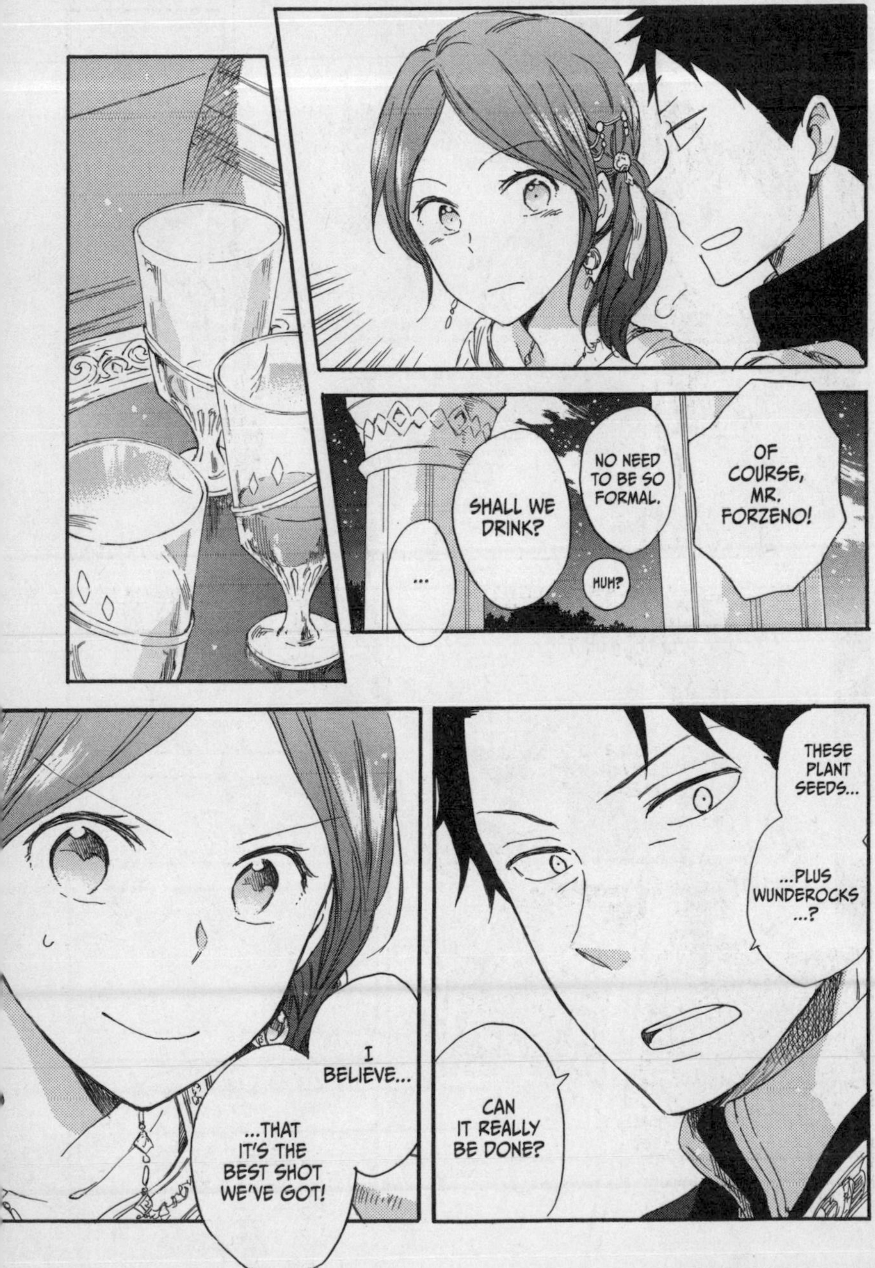
OF COURSE, MR. FORZENO!
NO NEED TO BE SO FORMAL.
HUH?
SHALL WE DRINK?
...
THESE PLANT SEEDS...
...PLUS WUNDEROCKS ...?
CAN IT REALLY BE DONE?
I BELIEVE...
...THAT IT'S THE BEST SHOT WE'VE GOT!

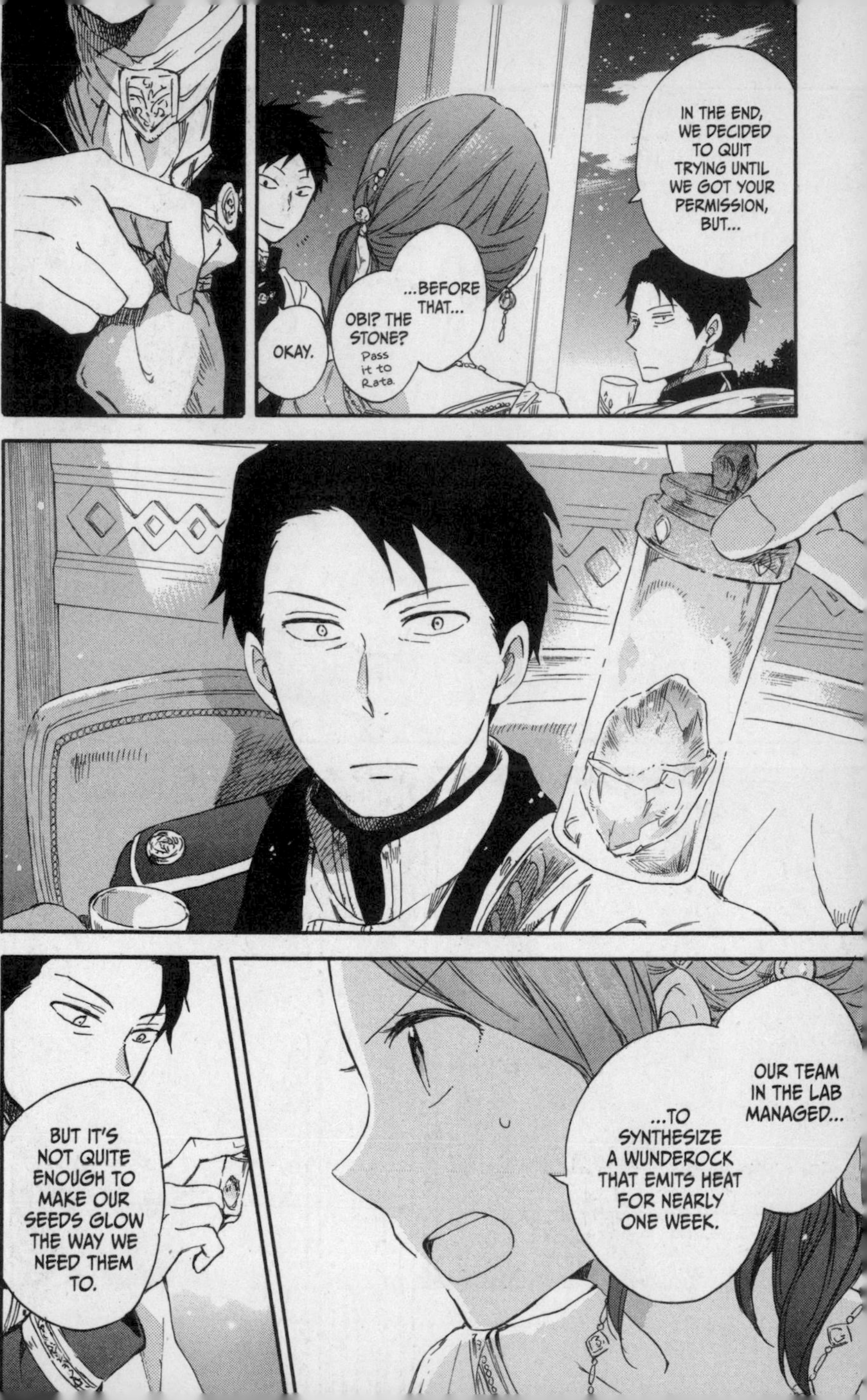
IN THE END, WE DECIDED TO QUIT TRYING UNTIL WE GOT YOUR PERMISSION, BUT...
...BEFORE THAT...
OBI? THE STONE?
Pass it to Rata.
OKAY.
OUR TEAM IN THE LAB MANAGED...
...TO SYNTHESIZE A WUNDEROCK THAT EMITS HEAT FOR NEARLY ONE WEEK.
BUT IT'S NOT QUITE ENOUGH TO MAKE OUR SEEDS GLOW THE WAY WE NEED THEM TO.

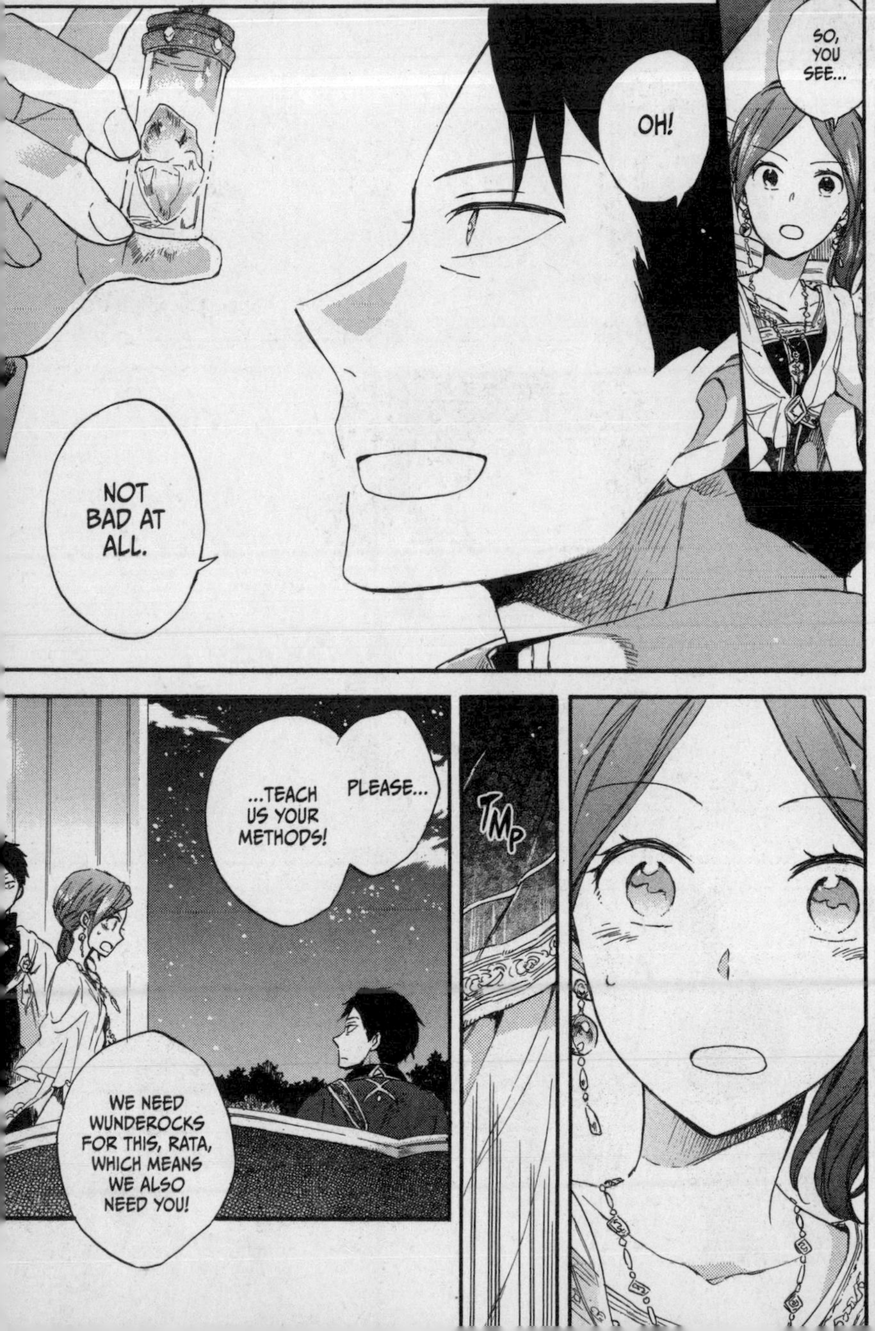
SO, YOU SEE...
OH!
NOT BAD AT ALL.
TMP
PLEASE...
...TEACH US YOUR METHODS!
WE NEED WUNDEROCKS FOR THIS, RATA, WHICH MEANS WE ALSO NEED YOU!

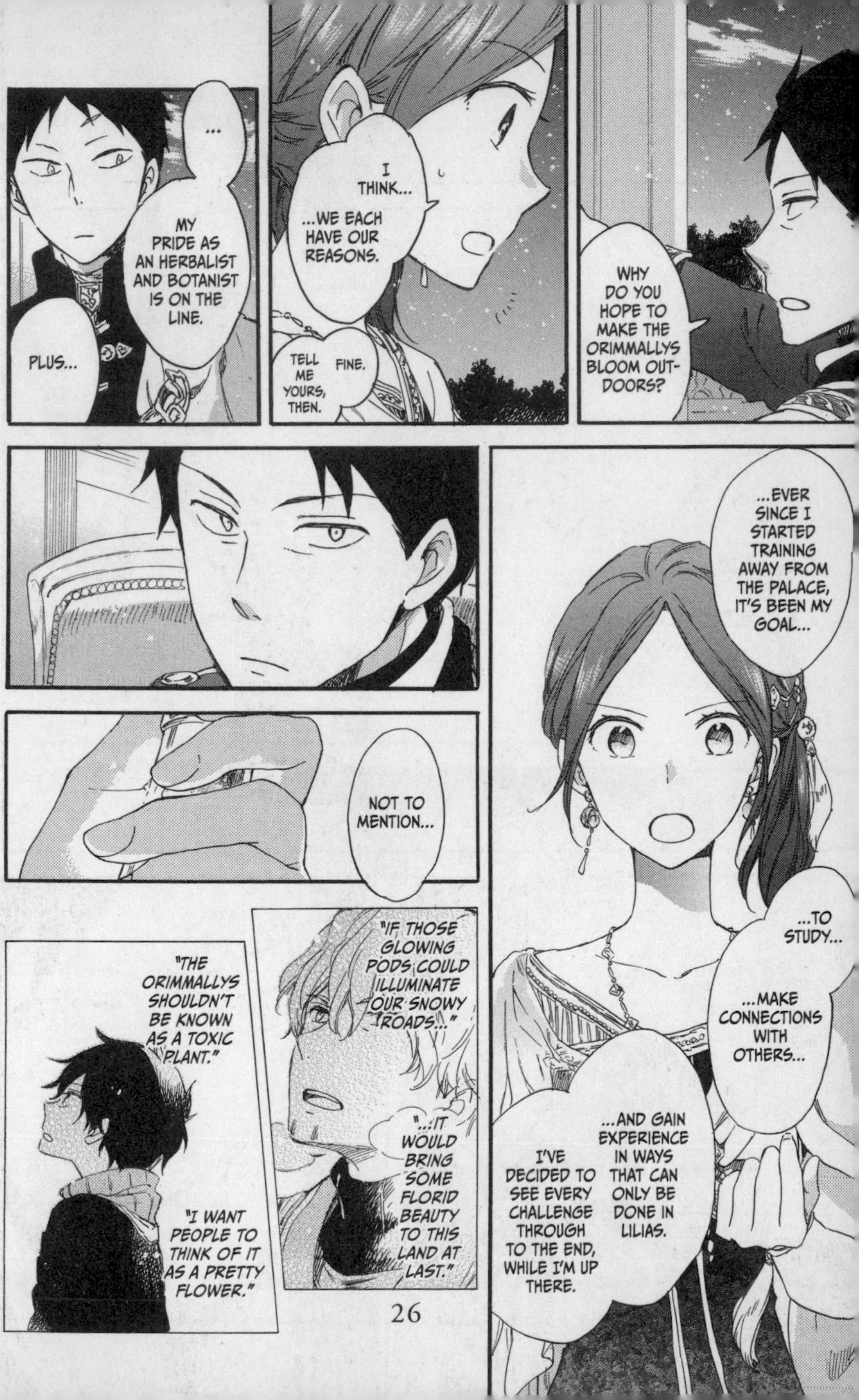
WHY DO YOU HOPE TO MAKE THE ORIMMALLYS BLOOM OUT-DOORS?
I THINK...
...WE EACH HAVE OUR REASONS.
FINE.
TELL ME YOURS, THEN.
...
MY PRIDE AS AN HERBALIST AND BOTANIST IS ON THE LINE.
PLUS...
...EVER SINCE I STARTED TRAINING AWAY FROM THE PALACE, IT'S BEEN MY GOAL...
...TO STUDY...
...MAKE CONNECTIONS WITH OTHERS...
...AND GAIN EXPERIENCE IN WAYS THAT CAN ONLY BE DONE IN LILIAS.
I'VE DECIDED TO SEE EVERY CHALLENGE THROUGH TO THE END, WHILE I'M UP THERE.
NOT TO MENTION...
"IF THOSE GLOWING PODS COULD ILLUMINATE OUR SNOWY ROADS..."
"...IT WOULD BRING SOME FLORID BEAUTY TO THIS LAND AT LAST."
"THE ORIMMALLYS SHOULDN'T BE KNOWN AS A TOXIC PLANT."
"I WANT PEOPLE TO THINK OF IT AS A PRETTY FLOWER."

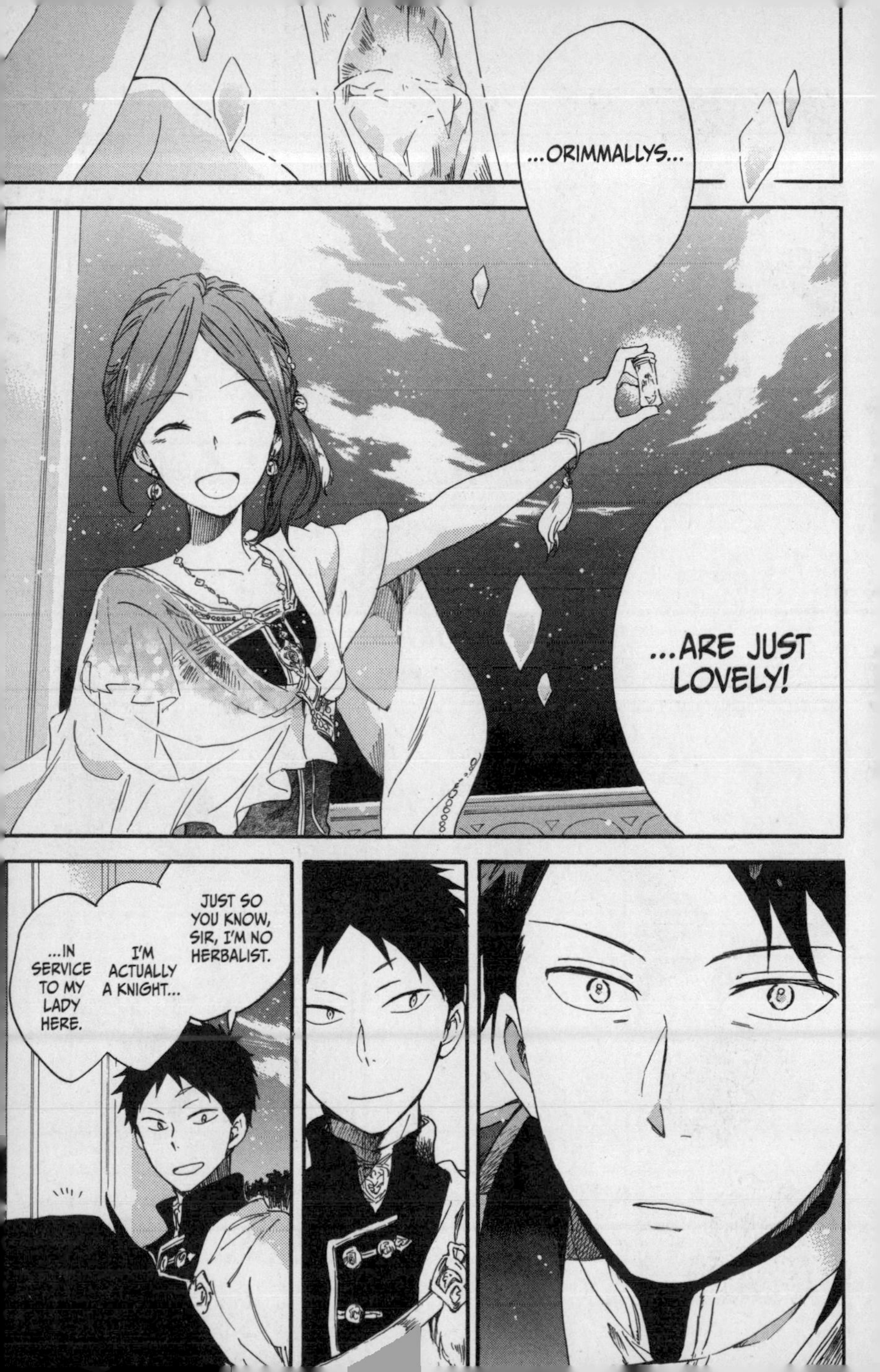
...ORIMMALLYS...
...ARE JUST LOVELY!
JUST SO YOU KNOW, SIR, I'M NO HERBALIST.
I'M ACTUALLY A KNIGHT...
...IN SERVICE TO MY LADY HERE.

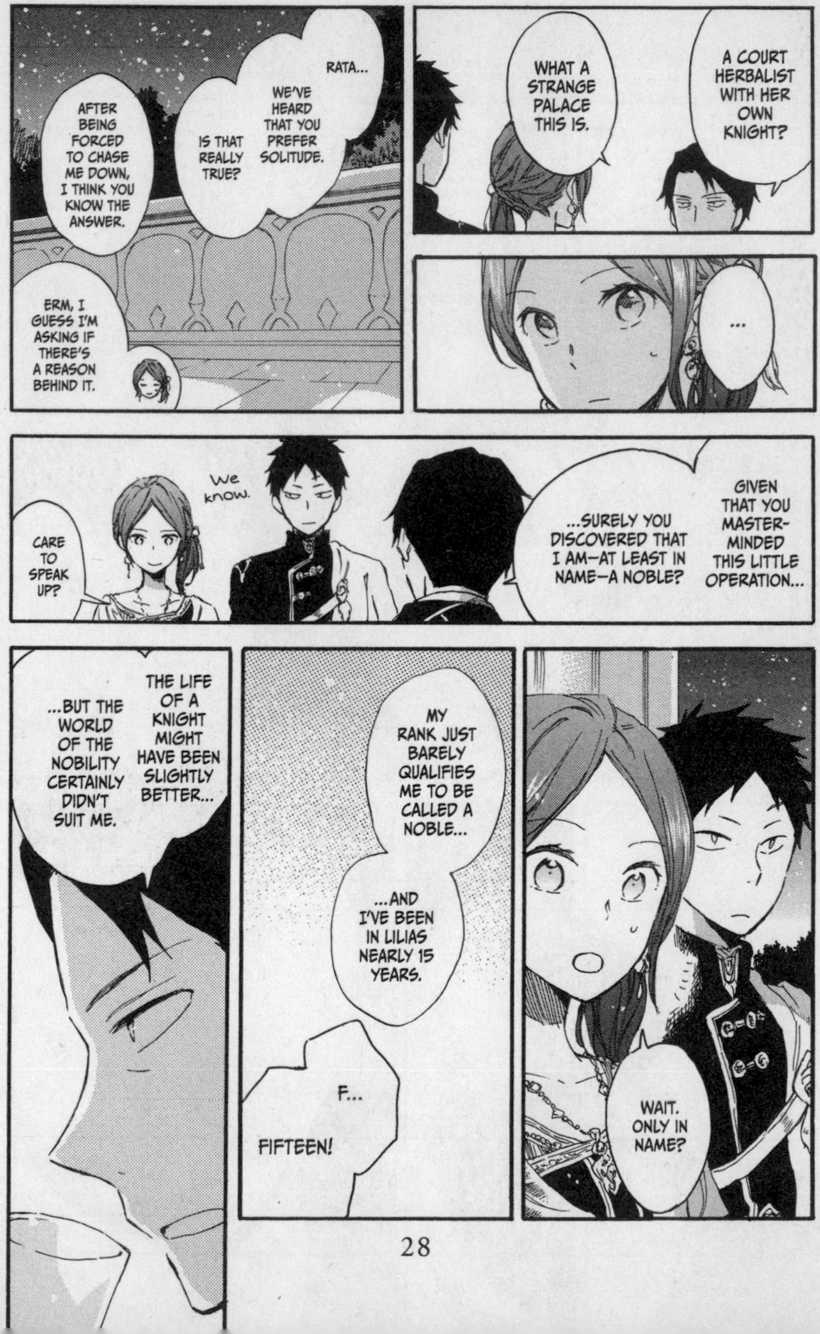
A COURT HERBALIST WITH HER OWN KNIGHT?
WHAT A STRANGE PALACE THIS IS.
...
RATA...
WE'VE HEARD THAT YOU PREFER SOLITUDE.
IS THAT REALLY TRUE?
AFTER BEING FORCED TO CHASE ME DOWN, I THINK YOU KNOW THE ANSWER.
ERM, I GUESS I'M ASKING IF THERE'S A REASON BEHIND IT.
GIVEN THAT YOU MASTER-MINDED THIS LITTLE OPERATION...
...SURELY YOU DISCOVERED THAT I AM—AT LEAST IN NAME—A NOBLE?
We know.
CARE TO SPEAK UP?
WAIT. ONLY IN NAME?
MY RANK JUST BARELY QUALIFIES ME TO BE CALLED A NOBLE...
...AND I'VE BEEN IN LILIAS NEARLY 15 YEARS.
F...
FIFTEEN!
THE LIFE OF A KNIGHT MIGHT HAVE BEEN SLIGHTLY BETTER...
...BUT THE WORLD OF THE NOBILITY CERTAINLY DIDN'T SUIT ME.

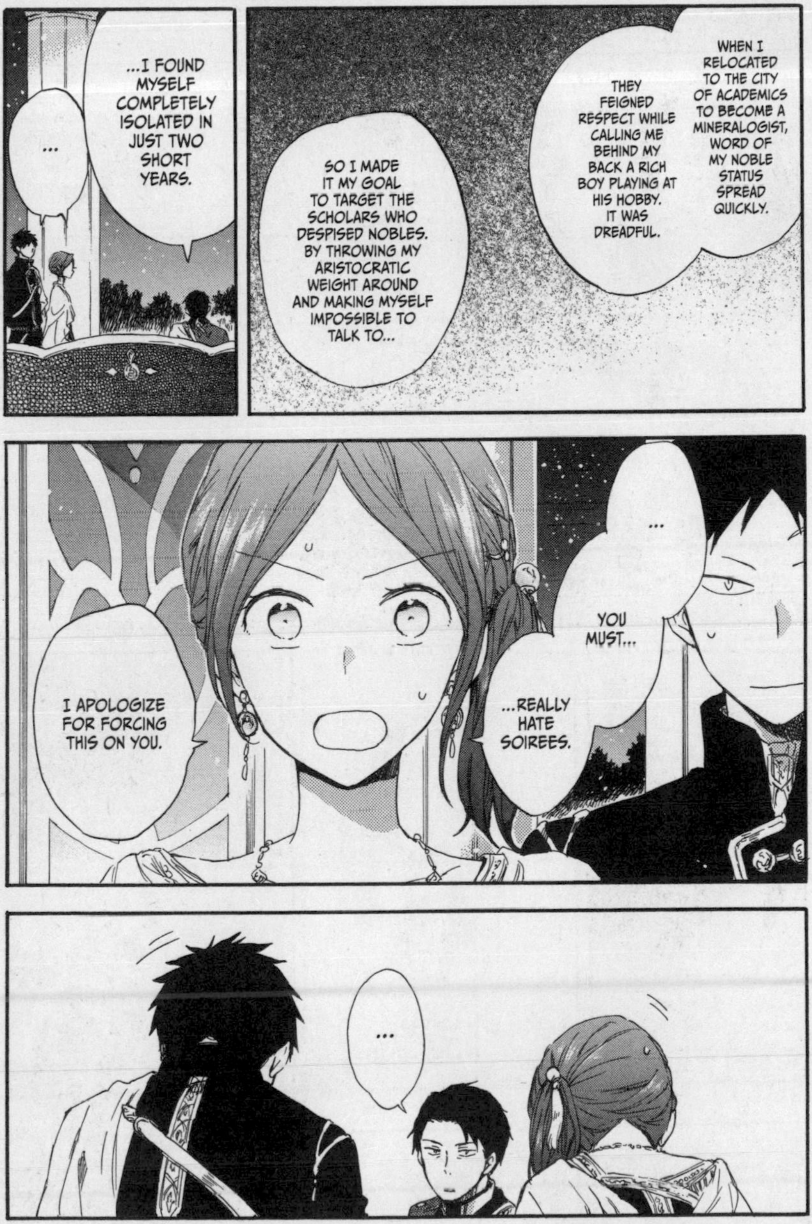
WHEN I RELOCATED TO THE CITY OF ACADEMICS TO BECOME A MINERALOGIST, WORD OF MY NOBLE STATUS SPREAD QUICKLY.
THEY FEIGNED RESPECT WHILE CALLING ME BEHIND MY BACK A RICH BOY PLAYING AT HIS HOBBY. IT WAS DREADFUL.
SO I MADE IT MY GOAL TO TARGET THE SCHOLARS WHO DESPISED NOBLES. BY THROWING MY ARISTOCRATIC WEIGHT AROUND AND MAKING MYSELF IMPOSSIBLE TO TALK TO...
...I FOUND MYSELF COMPLETELY ISOLATED IN JUST TWO SHORT YEARS.
...
...
YOU MUST...
...REALLY HATE SOIREES.
I APOLOGIZE FOR FORCING THIS ON YOU.
...

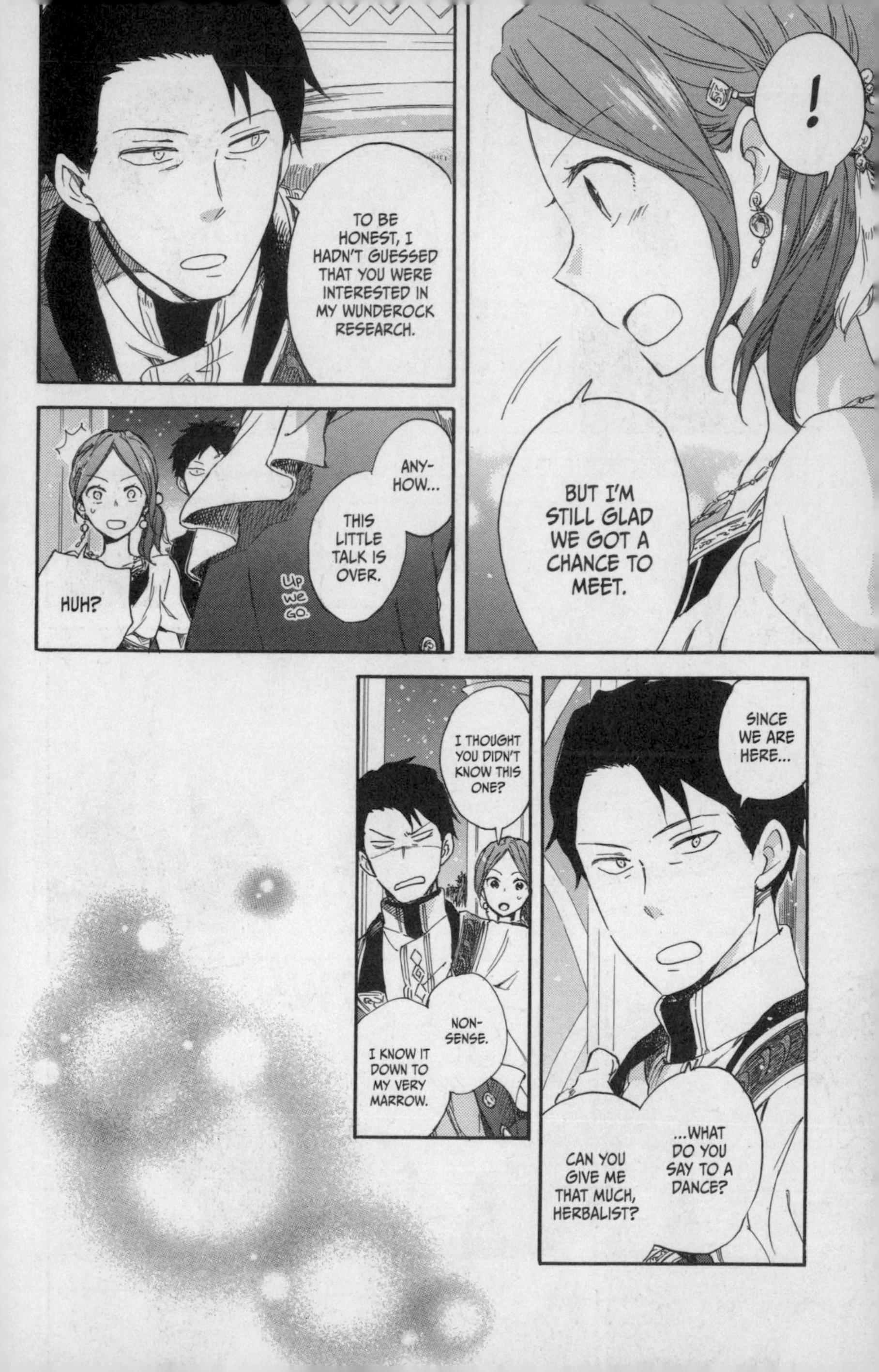
!
BUT I'M STILL GLAD WE GOT A CHANCE TO MEET.
TO BE HONEST, I HADN'T GUESSED THAT YOU WERE INTERESTED IN MY WUNDEROCK RESEARCH.
ANY-HOW...
THIS LITTLE TALK IS OVER.
Up we go.
HUH?
SINCE WE ARE HERE...
...WHAT DO YOU SAY TO A DANCE?
CAN YOU GIVE ME THAT MUCH, HERBALIST?
I THOUGHT YOU DIDN'T KNOW THIS ONE?
NON-SENSE.
I KNOW IT DOWN TO MY VERY MARROW.

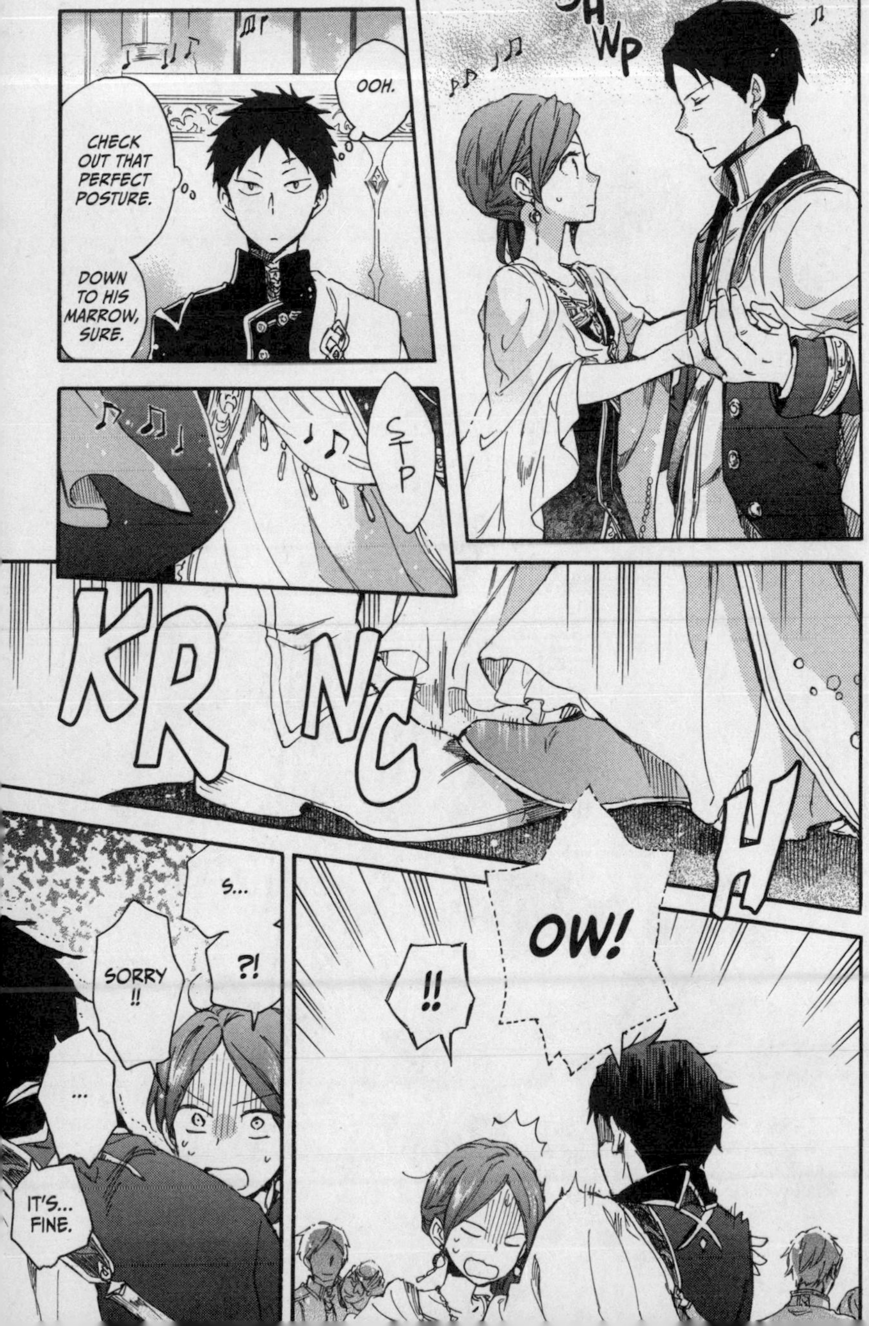
SHWP
OOH.
CHECK OUT THAT PERFECT POSTURE.
DOWN TO HIS MARROW, SURE.
STP
KR
NC
H
OW!
!!
S...
?!
SORRY!!
...
IT'S... FINE.

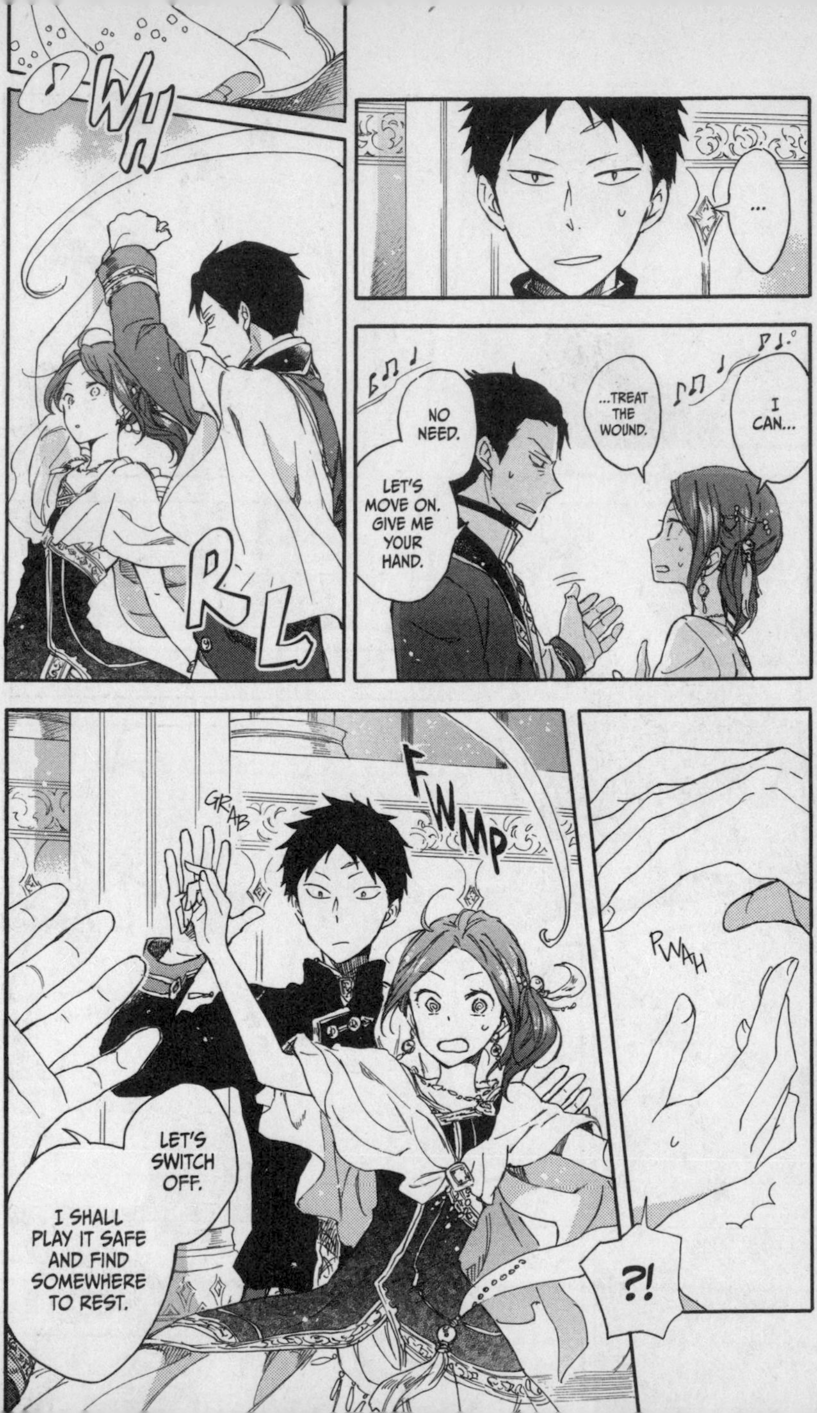
...
I CAN...
...TREAT THE WOUND.
NO NEED.
LET'S MOVE ON. GIVE ME YOUR HAND.
WH
RL
PWAH
?!
FWMP
GRAB
LET'S SWITCH OFF.
I SHALL PLAY IT SAFE AND FIND SOMEWHERE TO REST.

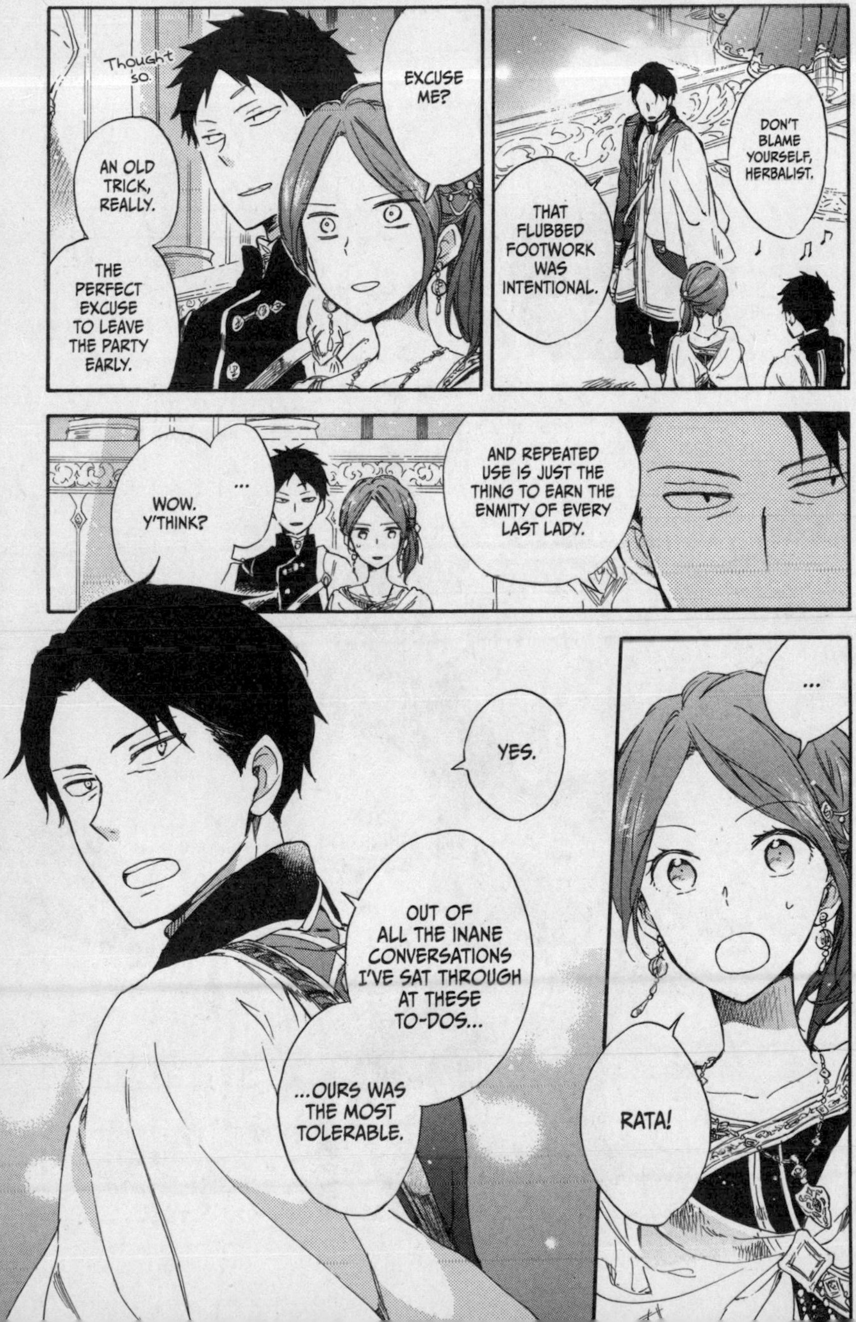
DON'T BLAME YOURSELF, HERBALIST.
THAT FLUBBED FOOTWORK WAS INTENTIONAL.
EXCUSE ME?
Thought so.
AN OLD TRICK, REALLY.
THE PERFECT EXCUSE TO LEAVE THE PARTY EARLY.
AND REPEATED USE IS JUST THE THING TO EARN THE ENMITY OF EVERY LAST LADY.
...
WOW. Y'THINK?
...
RATA!
YES.
OUT OF ALL THE INANE CONVERSATIONS I'VE SAT THROUGH AT THESE TO-DOS...
...OURS WAS THE MOST TOLERABLE.

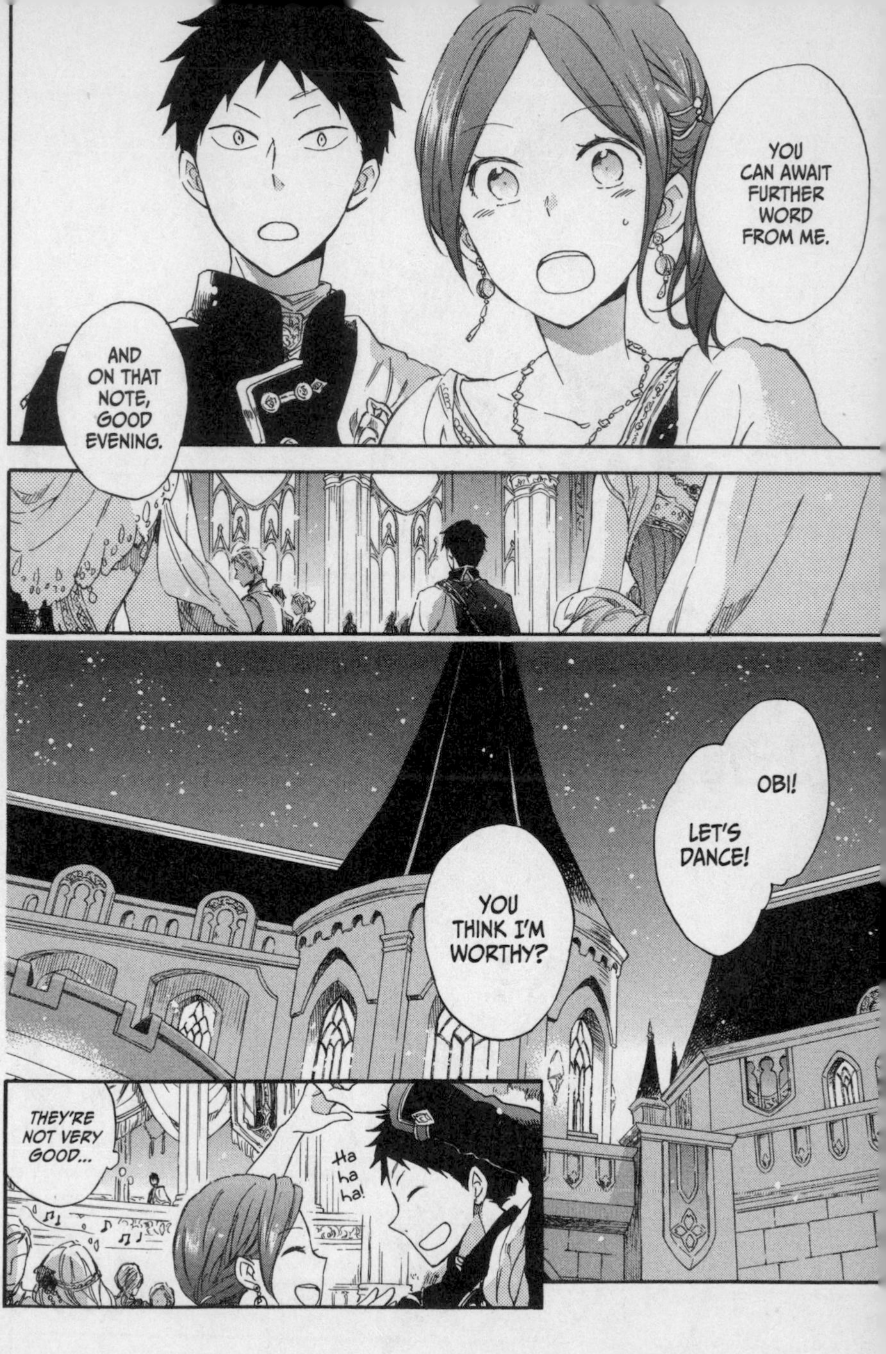
YOU CAN AWAIT FURTHER WORD FROM ME.
AND ON THAT NOTE, GOOD EVENING.
OBI!
LET'S DANCE!
YOU THINK I'M WORTHY?
Ha ha ha!
THEY'RE NOT VERY GOOD...

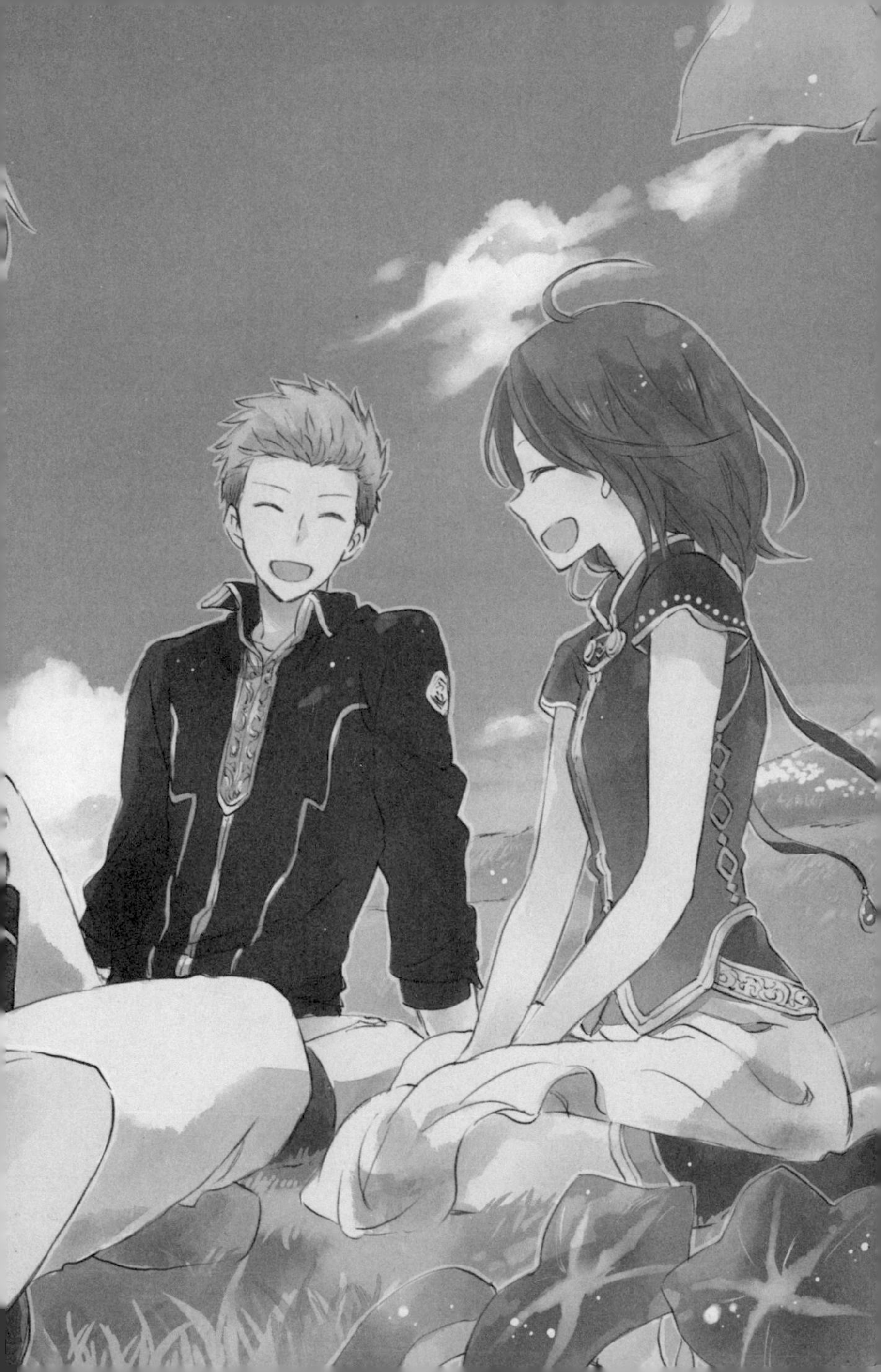

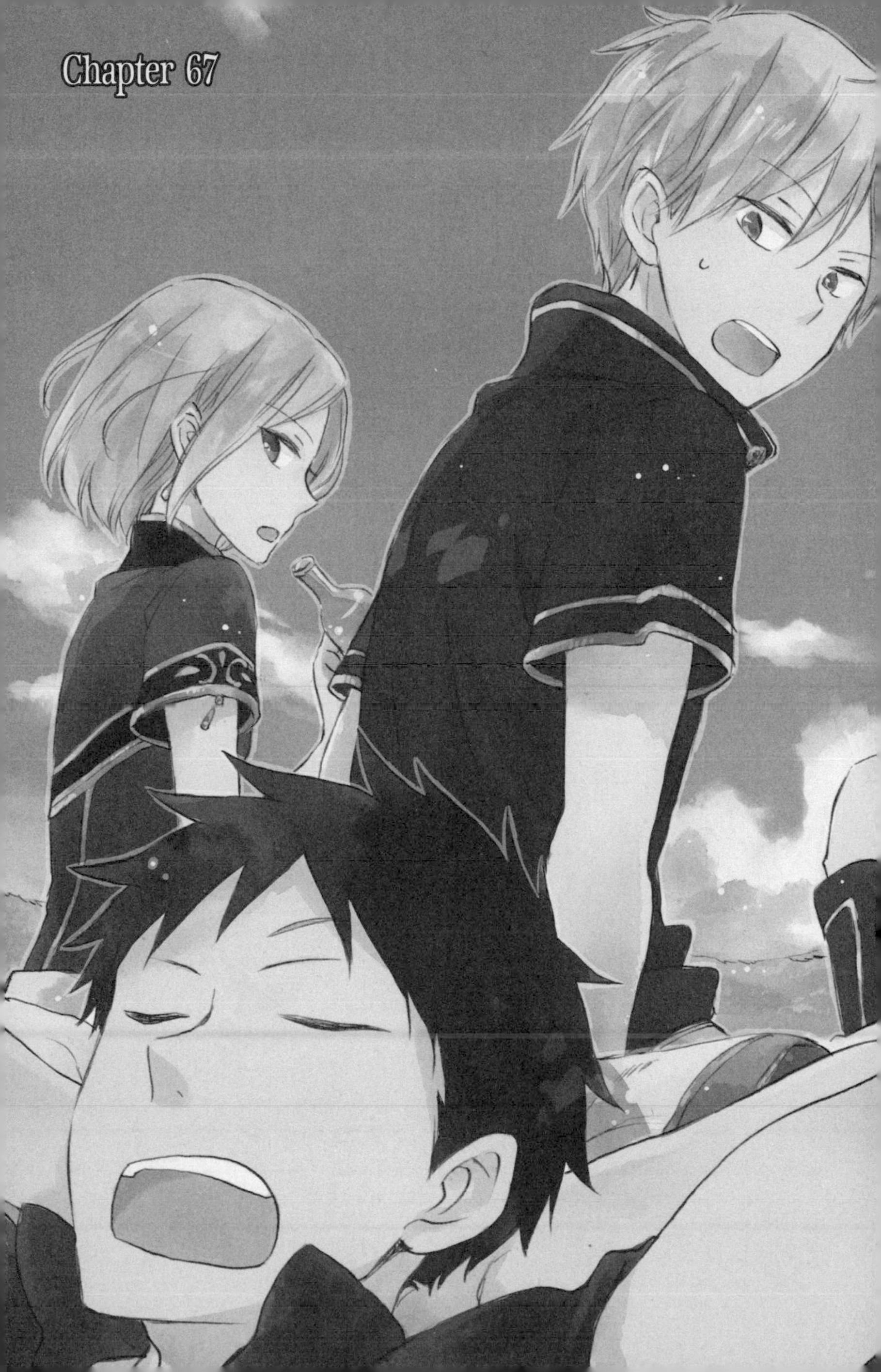
Chapter 67

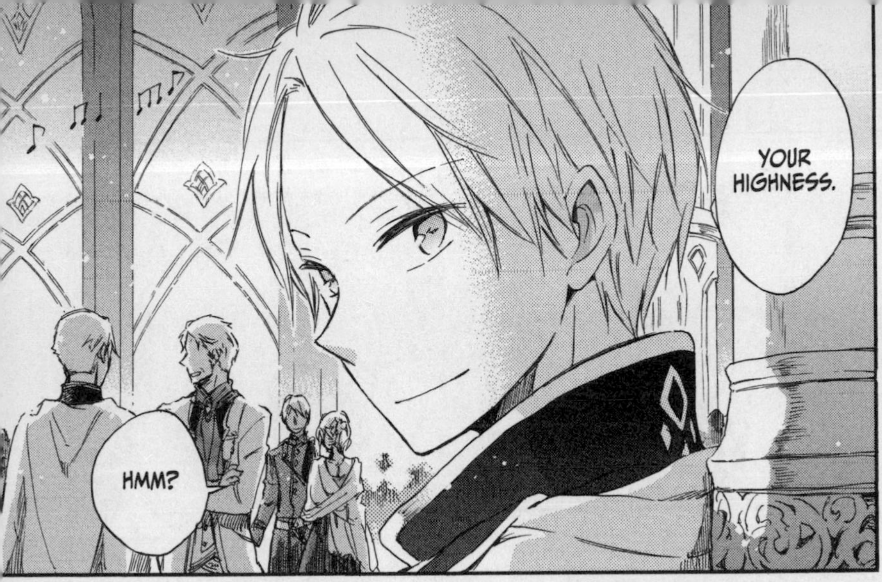
YOUR HIGHNESS.
HMM?

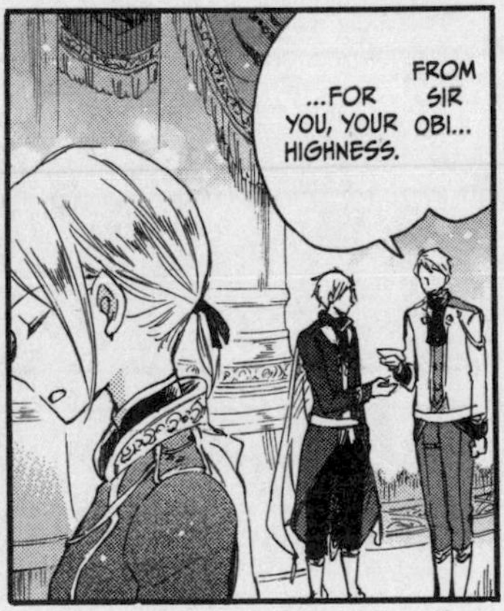
FROM SIR OBI...
...FOR YOU, YOUR HIGHNESS.

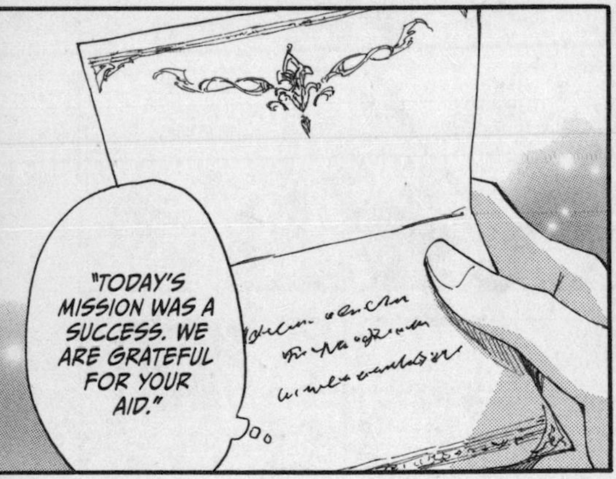
"TODAY'S MISSION WAS A SUCCESS. WE ARE GRATEFUL FOR YOUR AID."

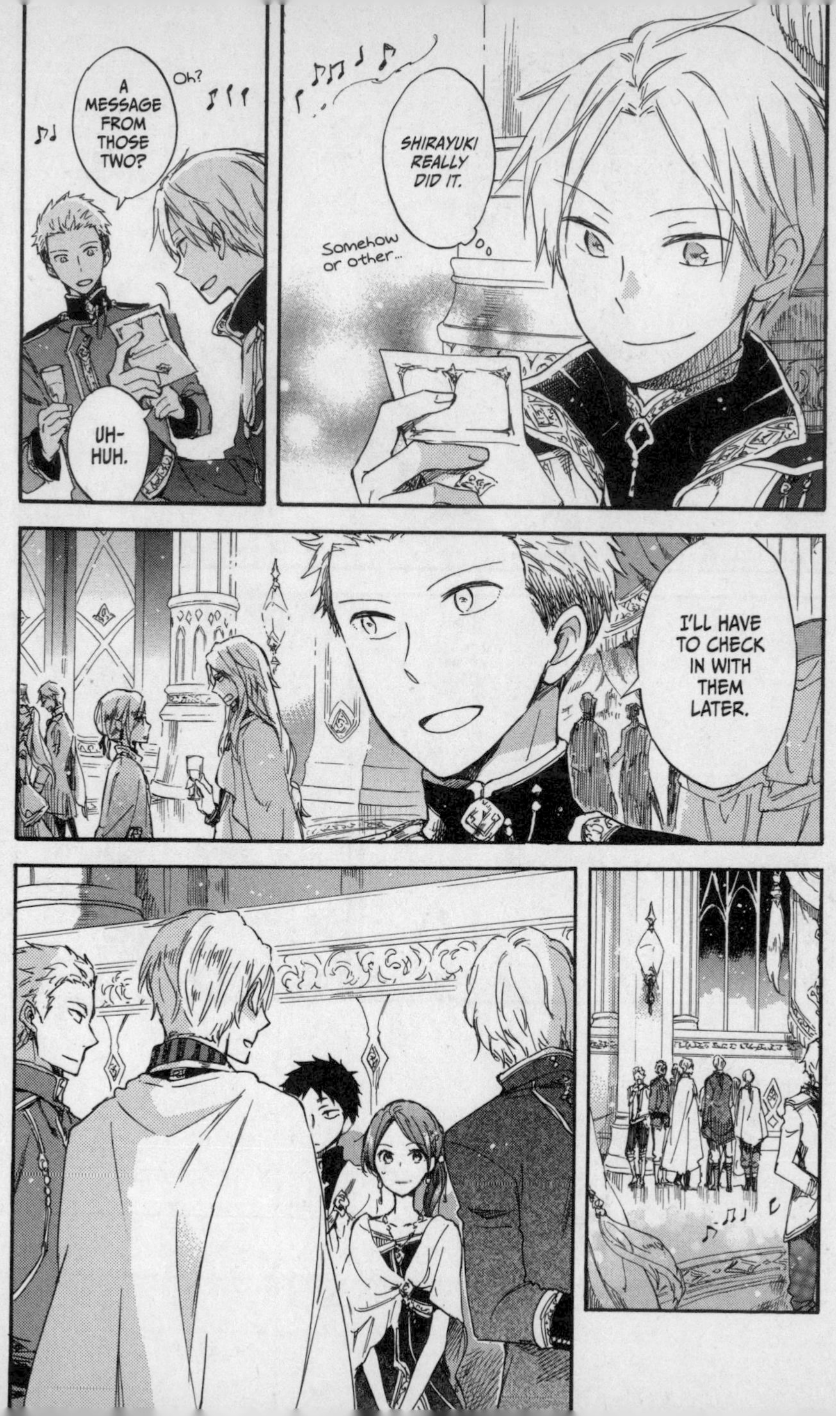
SHIRAYUKI REALLY DID IT.
Somehow or other...
Oh?
A MESSAGE FROM THOSE TWO?
UH-HUH.
I'LL HAVE TO CHECK IN WITH THEM LATER.

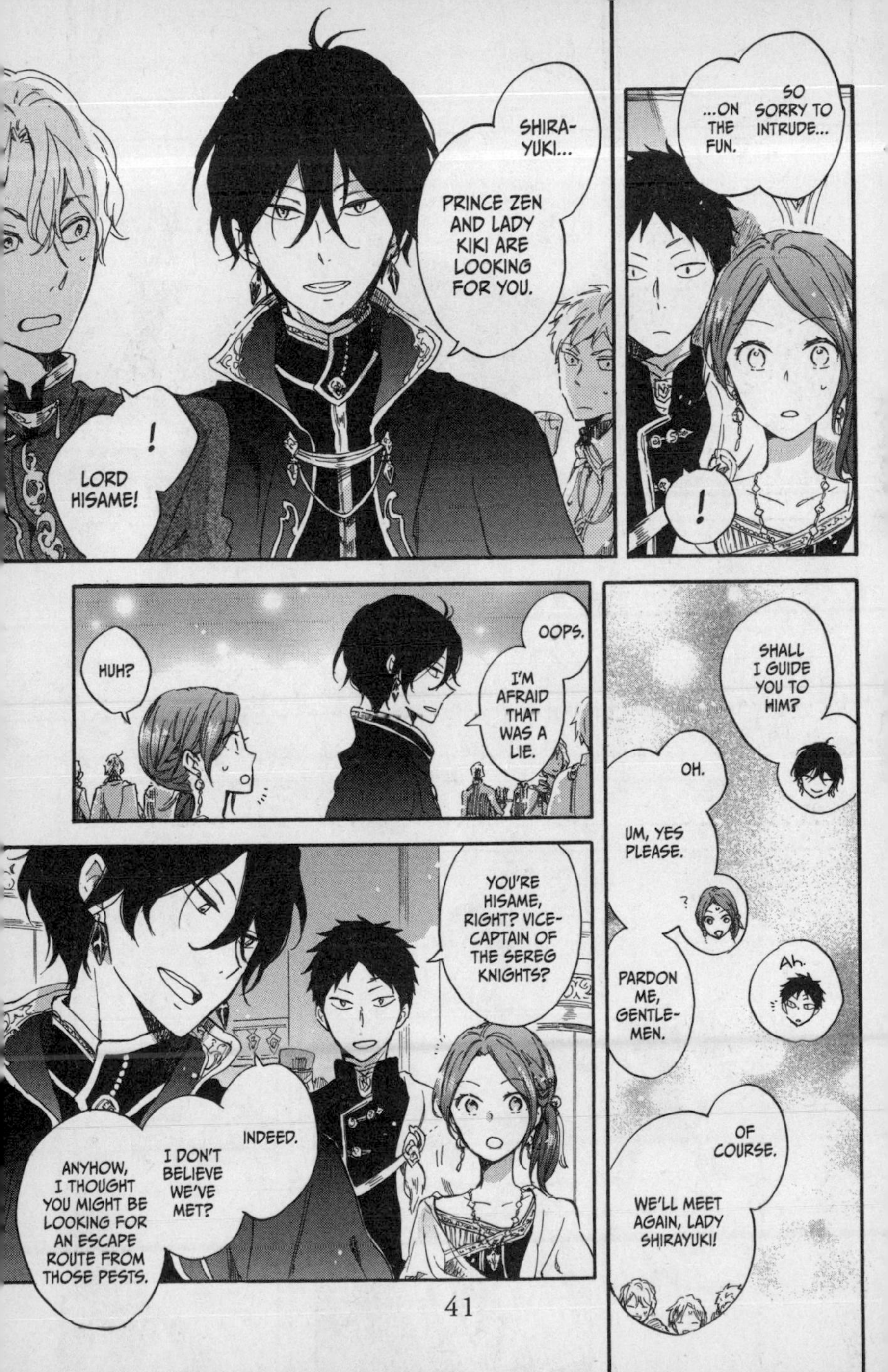
SO SORRY TO INTRUDE...
...ON THE FUN.
!
SHIRA-YUKI...
PRINCE ZEN AND LADY KIKI ARE LOOKING FOR YOU.
!
LORD HISAME!
SHALL I GUIDE YOU TO HIM?
OH.
UM, YES PLEASE.
Ah.
PARDON ME, GENTLEMEN.
OF COURSE.
WE'LL MEET AGAIN, LADY SHIRAYUKI!
OOPS.
I'M AFRAID THAT WAS A LIE.
HUH?
YOU'RE HISAME, RIGHT? VICE-CAPTAIN OF THE SEREG KNIGHTS?
INDEED.
I DON'T BELIEVE WE'VE MET?
ANYHOW, I THOUGHT YOU MIGHT BE LOOKING FOR AN ESCAPE ROUTE FROM THOSE PESTS.

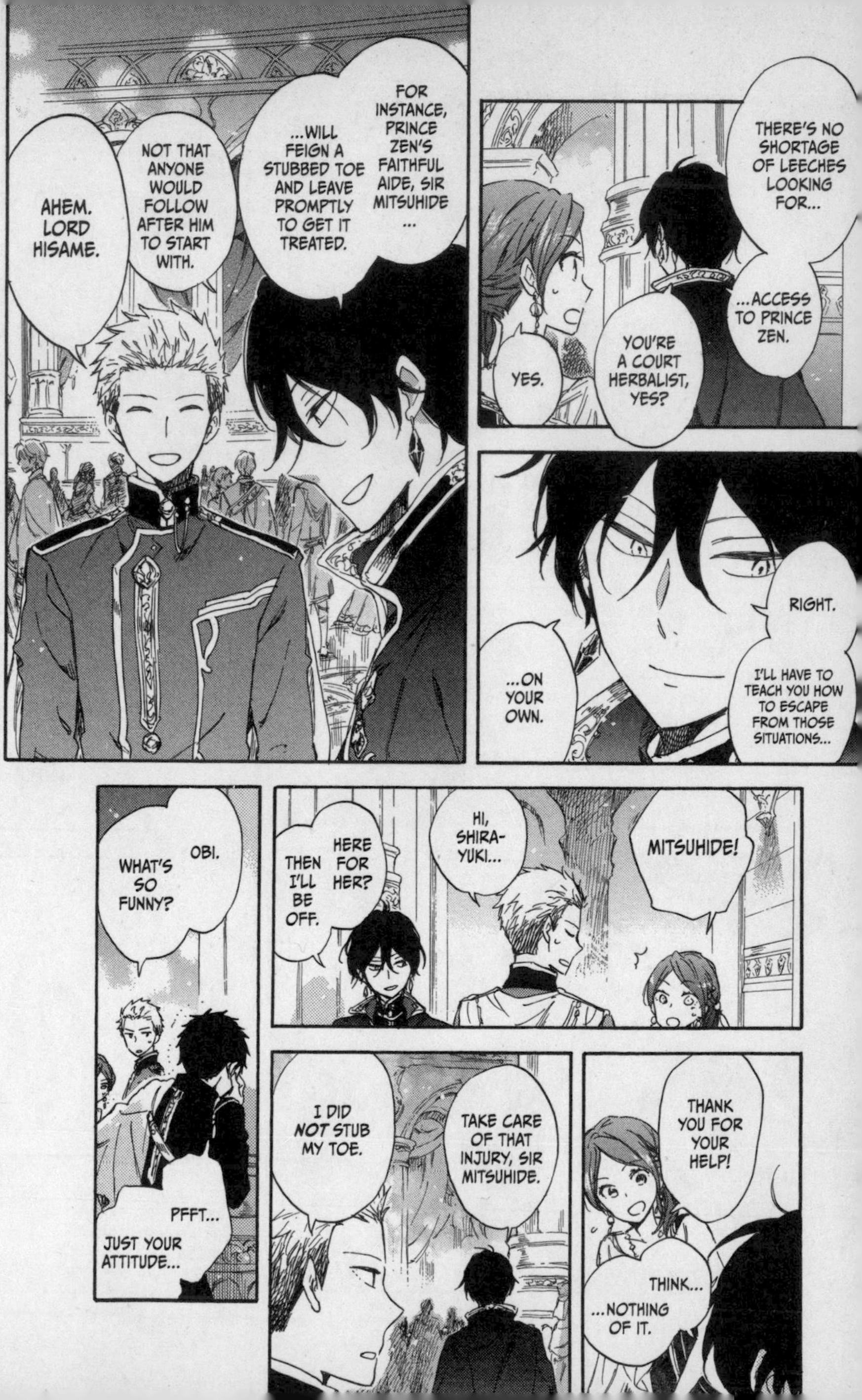
THERE'S NO SHORTAGE OF LEECHES LOOKING FOR...
...ACCESS TO PRINCE ZEN.
YOU'RE A COURT HERBALIST, YES?
YES.
RIGHT.
I'LL HAVE TO TEACH YOU HOW TO ESCAPE FROM THOSE SITUATIONS...
...ON YOUR OWN.
FOR INSTANCE, PRINCE ZEN'S FAITHFUL AIDE, SIR MITSUHIDE...
...WILL FEIGN A STUBBED TOE AND LEAVE PROMPTLY TO GET IT TREATED.
NOT THAT ANYONE WOULD FOLLOW AFTER HIM TO START WITH.
AHEM. LORD HISAME.
MITSUHIDE!
HI, SHIRA-YUKI...
HERE FOR HER?
THEN I'LL BE OFF.
THANK YOU FOR YOUR HELP!
THINK...
...NOTHING OF IT.
TAKE CARE OF THAT INJURY, SIR MITSUHIDE.
I DID *NOT* STUB MY TOE.
OBI.
WHAT'S SO FUNNY?
PFFT...
JUST YOUR ATTITUDE...

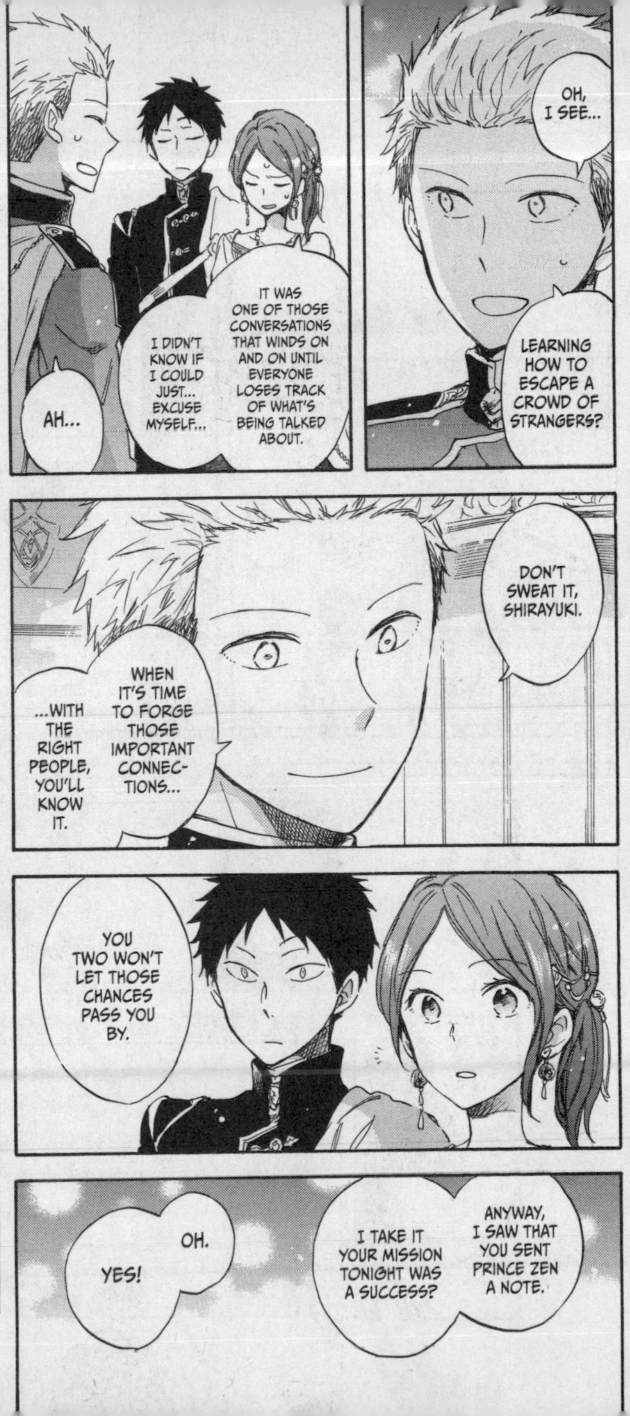
OH, I SEE...
LEARNING HOW TO ESCAPE A CROWD OF STRANGERS?
IT WAS ONE OF THOSE CONVERSATIONS THAT WINDS ON AND ON UNTIL EVERYONE LOSES TRACK OF WHAT'S BEING TALKED ABOUT.
I DIDN'T KNOW IF I COULD JUST... EXCUSE MYSELF...
AH...
DON'T SWEAT IT, SHIRAYUKI.
WHEN IT'S TIME TO FORGE THOSE IMPORTANT CONNEC-TIONS...
...WITH THE RIGHT PEOPLE, YOU'LL KNOW IT.
YOU TWO WON'T LET THOSE CHANCES PASS YOU BY.
ANYWAY, I SAW THAT YOU SENT PRINCE ZEN A NOTE.
I TAKE IT YOUR MISSION TONIGHT WAS A SUCCESS?
OH.
YES!

2

CHAPTER TALK

Chapter 66

Hisame, Shirayuki and Obi finally came face-to-face. I wasn't sure that we'd ever get this scene, but I'm glad that we did.

Earlier, Kiki surmised that Obi and Hisame wouldn't get along at all, but weirdly enough, that didn't seem to be the case.

Still, Obi is firmly on Mitsuhide's side. He's just not the type to step in when old rivals start butting heads. He'd rather watch how things play out while holding back his laughter.

And I can't even imagine Zen and Hisame talking at all.

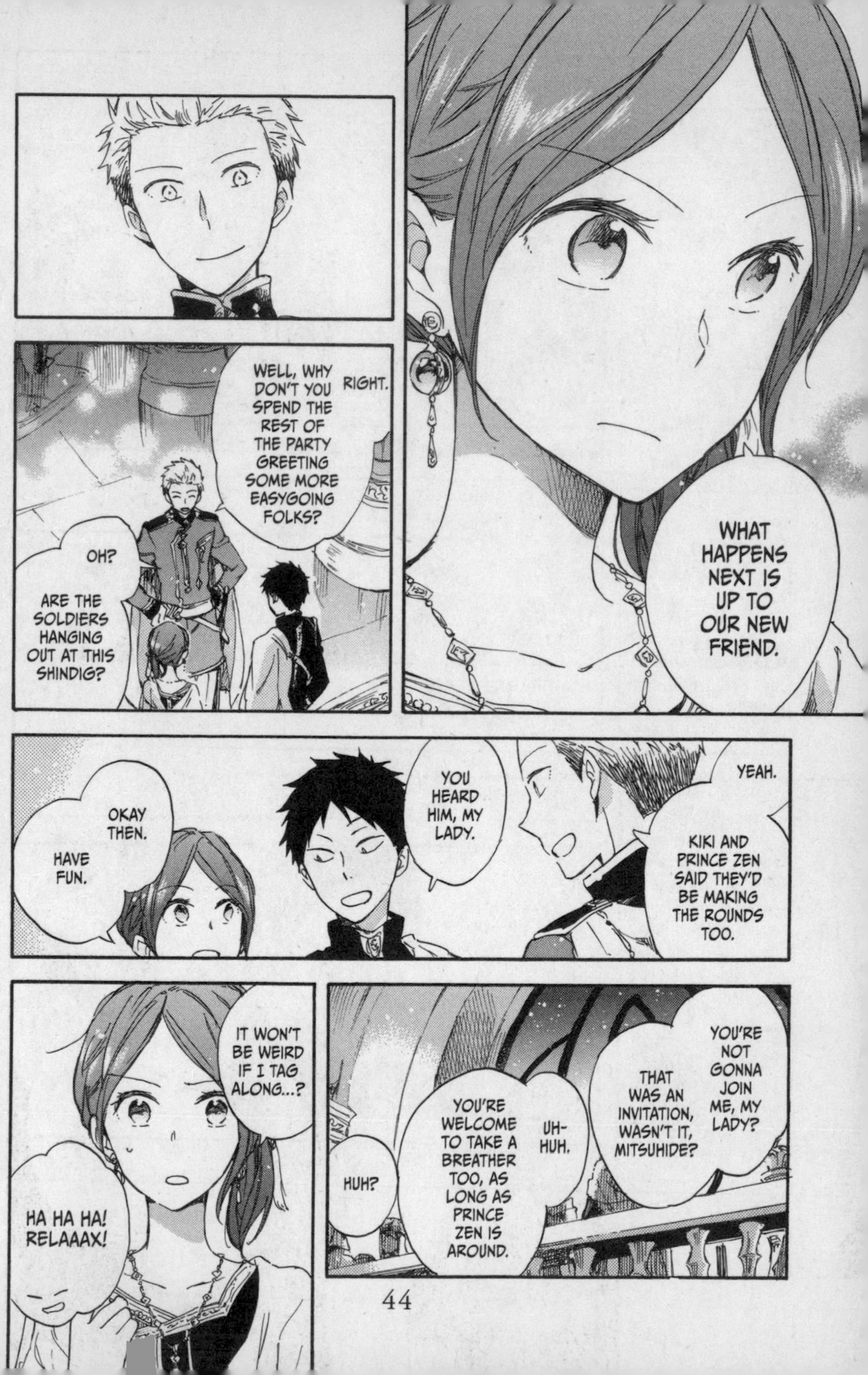
WHAT HAPPENS NEXT IS UP TO OUR NEW FRIEND.
RIGHT.
WELL, WHY DON'T YOU SPEND THE REST OF THE PARTY GREETING SOME MORE EASYGOING FOLKS?
OH?
ARE THE SOLDIERS HANGING OUT AT THIS SHINDIG?
YEAH.
KIKI AND PRINCE ZEN SAID THEY'D BE MAKING THE ROUNDS TOO.
YOU HEARD HIM, MY LADY.
OKAY THEN.
HAVE FUN.
YOU'RE NOT GONNA JOIN ME, MY LADY?
THAT WAS AN INVITATION, WASN'T IT, MITSUHIDE?
UH-HUH.
YOU'RE WELCOME TO TAKE A BREATHER TOO, AS LONG AS PRINCE ZEN IS AROUND.
HUH?
IT WON'T BE WEIRD IF I TAG ALONG...?
HA HA HA! RELAAAX!

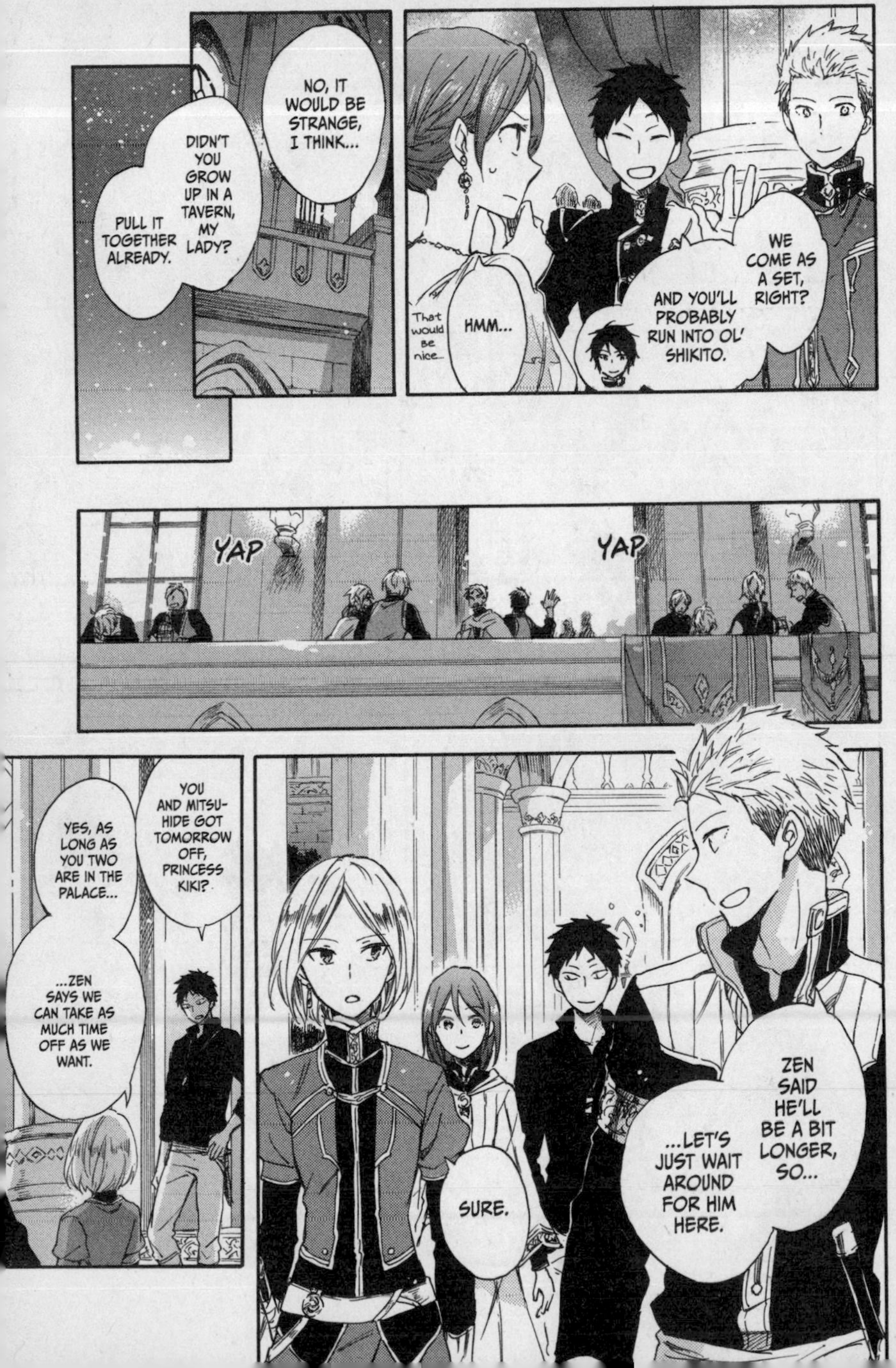
WE COME AS A SET, RIGHT?
AND YOU'LL PROBABLY RUN INTO OL' SHIKITO.
HMM...
That would be nice...
NO, IT WOULD BE STRANGE, I THINK...
DIDN'T YOU GROW UP IN A TAVERN, MY LADY?
PULL IT TOGETHER ALREADY.
YAP
YAP
ZEN SAID HE'LL BE A BIT LONGER, SO...
...LET'S JUST WAIT AROUND FOR HIM HERE.
SURE.
YOU AND MITSU-HIDE GOT TOMORROW OFF, PRINCESS KIKI?
YES, AS LONG AS YOU TWO ARE IN THE PALACE...
...ZEN SAYS WE CAN TAKE AS MUCH TIME OFF AS WE WANT.

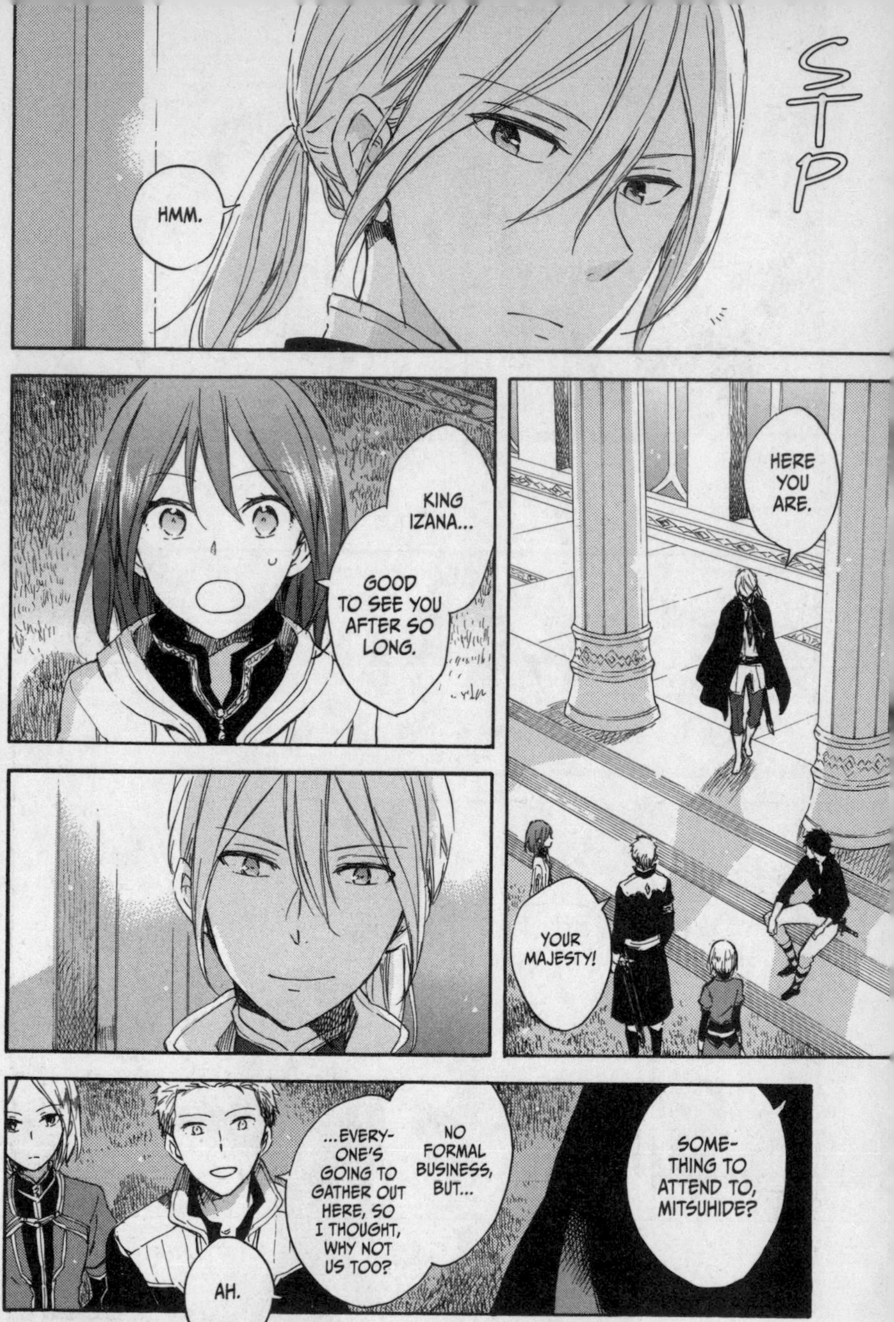
STP
HMM.
HERE YOU ARE.
YOUR MAJESTY!
KING IZANA...
GOOD TO SEE YOU AFTER SO LONG.
SOME-THING TO ATTEND TO, MITSUHIDE?
NO FORMAL BUSINESS, BUT...
...EVERY-ONE'S GOING TO GATHER OUT HERE, SO I THOUGHT, WHY NOT US TOO?
AH.

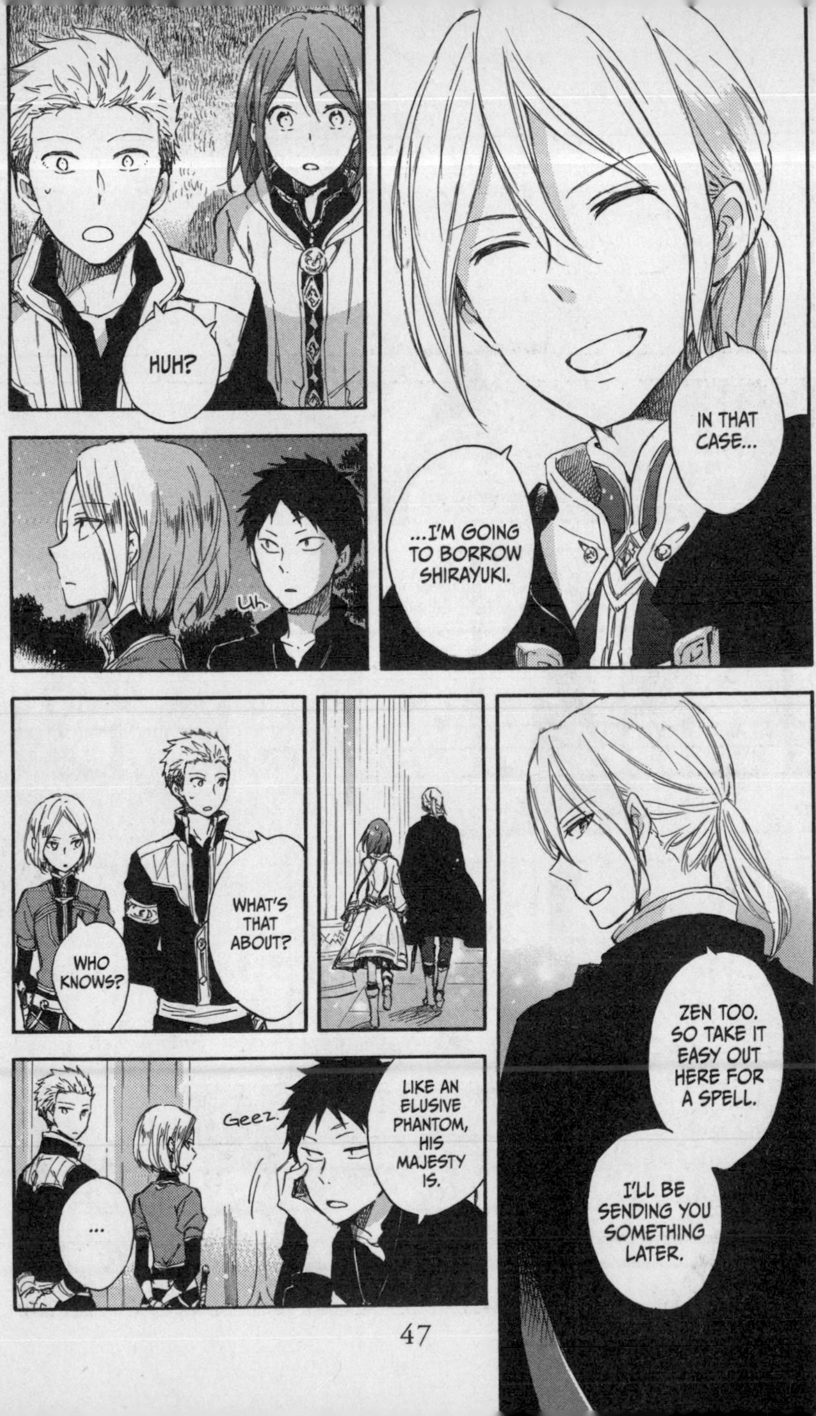
IN THAT CASE...
...I'M GOING TO BORROW SHIRAYUKI.
HUH?
Uh.
ZEN TOO. SO TAKE IT EASY OUT HERE FOR A SPELL.
I'LL BE SENDING YOU SOMETHING LATER.
WHAT'S THAT ABOUT?
WHO KNOWS?
LIKE AN ELUSIVE PHANTOM, HIS MAJESTY IS.
Geez.
...

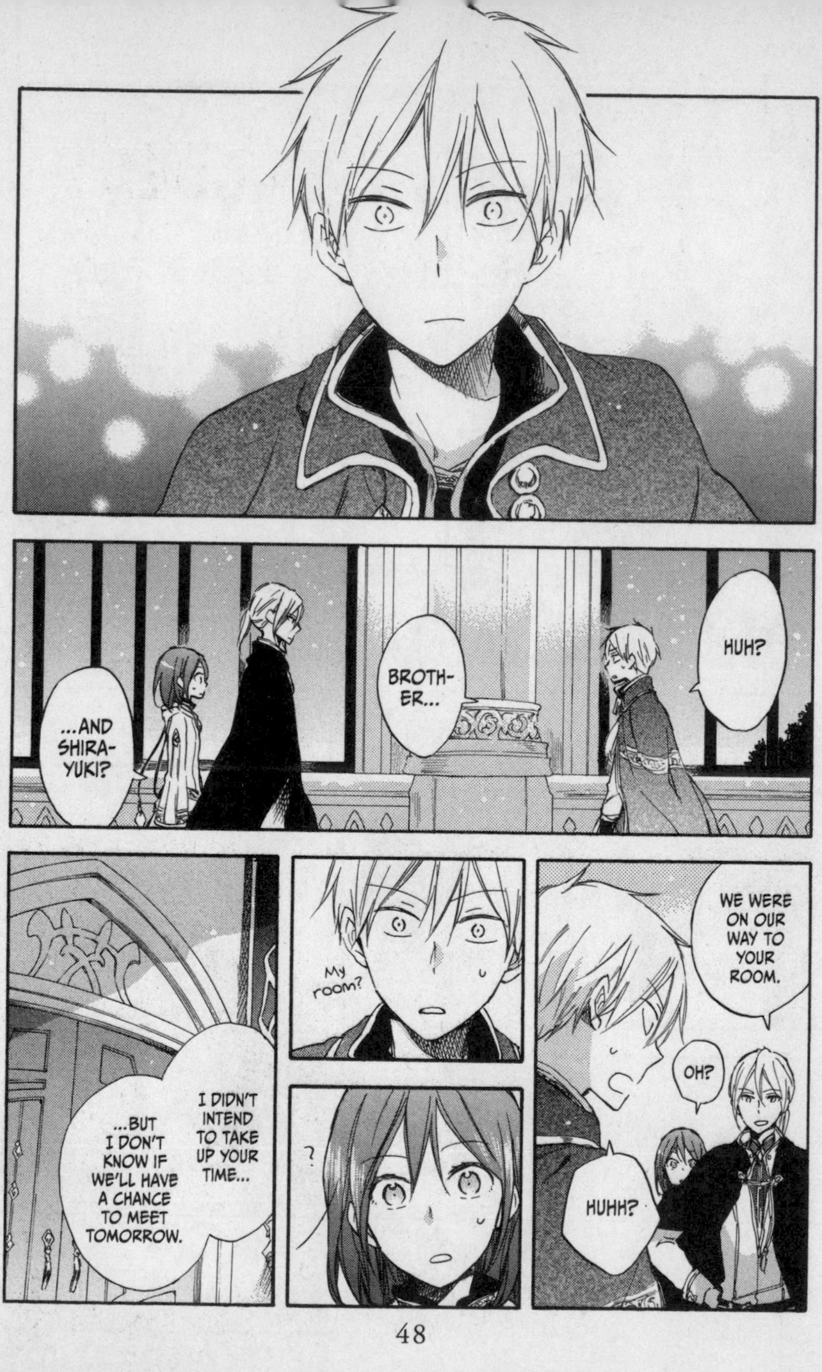
HUH?
BROTH-ER...
...AND SHIRA-YUKI?
WE WERE ON OUR WAY TO YOUR ROOM.
OH?
HUHH?
My room?
?
I DIDN'T INTEND TO TAKE UP YOUR TIME...
...BUT I DON'T KNOW IF WE'LL HAVE A CHANCE TO MEET TOMORROW.

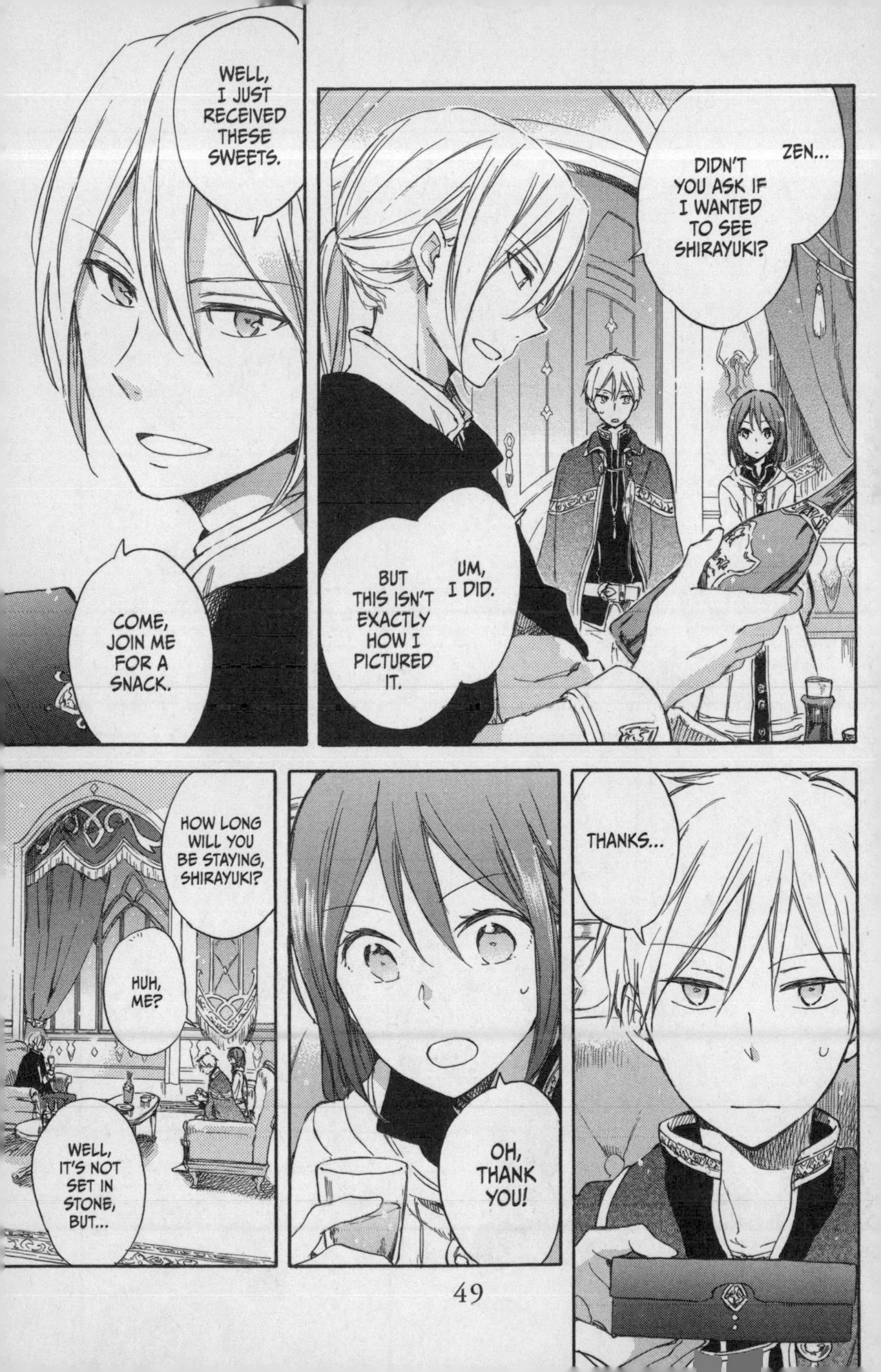
ZEN...
DIDN'T YOU ASK IF I WANTED TO SEE SHIRAYUKI?
UM, I DID.
BUT THIS ISN'T EXACTLY HOW I PICTURED IT.
WELL, I JUST RECEIVED THESE SWEETS.
COME, JOIN ME FOR A SNACK.
THANKS...
OH, THANK YOU!
HOW LONG WILL YOU BE STAYING, SHIRAYUKI?
HUH, ME?
WELL, IT'S NOT SET IN STONE, BUT...

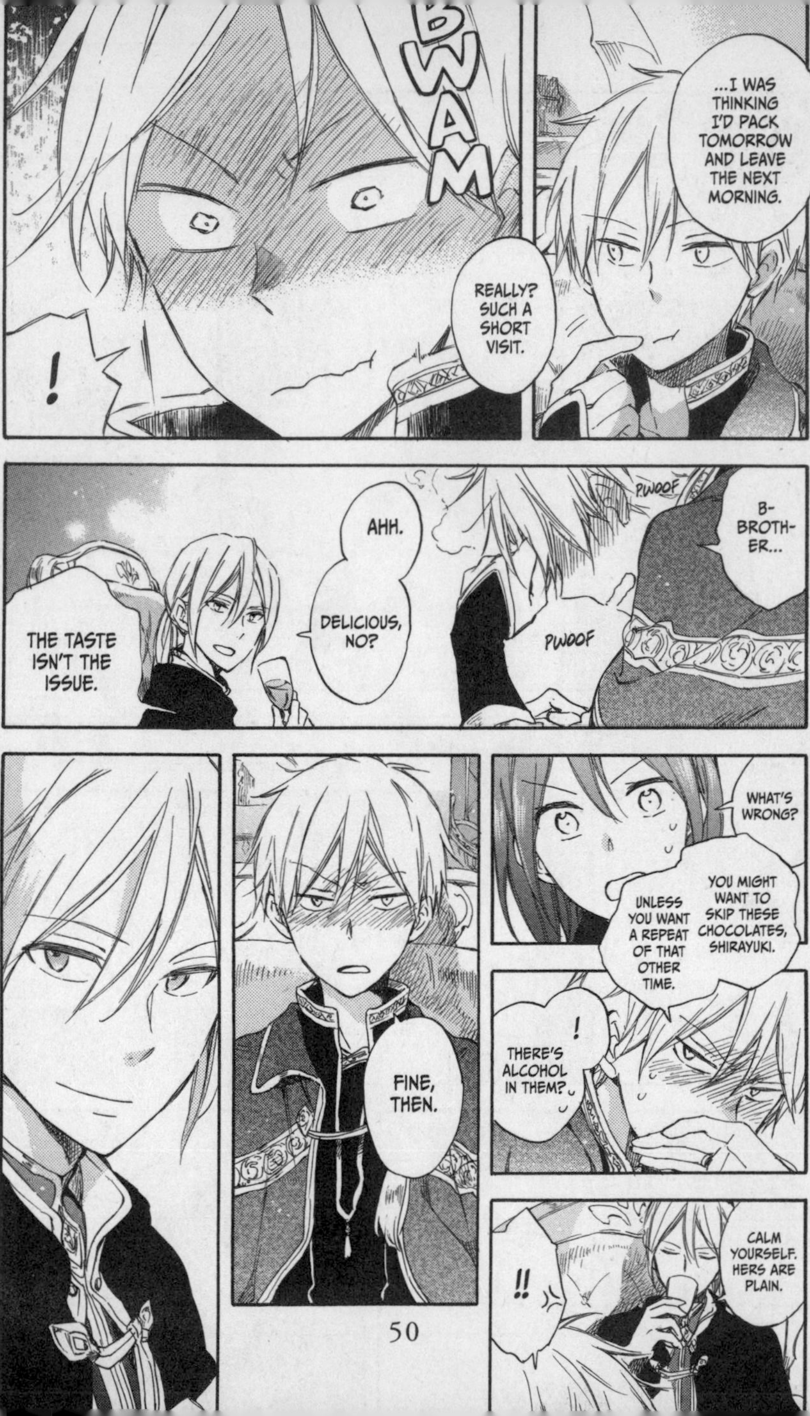
...I WAS THINKING I'D PACK TOMORROW AND LEAVE THE NEXT MORNING.
REALLY? SUCH A SHORT VISIT.
BWAM
!
B-BROTH-ER...
PWOOF
PWOOF
AHH.
DELICIOUS, NO?
THE TASTE ISN'T THE ISSUE.
WHAT'S WRONG?
YOU MIGHT WANT TO SKIP THESE CHOCOLATES, SHIRAYUKI.
UNLESS YOU WANT A REPEAT OF THAT OTHER TIME.
!
THERE'S ALCOHOL IN THEM?
CALM YOURSELF. HERS ARE PLAIN.
!!
FINE, THEN.

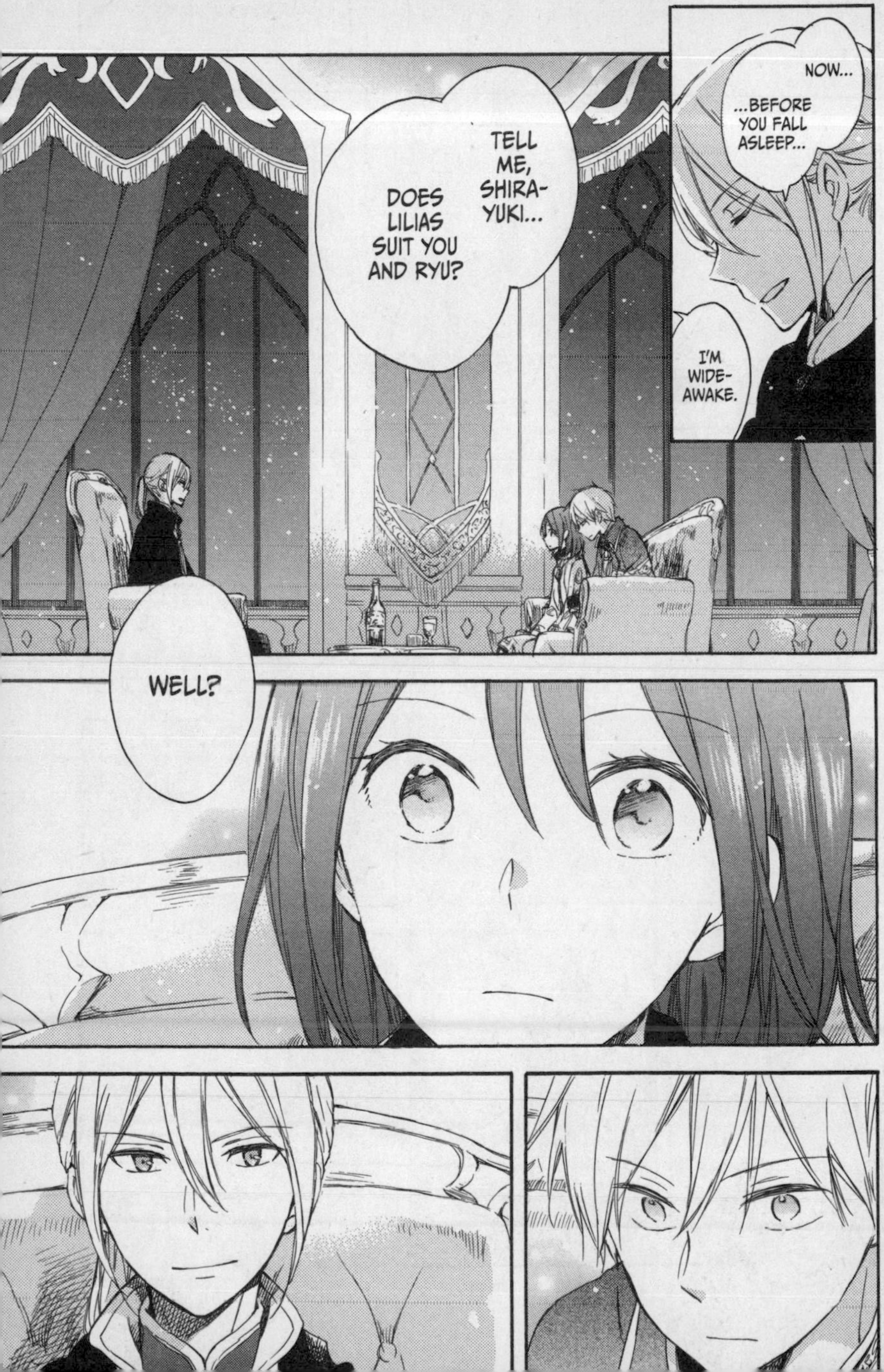
NOW...
...BEFORE YOU FALL ASLEEP...
I'M WIDE-AWAKE.
TELL ME, SHIRA-YUKI...
DOES LILIAS SUIT YOU AND RYU?
WELL?

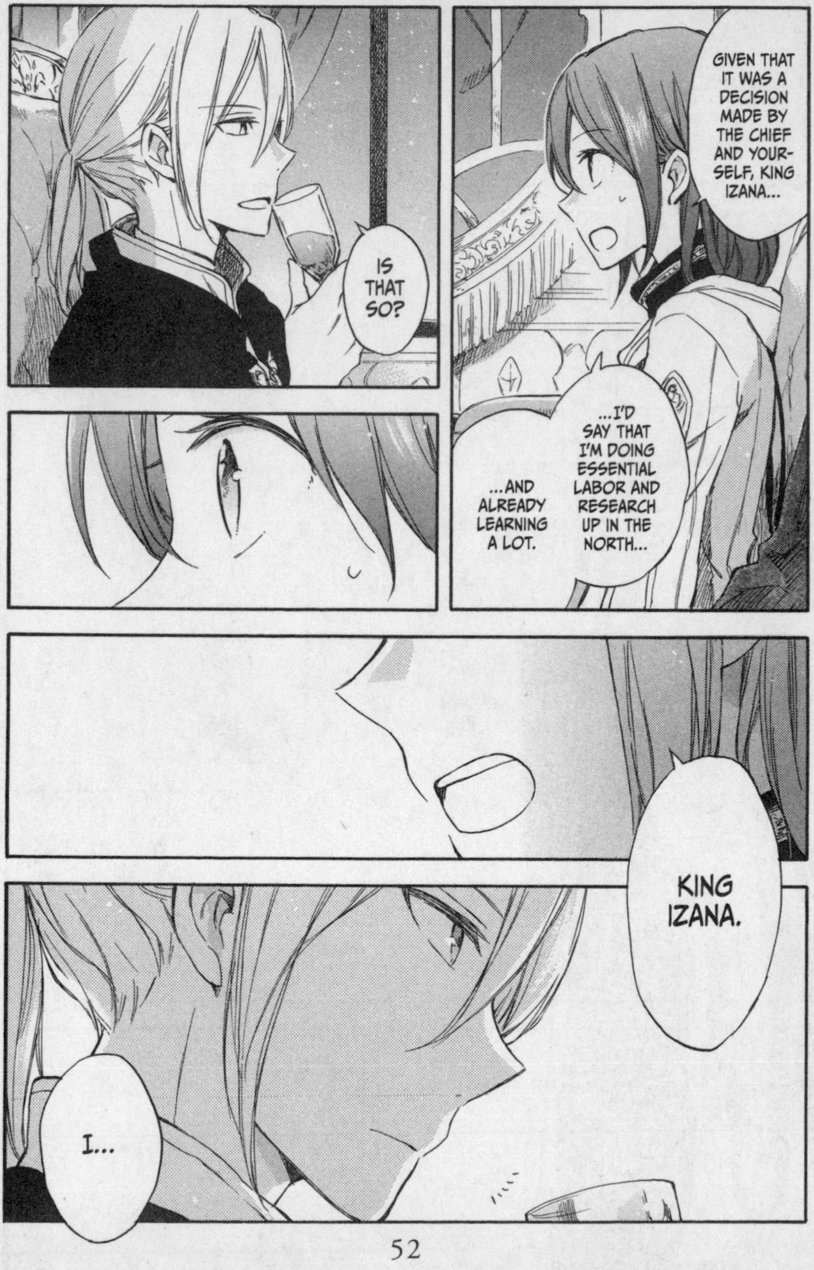

GIVEN THAT IT WAS A DECISION MADE BY THE CHIEF AND YOURSELF, KING IZANA...
...I'D SAY THAT I'M DOING ESSENTIAL LABOR AND RESEARCH UP IN THE NORTH...
...AND ALREADY LEARNING A LOT.
IS THAT SO?
KING IZANA.
I...

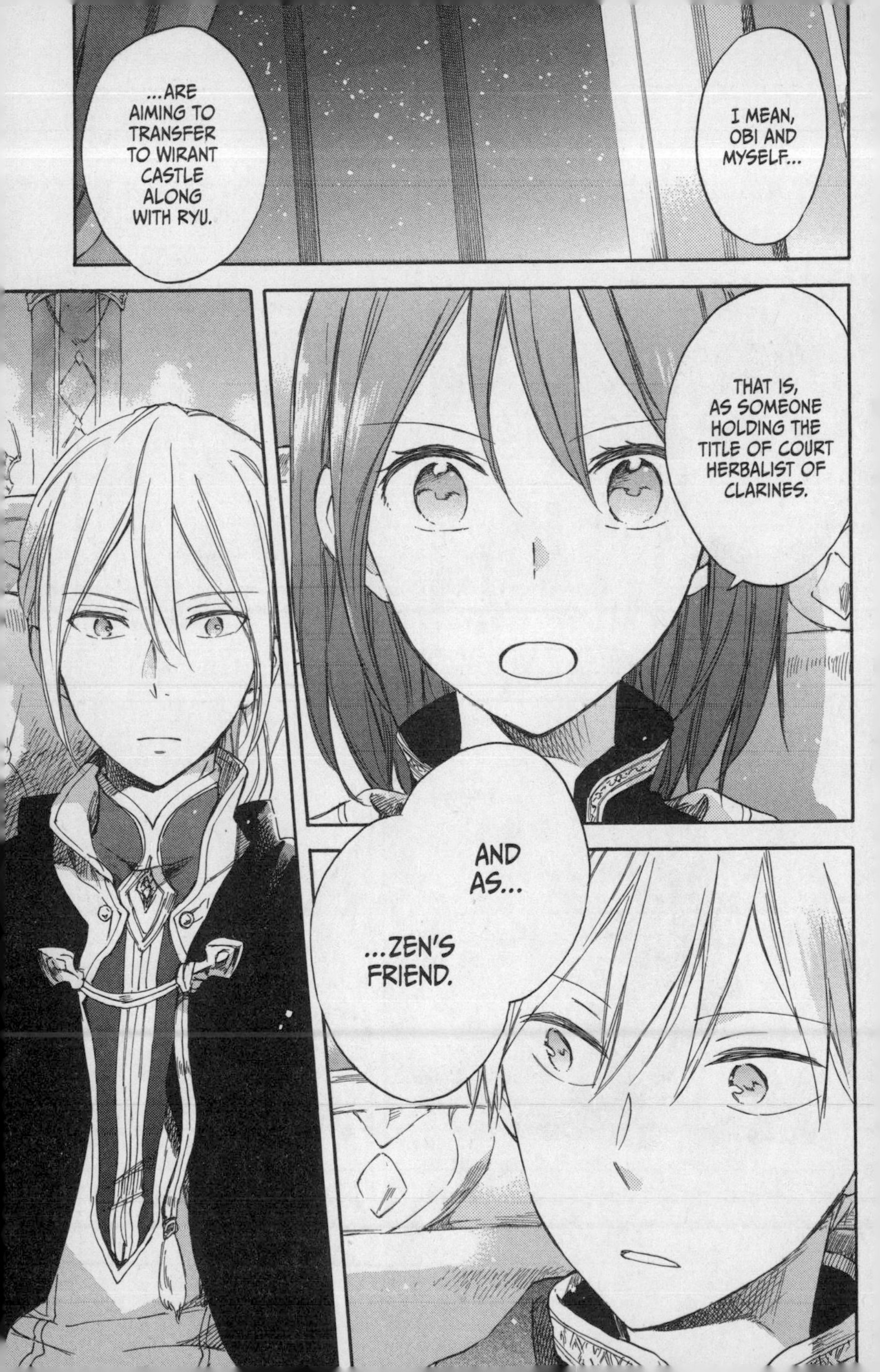
I MEAN, OBI AND MYSELF...
...ARE AIMING TO TRANSFER TO WIRANT CASTLE ALONG WITH RYU.
THAT IS, AS SOMEONE HOLDING THE TITLE OF COURT HERBALIST OF CLARINES.
AND AS...
...ZEN'S FRIEND.

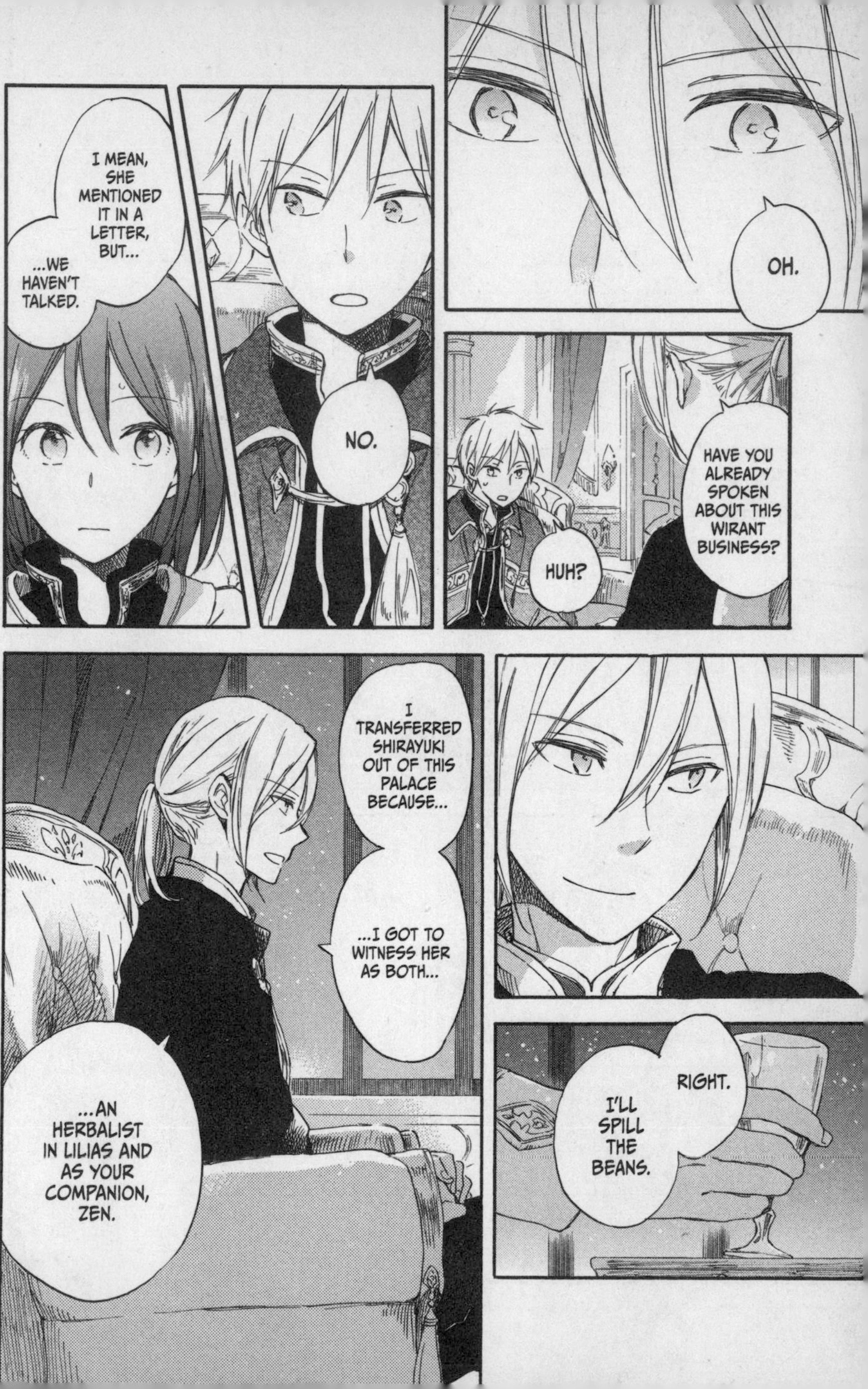
OH.
HAVE YOU ALREADY SPOKEN ABOUT THIS WIRANT BUSINESS?
HUH?
NO.
I MEAN, SHE MENTIONED IT IN A LETTER, BUT...
...WE HAVEN'T TALKED.
RIGHT.
I'LL SPILL THE BEANS.
I TRANSFERRED SHIRAYUKI OUT OF THIS PALACE BECAUSE...
...I GOT TO WITNESS HER AS BOTH...
...AN HERBALIST IN LILIAS AND AS YOUR COMPANION, ZEN.

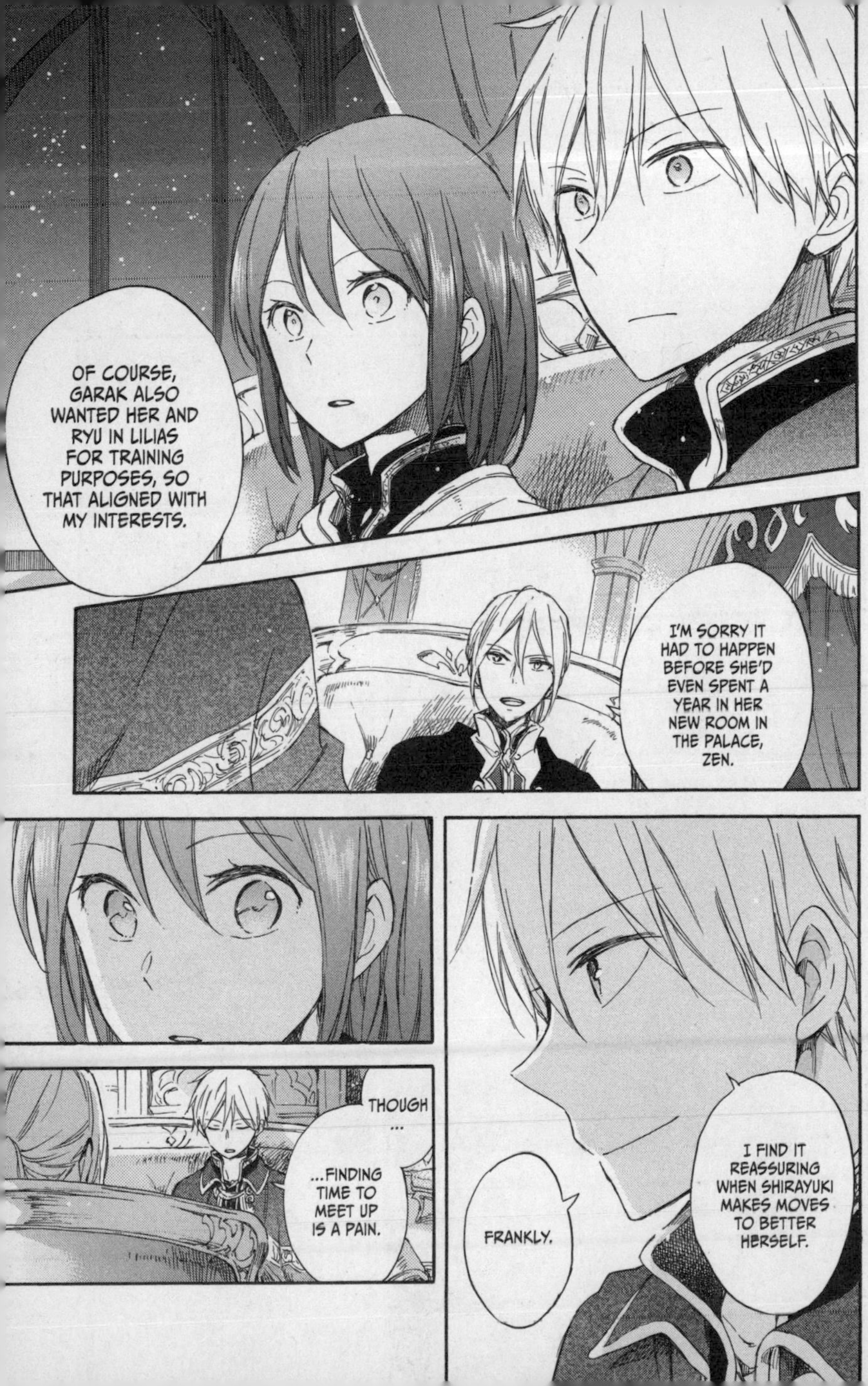
OF COURSE, GARAK ALSO WANTED HER AND RYU IN LILIAS FOR TRAINING PURPOSES, SO THAT ALIGNED WITH MY INTERESTS.
I'M SORRY IT HAD TO HAPPEN BEFORE SHE'D EVEN SPENT A YEAR IN HER NEW ROOM IN THE PALACE, ZEN.
I FIND IT REASSURING WHEN SHIRAYUKI MAKES MOVES TO BETTER HERSELF.
FRANKLY.
THOUGH ...
...FINDING TIME TO MEET UP IS A PAIN.

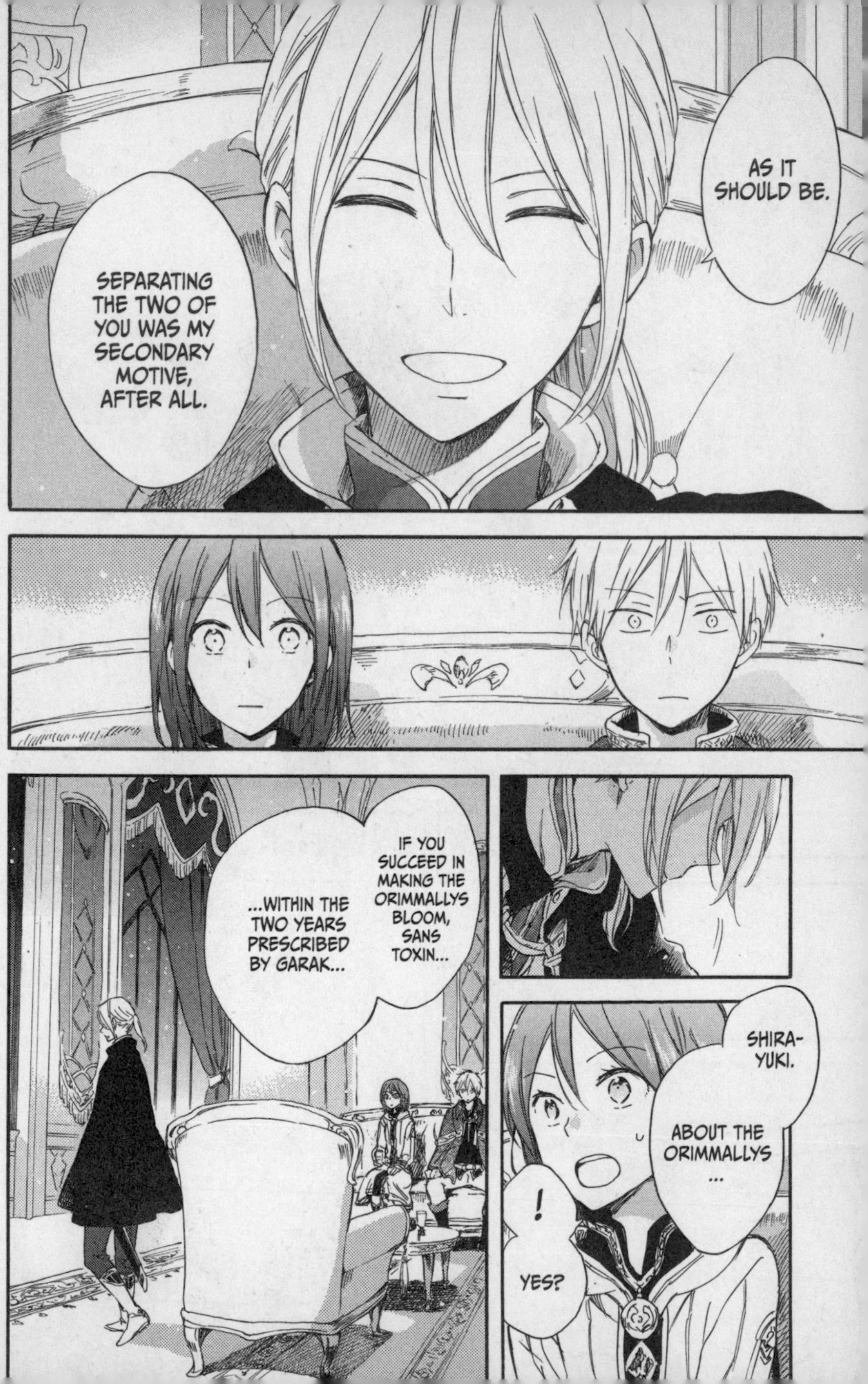
AS IT SHOULD BE.
SEPARATING THE TWO OF YOU WAS MY SECONDARY MOTIVE, AFTER ALL.
SHIRA-YUKI.
ABOUT THE ORIMMALLYS ...
!
YES?
IF YOU SUCCEED IN MAKING THE ORIMMALLYS BLOOM, SANS TOXIN...
...WITHIN THE TWO YEARS PRESCRIBED BY GARAK...

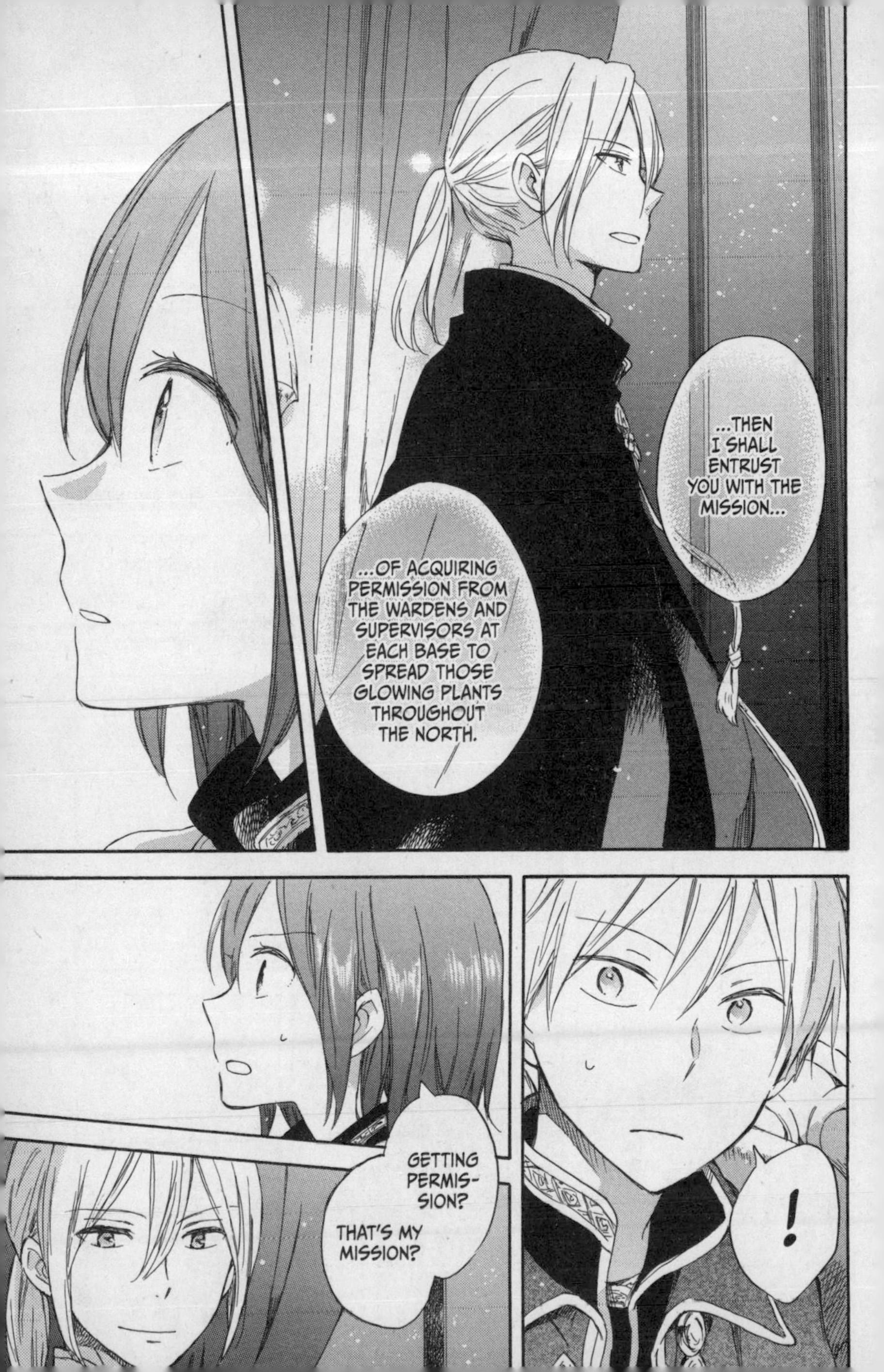
...THEN I SHALL ENTRUST YOU WITH THE MISSION...
...OF ACQUIRING PERMISSION FROM THE WARDENS AND SUPERVISORS AT EACH BASE TO SPREAD THOSE GLOWING PLANTS THROUGHOUT THE NORTH.
!
GETTING PERMIS-SION?
THAT'S MY MISSION?

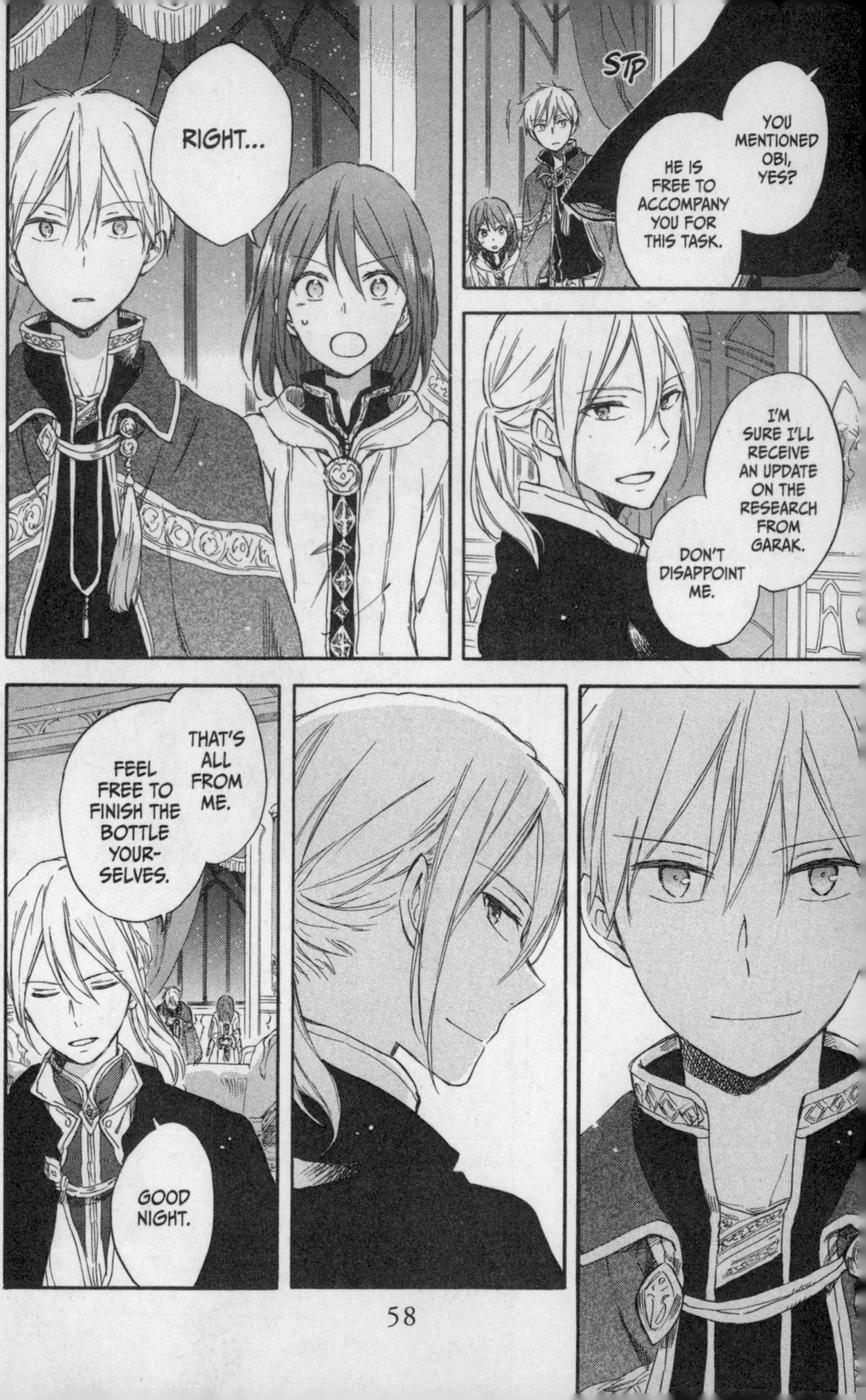
STP
YOU MENTIONED OBI, YES?
HE IS FREE TO ACCOMPANY YOU FOR THIS TASK.
I'M SURE I'LL RECEIVE AN UPDATE ON THE RESEARCH FROM GARAK.
DON'T DISAPPOINT ME.
RIGHT...
THAT'S ALL FROM ME.
FEEL FREE TO FINISH THE BOTTLE YOUR-SELVES.
GOOD NIGHT.

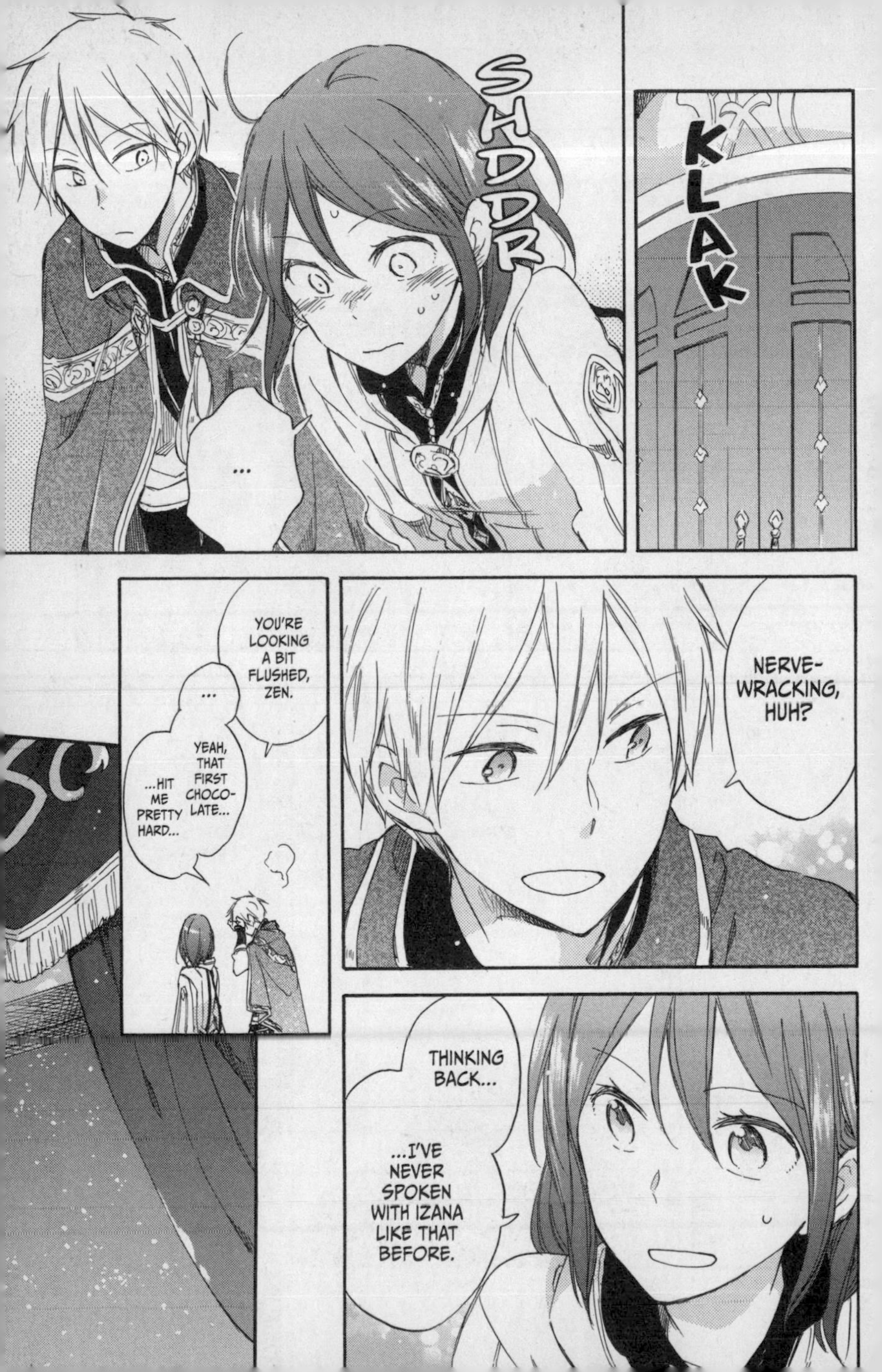
KLAK
SHDDR
...
NERVE-WRACKING, HUH?
YOU'RE LOOKING A BIT FLUSHED, ZEN.
...
YEAH, THAT FIRST CHOCOLATE...
...HIT ME PRETTY HARD...
THINKING BACK...
...I'VE NEVER SPOKEN WITH IZANA LIKE THAT BEFORE.

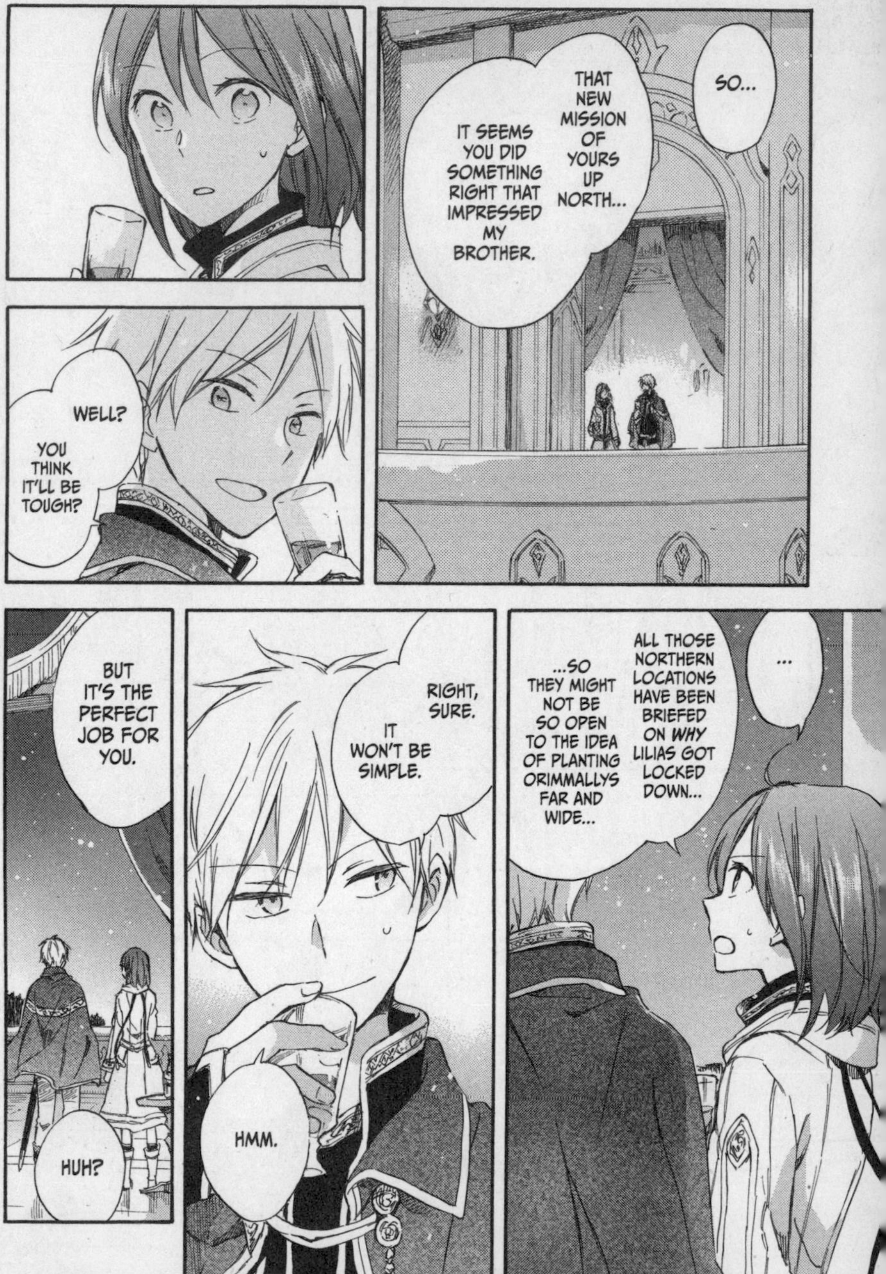
SO...
THAT NEW MISSION OF YOURS UP NORTH...
IT SEEMS YOU DID SOMETHING RIGHT THAT IMPRESSED MY BROTHER.
WELL?
YOU THINK IT'LL BE TOUGH?
...
ALL THOSE NORTHERN LOCATIONS HAVE BEEN BRIEFED ON *WHY* LILIAS GOT LOCKED DOWN...
...SO THEY MIGHT NOT BE SO OPEN TO THE IDEA OF PLANTING ORIMMALLYS FAR AND WIDE...
RIGHT, SURE.
IT WON'T BE SIMPLE.
HMM.
BUT IT'S THE PERFECT JOB FOR YOU.
HUH?

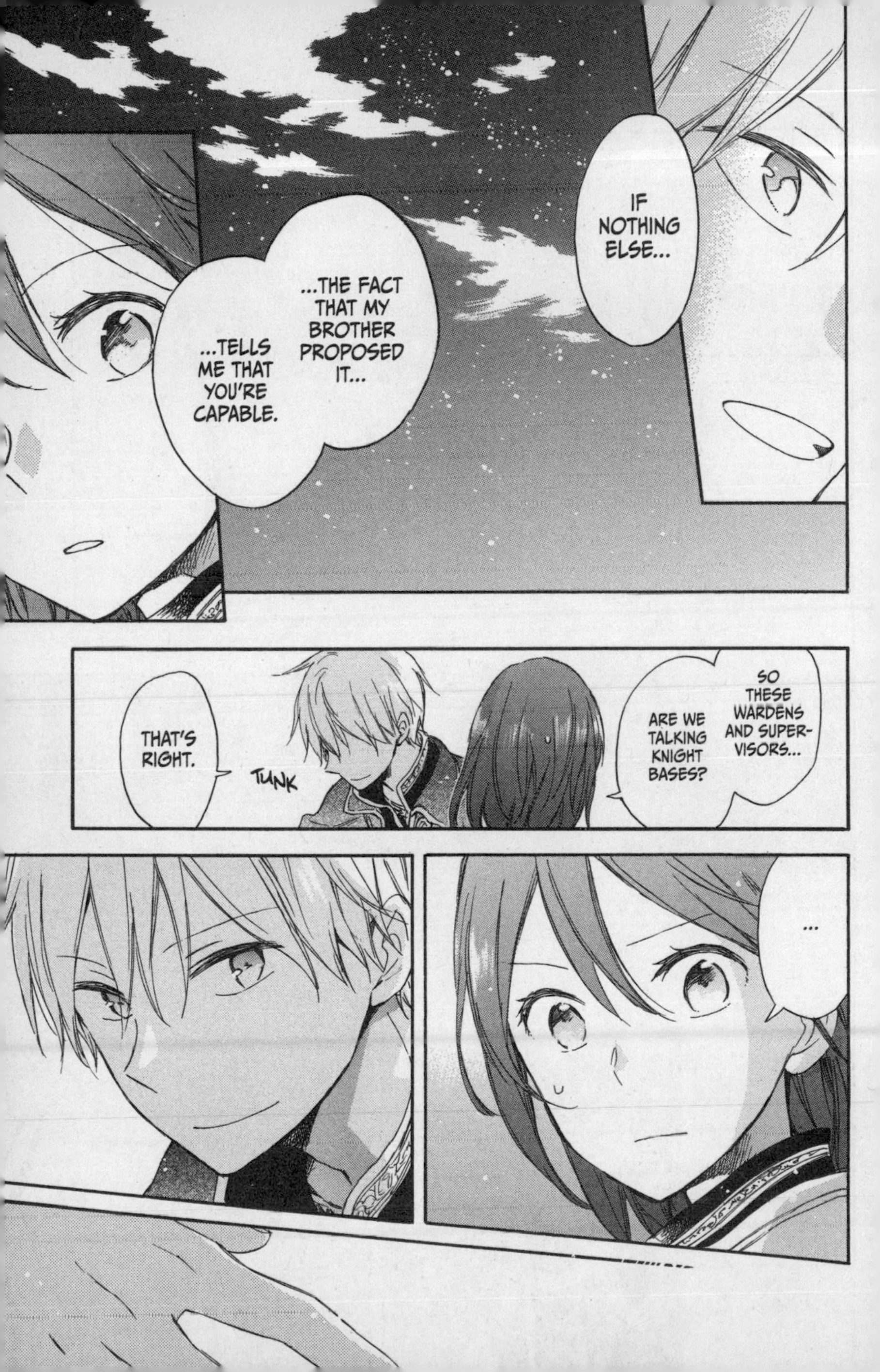
IF NOTHING ELSE...
...THE FACT THAT MY BROTHER PROPOSED IT...
...TELLS ME THAT YOU'RE CAPABLE.
SO THESE WARDENS AND SUPER-VISORS...
ARE WE TALKING KNIGHT BASES?
TUNK
THAT'S RIGHT.
...

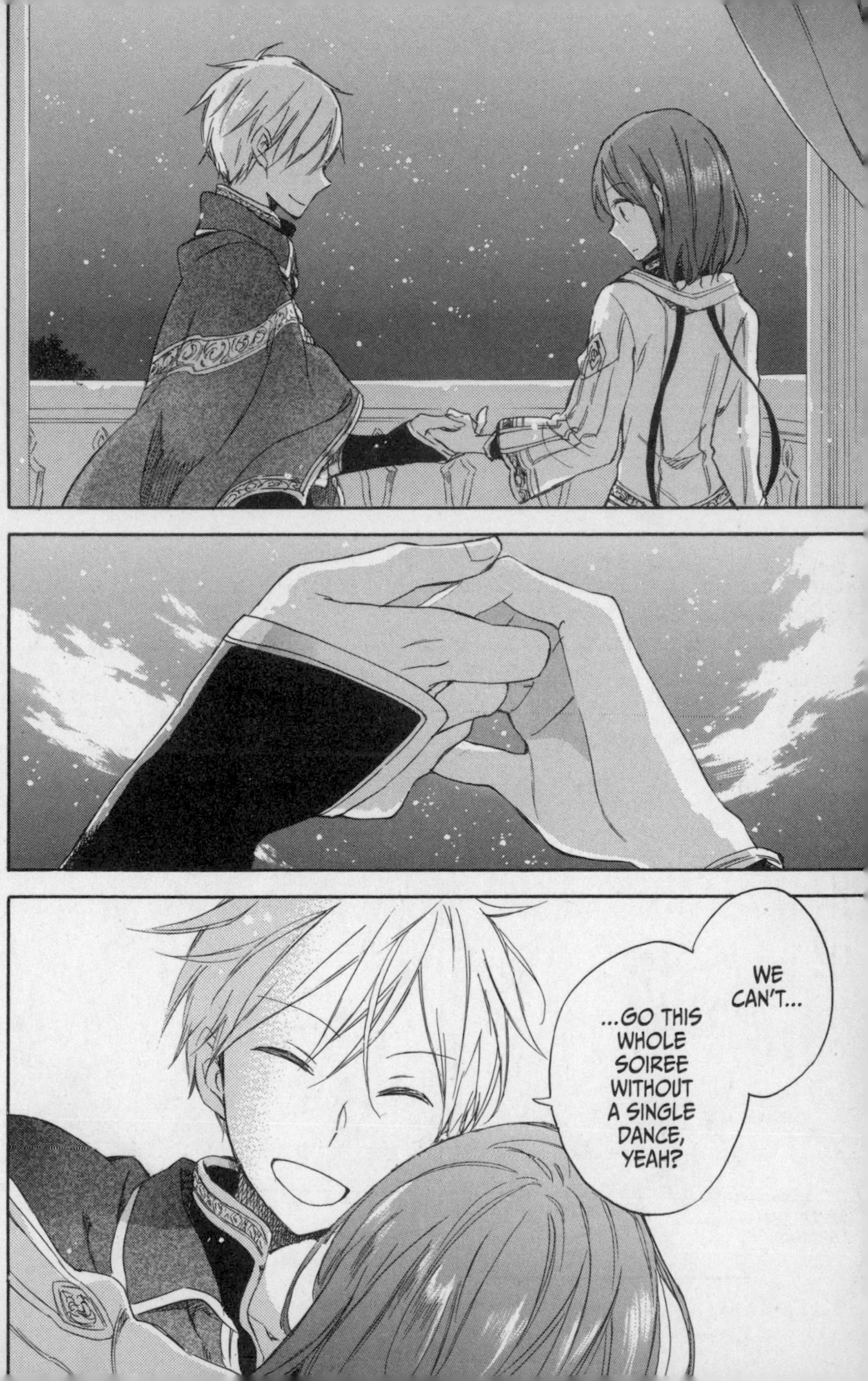
WE CAN'T...
...GO THIS WHOLE SOIREE WITHOUT A SINGLE DANCE, YEAH?

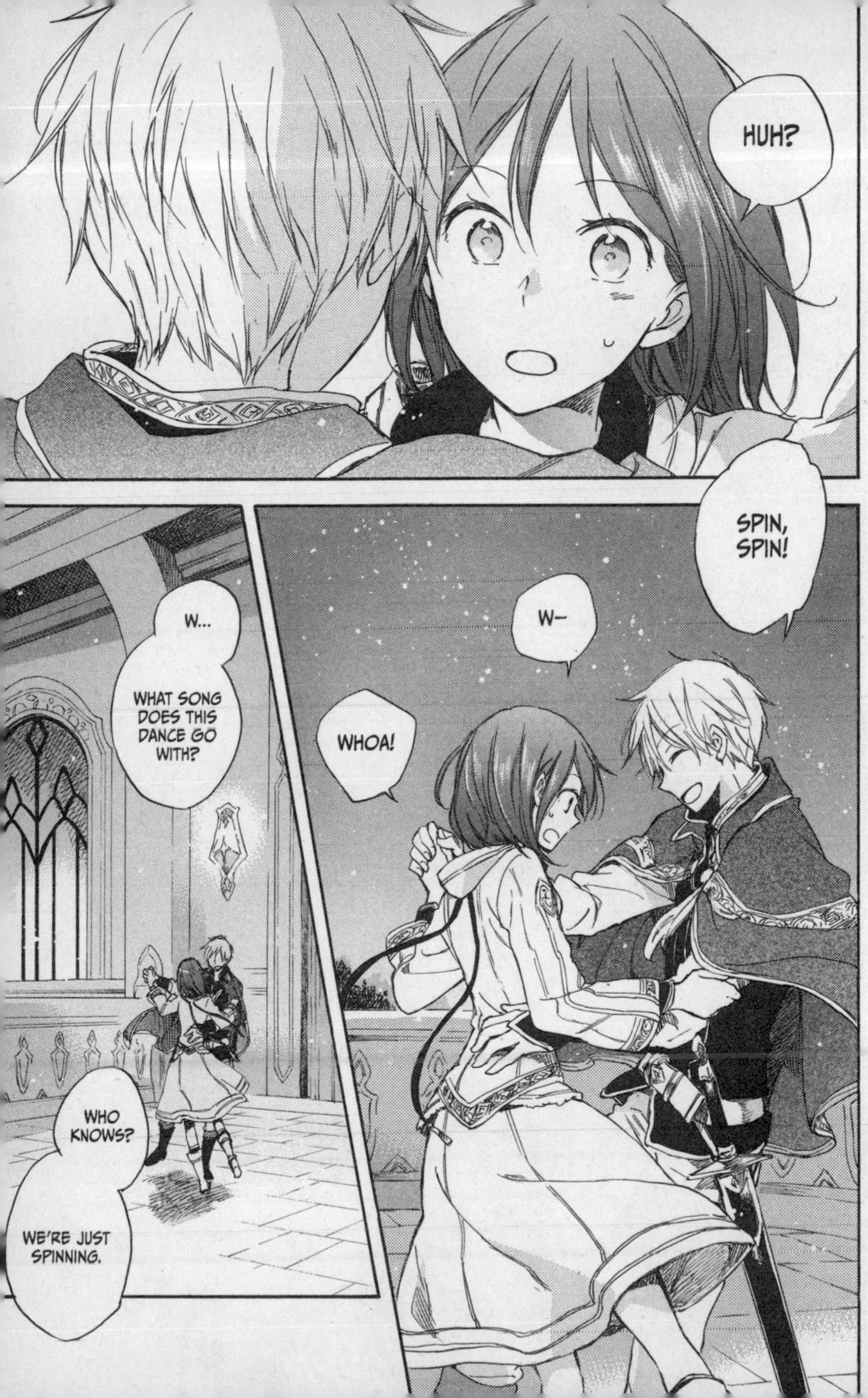
HUH?
SPIN, SPIN!
W–
WHOA!
W...
WHAT SONG DOES THIS DANCE GO WITH?
WHO KNOWS?
WE'RE JUST SPINNING.

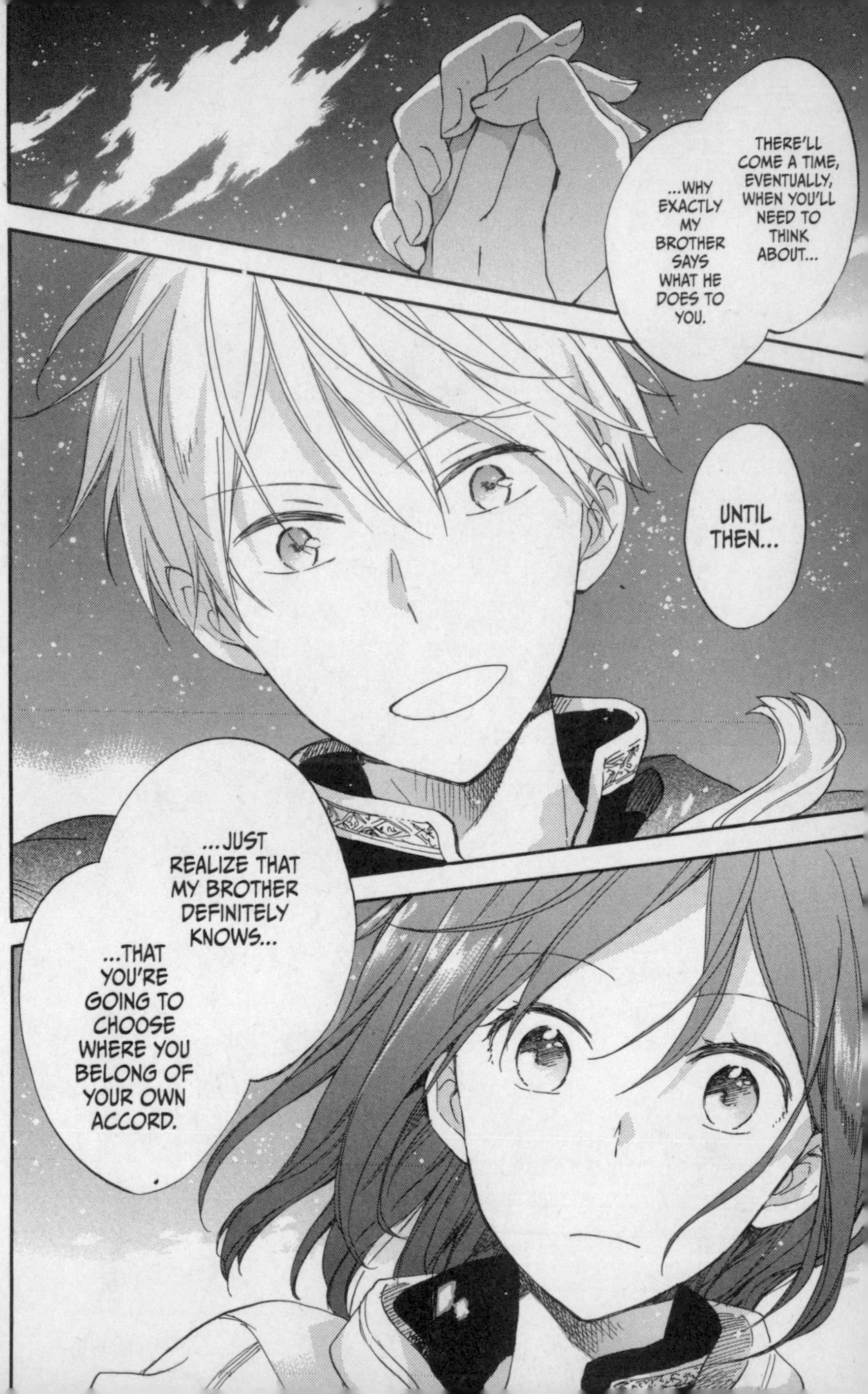
THERE'LL COME A TIME, EVENTUALLY, WHEN YOU'LL NEED TO THINK ABOUT...
...WHY EXACTLY MY BROTHER SAYS WHAT HE DOES TO YOU.
UNTIL THEN...
...JUST REALIZE THAT MY BROTHER DEFINITELY KNOWS...
...THAT YOU'RE GOING TO CHOOSE WHERE YOU BELONG OF YOUR OWN ACCORD.

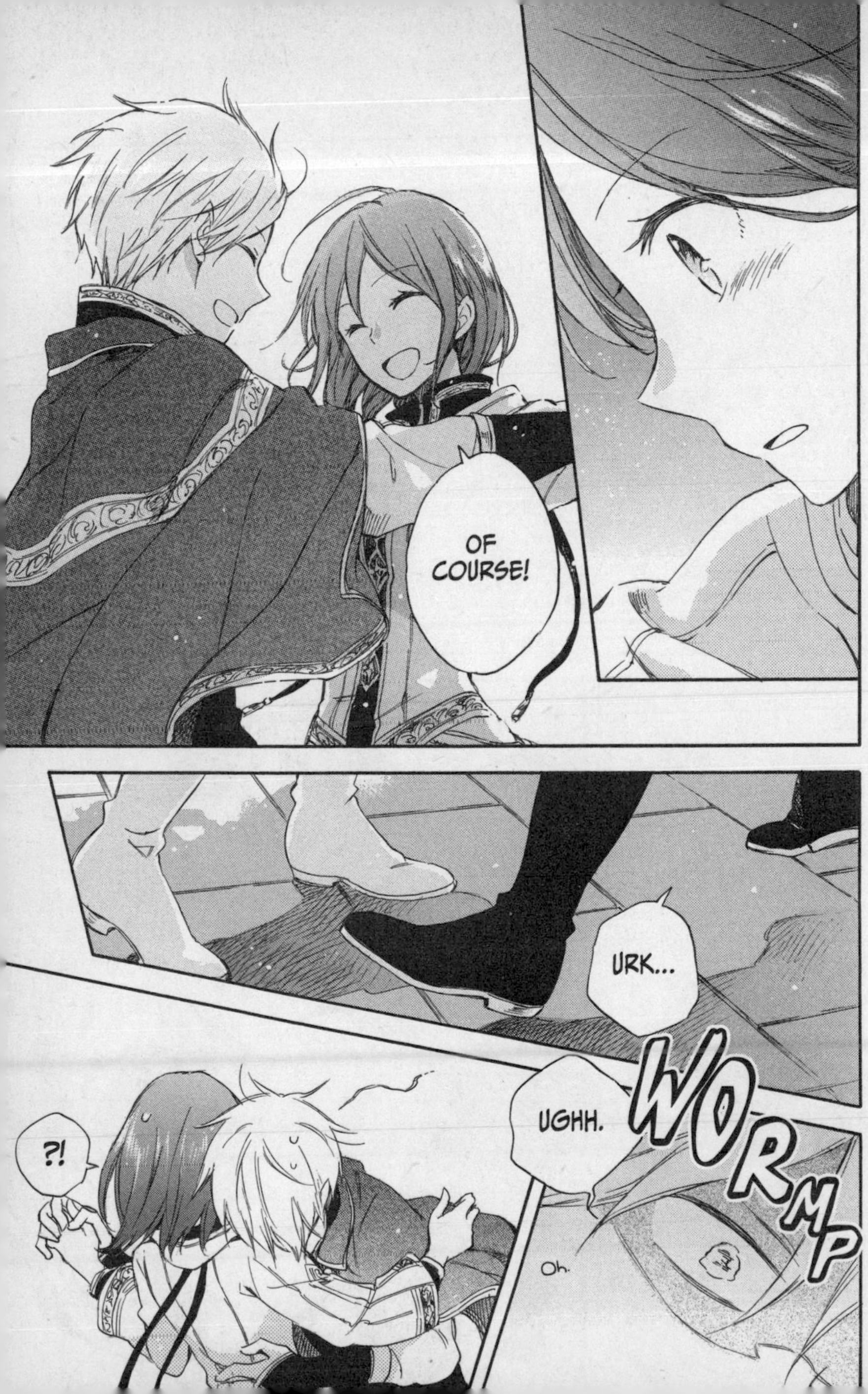
OF COURSE!
URK...
WORMP
Oh.
UGHH.
?!

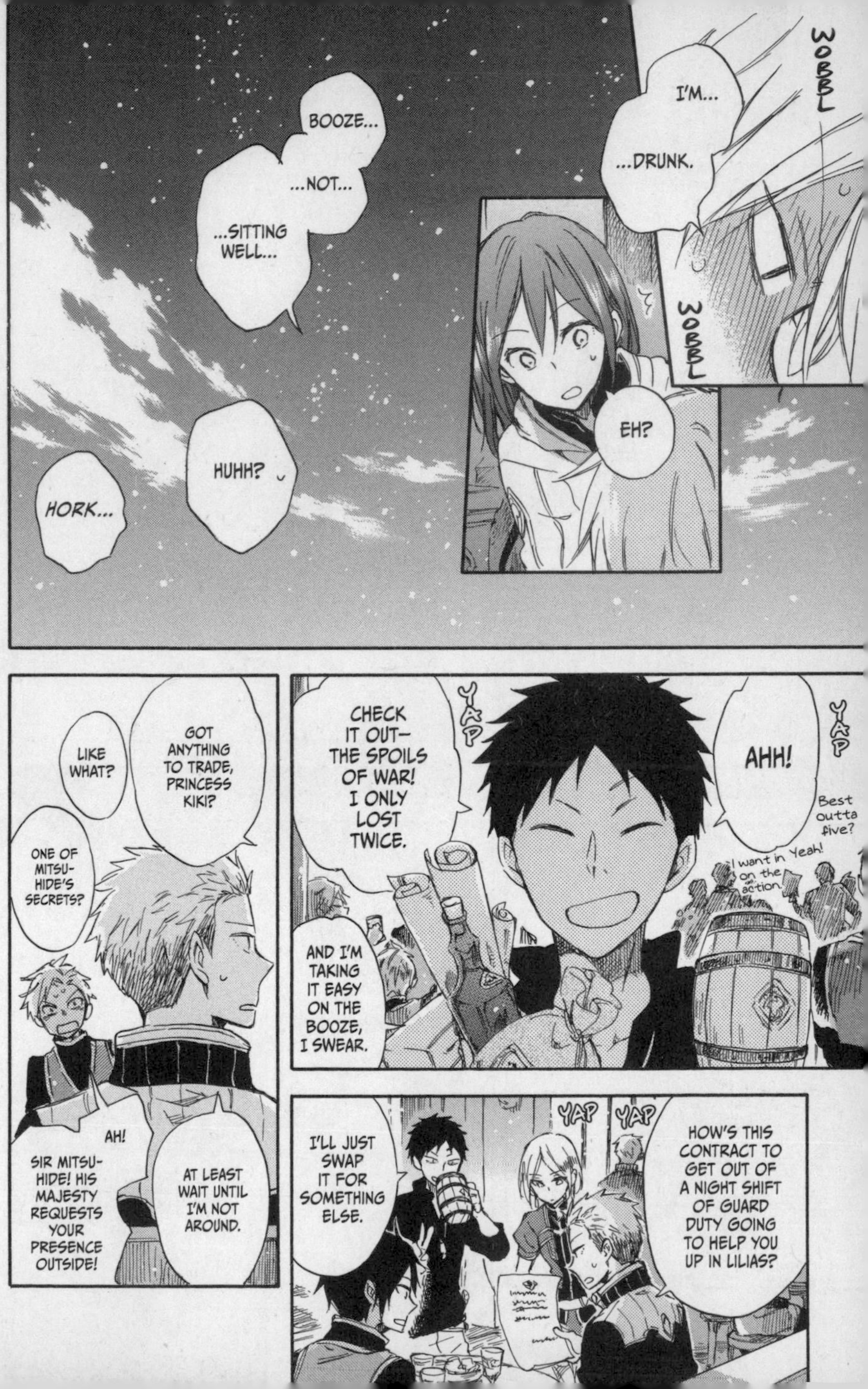
WOBBL
I'M... ...DRUNK.
WOBBL
EH?
BOOZE...
...NOT...
...SITTING WELL...
HUHH?
HORK...
YAP
AHH!
Best outta five?
Yeah!
I want in on the action.
CHECK IT OUT— THE SPOILS OF WAR! I ONLY LOST TWICE.
YAP
AND I'M TAKING IT EASY ON THE BOOZE, I SWEAR.
HOW'S THIS CONTRACT TO GET OUT OF A NIGHT SHIFT OF GUARD DUTY GOING TO HELP YOU UP IN LILIAS?
YAP YAP
I'LL JUST SWAP IT FOR SOMETHING ELSE.
GOT ANYTHING TO TRADE, PRINCESS KIKI?
LIKE WHAT?
ONE OF MITSU-HIDE'S SECRETS?
AT LEAST WAIT UNTIL I'M NOT AROUND.
AH!
SIR MITSU-HIDE! HIS MAJESTY REQUESTS YOUR PRESENCE OUTSIDE!

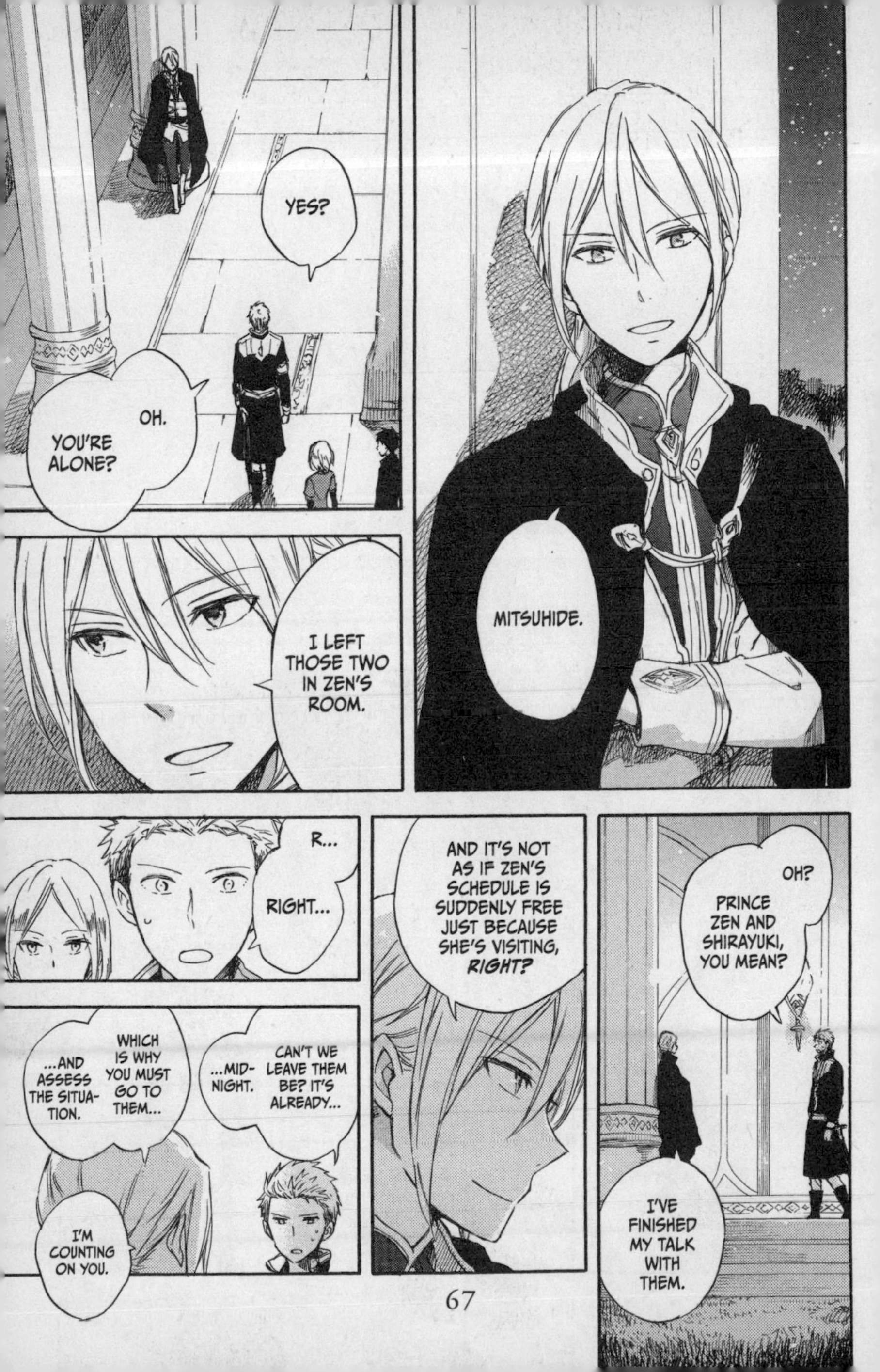

MITSUHIDE.
YES?
OH. YOU'RE ALONE?
I LEFT THOSE TWO IN ZEN'S ROOM.
OH? PRINCE ZEN AND SHIRAYUKI, YOU MEAN?
I'VE FINISHED MY TALK WITH THEM.
AND IT'S NOT AS IF ZEN'S SCHEDULE IS SUDDENLY FREE JUST BECAUSE SHE'S VISITING, *RIGHT?*
R... RIGHT...
CAN'T WE LEAVE THEM BE? IT'S ALREADY...
...MIDNIGHT.
WHICH IS WHY YOU MUST GO TO THEM...
...AND ASSESS THE SITUATION.
I'M COUNTING ON YOU.

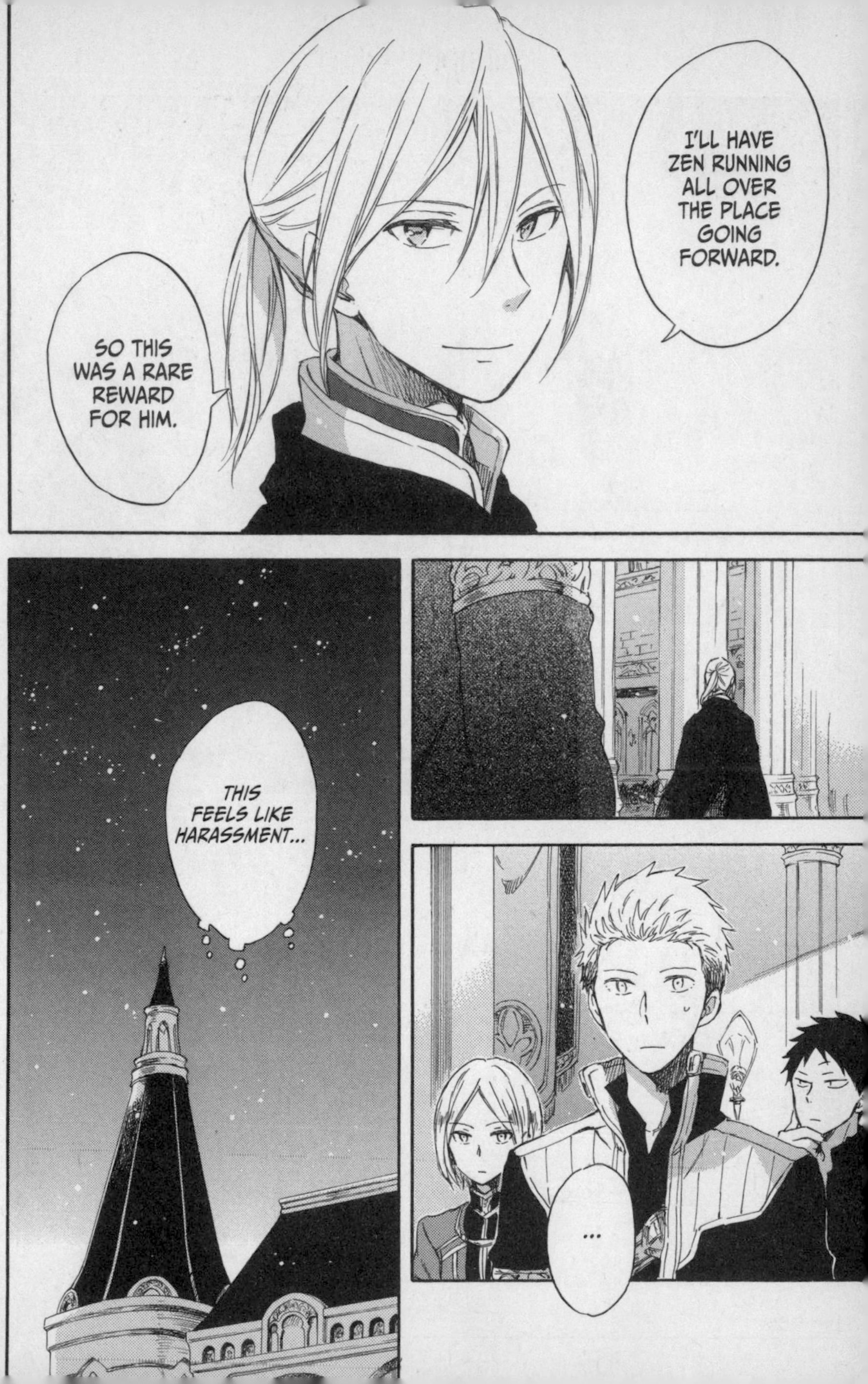
I'LL HAVE ZEN RUNNING ALL OVER THE PLACE GOING FORWARD.
SO THIS WAS A RARE REWARD FOR HIM.
...
THIS FEELS LIKE HARASSMENT...

Chapter 68

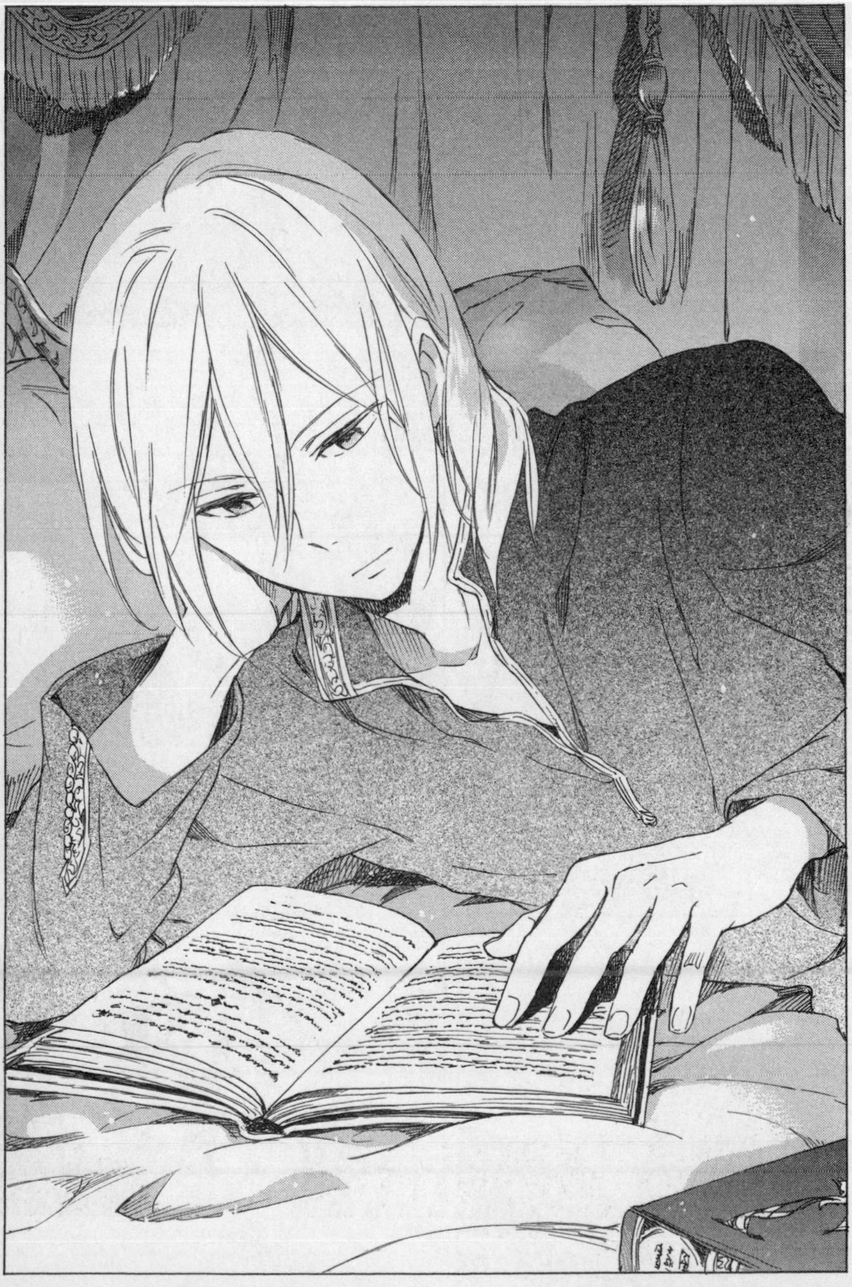

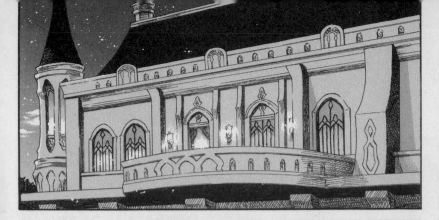

UGH...

HEAD'S
...
... SPINNING.

ZEN...
YOU
OKAY?

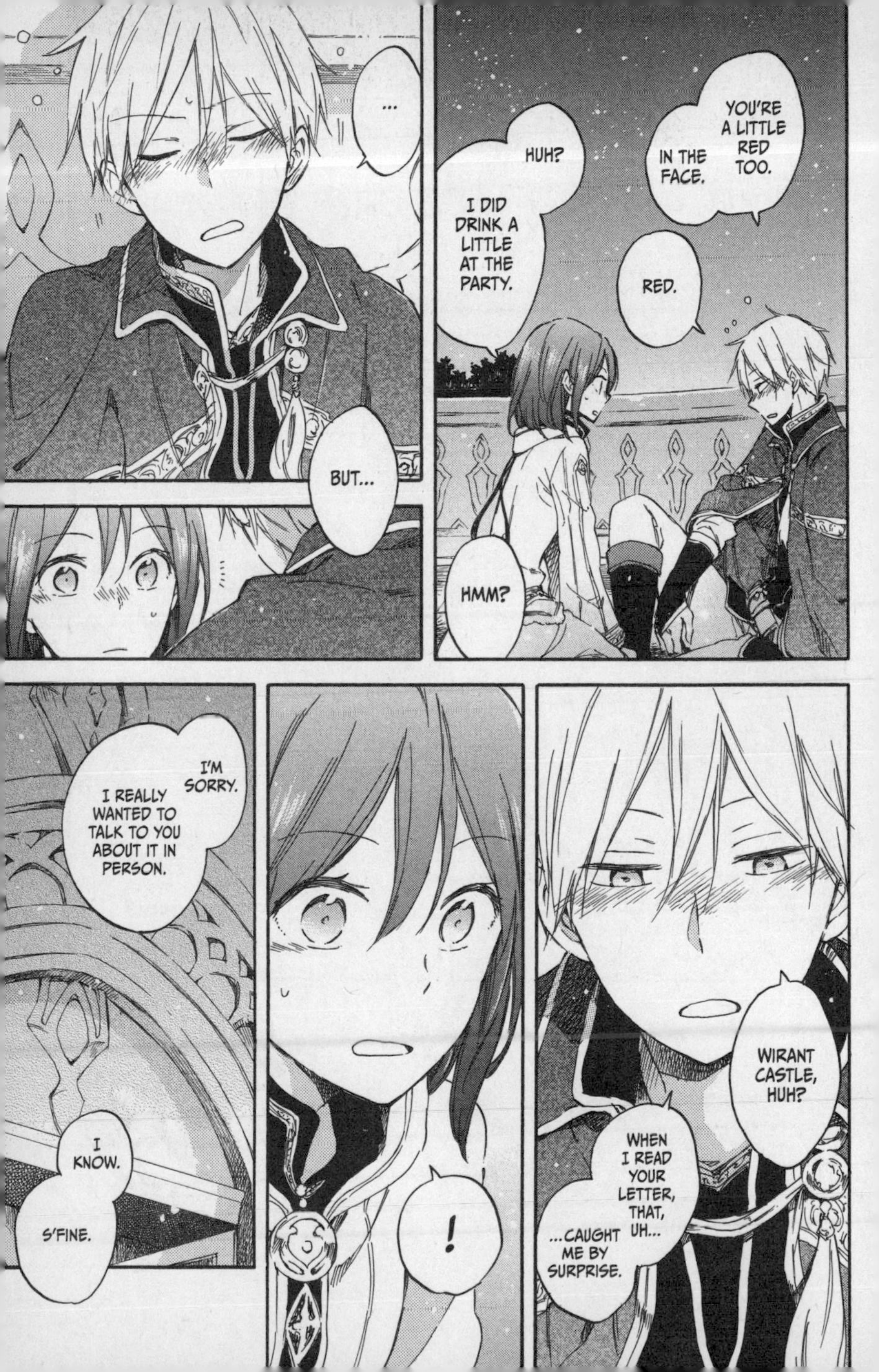
YOU'RE A LITTLE RED TOO.
IN THE FACE.
HUH?
I DID DRINK A LITTLE AT THE PARTY.
RED.
HMM?
...
BUT...
WIRANT CASTLE, HUH?
WHEN I READ YOUR LETTER, THAT, UH...
...CAUGHT ME BY SURPRISE.
!
I'M SORRY.
I REALLY WANTED TO TALK TO YOU ABOUT IT IN PERSON.
I KNOW.
S'FINE.

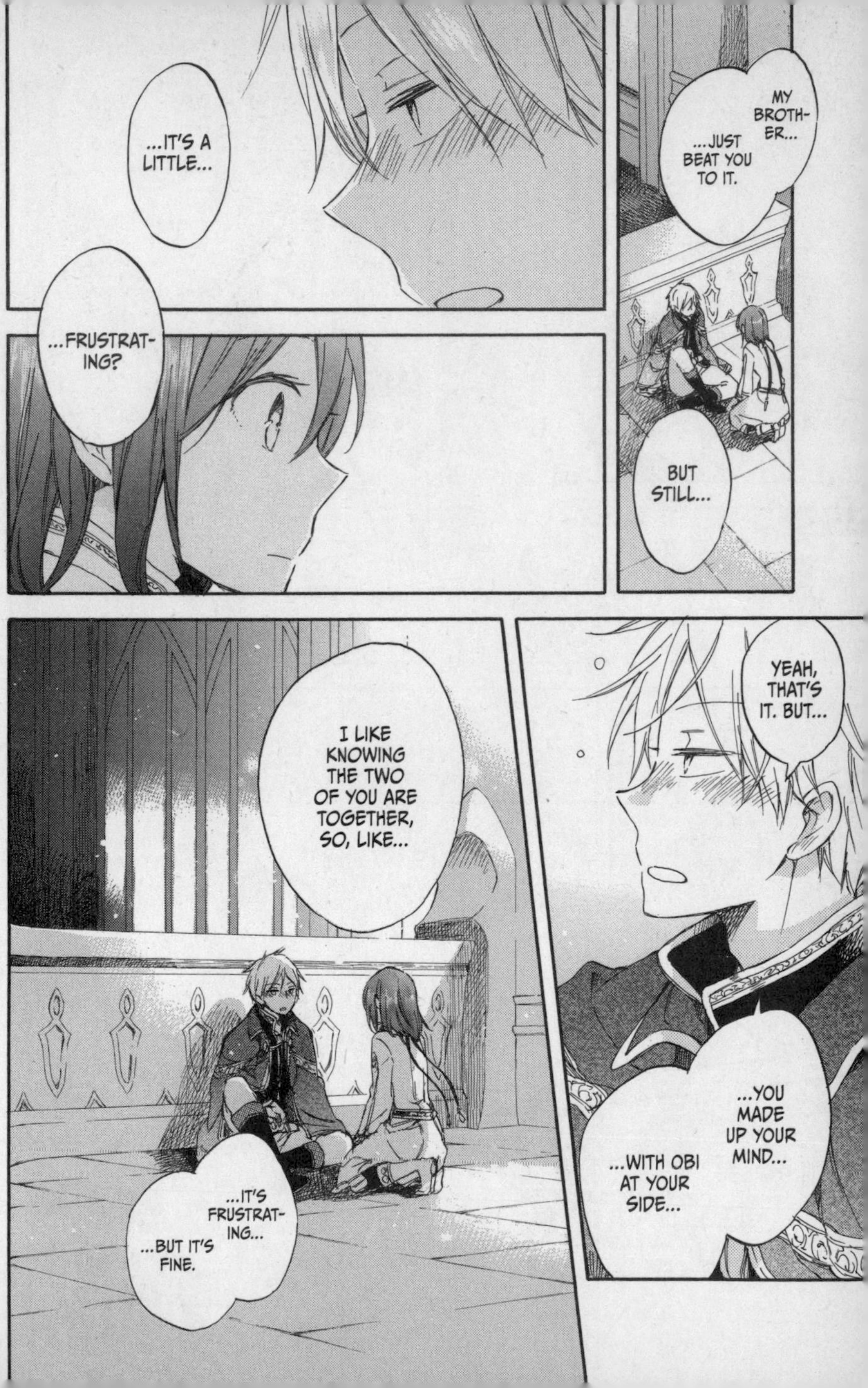
MY BROTHER...
...JUST BEAT YOU TO IT.
BUT STILL...
...IT'S A LITTLE...
...FRUSTRATING?
YEAH, THAT'S IT. BUT...
...YOU MADE UP YOUR MIND...
...WITH OBI AT YOUR SIDE...
I LIKE KNOWING THE TWO OF YOU ARE TOGETHER, SO, LIKE...
...IT'S FRUSTRATING...
...BUT IT'S FINE.

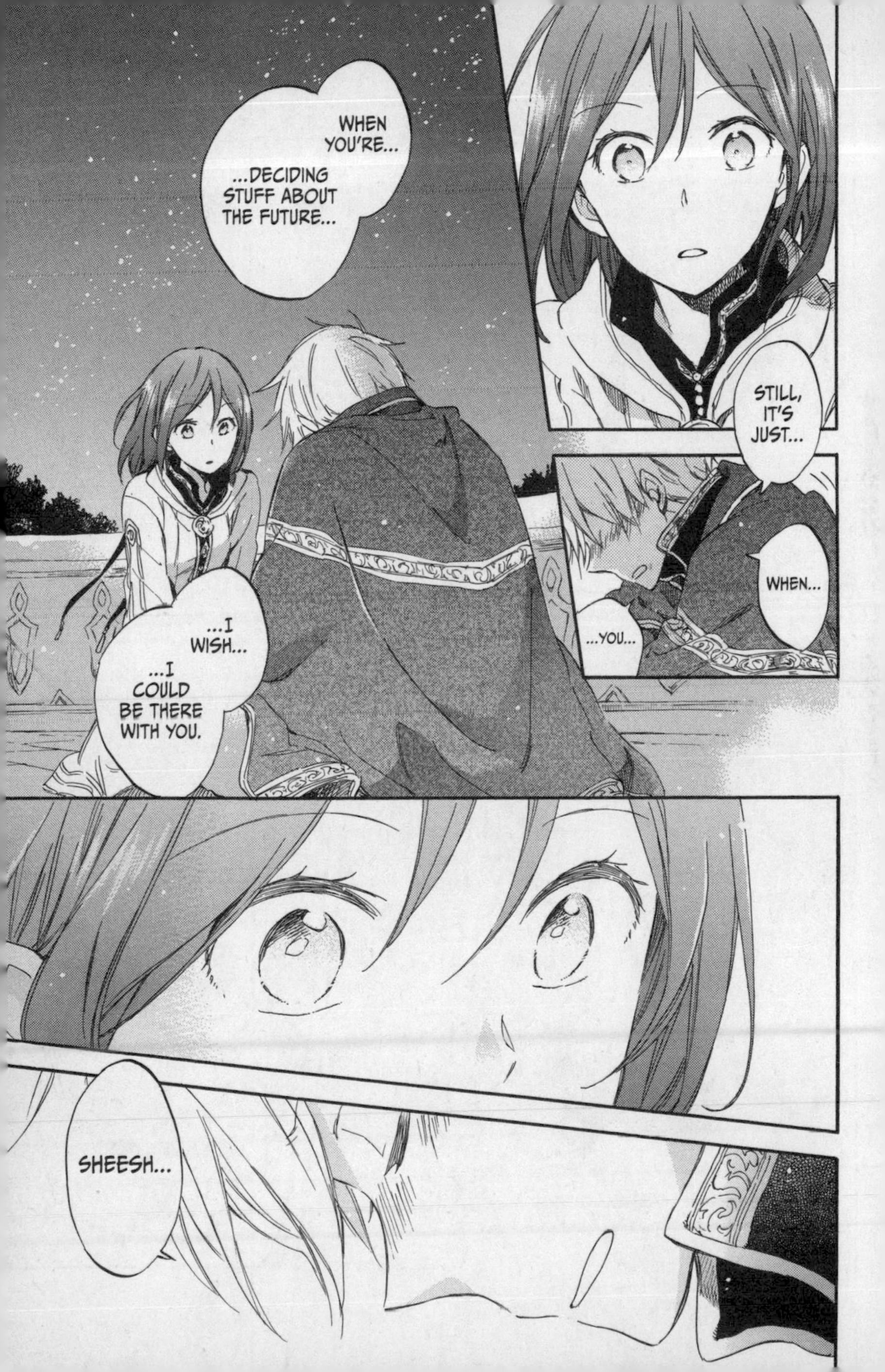
STILL, IT'S JUST...
WHEN...
...YOU...
WHEN YOU'RE...
...DECIDING STUFF ABOUT THE FUTURE...
...I WISH...
...I COULD BE THERE WITH YOU.
SHEESH...

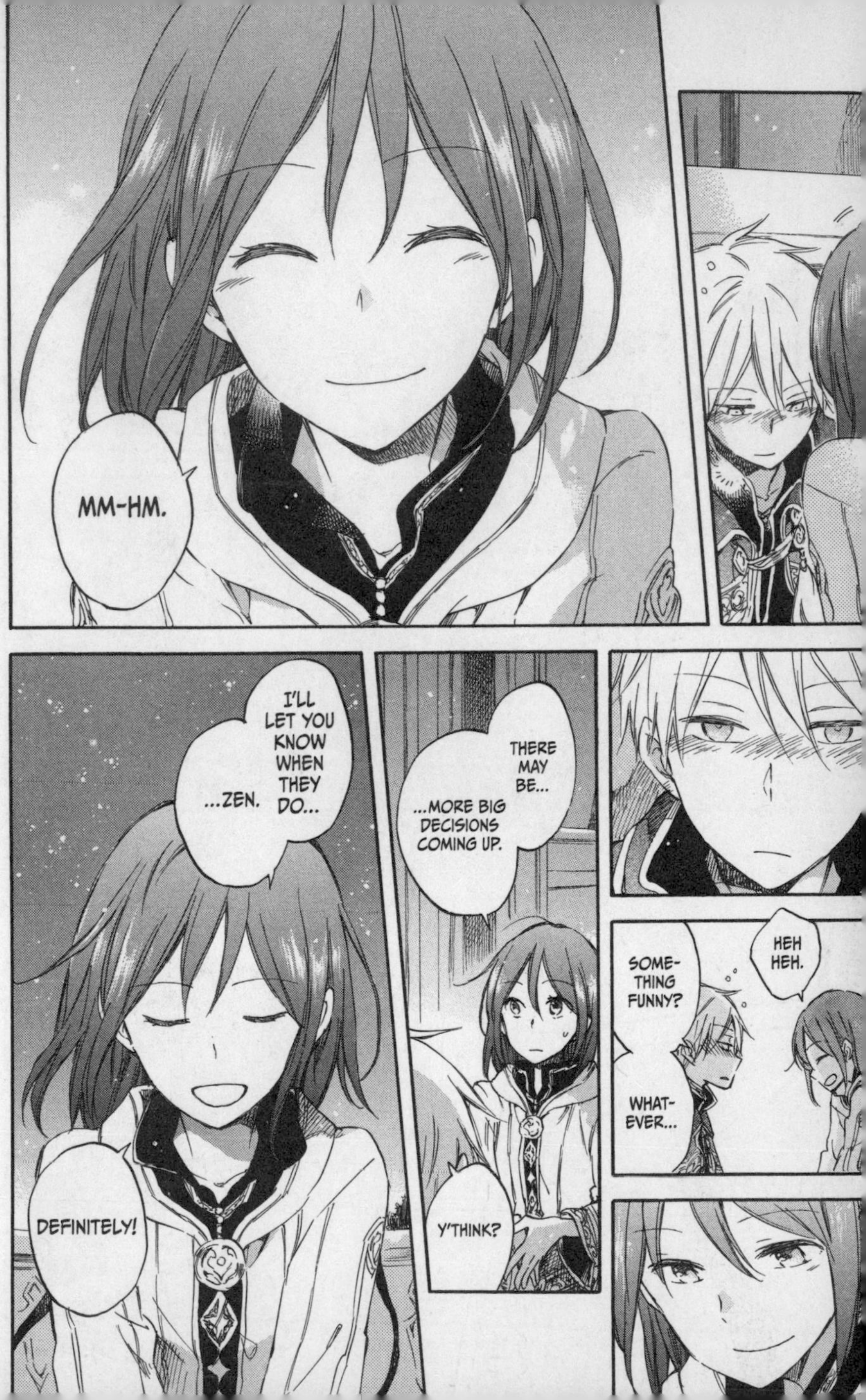
MM-HM.
HEH HEH.
SOME-THING FUNNY?
WHAT-EVER...
THERE MAY BE...
...MORE BIG DECISIONS COMING UP.
Y'THINK?
I'LL LET YOU KNOW WHEN THEY DO...
...ZEN.
DEFINITELY!

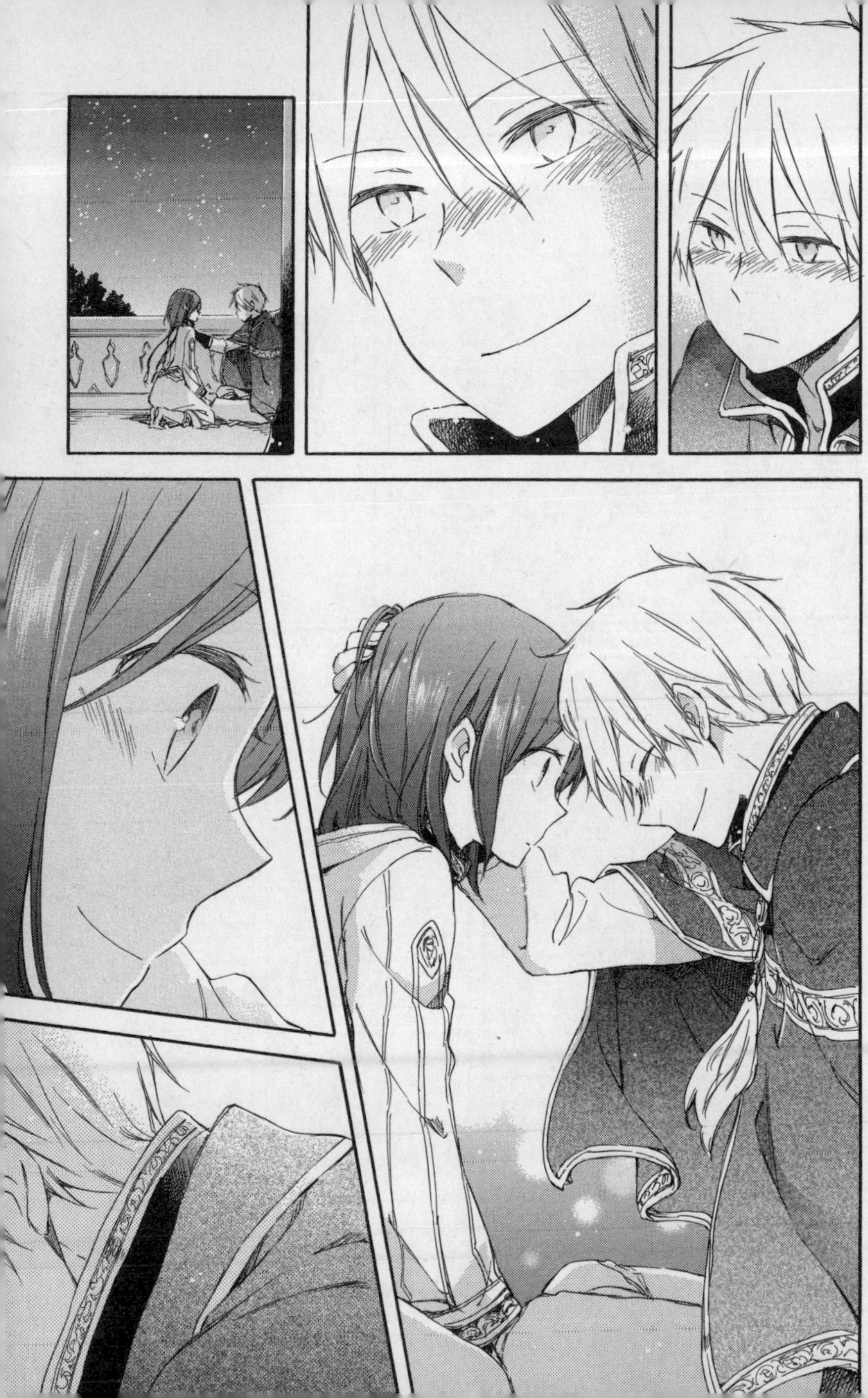

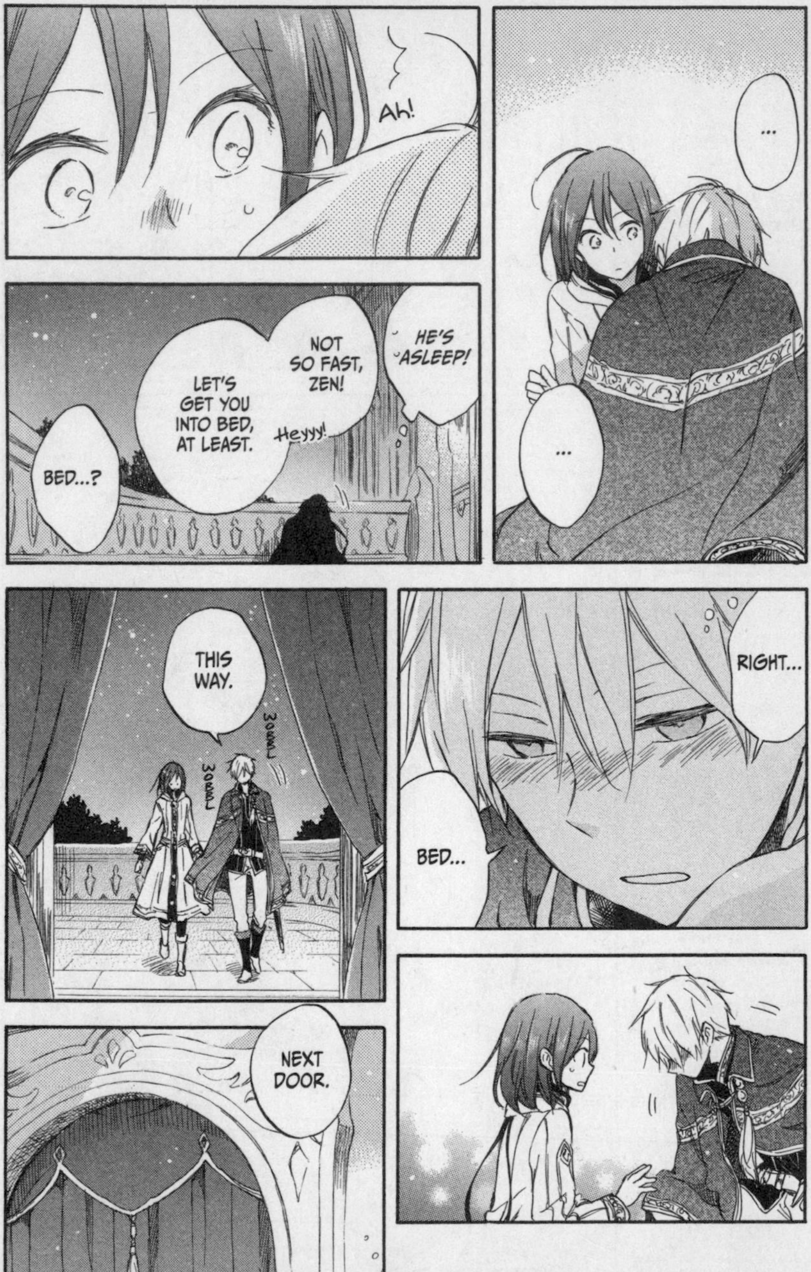
...
...
Ah!
HE'S ASLEEP!
NOT SO FAST, ZEN!
Heyyy!
LET'S GET YOU INTO BED, AT LEAST.
BED...?
RIGHT...
BED...
THIS WAY.
WOBBL
WOBBL
NEXT DOOR.

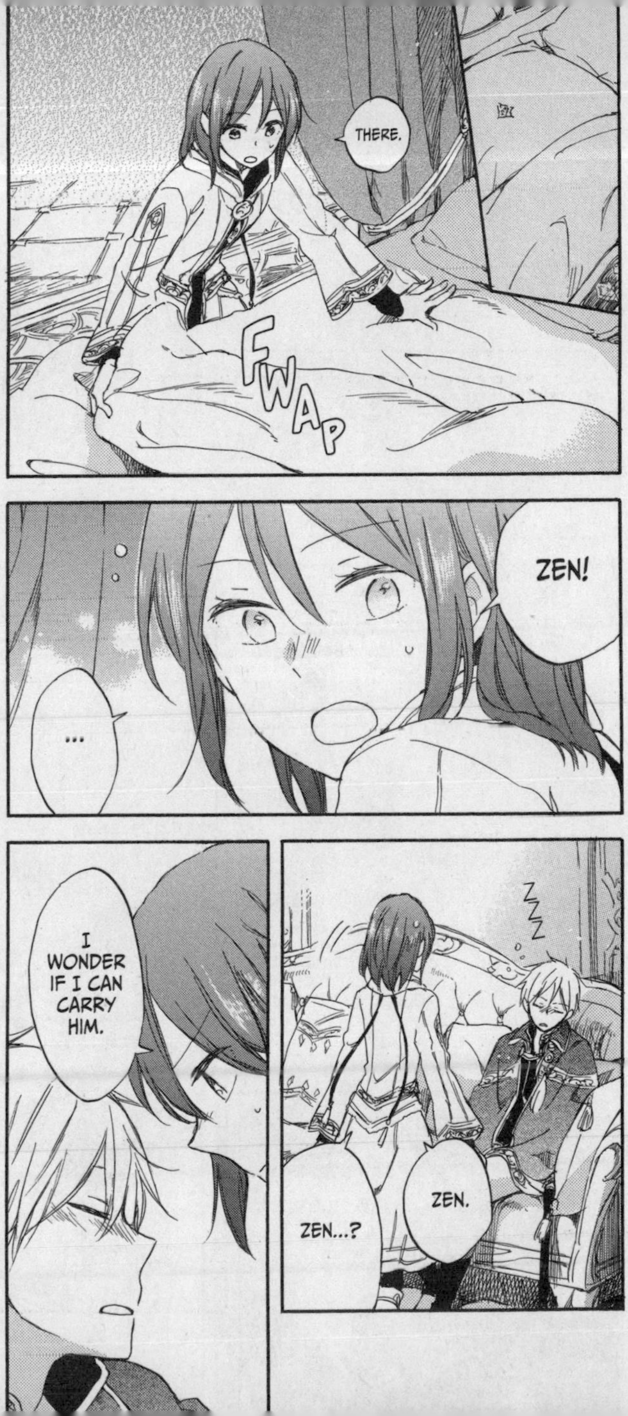
THERE.
FWAP
ZEN!
...
ZZZ
ZEN.
ZEN...?
I WONDER IF I CAN CARRY HIM.

3

CHAPTER TALK

Chapter 67

Izana didn't mention it, but the chocolates were likely a gift from Queen Dowager Haruto.

By the way, King Izana ate one himself, then gave the rest to Lord Zakura and the booze-loving Garak, who both happened to be nearby.

Higata will have his work cut out for him.

Maybe Zen gave his portion to Mitsuhide...?

Sometimes I have trouble separating Zakura and Garak (Ga-ra-ku, in Japanese). Zakura. Garaku. Zaraku. Gakura. Or maybe that's just me!

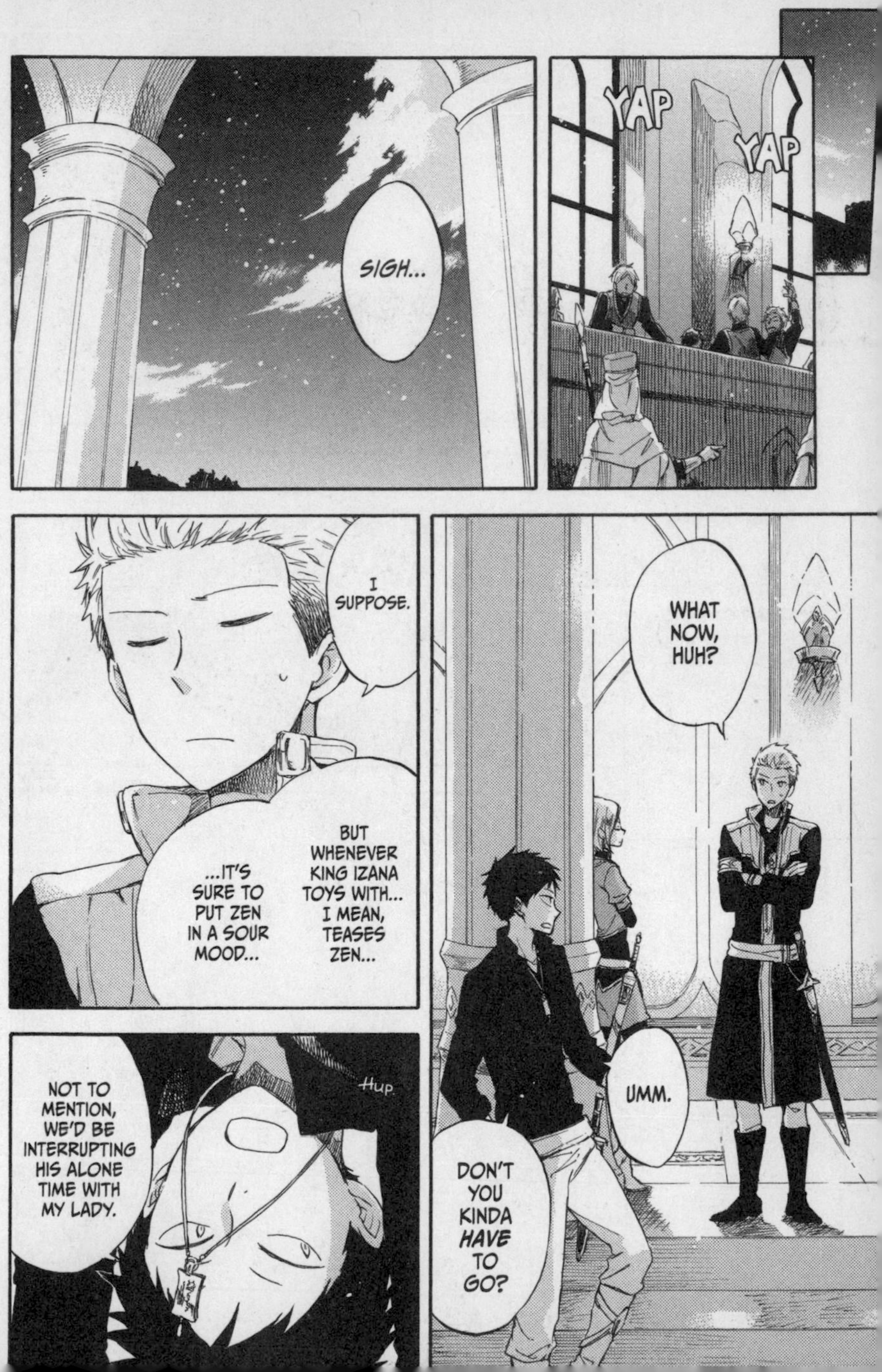
YAP
YAP
SIGH...
WHAT NOW, HUH?
UMM.
DON'T YOU KINDA HAVE TO GO?
I SUPPOSE.
BUT WHENEVER KING IZANA TOYS WITH... I MEAN, TEASES ZEN...
...IT'S SURE TO PUT ZEN IN A SOUR MOOD...
Hup.
NOT TO MENTION, WE'D BE INTERRUPTING HIS ALONE TIME WITH MY LADY.

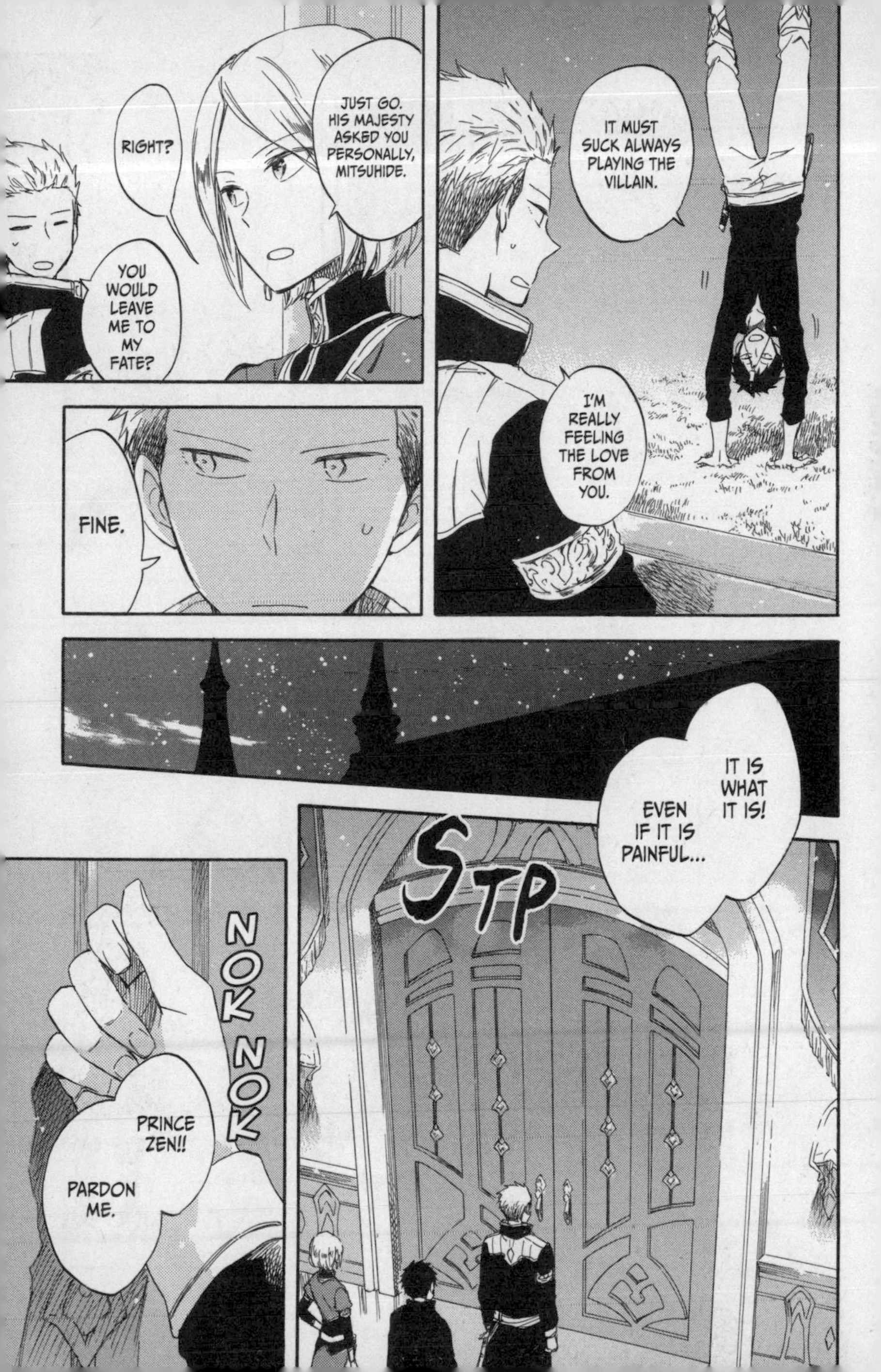
IT MUST SUCK ALWAYS PLAYING THE VILLAIN.
I'M REALLY FEELING THE LOVE FROM YOU.
JUST GO. HIS MAJESTY ASKED YOU PERSONALLY, MITSUHIDE.
RIGHT?
YOU WOULD LEAVE ME TO MY FATE?
FINE.
IT IS WHAT IT IS!
EVEN IF IT IS PAINFUL...
STP
NOK NOK
PRINCE ZEN!!
PARDON ME.

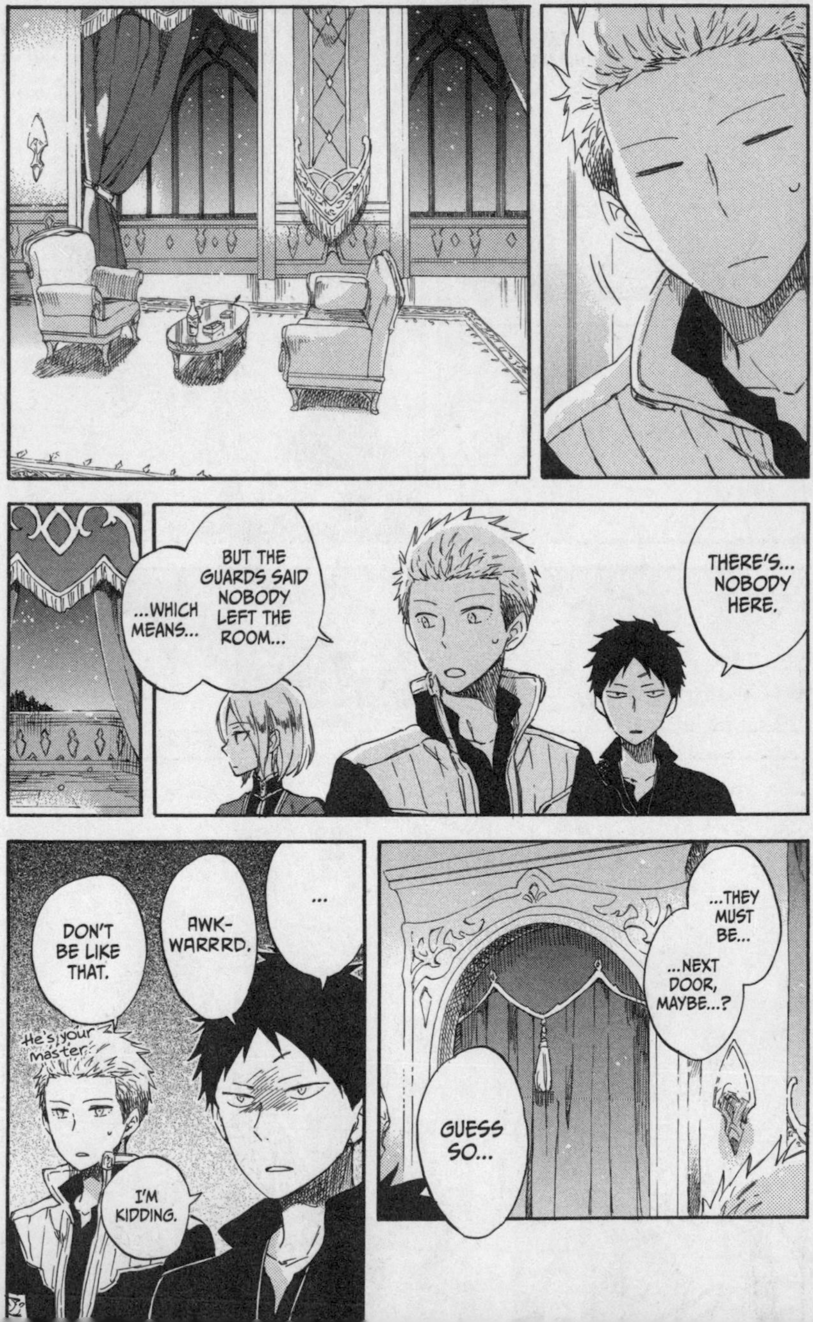
THERE'S... NOBODY HERE.
BUT THE GUARDS SAID NOBODY LEFT THE ROOM...
...WHICH MEANS...
...THEY MUST BE...
...NEXT DOOR, MAYBE...?
GUESS SO...
...
AWK-WARRRD.
DON'T BE LIKE THAT.
He's your master.
I'M KIDDING.

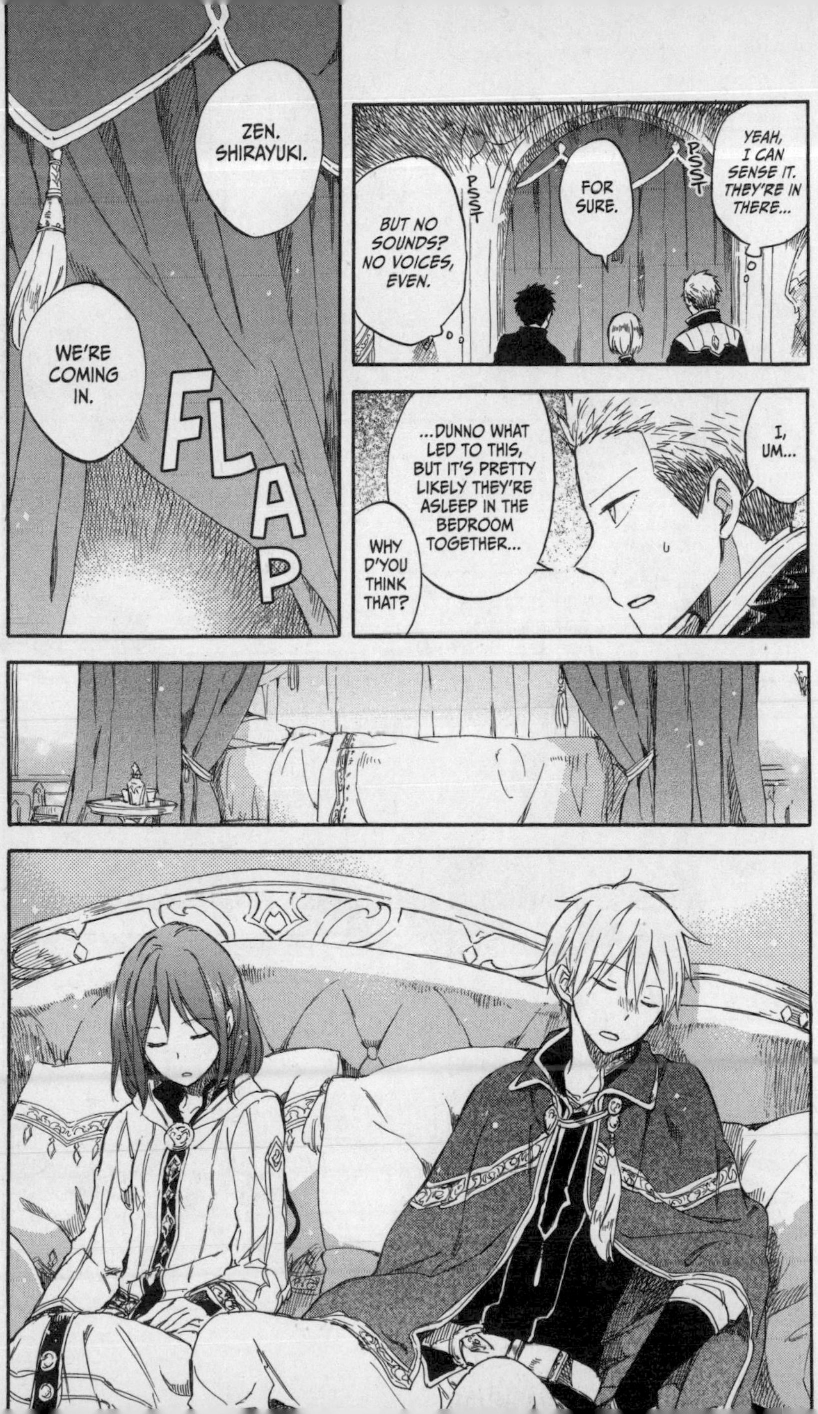
YEAH, I CAN SENSE IT. THEY'RE IN THERE...
PSST
FOR SURE.
PSST
BUT NO SOUNDS? NO VOICES, EVEN.
I, UM...
...DUNNO WHAT LED TO THIS, BUT IT'S PRETTY LIKELY THEY'RE ASLEEP IN THE BEDROOM TOGETHER...
WHY D'YOU THINK THAT?
ZEN. SHIRAYUKI.
WE'RE COMING IN.
FLAP

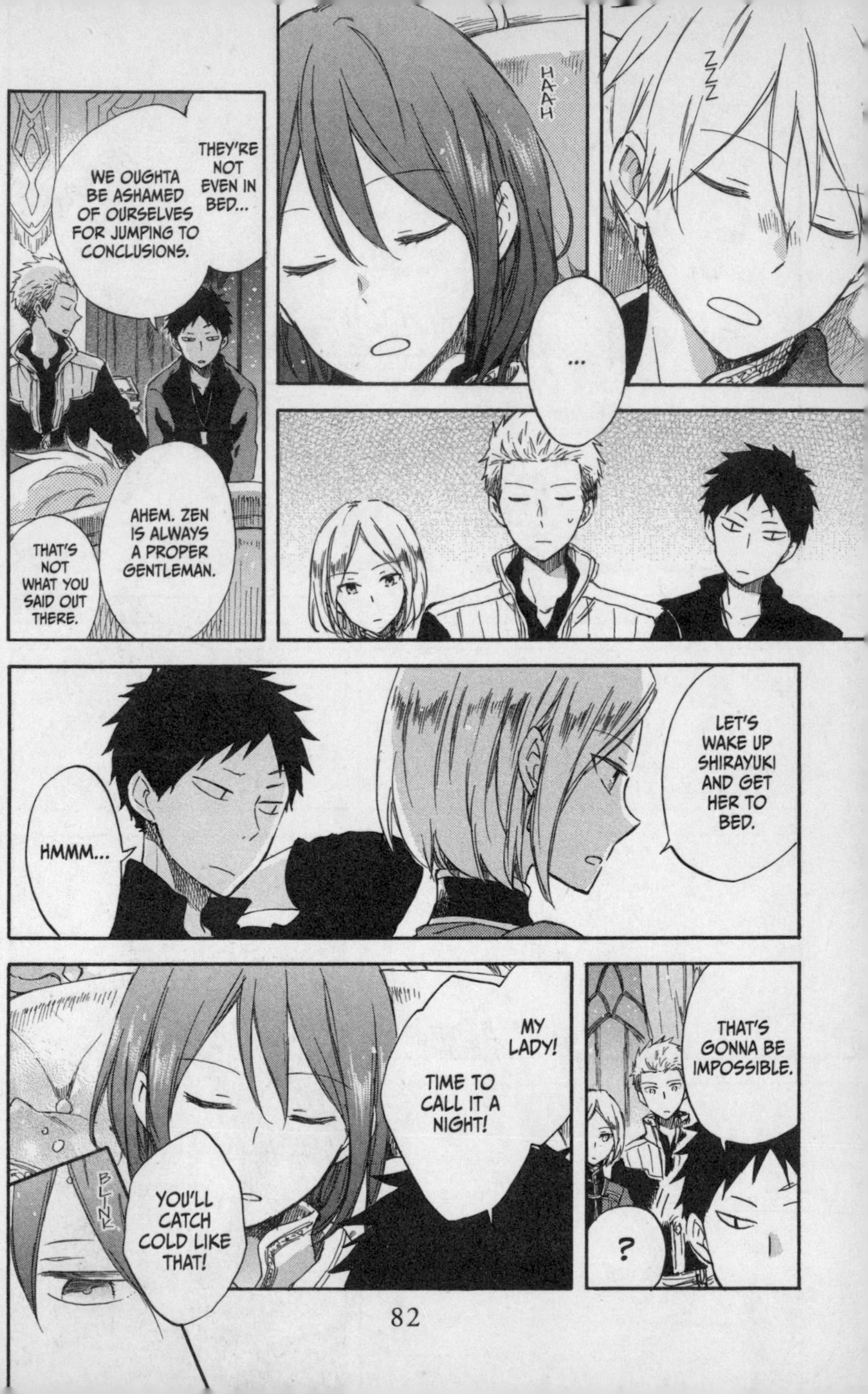
ZZZ
HAAH
...
THEY'RE NOT EVEN IN BED...
WE OUGHTA BE ASHAMED OF OURSELVES FOR JUMPING TO CONCLUSIONS.
AHEM. ZEN IS ALWAYS A PROPER GENTLEMAN.
THAT'S NOT WHAT YOU SAID OUT THERE.
LET'S WAKE UP SHIRAYUKI AND GET HER TO BED.
HMMM...
THAT'S GONNA BE IMPOSSIBLE.
?
MY LADY!
TIME TO CALL IT A NIGHT!
BLINK
YOU'LL CATCH COLD LIKE THAT!

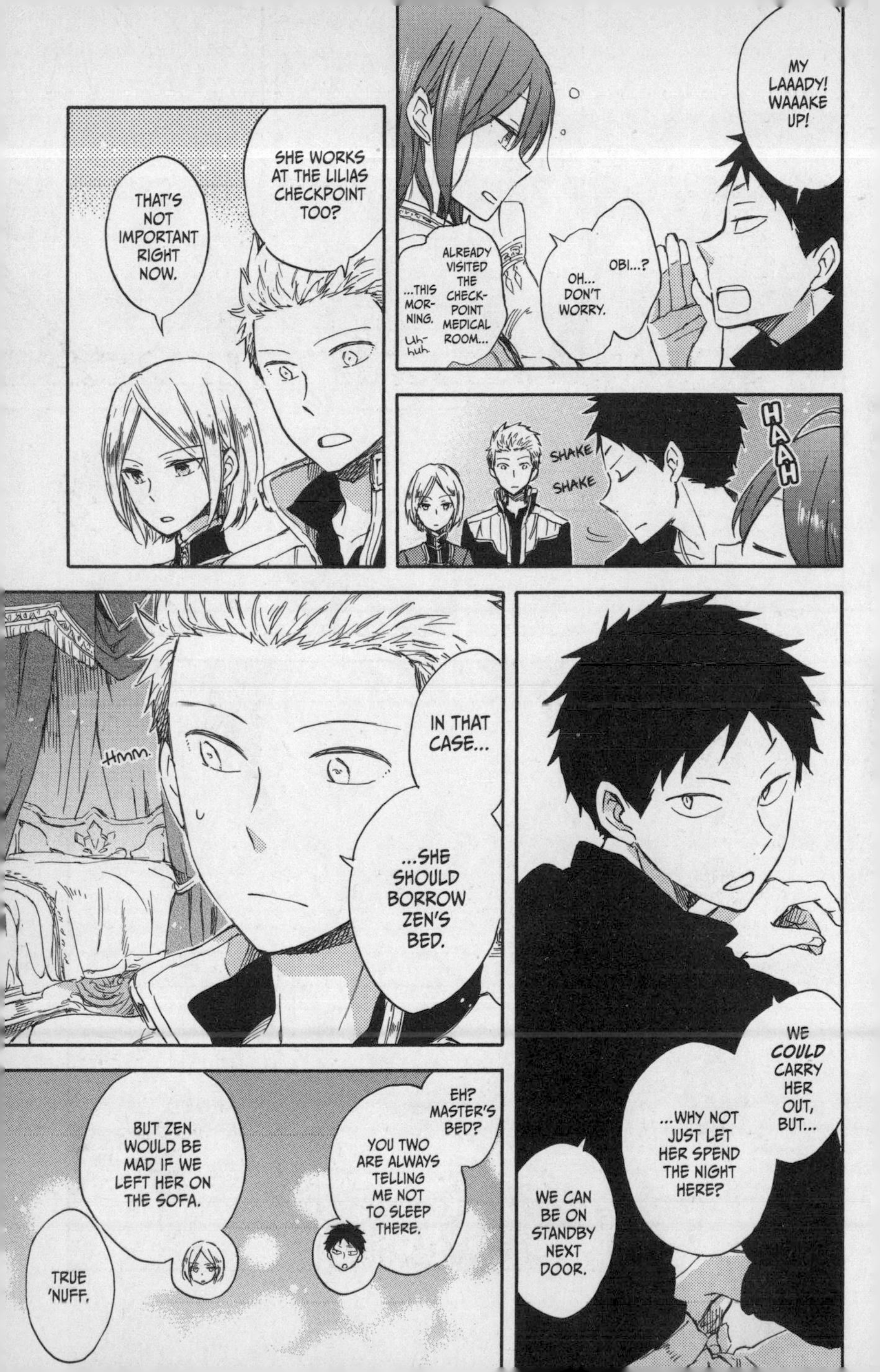
MY LAAADY! WAAAKE UP!
OBI...?
OH... DON'T WORRY.
ALREADY VISITED THE CHECKPOINT MEDICAL ROOM...
...THIS MORNING.
Uh-huh.
HAAAH
SHAKE
SHAKE
SHE WORKS AT THE LILIAS CHECKPOINT TOO?
THAT'S NOT IMPORTANT RIGHT NOW.
WE COULD CARRY HER OUT, BUT...
...WHY NOT JUST LET HER SPEND THE NIGHT HERE?
WE CAN BE ON STANDBY NEXT DOOR.
IN THAT CASE...
...SHE SHOULD BORROW ZEN'S BED.
Hmm.
EH? MASTER'S BED?
YOU TWO ARE ALWAYS TELLING ME NOT TO SLEEP THERE.
BUT ZEN WOULD BE MAD IF WE LEFT HER ON THE SOFA.
TRUE 'NUFF.

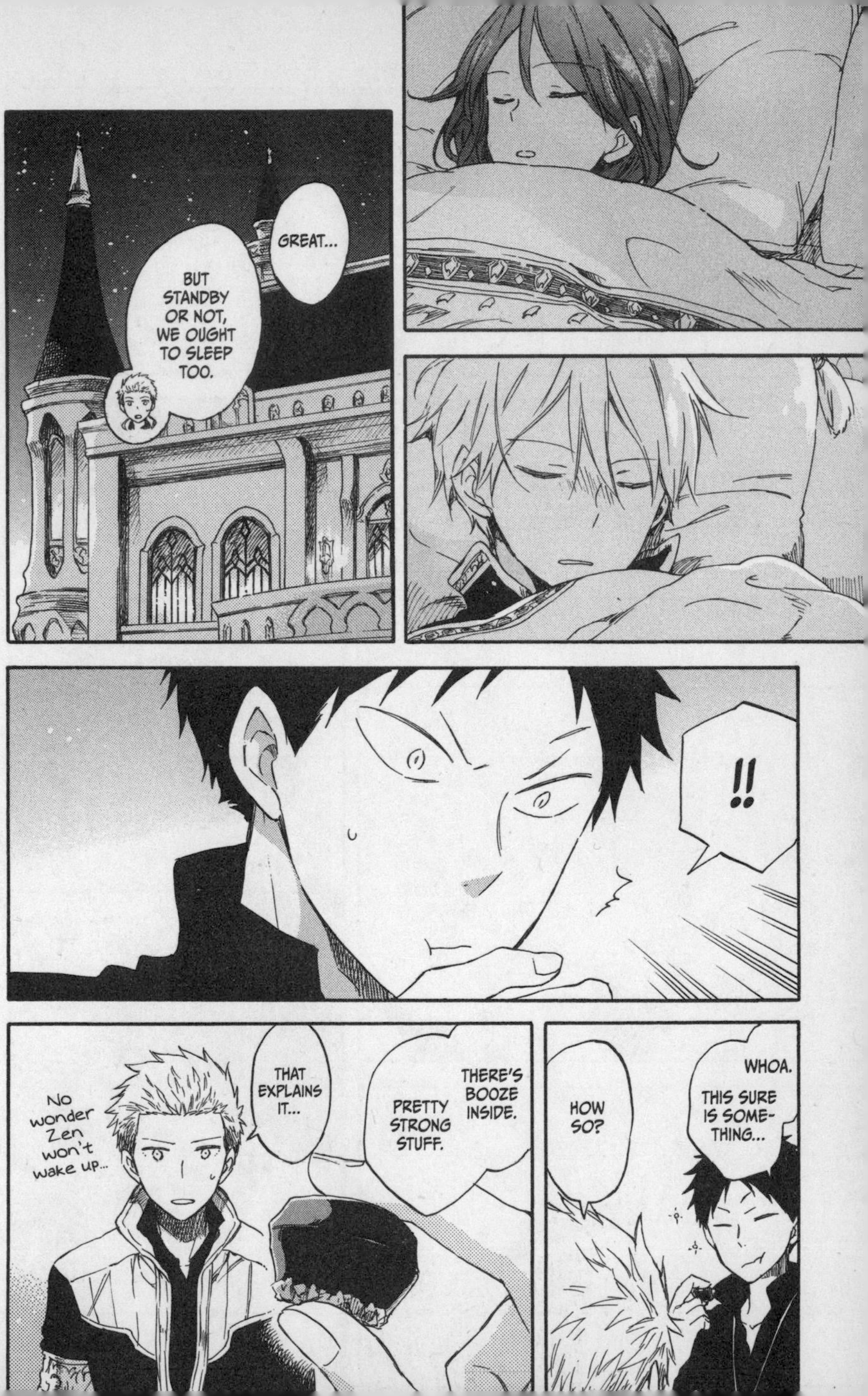
GREAT...
BUT STANDBY OR NOT, WE OUGHT TO SLEEP TOO.
!!
WHOA.
THIS SURE IS SOME-THING...
HOW SO?
THERE'S BOOZE INSIDE.
PRETTY STRONG STUFF.
THAT EXPLAINS IT...
No wonder Zen won't wake up...

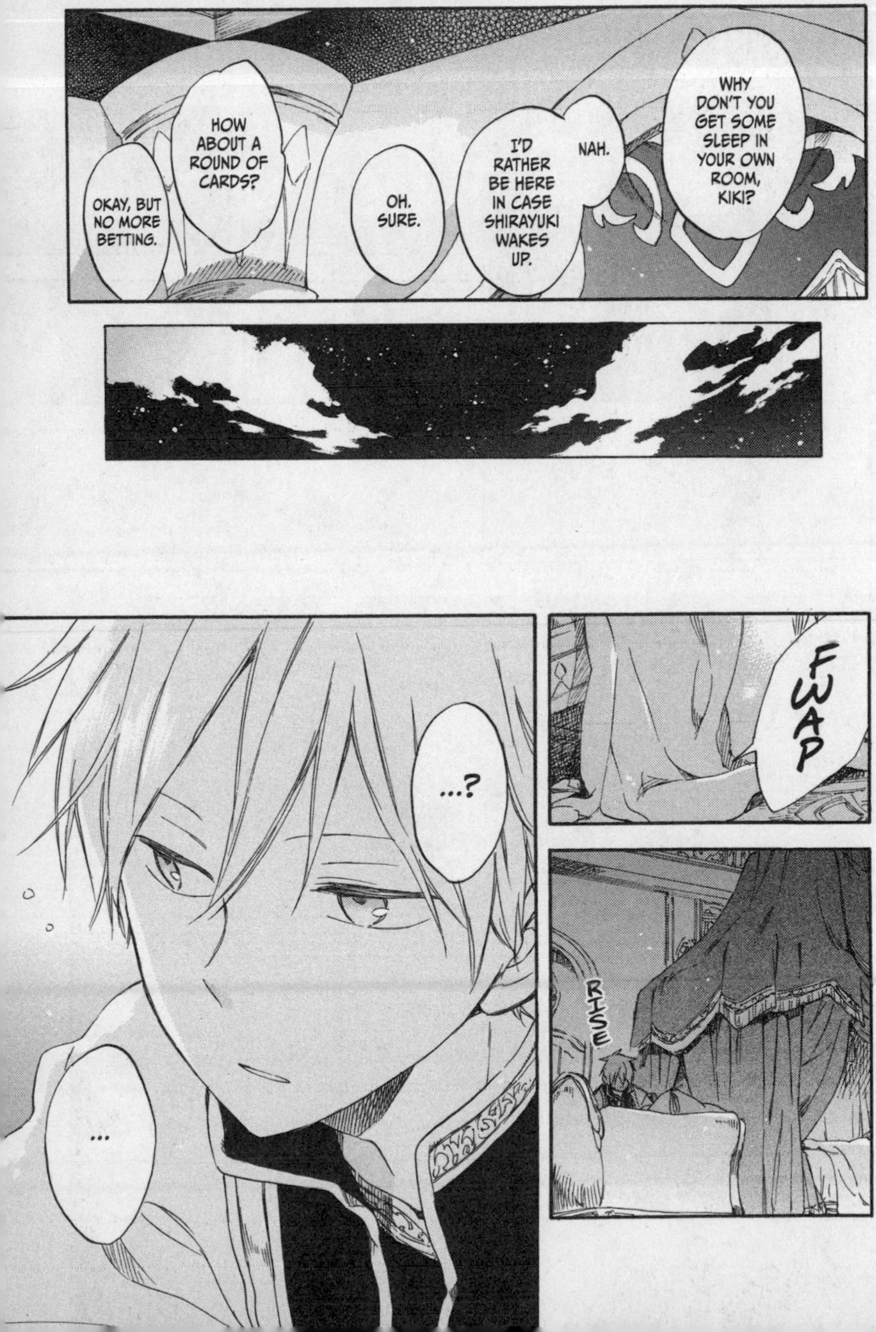
WHY DON'T YOU GET SOME SLEEP IN YOUR OWN ROOM, KIKI?
NAH.
I'D RATHER BE HERE IN CASE SHIRAYUKI WAKES UP.
OH. SURE.
HOW ABOUT A ROUND OF CARDS?
OKAY, BUT NO MORE BETTING.
FWAP
RISE
...?
...

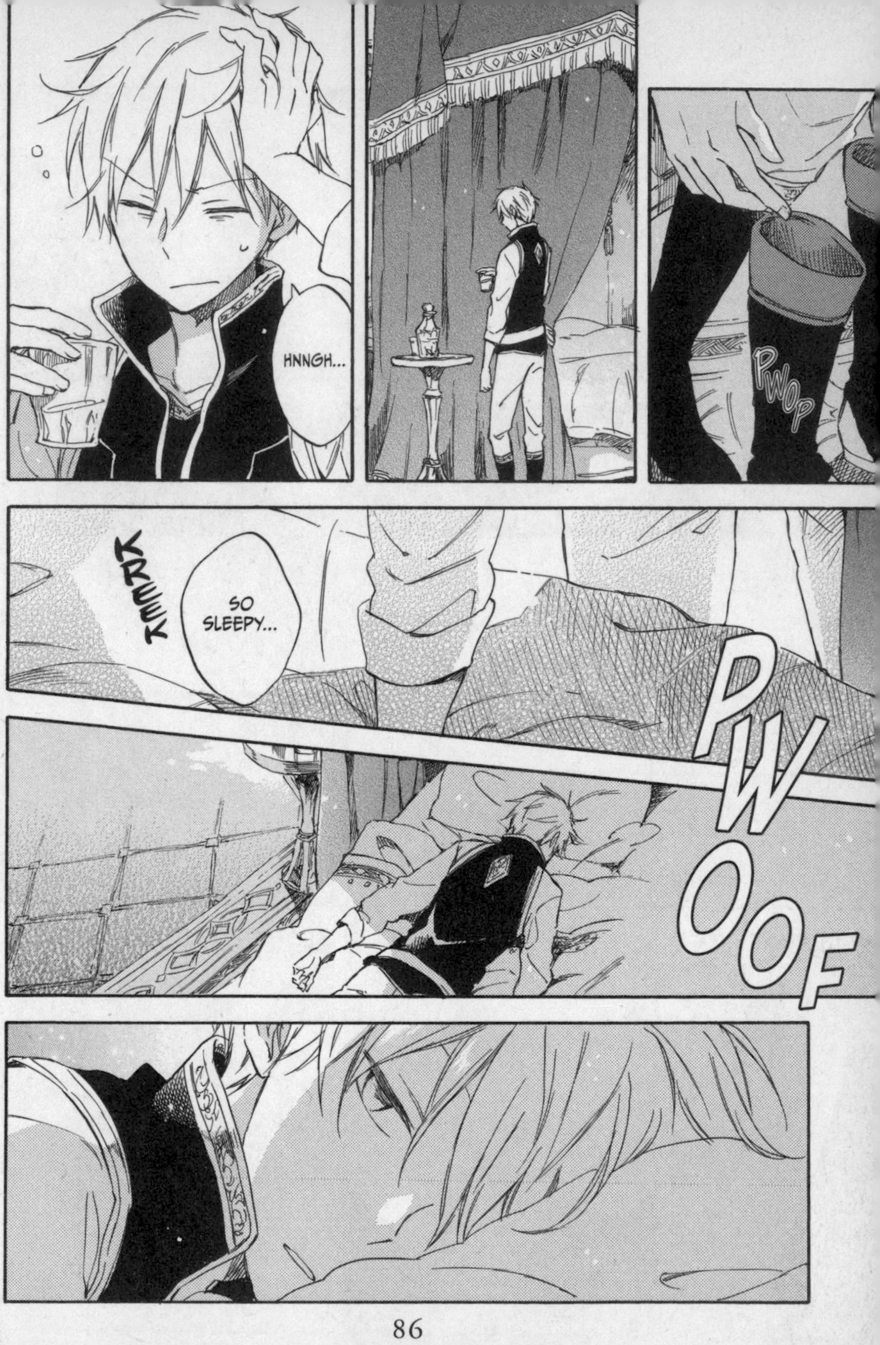
PWOP
HNNGH...
SO SLEEPY...
KREEK
PWOOF

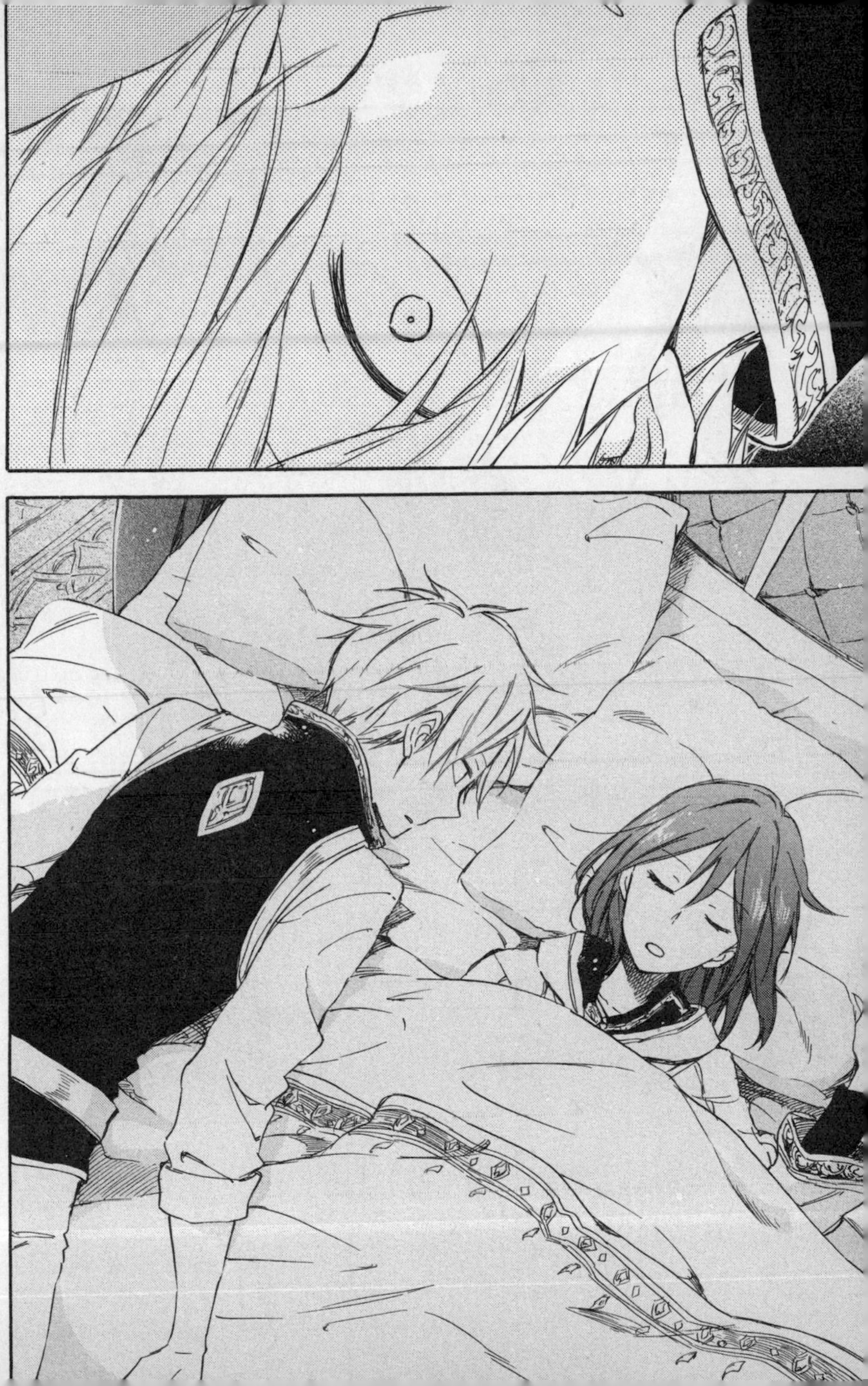

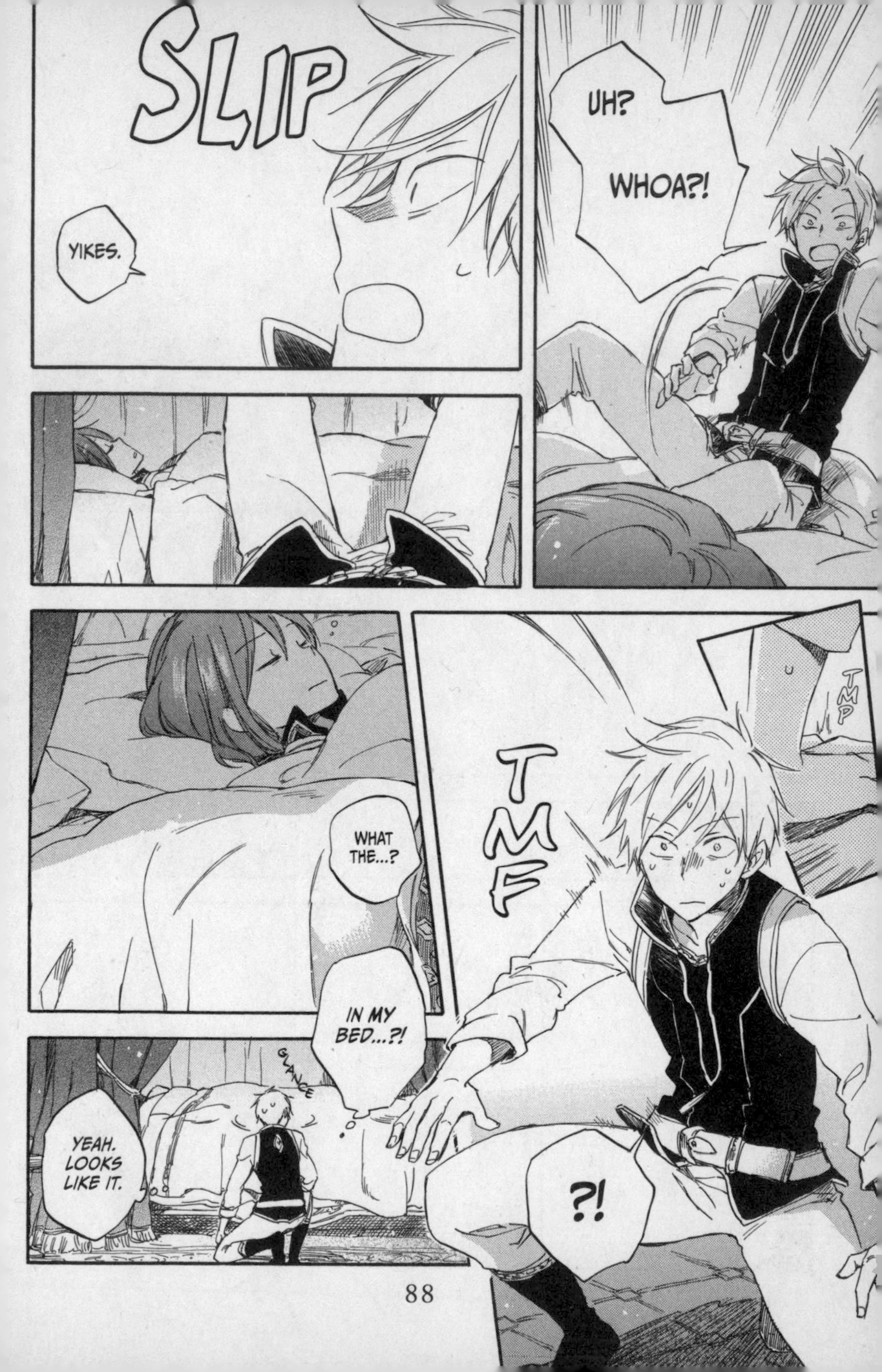
UH?
WHOA?!
SLIP
YIKES.
TMP
TMF
?!
WHAT THE...?
IN MY BED...?!
GLANCE
YEAH. LOOKS LIKE IT.

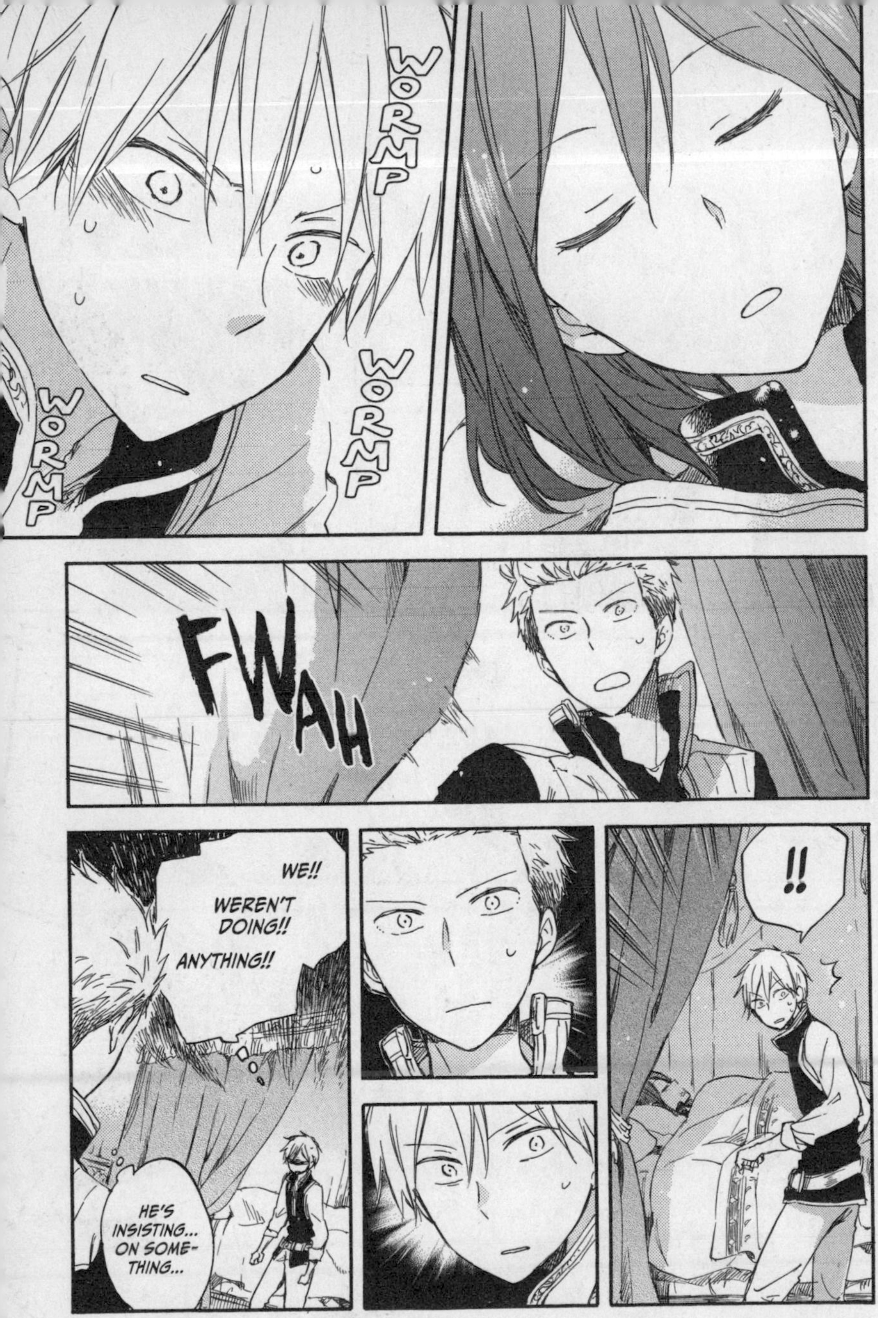
WORMP
WORMP
WORMP
FWAH
!!
WE!! WEREN'T DOING!! ANYTHING!!
HE'S INSISTING... ON SOMETHING...

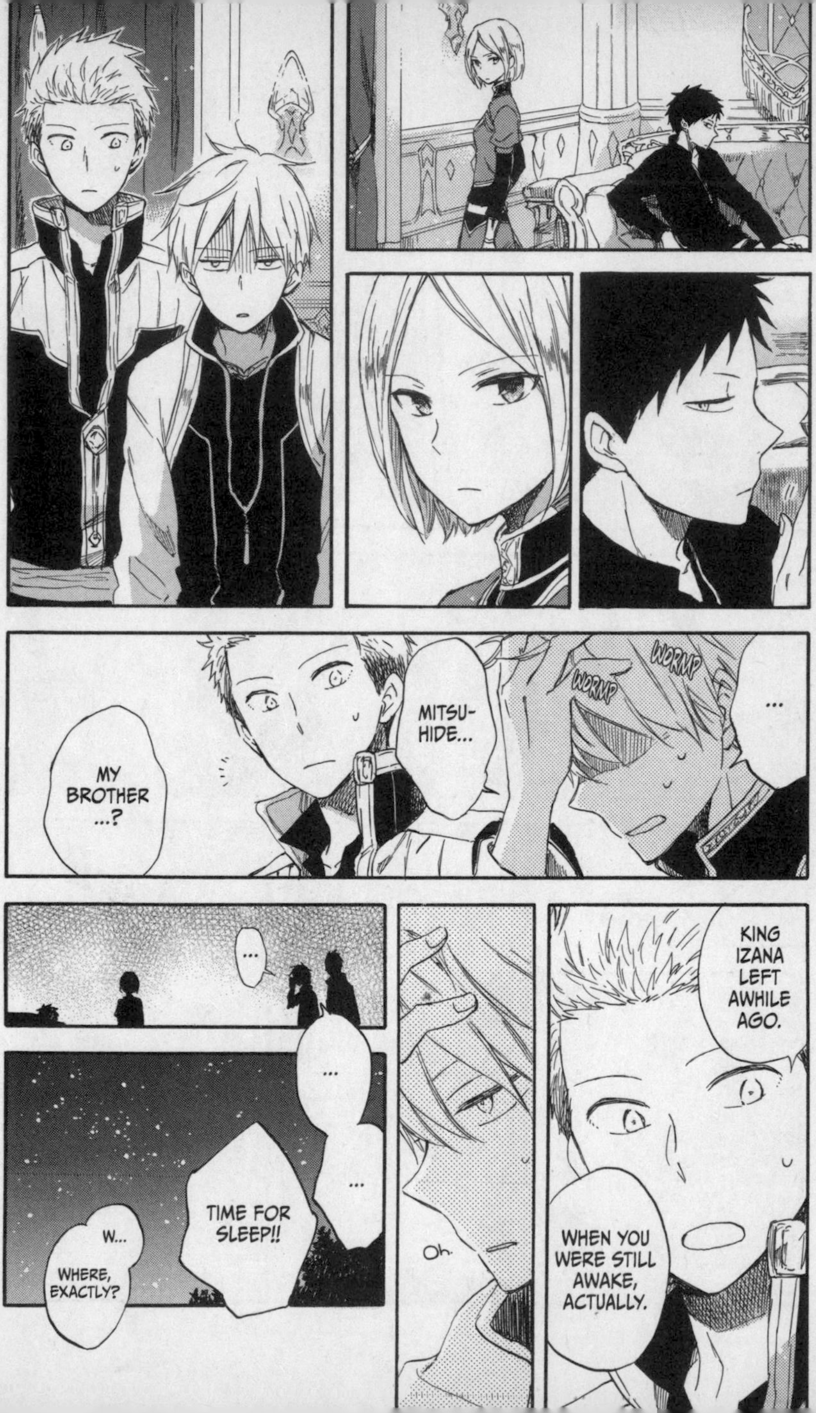
...
WORMP
WORMP
MITSU-HIDE...
MY BROTHER ...?
KING IZANA LEFT AWHILE AGO.
WHEN YOU WERE STILL AWAKE, ACTUALLY.
Oh.
...
...
...
TIME FOR SLEEP!!
W...
WHERE, EXACTLY?

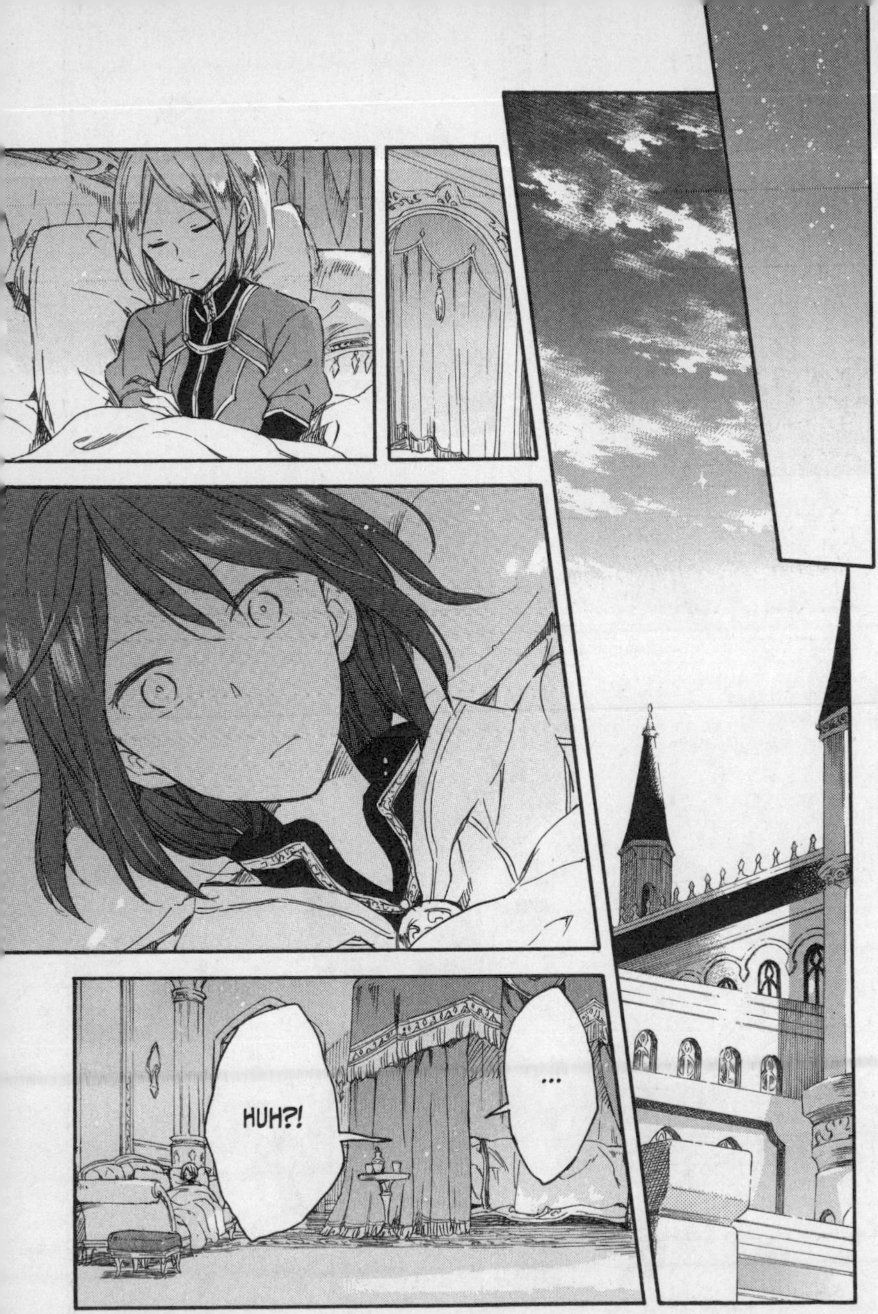
...
HUH?!

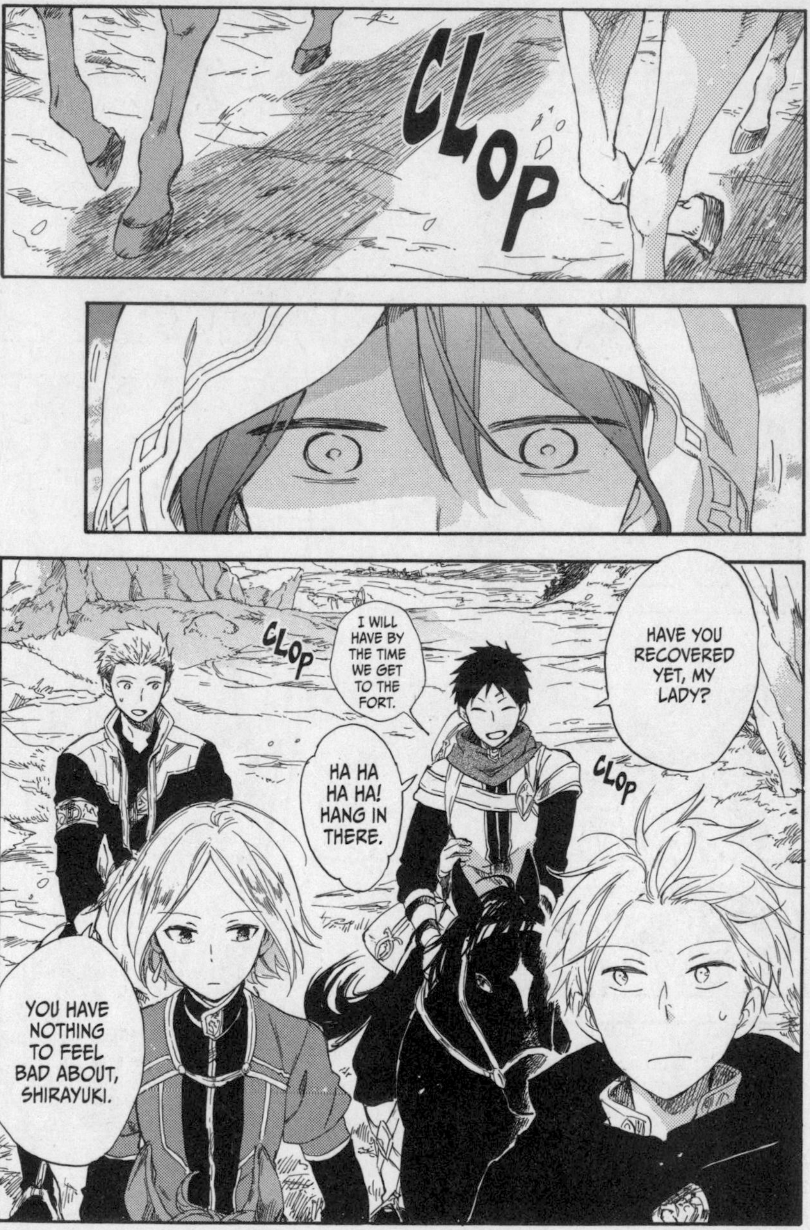
CLOP
HAVE YOU RECOVERED YET, MY LADY?
CLOP
I WILL HAVE BY THE TIME WE GET TO THE FORT.
HA HA HA HA! HANG IN THERE.
CLOP
YOU HAVE NOTHING TO FEEL BAD ABOUT, SHIRAYUKI.

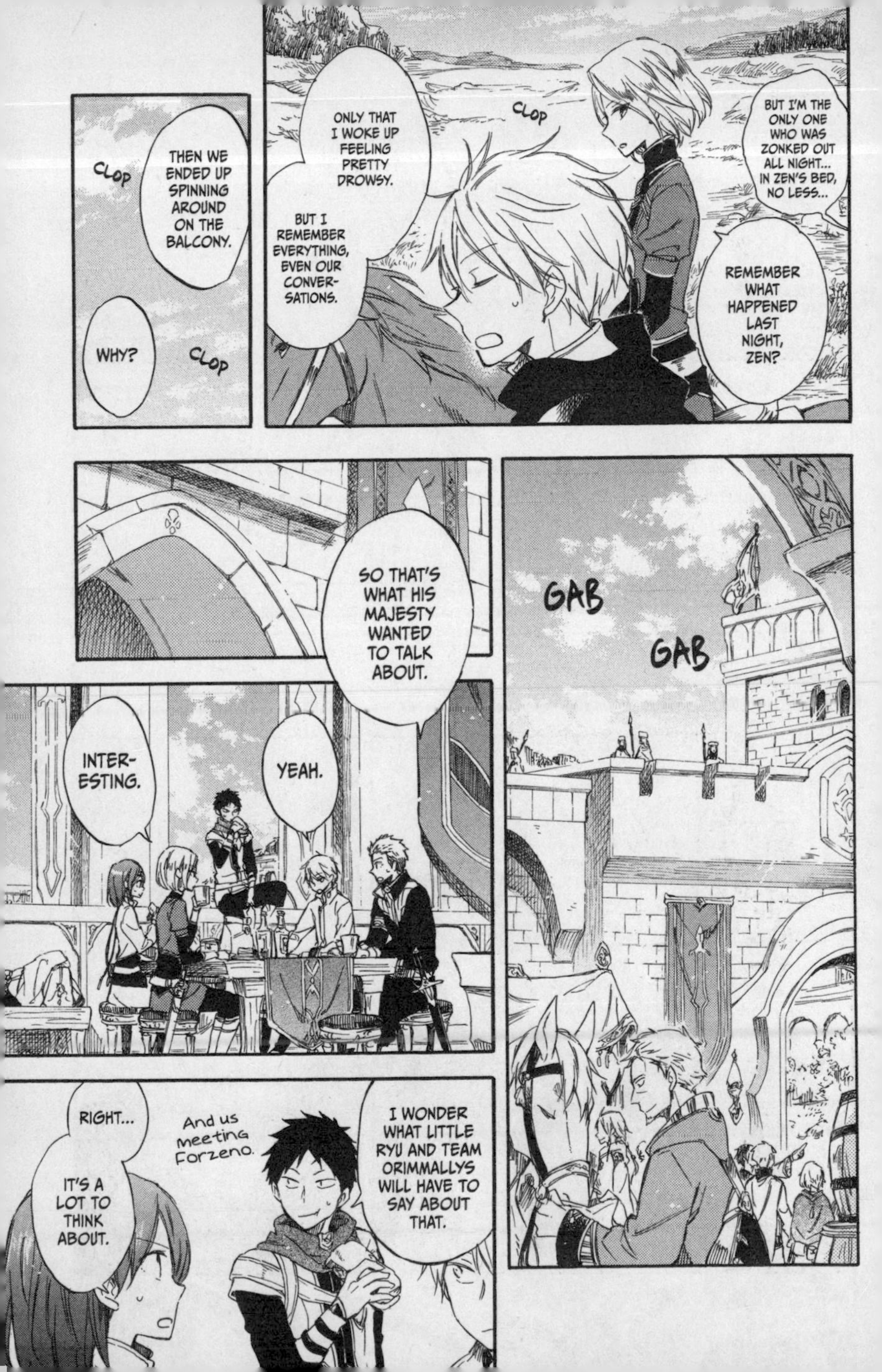
BUT I'M THE ONLY ONE WHO WAS ZONKED OUT ALL NIGHT... IN ZEN'S BED, NO LESS...
REMEMBER WHAT HAPPENED LAST NIGHT, ZEN?
CLOP
ONLY THAT I WOKE UP FEELING PRETTY DROWSY.
BUT I REMEMBER EVERYTHING, EVEN OUR CONVERSATIONS.
THEN WE ENDED UP SPINNING AROUND ON THE BALCONY.
CLOP
WHY?
CLOP
GAB
GAB
SO THAT'S WHAT HIS MAJESTY WANTED TO TALK ABOUT.
YEAH.
INTER-ESTING.
I WONDER WHAT LITTLE RYU AND TEAM ORIMMALLYS WILL HAVE TO SAY ABOUT THAT.
And us meeting Forzeno.
RIGHT...
IT'S A LOT TO THINK ABOUT.

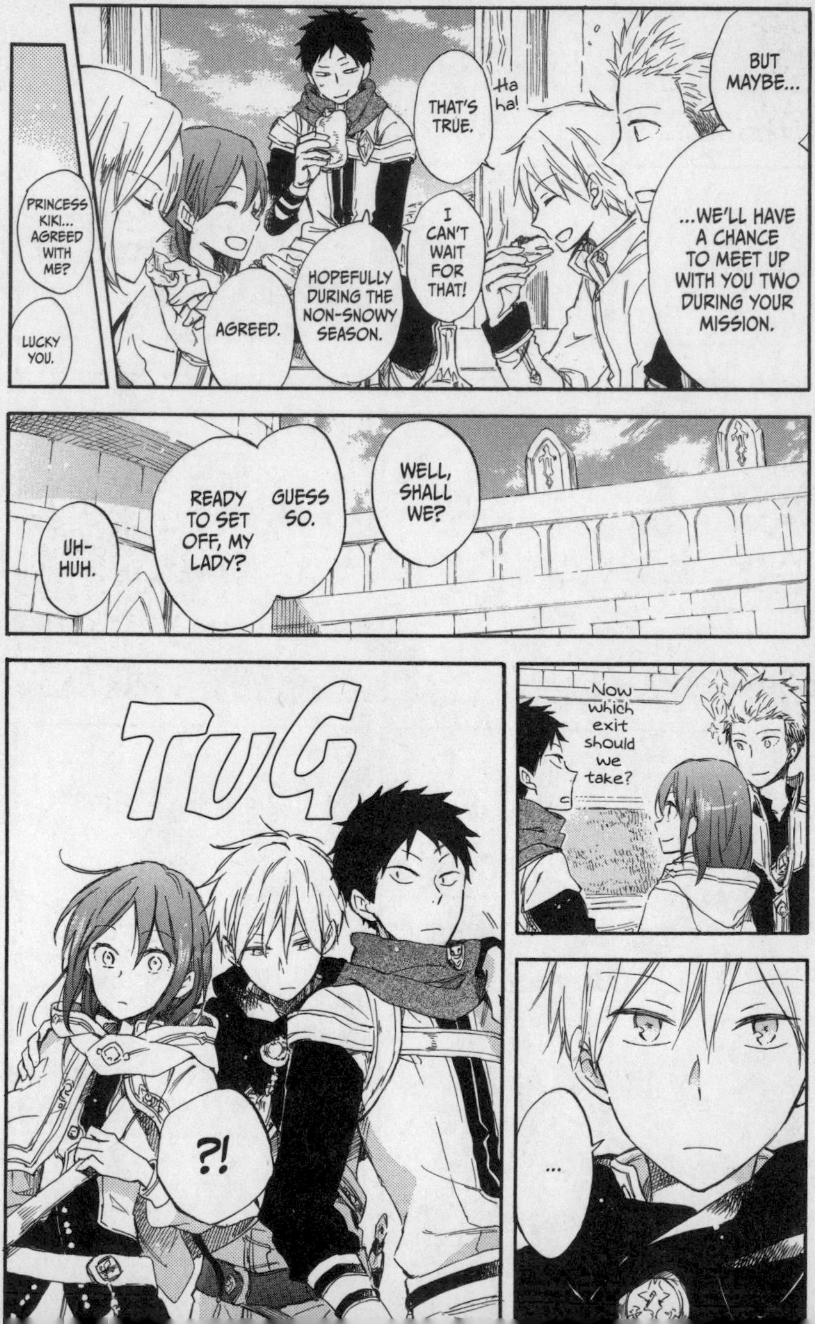
BUT MAYBE...
...WE'LL HAVE A CHANCE TO MEET UP WITH YOU TWO DURING YOUR MISSION.
Ha ha!
THAT'S TRUE.
I CAN'T WAIT FOR THAT!
HOPEFULLY DURING THE NON-SNOWY SEASON.
AGREED.
PRINCESS KIKI... AGREED WITH ME?
LUCKY YOU.
WELL, SHALL WE?
GUESS SO.
READY TO SET OFF, MY LADY?
UH-HUH.
Now which exit should we take?
...
TUG
?!

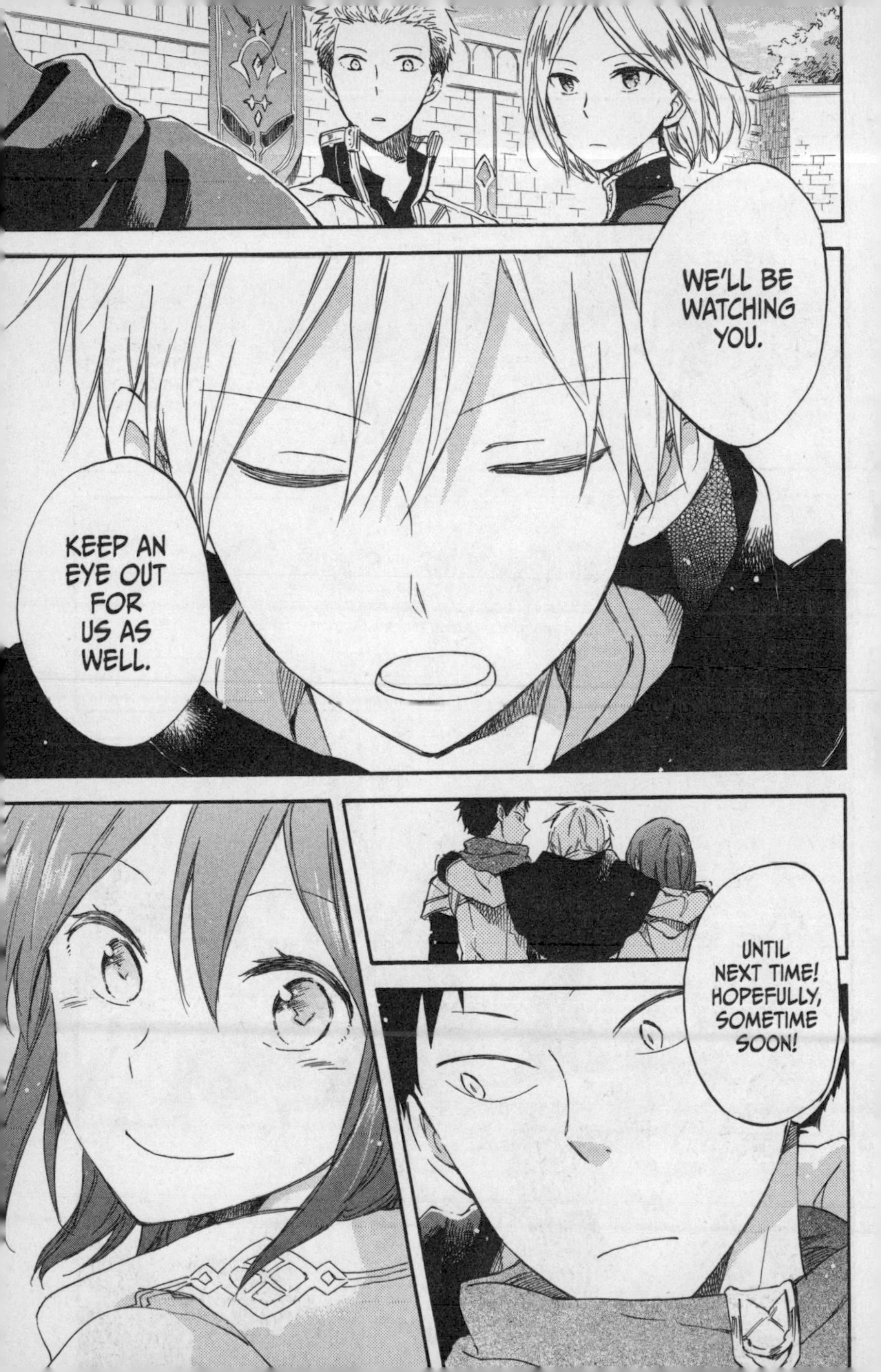
WE'LL BE WATCHING YOU.
KEEP AN EYE OUT FOR US AS WELL.
UNTIL NEXT TIME! HOPEFULLY, SOMETIME SOON!

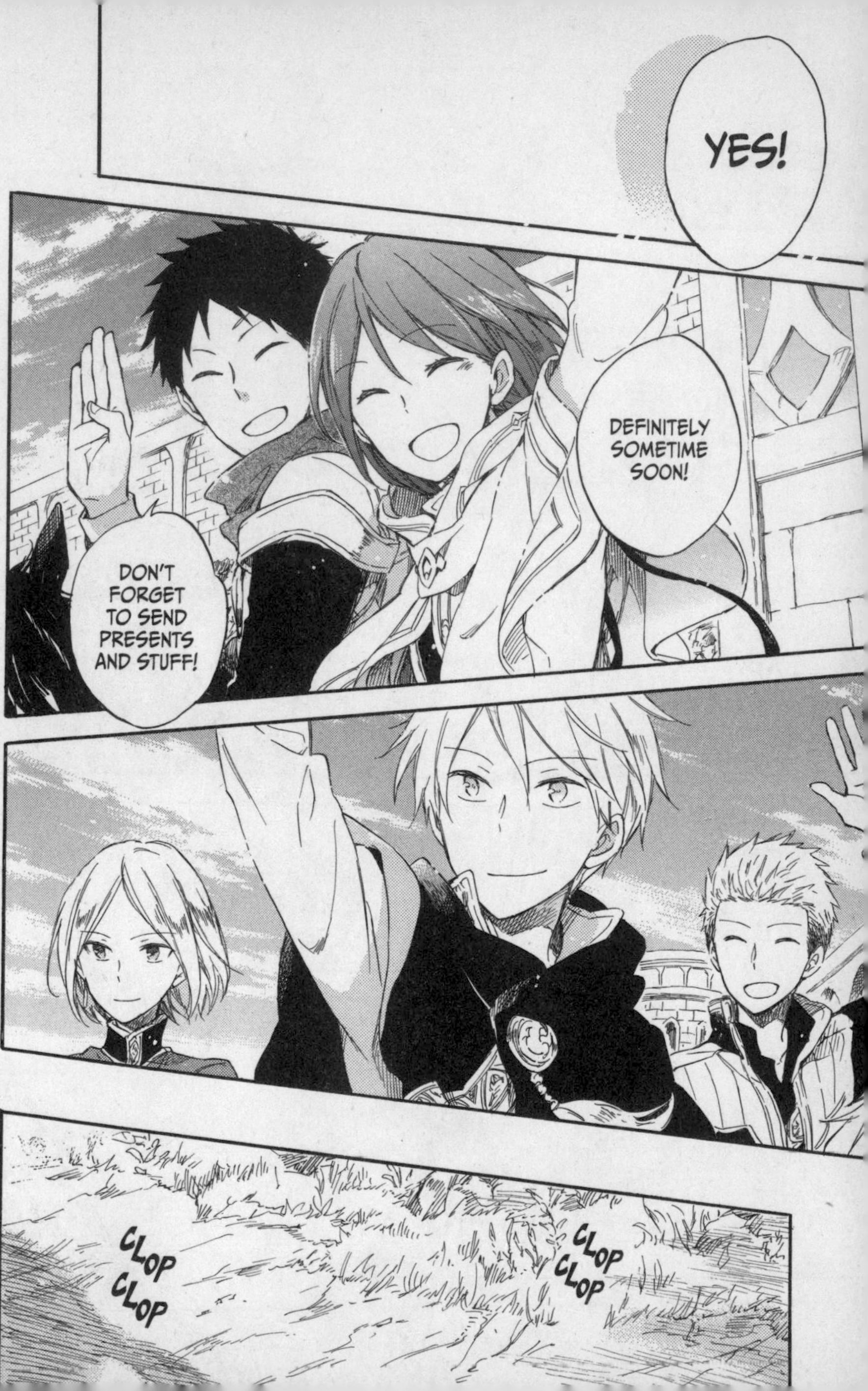
YES!
DEFINITELY SOMETIME SOON!
DON'T FORGET TO SEND PRESENTS AND STUFF!
CLOP CLOP
CLOP CLOP

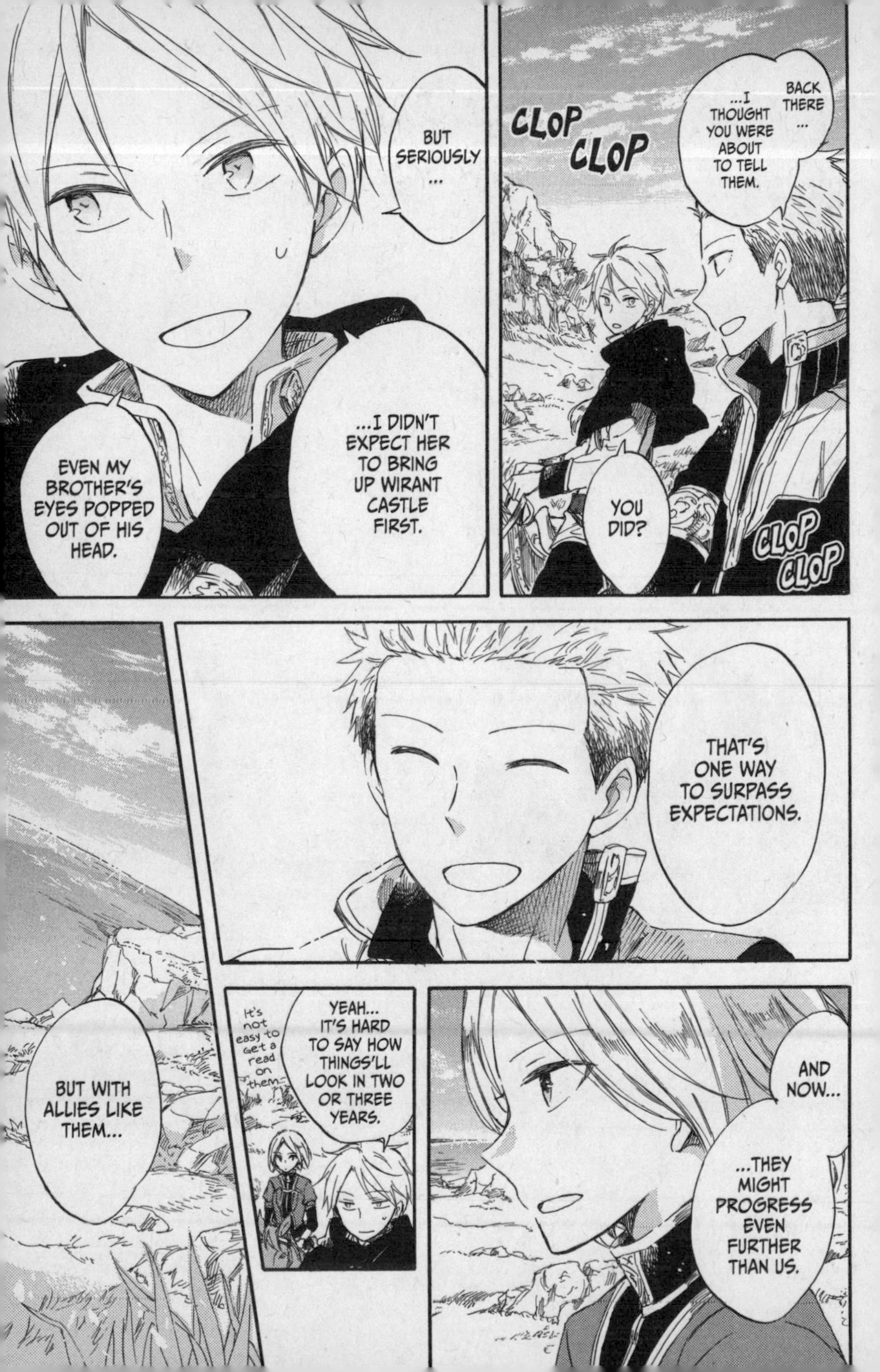
BACK THERE ...
...I THOUGHT YOU WERE ABOUT TO TELL THEM.
CLOP CLOP
YOU DID?
CLOP CLOP
BUT SERIOUSLY ...
...I DIDN'T EXPECT HER TO BRING UP WIRANT CASTLE FIRST.
EVEN MY BROTHER'S EYES POPPED OUT OF HIS HEAD.
THAT'S ONE WAY TO SURPASS EXPECTATIONS.
AND NOW...
...THEY MIGHT PROGRESS EVEN FURTHER THAN US.
YEAH... IT'S HARD TO SAY HOW THINGS'LL LOOK IN TWO OR THREE YEARS.
It's not easy to get a read on them...
BUT WITH ALLIES LIKE THEM...

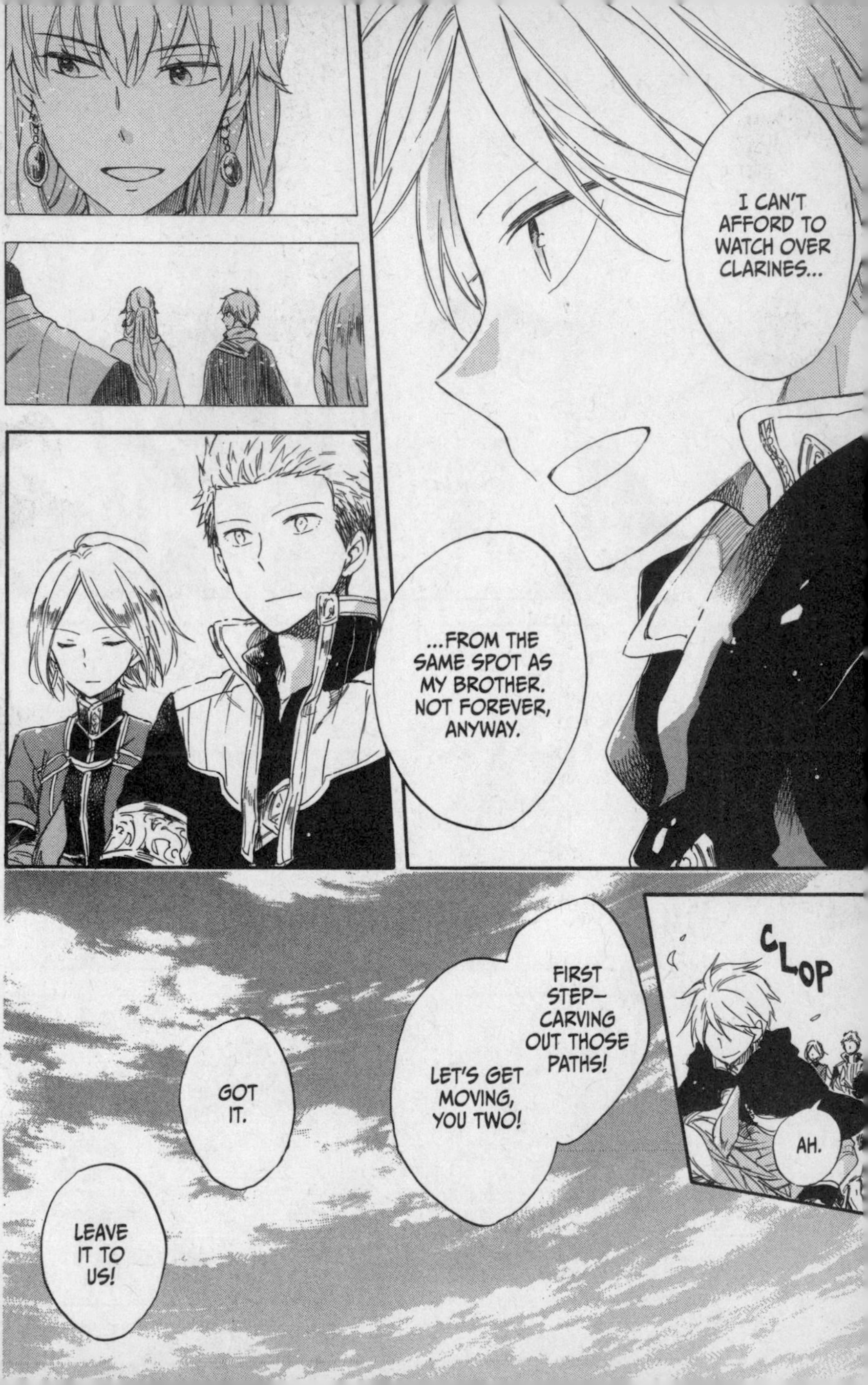
I CAN'T AFFORD TO WATCH OVER CLARINES...
...FROM THE SAME SPOT AS MY BROTHER. NOT FOREVER, ANYWAY.
CLOP
AH.
FIRST STEP— CARVING OUT THOSE PATHS!
LET'S GET MOVING, YOU TWO!
GOT IT.
LEAVE IT TO US!

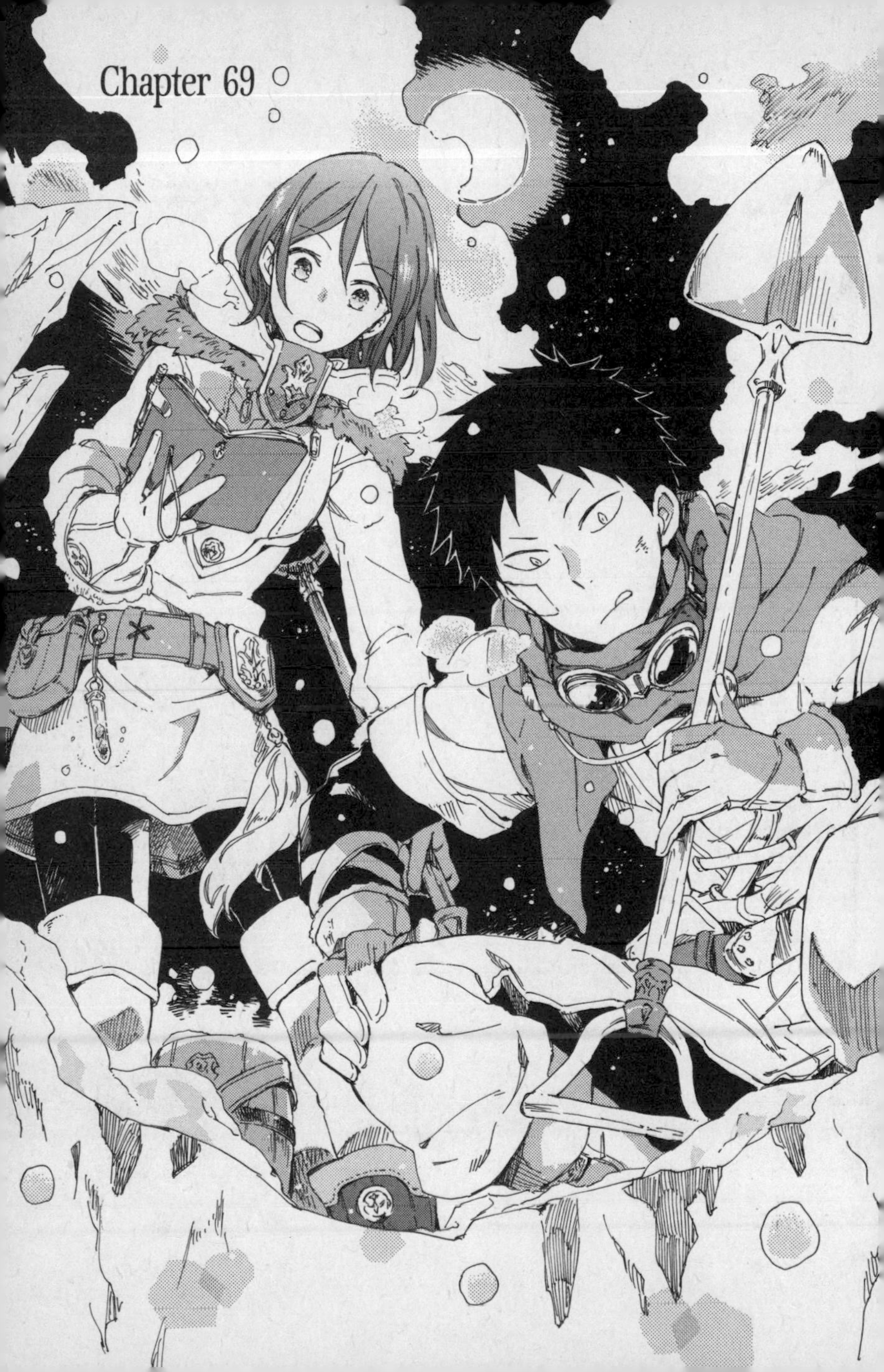
Chapter 69

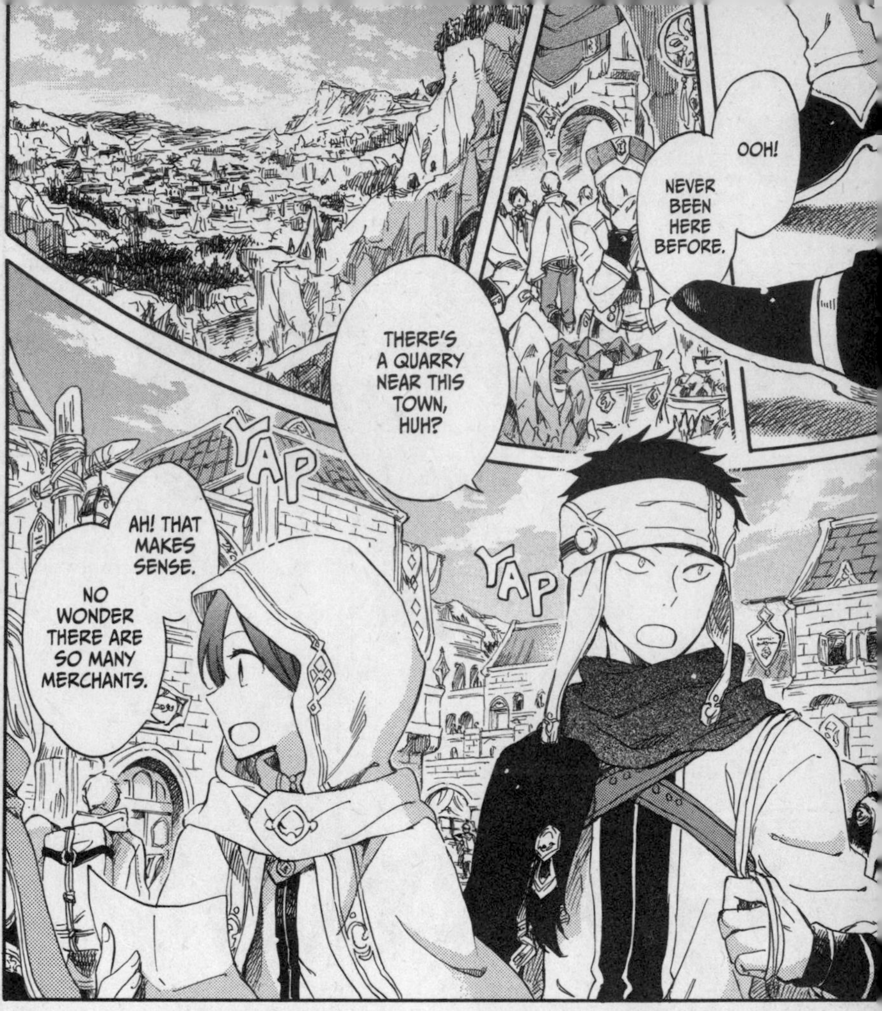
OOH!
NEVER BEEN HERE BEFORE.
THERE'S A QUARRY NEAR THIS TOWN, HUH?
YAP
YAP
AH! THAT MAKES SENSE.
NO WONDER THERE ARE SO MANY MERCHANTS.

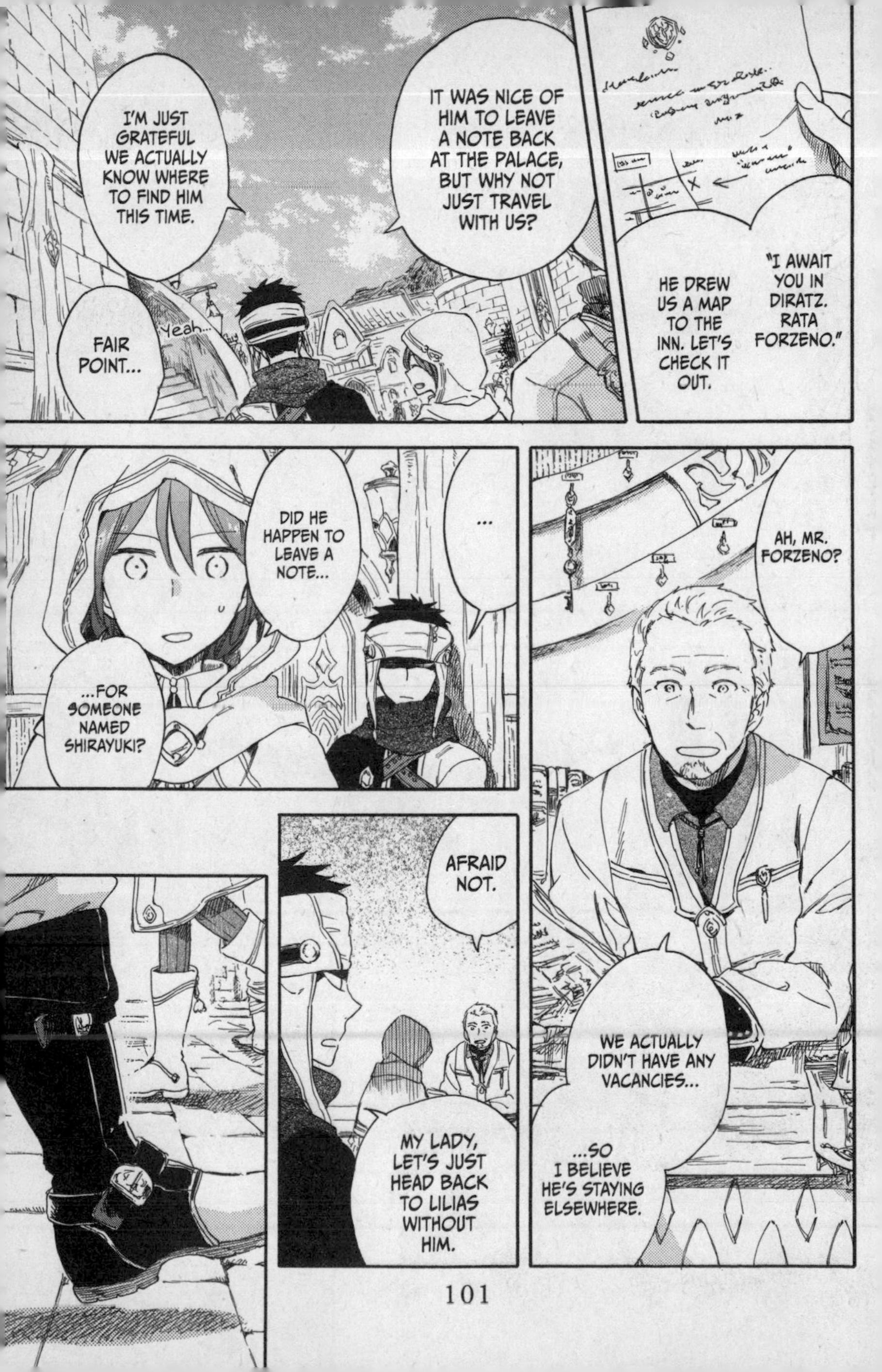
"I AWAIT YOU IN DIRATZ. RATA FORZENO."
HE DREW US A MAP TO THE INN. LET'S CHECK IT OUT.
IT WAS NICE OF HIM TO LEAVE A NOTE BACK AT THE PALACE, BUT WHY NOT JUST TRAVEL WITH US?
I'M JUST GRATEFUL WE ACTUALLY KNOW WHERE TO FIND HIM THIS TIME.
Yeah...
FAIR POINT...
AH, MR. FORZENO?
WE ACTUALLY DIDN'T HAVE ANY VACANCIES...
...SO I BELIEVE HE'S STAYING ELSEWHERE.
...
DID HE HAPPEN TO LEAVE A NOTE...
...FOR SOMEONE NAMED SHIRAYUKI?
AFRAID NOT.
MY LADY, LET'S JUST HEAD BACK TO LILIAS WITHOUT HIM.

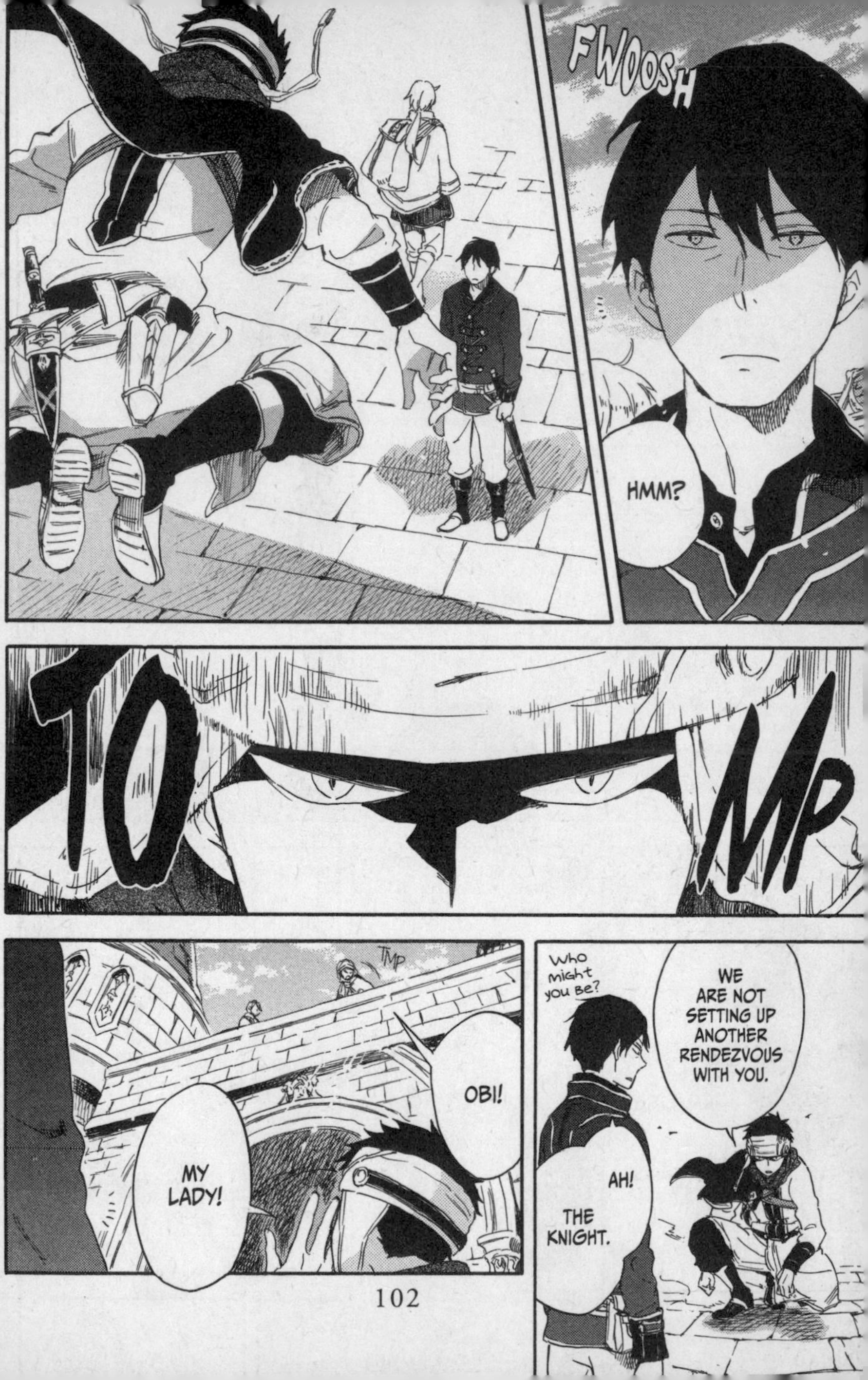
FWOOSH
HMM?
TOMP
WE ARE NOT SETTING UP ANOTHER RENDEZVOUS WITH YOU.
Who might you be?
AH! THE KNIGHT.
TMP
OBI!
MY LADY!

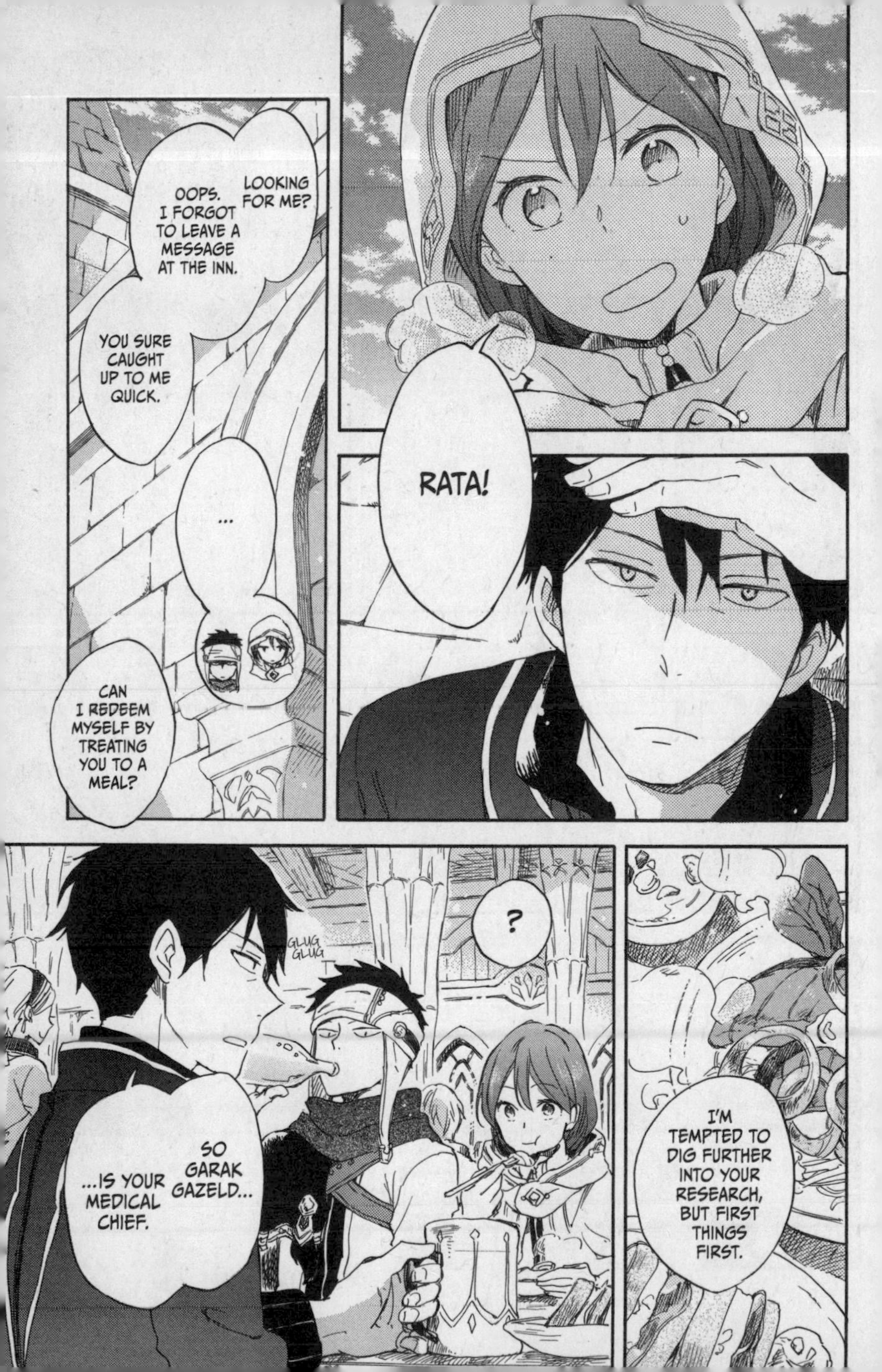
RATA!
LOOKING FOR ME?
OOPS. I FORGOT TO LEAVE A MESSAGE AT THE INN.
YOU SURE CAUGHT UP TO ME QUICK.
...
CAN I REDEEM MYSELF BY TREATING YOU TO A MEAL?
I'M TEMPTED TO DIG FURTHER INTO YOUR RESEARCH, BUT FIRST THINGS FIRST.
?
GLUG GLUG
SO GARAK GAZELD...
...IS YOUR MEDICAL CHIEF.

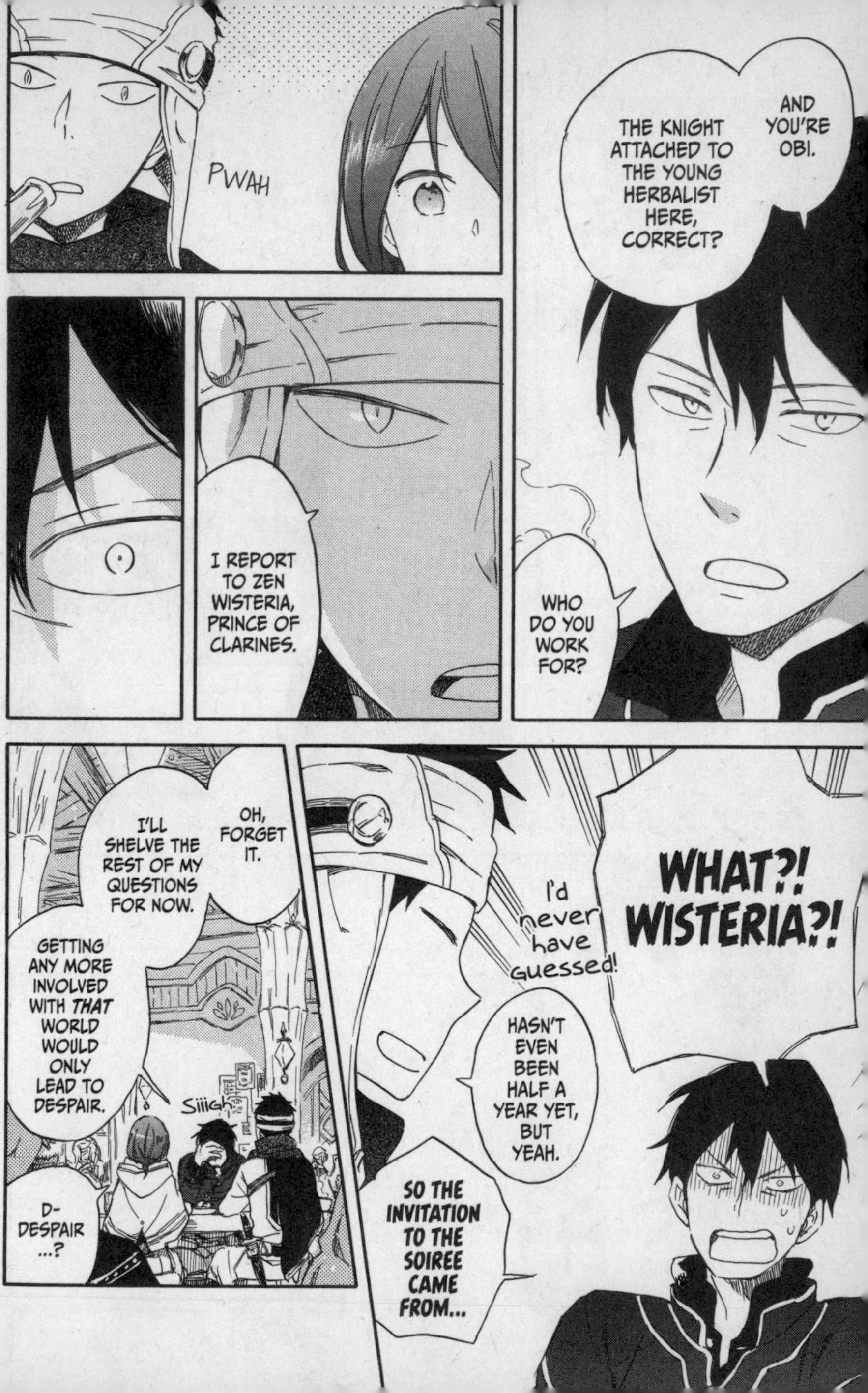
AND YOU'RE OBI.
THE KNIGHT ATTACHED TO THE YOUNG HERBALIST HERE, CORRECT?
WHO DO YOU WORK FOR?
PWAH
I REPORT TO ZEN WISTERIA, PRINCE OF CLARINES.
WHAT?! WISTERIA?!
I'd never have guessed!
HASN'T EVEN BEEN HALF A YEAR YET, BUT YEAH.
SO THE INVITATION TO THE SOIREE CAME FROM...
OH, FORGET IT.
I'LL SHELVE THE REST OF MY QUESTIONS FOR NOW.
GETTING ANY MORE INVOLVED WITH *THAT* WORLD WOULD ONLY LEAD TO DESPAIR.
Siiigh
D-DESPAIR...?

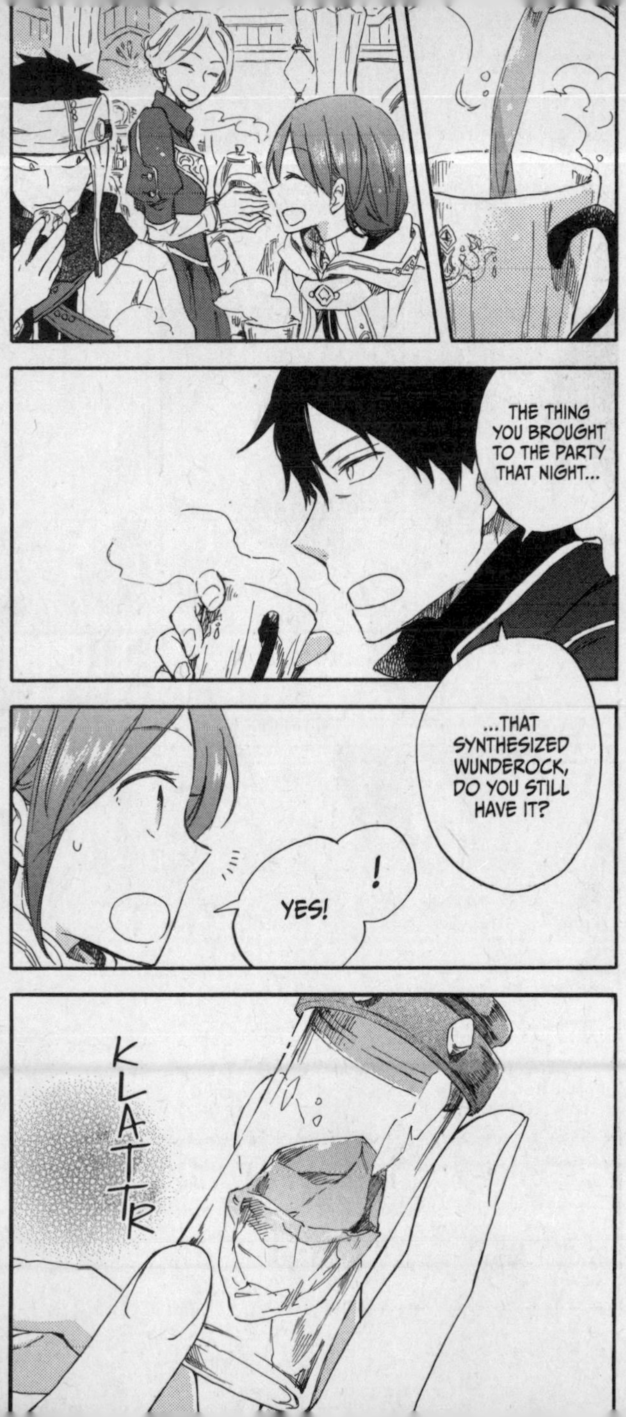
THE THING YOU BROUGHT TO THE PARTY THAT NIGHT...
...THAT SYNTHESIZED WUNDEROCK, DO YOU STILL HAVE IT?
!
YES!
KLATTR

4

CHAPTER TALK

Chapter 68

Shirayuki and Obi spent four nights at the palace.

This chapter only covers one of those four nights...

Come to think of it, chapters 66 and 67 also took place that same night. Ahem. Yes, I knew that. I'm just glad those five got to enjoy themselves!

When this chapter ran in the magazine, the copy written on the title page (provided by my editor) said:

"Kindness from his majesty, the magnanimous King Izana?!"

Isn't that funny?

I don't think his majesty was thinking about Zen and Shirayuki at all, honestly! He got sleepy, so he went to bed. That's all.

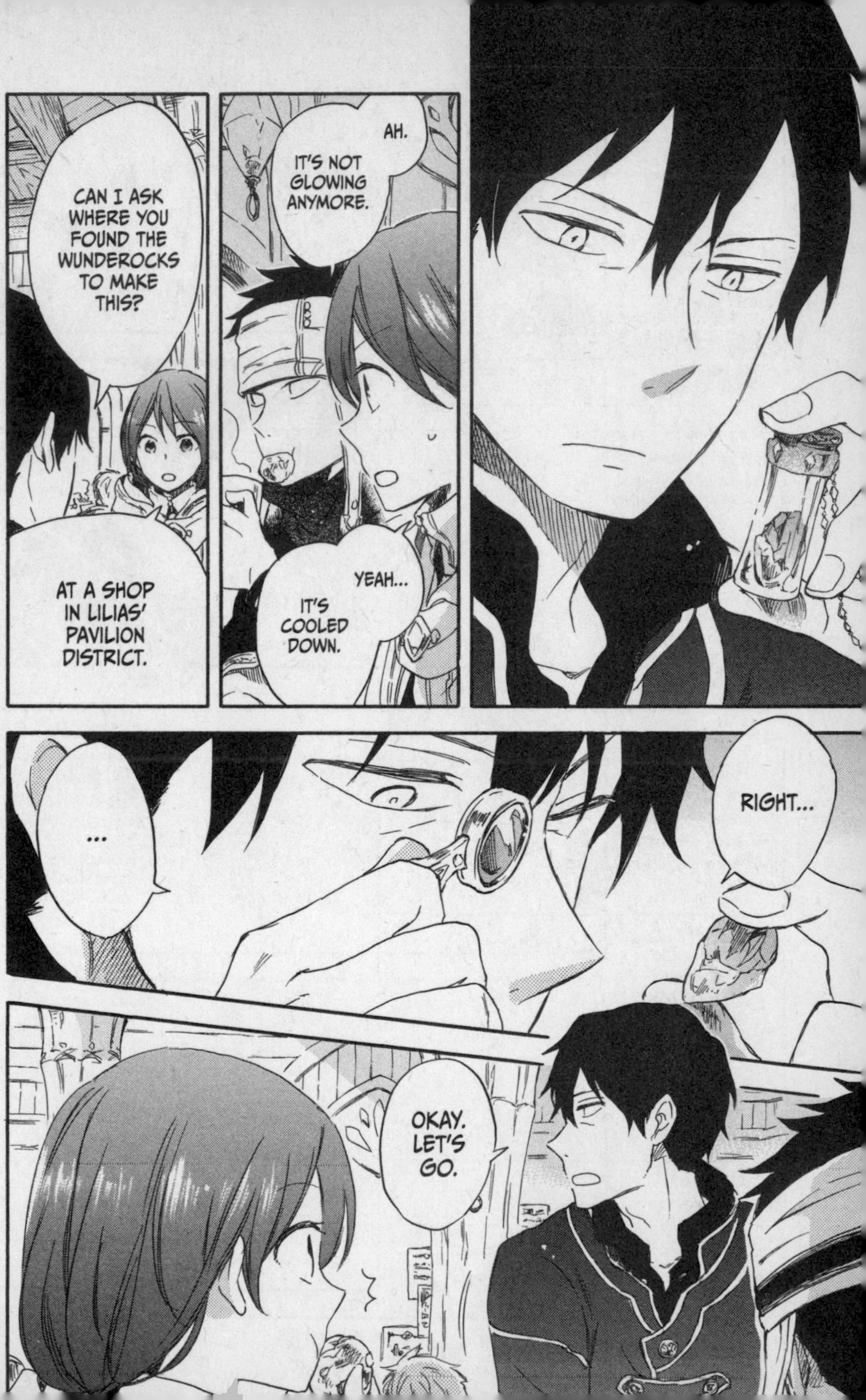
AH.
IT'S NOT GLOWING ANYMORE.
YEAH... IT'S COOLED DOWN.
CAN I ASK WHERE YOU FOUND THE WUNDEROCKS TO MAKE THIS?
AT A SHOP IN LILIAS' PAVILION DISTRICT.
RIGHT...
...
OKAY. LET'S GO.

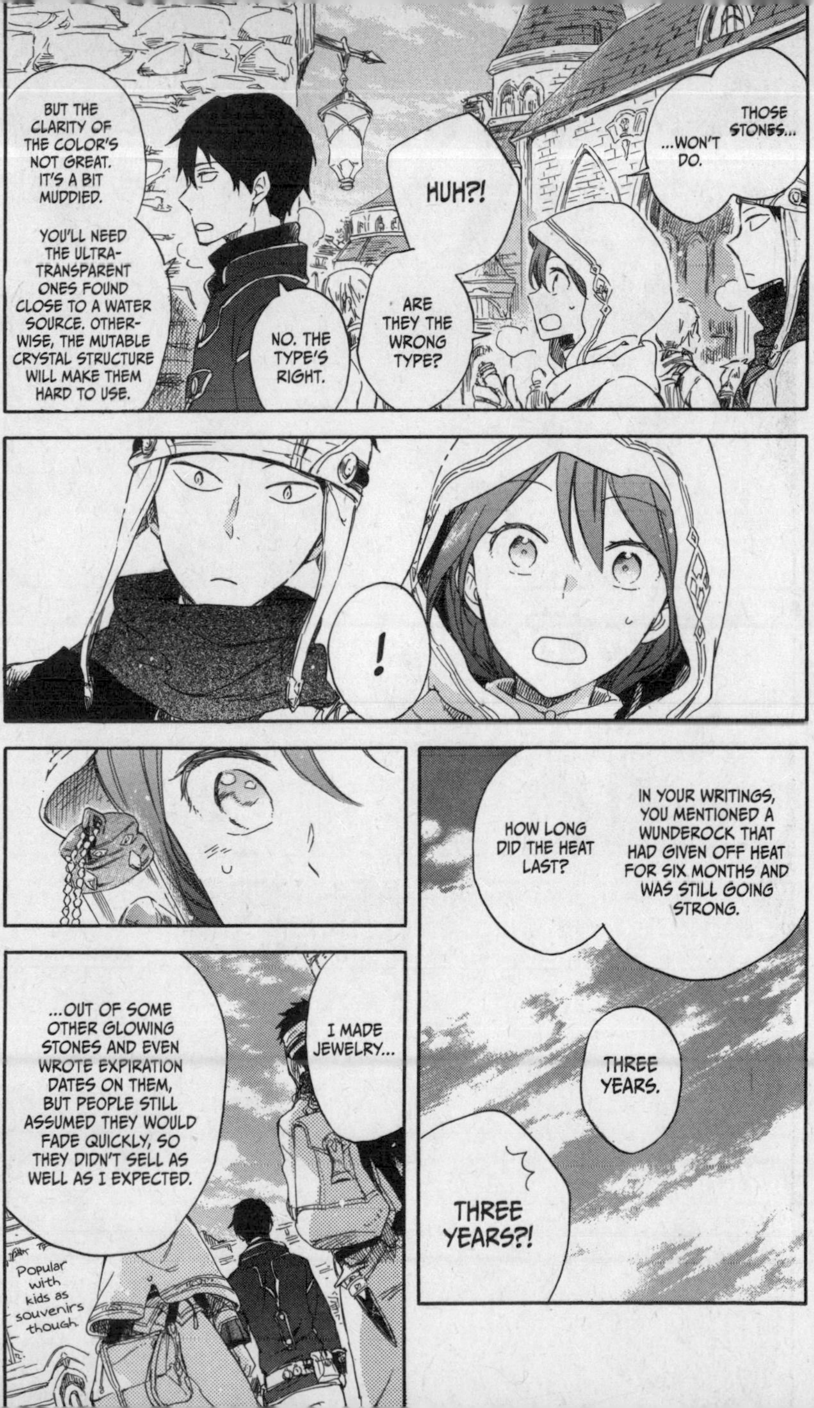
THOSE STONES...
...WON'T DO.
HUH?!
ARE THEY THE WRONG TYPE?
NO. THE TYPE'S RIGHT.
BUT THE CLARITY OF THE COLOR'S NOT GREAT. IT'S A BIT MUDDIED.
YOU'LL NEED THE ULTRA-TRANSPARENT ONES FOUND CLOSE TO A WATER SOURCE. OTHER-WISE, THE MUTABLE CRYSTAL STRUCTURE WILL MAKE THEM HARD TO USE.
!
IN YOUR WRITINGS, YOU MENTIONED A WUNDEROCK THAT HAD GIVEN OFF HEAT FOR SIX MONTHS AND WAS STILL GOING STRONG.
HOW LONG DID THE HEAT LAST?
THREE YEARS.
THREE YEARS?!
I MADE JEWELRY...
...OUT OF SOME OTHER GLOWING STONES AND EVEN WROTE EXPIRATION DATES ON THEM, BUT PEOPLE STILL ASSUMED THEY WOULD FADE QUICKLY, SO THEY DIDN'T SELL AS WELL AS I EXPECTED.
Popular with kids as souvenirs though.

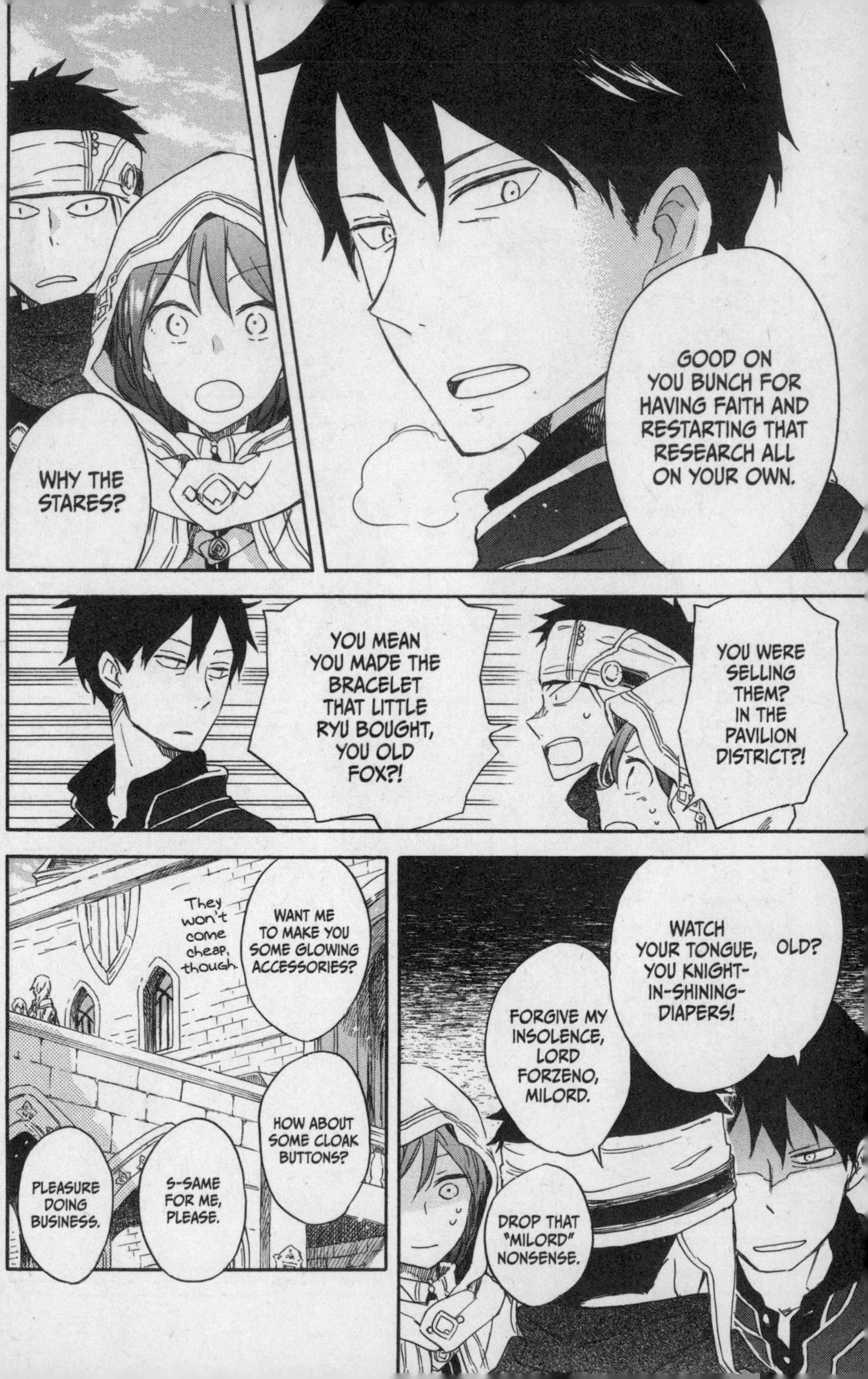
GOOD ON YOU BUNCH FOR HAVING FAITH AND RESTARTING THAT RESEARCH ALL ON YOUR OWN.
WHY THE STARES?
YOU WERE SELLING THEM? IN THE PAVILION DISTRICT?!
YOU MEAN YOU MADE THE BRACELET THAT LITTLE RYU BOUGHT, YOU OLD FOX?!
OLD?
WATCH YOUR TONGUE, YOU KNIGHT-IN-SHINING-DIAPERS!
FORGIVE MY INSOLENCE, LORD FORZENO, MILORD.
DROP THAT "MILORD" NONSENSE.
WANT ME TO MAKE YOU SOME GLOWING ACCESSORIES?
They won't come cheap, though.
HOW ABOUT SOME CLOAK BUTTONS?
S-SAME FOR ME, PLEASE.
PLEASURE DOING BUSINESS.

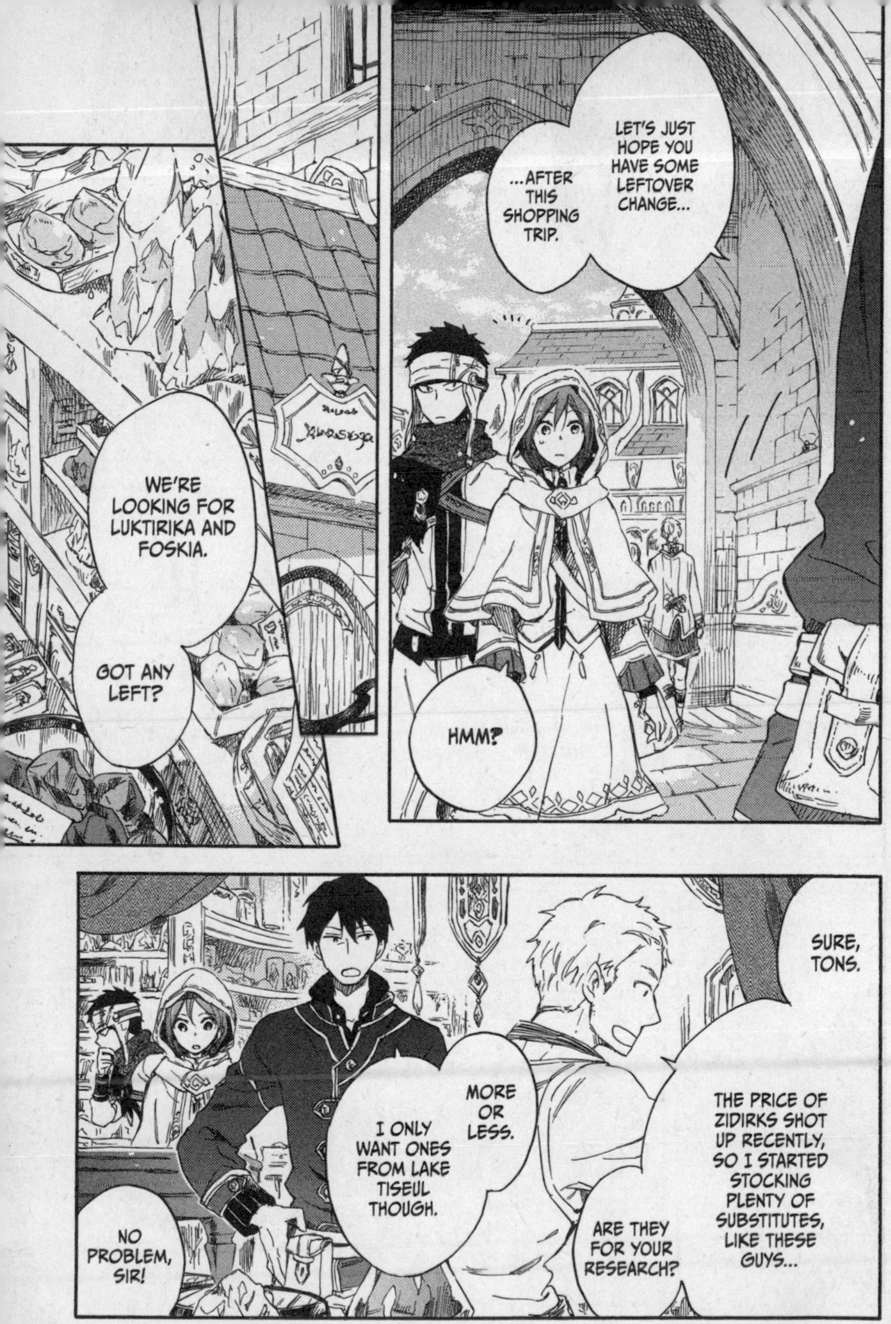
LET'S JUST HOPE YOU HAVE SOME LEFTOVER CHANGE...
...AFTER THIS SHOPPING TRIP.
HMM?
WE'RE LOOKING FOR LUKTIRIKA AND FOSKIA.
GOT ANY LEFT?
SURE, TONS.
THE PRICE OF ZIDIRKS SHOT UP RECENTLY, SO I STARTED STOCKING PLENTY OF SUBSTITUTES, LIKE THESE GUYS...
ARE THEY FOR YOUR RESEARCH?
MORE OR LESS.
I ONLY WANT ONES FROM LAKE TISEUL THOUGH.
NO PROBLEM, SIR!

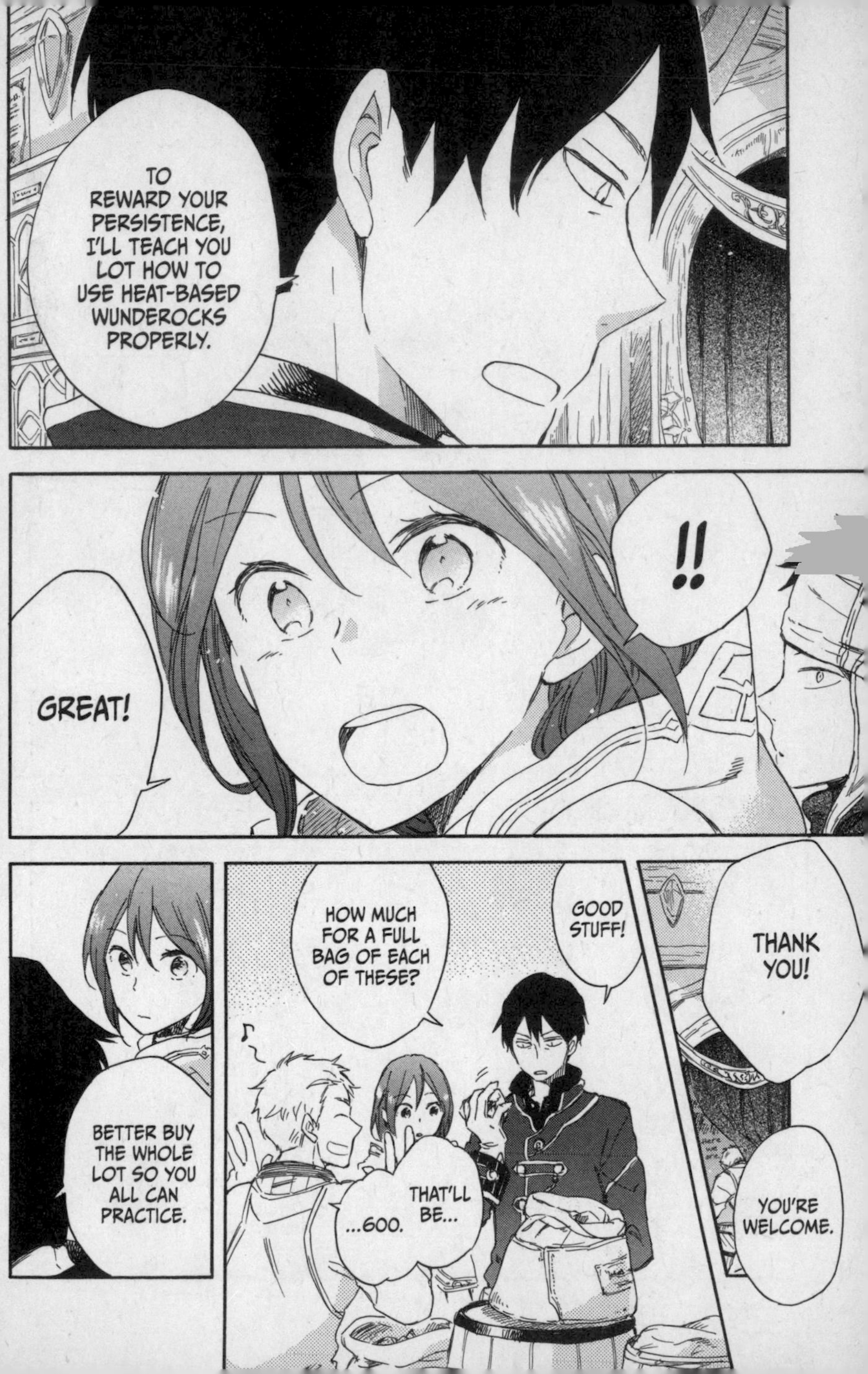
TO REWARD YOUR PERSISTENCE, I'LL TEACH YOU LOT HOW TO USE HEAT-BASED WUNDEROCKS PROPERLY.
!!
GREAT!
THANK YOU!
YOU'RE WELCOME.
GOOD STUFF!
HOW MUCH FOR A FULL BAG OF EACH OF THESE?
THAT'LL BE...
...600.
BETTER BUY THE WHOLE LOT SO YOU ALL CAN PRACTICE.

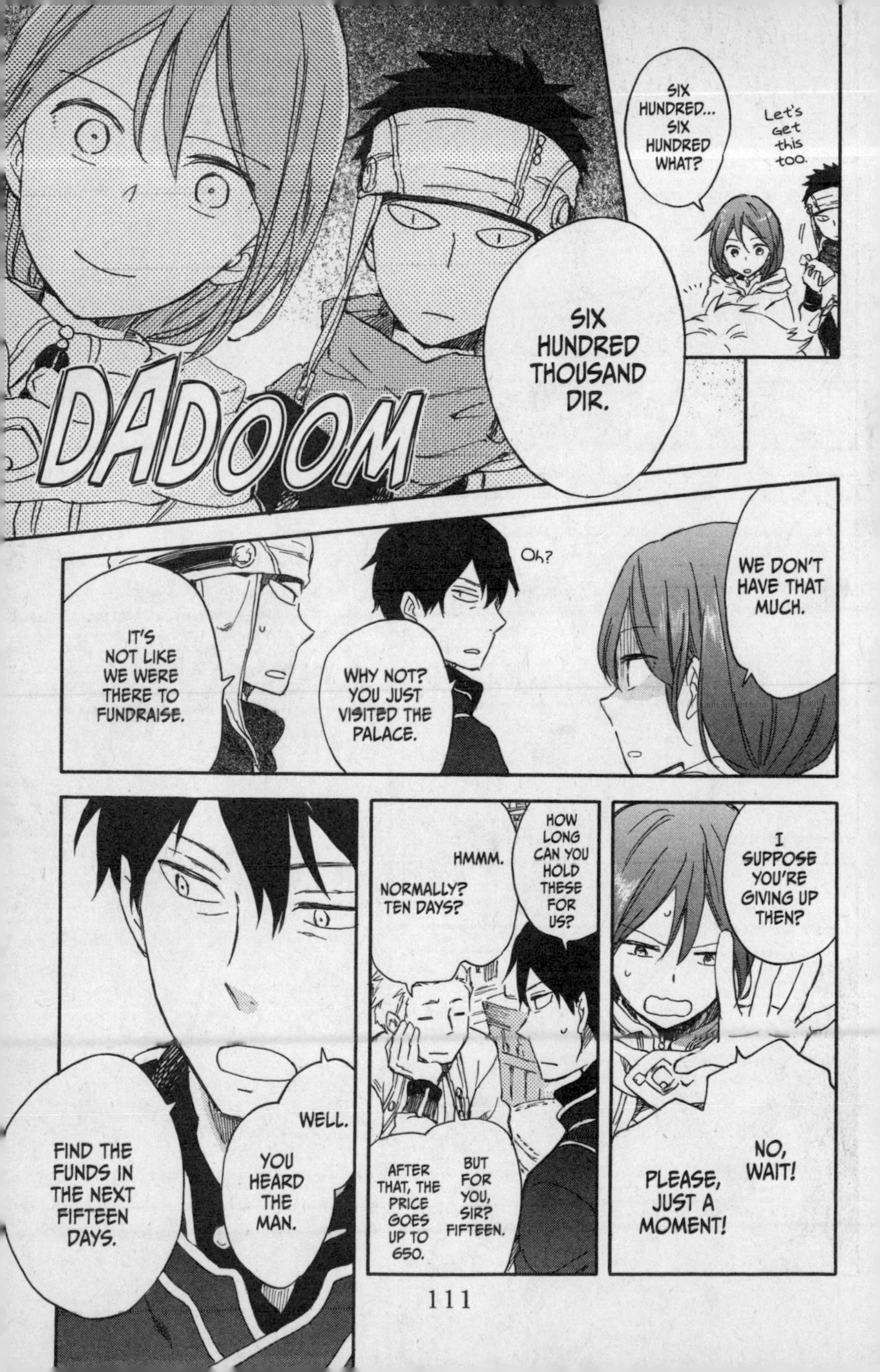
Let's get this too.
SIX HUNDRED... SIX HUNDRED WHAT?
SIX HUNDRED THOUSAND DIR.
DADOOM
WE DON'T HAVE THAT MUCH.
Oh?
WHY NOT? YOU JUST VISITED THE PALACE.
IT'S NOT LIKE WE WERE THERE TO FUNDRAISE.
I SUPPOSE YOU'RE GIVING UP THEN?
NO, WAIT!
PLEASE, JUST A MOMENT!
HOW LONG CAN YOU HOLD THESE FOR US?
HMMM.
NORMALLY? TEN DAYS?
BUT FOR YOU, SIR? FIFTEEN.
AFTER THAT, THE PRICE GOES UP TO 650.
WELL.
YOU HEARD THE MAN.
FIND THE FUNDS IN THE NEXT FIFTEEN DAYS.

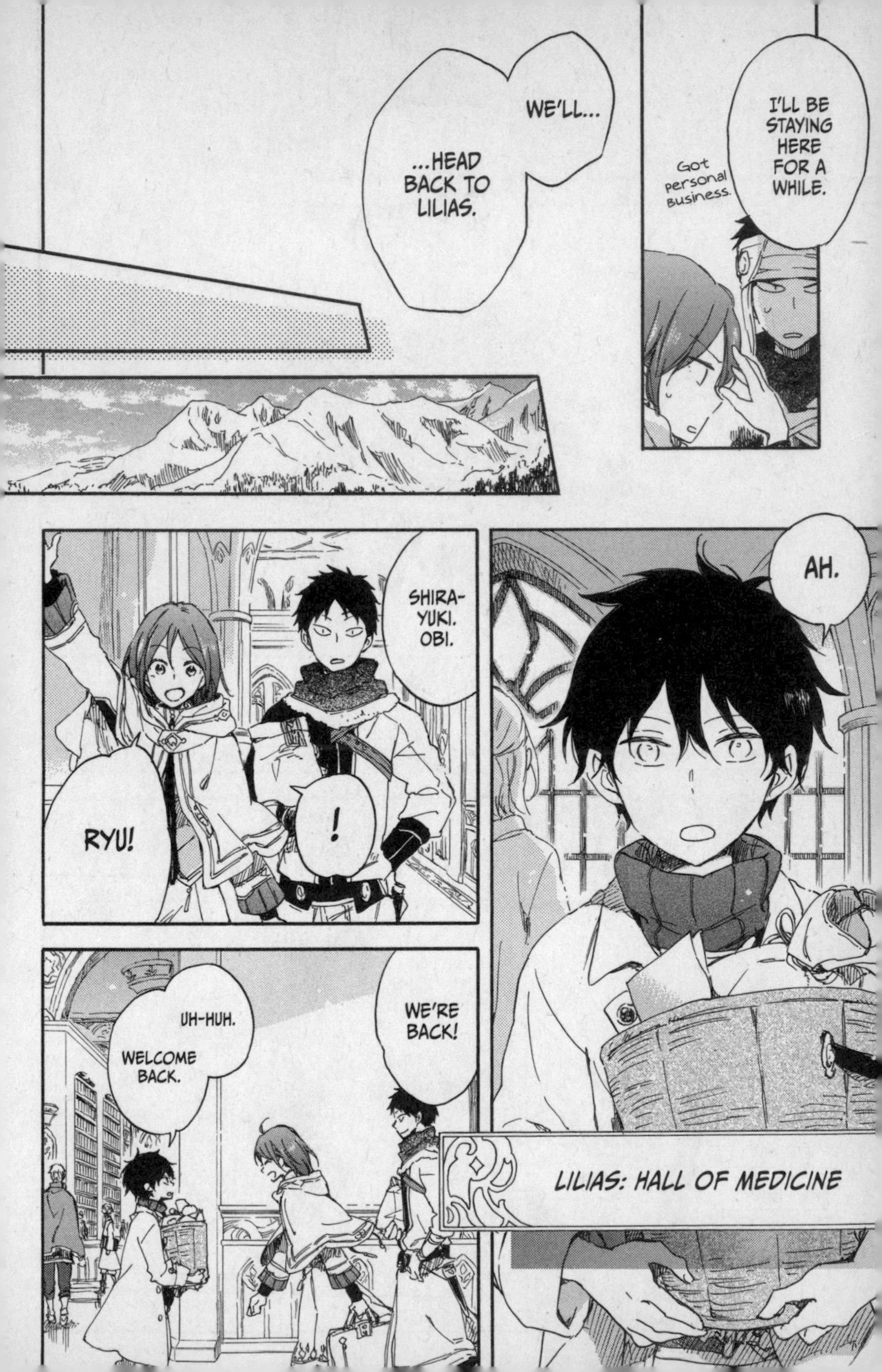

I'LL BE STAYING HERE FOR A WHILE.
Got personal business.
WE'LL...
...HEAD BACK TO LILIAS.
AH.
LILIAS: HALL OF MEDICINE
SHIRA-YUKI. OBI.
RYU!
!
WE'RE BACK!
UH-HUH.
WELCOME BACK.

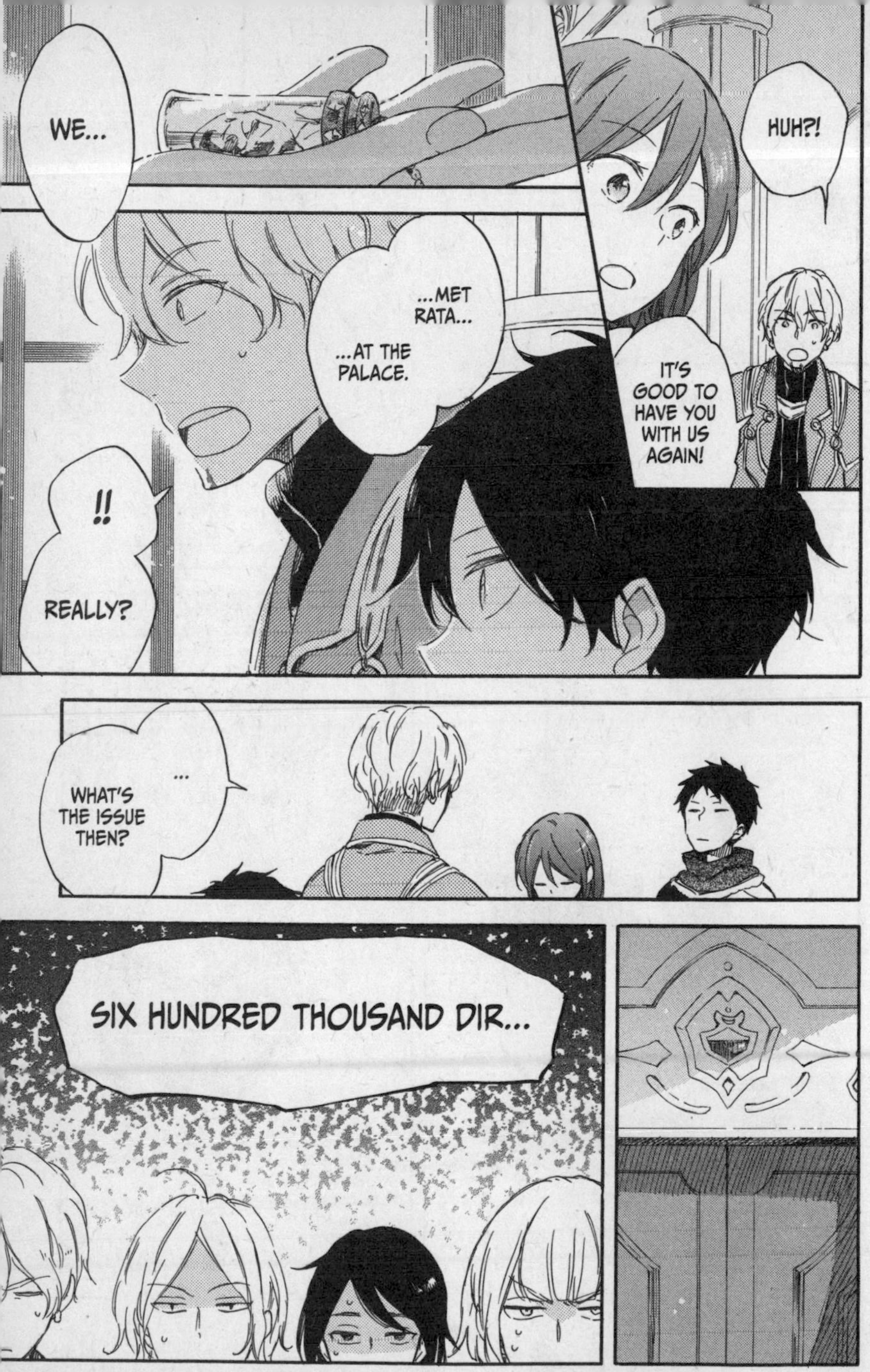
HUH?!
IT'S GOOD TO HAVE YOU WITH US AGAIN!
WE...
...MET RATA...
...AT THE PALACE.
!!
REALLY?
...
WHAT'S THE ISSUE THEN?
SIX HUNDRED THOUSAND DIR...

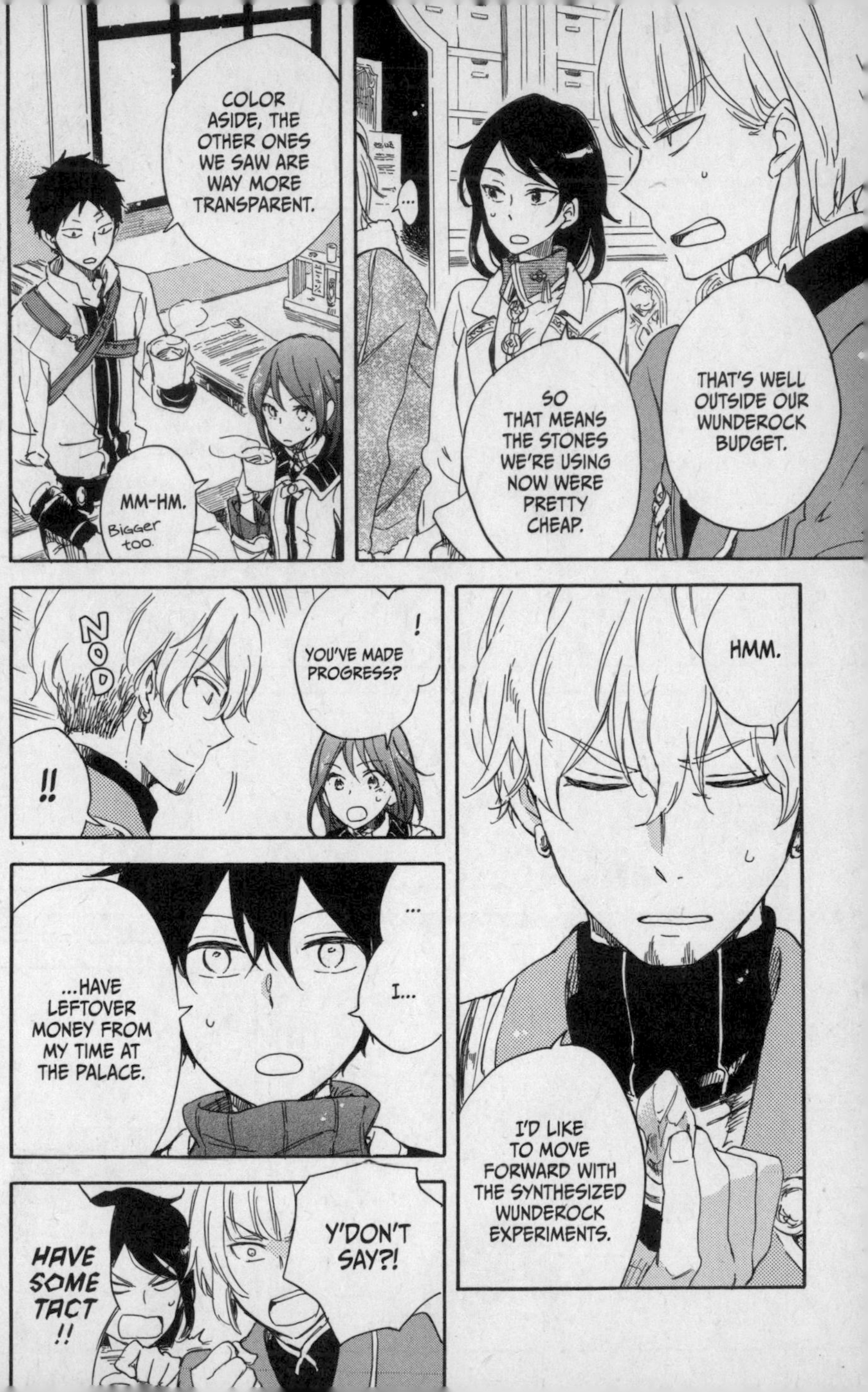
...
THAT'S WELL OUTSIDE OUR WUNDEROCK BUDGET.
SO THAT MEANS THE STONES WE'RE USING NOW WERE PRETTY CHEAP.
COLOR ASIDE, THE OTHER ONES WE SAW ARE WAY MORE TRANSPARENT.
MM-HM.
Bigger too.
HMM.
I'D LIKE TO MOVE FORWARD WITH THE SYNTHESIZED WUNDEROCK EXPERIMENTS.
!
YOU'VE MADE PROGRESS?
NOD
!!
...
I...
...HAVE LEFTOVER MONEY FROM MY TIME AT THE PALACE.
Y'DON'T SAY?!
HAVE SOME TACT !!

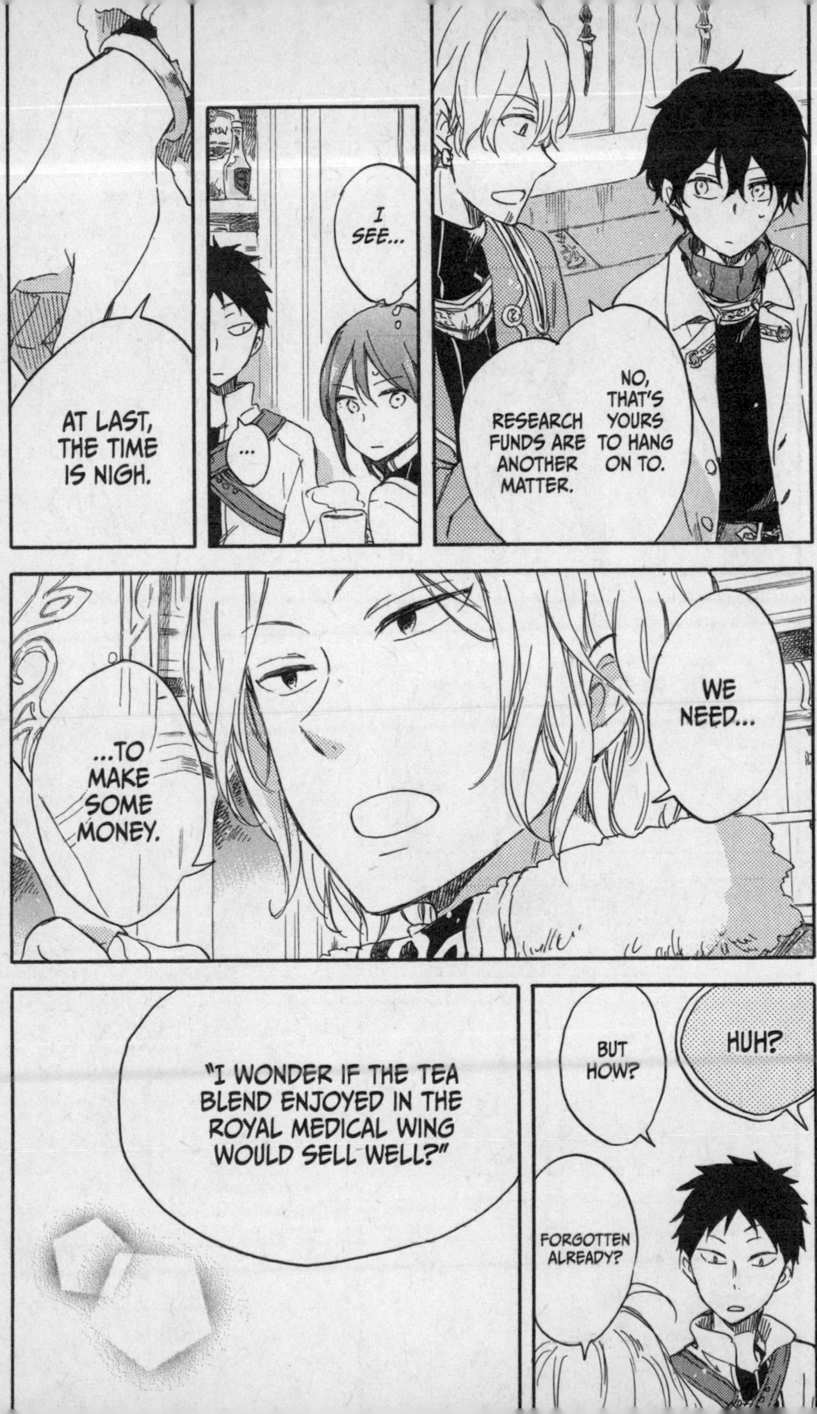
NO, THAT'S YOURS TO HANG ON TO.
RESEARCH FUNDS ARE ANOTHER MATTER.
I SEE...
...
AT LAST, THE TIME IS NIGH.
WE NEED...
...TO MAKE SOME MONEY.
HUH?
BUT HOW?
FORGOTTEN ALREADY?
"I WONDER IF THE TEA BLEND ENJOYED IN THE ROYAL MEDICAL WING WOULD SELL WELL?"

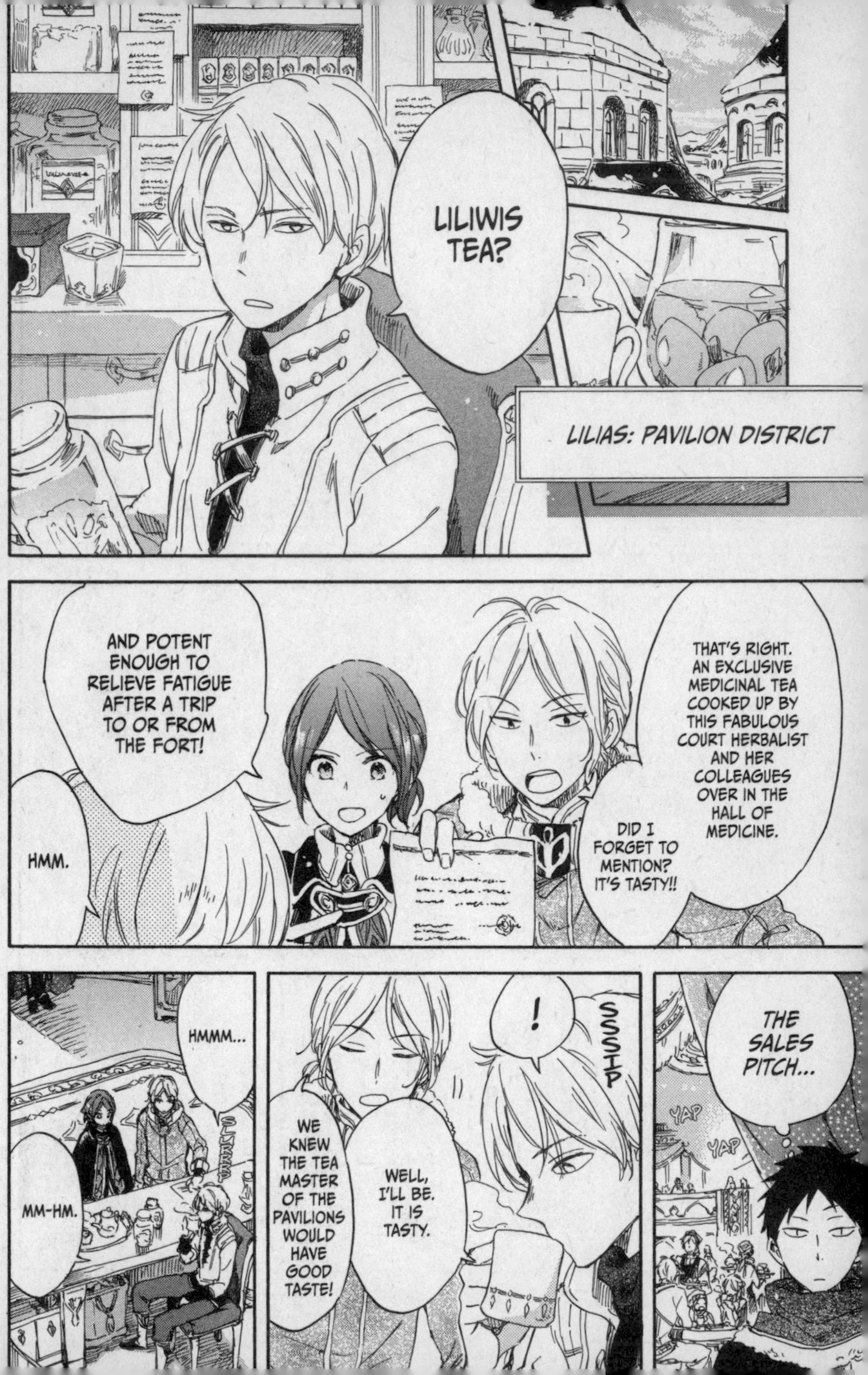
LILIWIS TEA?
LILIAS: PAVILION DISTRICT
THAT'S RIGHT. AN EXCLUSIVE MEDICINAL TEA COOKED UP BY THIS FABULOUS COURT HERBALIST AND HER COLLEAGUES OVER IN THE HALL OF MEDICINE.
DID I FORGET TO MENTION? IT'S TASTY!!
AND POTENT ENOUGH TO RELIEVE FATIGUE AFTER A TRIP TO OR FROM THE FORT!
HMM.
THE SALES PITCH...
YAP
YAP
!
SSSIP
WELL, I'LL BE. IT IS TASTY.
WE KNEW THE TEA MASTER OF THE PAVILIONS WOULD HAVE GOOD TASTE!
HMMM...
MM-HM.

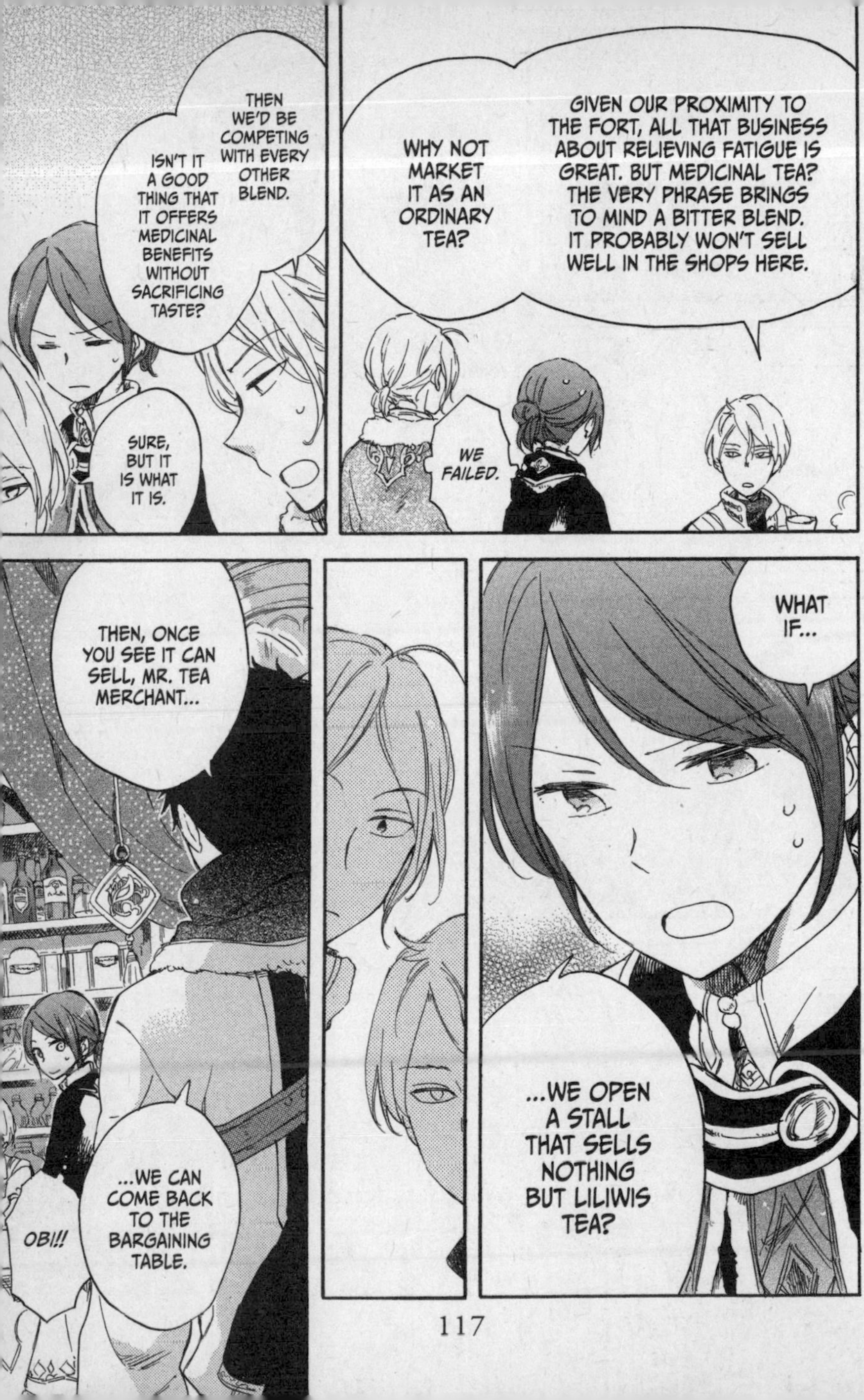
GIVEN OUR PROXIMITY TO THE FORT, ALL THAT BUSINESS ABOUT RELIEVING FATIGUE IS GREAT. BUT MEDICINAL TEA? THE VERY PHRASE BRINGS TO MIND A BITTER BLEND. IT PROBABLY WON'T SELL WELL IN THE SHOPS HERE.
WHY NOT MARKET IT AS AN ORDINARY TEA?
WE FAILED.
THEN WE'D BE COMPETING WITH EVERY OTHER BLEND.
ISN'T IT A GOOD THING THAT IT OFFERS MEDICINAL BENEFITS WITHOUT SACRIFICING TASTE?
SURE, BUT IT IS WHAT IT IS.
WHAT IF...
...WE OPEN A STALL THAT SELLS NOTHING BUT LILIWIS TEA?
THEN, ONCE YOU SEE IT CAN SELL, MR. TEA MERCHANT...
...WE CAN COME BACK TO THE BARGAINING TABLE.
OBI!!

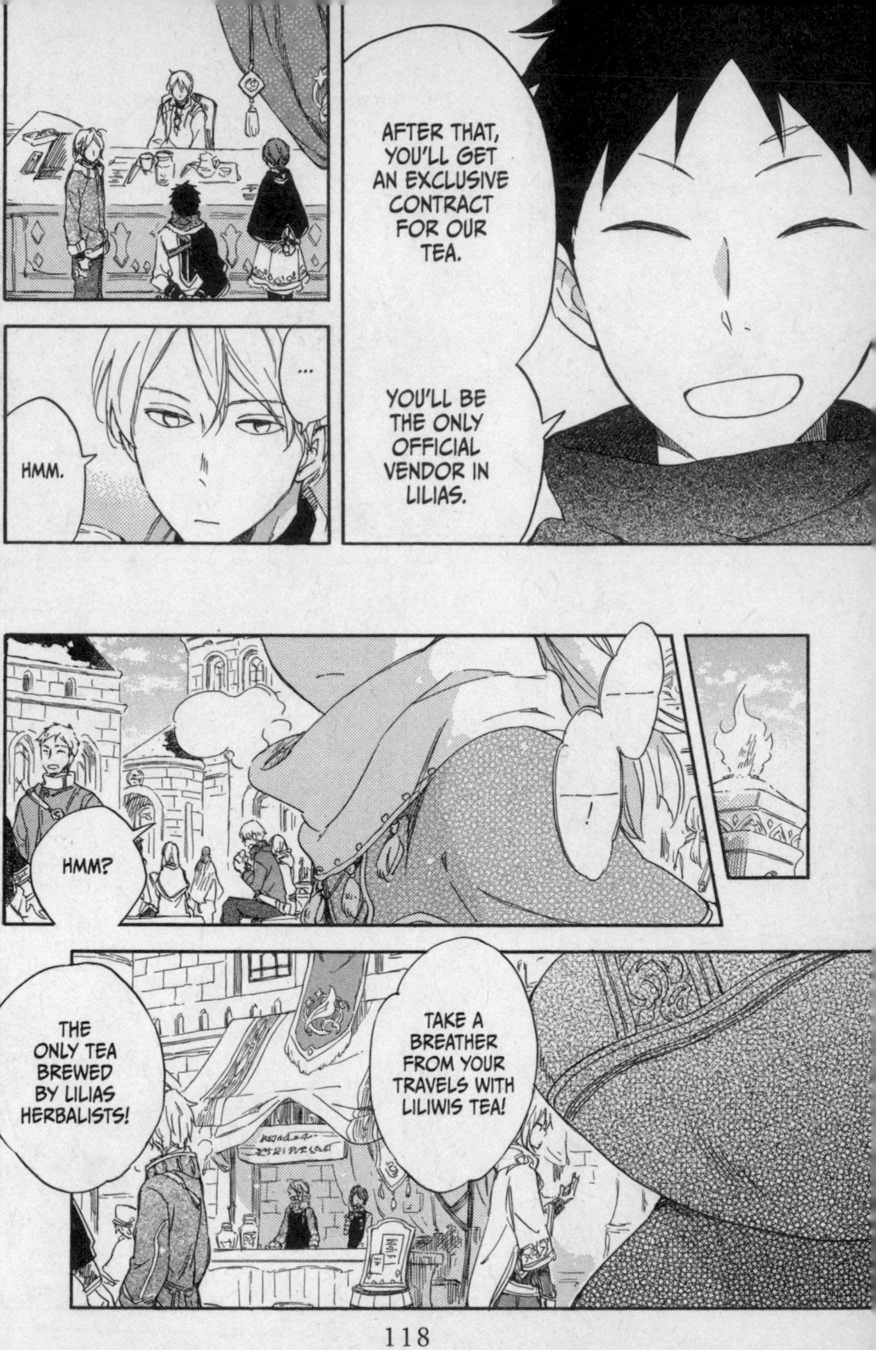
AFTER THAT, YOU'LL GET AN EXCLUSIVE CONTRACT FOR OUR TEA.
YOU'LL BE THE ONLY OFFICIAL VENDOR IN LILIAS.
...
HMM.
HMM?
TAKE A BREATHER FROM YOUR TRAVELS WITH LILIWIS TEA!
THE ONLY TEA BREWED BY LILIAS HERBALISTS!

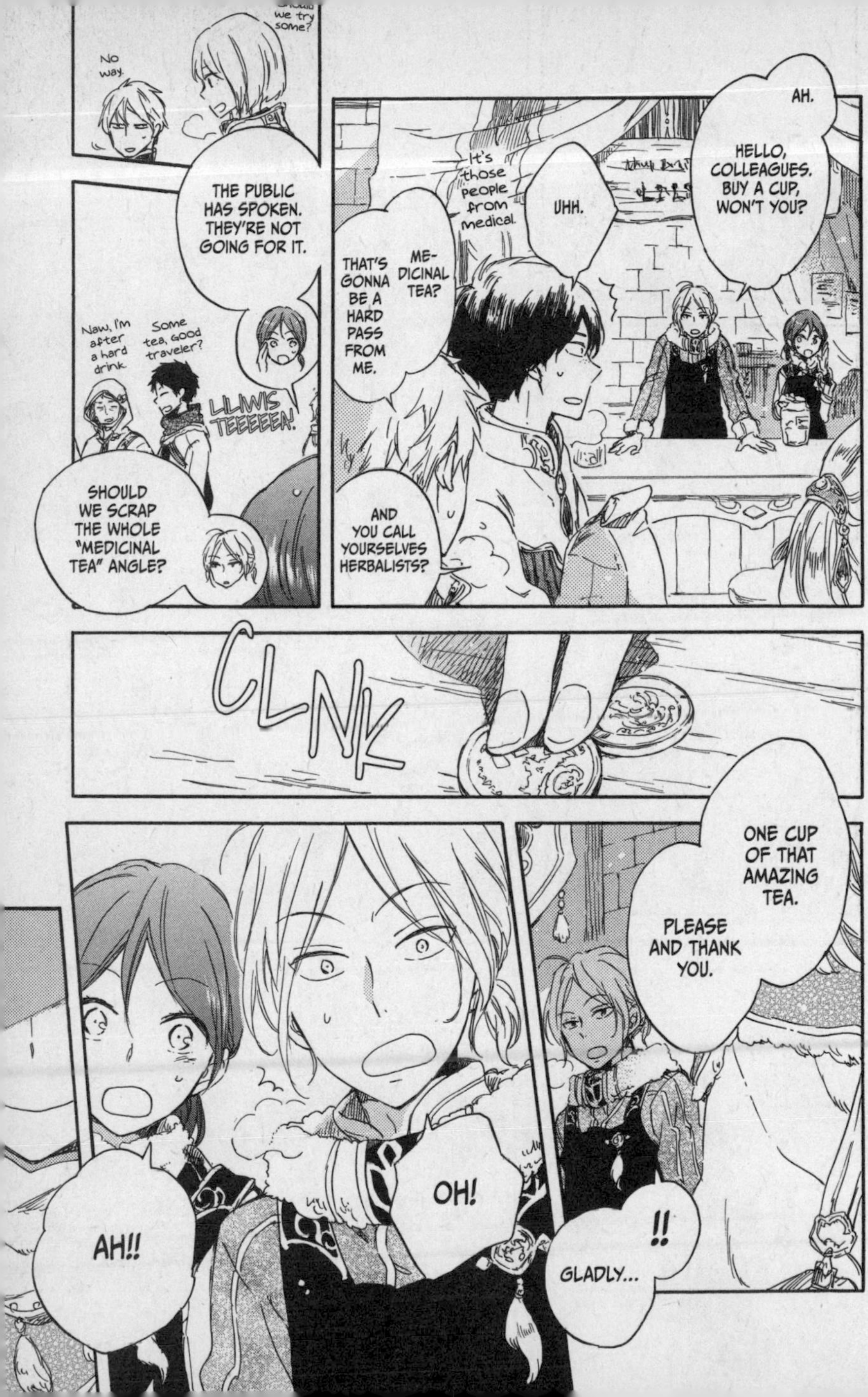
AH.
HELLO, COLLEAGUES. BUY A CUP, WON'T YOU?
UHH.
It's those people from medical.
ME-DICINAL TEA?
THAT'S GONNA BE A HARD PASS FROM ME.
AND YOU CALL YOURSELVES HERBALISTS?
Should we try some?
No way.
THE PUBLIC HAS SPOKEN. THEY'RE NOT GOING FOR IT.
LILIWIS TEEEEEA!
Some tea, good traveler?
Naw, I'm after a hard drink.
SHOULD WE SCRAP THE WHOLE "MEDICINAL TEA" ANGLE?
CLNK
ONE CUP OF THAT AMAZING TEA.
PLEASE AND THANK YOU.
!!
GLADLY...
OH!
AH!!

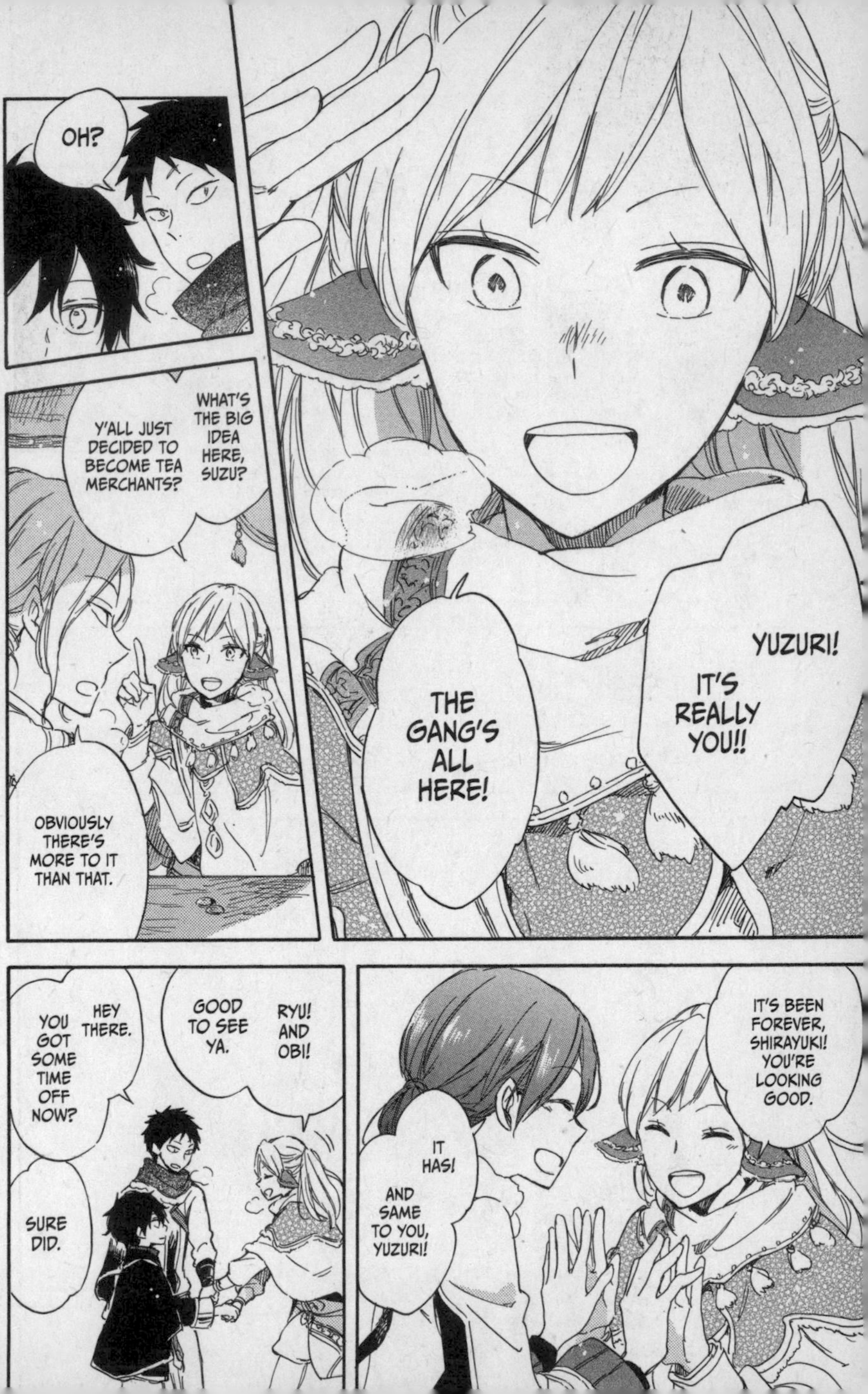
YUZURI! IT'S REALLY YOU!!
THE GANG'S ALL HERE!
OH?
WHAT'S THE BIG IDEA HERE, SUZU?
Y'ALL JUST DECIDED TO BECOME TEA MERCHANTS?
OBVIOUSLY THERE'S MORE TO IT THAN THAT.
IT'S BEEN FOREVER, SHIRAYUKI! YOU'RE LOOKING GOOD.
IT HAS!
AND SAME TO YOU, YUZURI!
RYU! AND OBI!
GOOD TO SEE YA.
HEY THERE.
YOU GOT SOME TIME OFF NOW?
SURE DID.

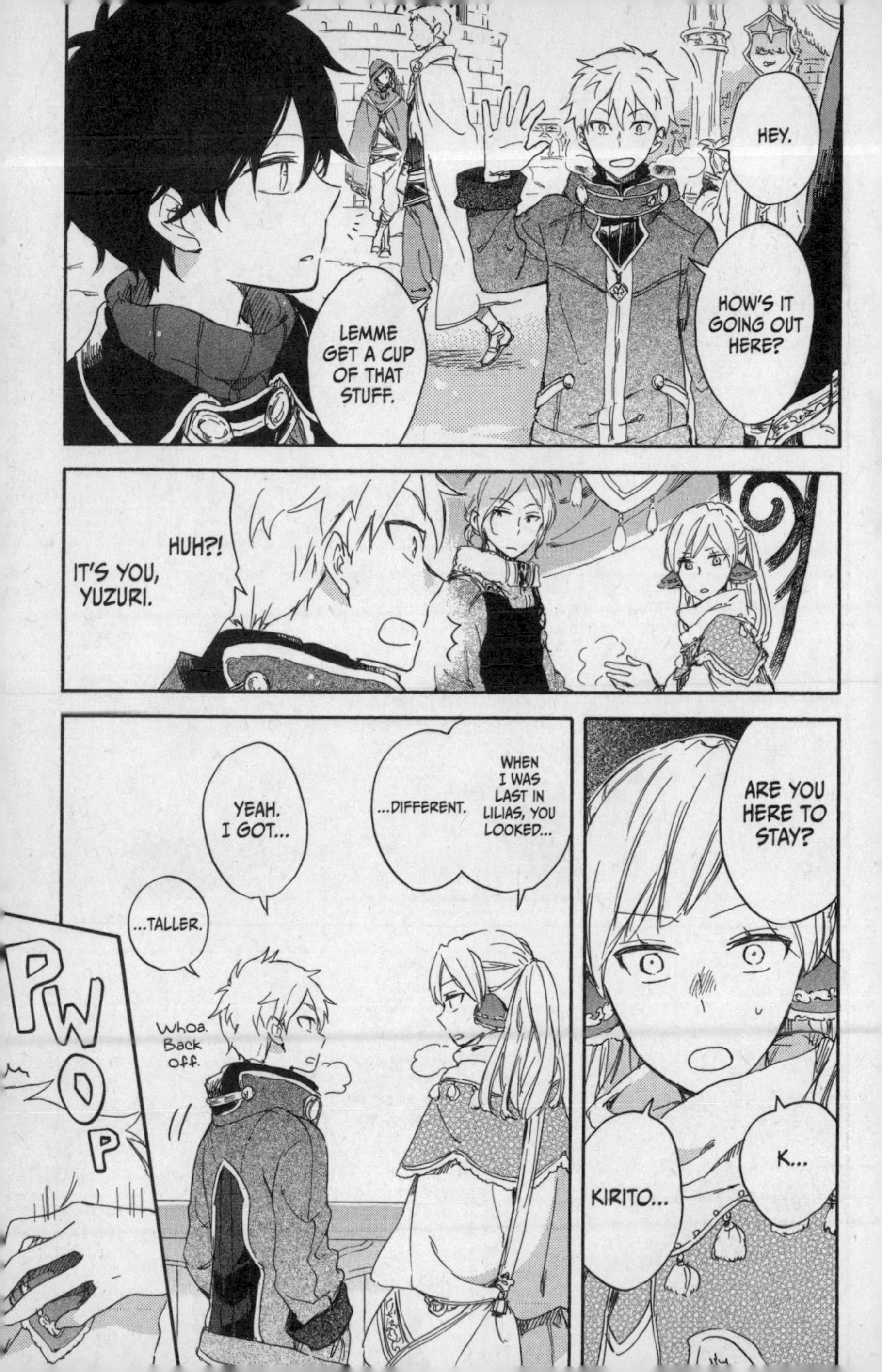
HEY.
HOW'S IT GOING OUT HERE?
LEMME GET A CUP OF THAT STUFF.
HUH?!
IT'S YOU, YUZURI.
ARE YOU HERE TO STAY?
K...
KIRITO...
WHEN I WAS LAST IN LILIAS, YOU LOOKED...
...DIFFERENT.
YEAH. I GOT...
...TALLER.
Whoa. Back off.
PWOP

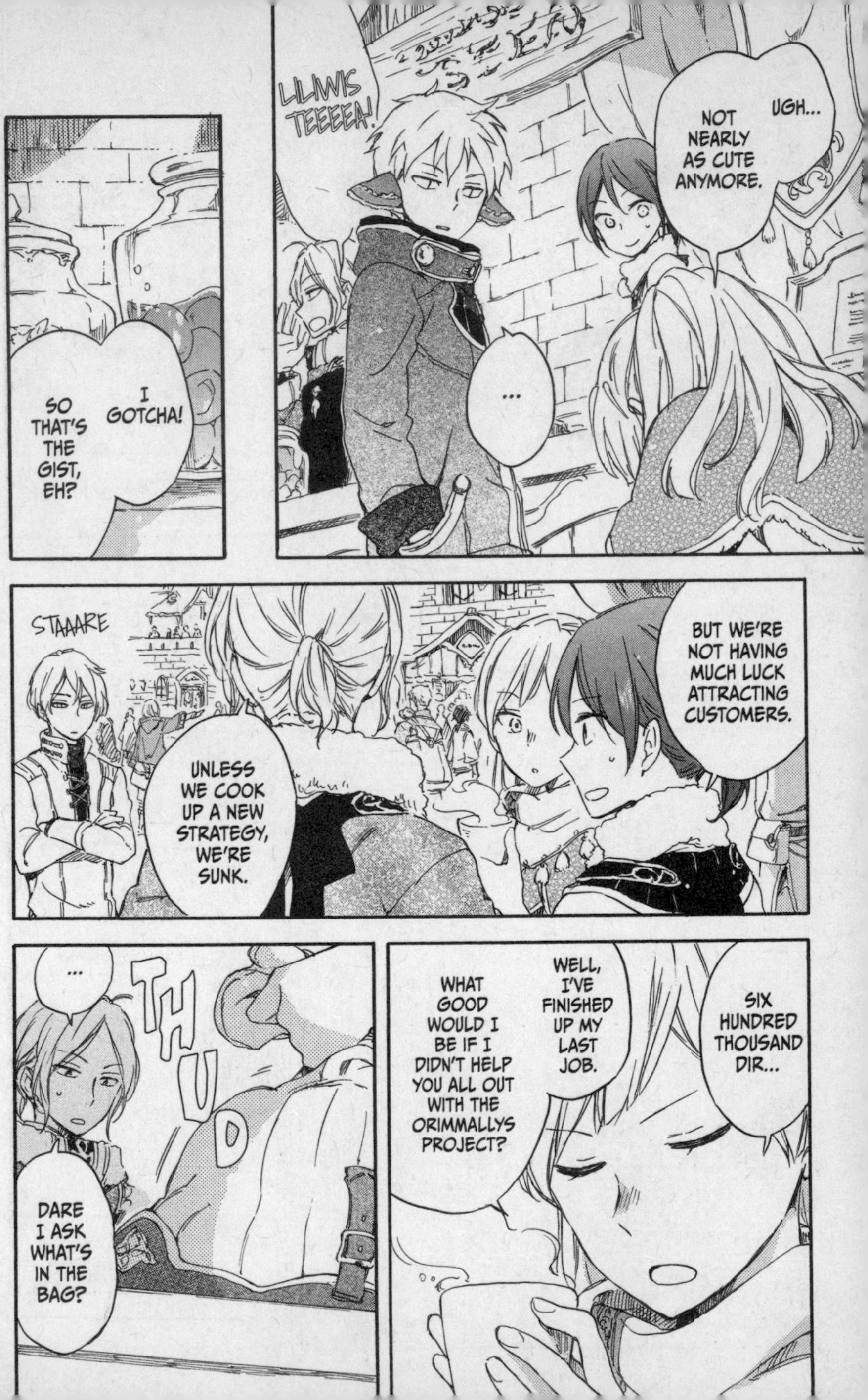
UGH... NOT NEARLY AS CUTE ANYMORE.
LILIWIS TEEEEA!
...
I GOTCHA!
SO THAT'S THE GIST, EH?
BUT WE'RE NOT HAVING MUCH LUCK ATTRACTING CUSTOMERS.
UNLESS WE COOK UP A NEW STRATEGY, WE'RE SUNK.
STAAARE
SIX HUNDRED THOUSAND DIR...
WELL, I'VE FINISHED UP MY LAST JOB.
WHAT GOOD WOULD I BE IF I DIDN'T HELP YOU ALL OUT WITH THE ORIMMALLYS PROJECT?
...
THUD
DARE I ASK WHAT'S IN THE BAG?

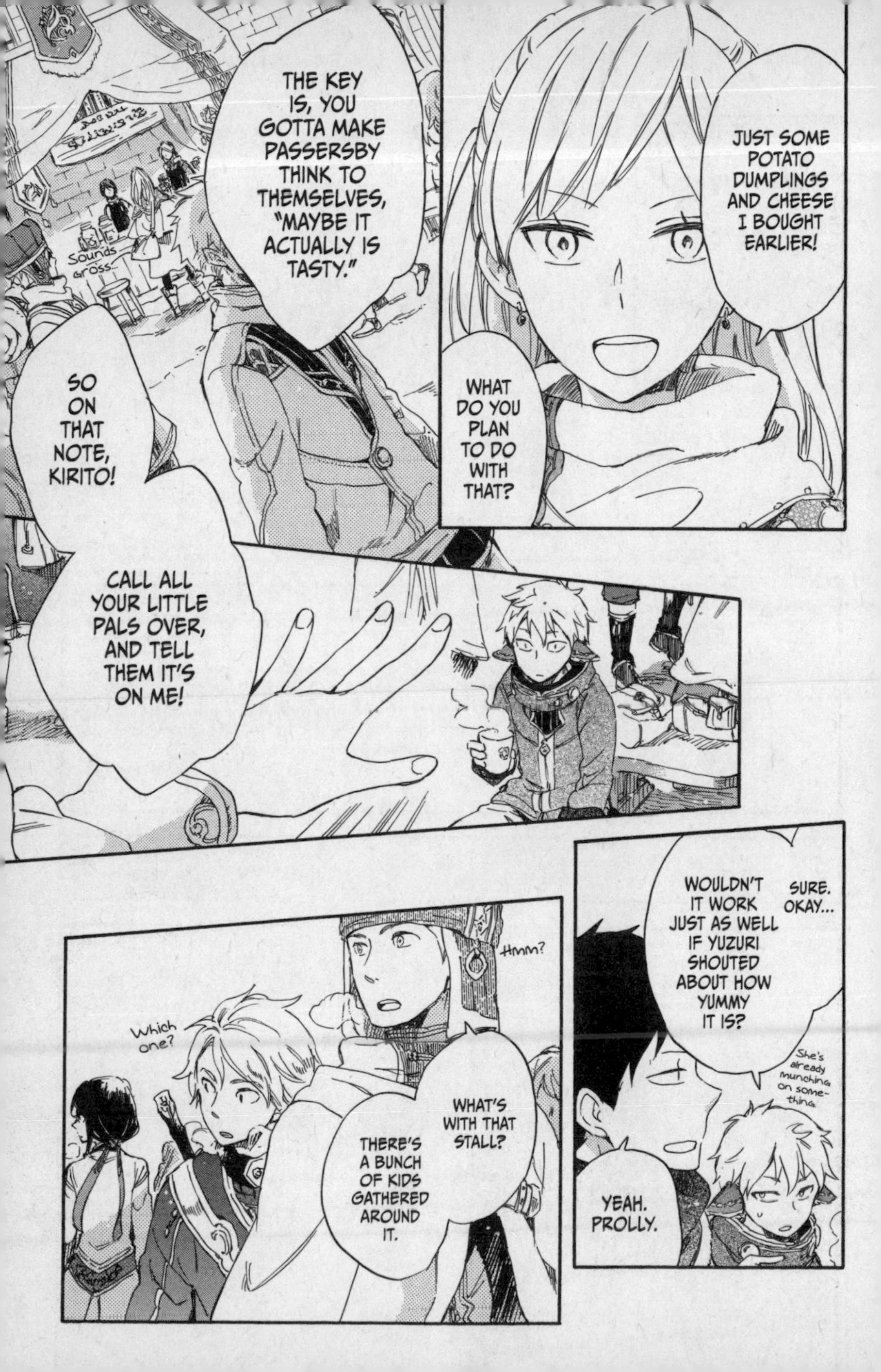
JUST SOME POTATO DUMPLINGS AND CHEESE I BOUGHT EARLIER!
WHAT DO YOU PLAN TO DO WITH THAT?
THE KEY IS, YOU GOTTA MAKE PASSERSBY THINK TO THEMSELVES, "MAYBE IT ACTUALLY IS TASTY."
Sounds gross...
SO ON THAT NOTE, KIRITO!
CALL ALL YOUR LITTLE PALS OVER, AND TELL THEM IT'S ON ME!
SURE. OKAY...
WOULDN'T IT WORK JUST AS WELL IF YUZURI SHOUTED ABOUT HOW YUMMY IT IS?
She's already munching on some-thing
YEAH. PROLLY.
Hmm?
WHAT'S WITH THAT STALL?
THERE'S A BUNCH OF KIDS GATHERED AROUND IT.
Which one?

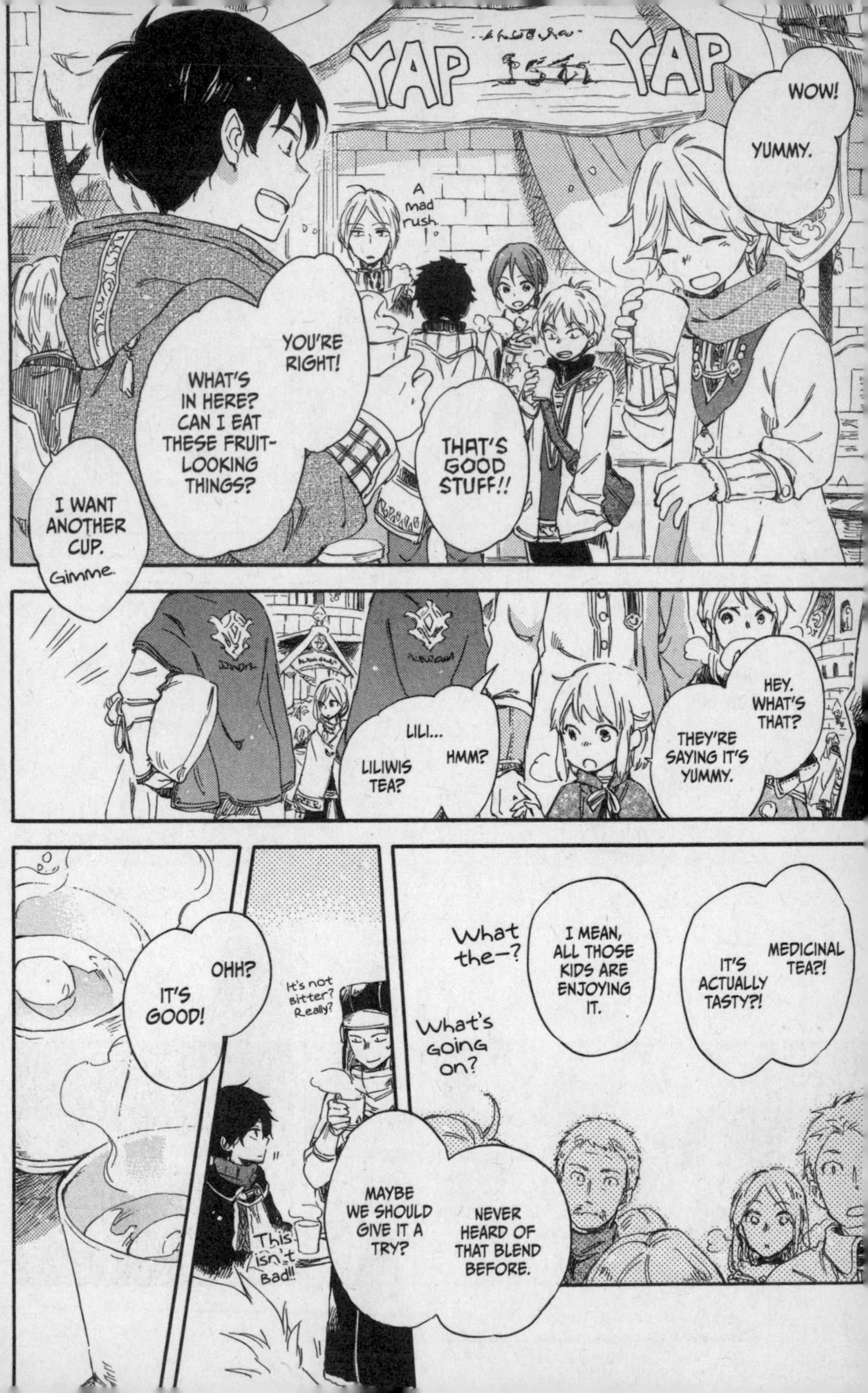
YAP YAP
WOW!
YUMMY.
A mad rush.
THAT'S GOOD STUFF!!
YOU'RE RIGHT!
WHAT'S IN HERE? CAN I EAT THESE FRUIT-LOOKING THINGS?
I WANT ANOTHER CUP.
Gimme.
HEY. WHAT'S THAT?
THEY'RE SAYING IT'S YUMMY.
LILI...
HMM?
LILIWIS TEA?
MEDICINAL TEA?!
IT'S ACTUALLY TASTY?!
I MEAN, ALL THOSE KIDS ARE ENJOYING IT.
What the–?
What's going on?
NEVER HEARD OF THAT BLEND BEFORE.
MAYBE WE SHOULD GIVE IT A TRY?
It's not bitter? Really?
This isn't bad!!
OHH?
IT'S GOOD!

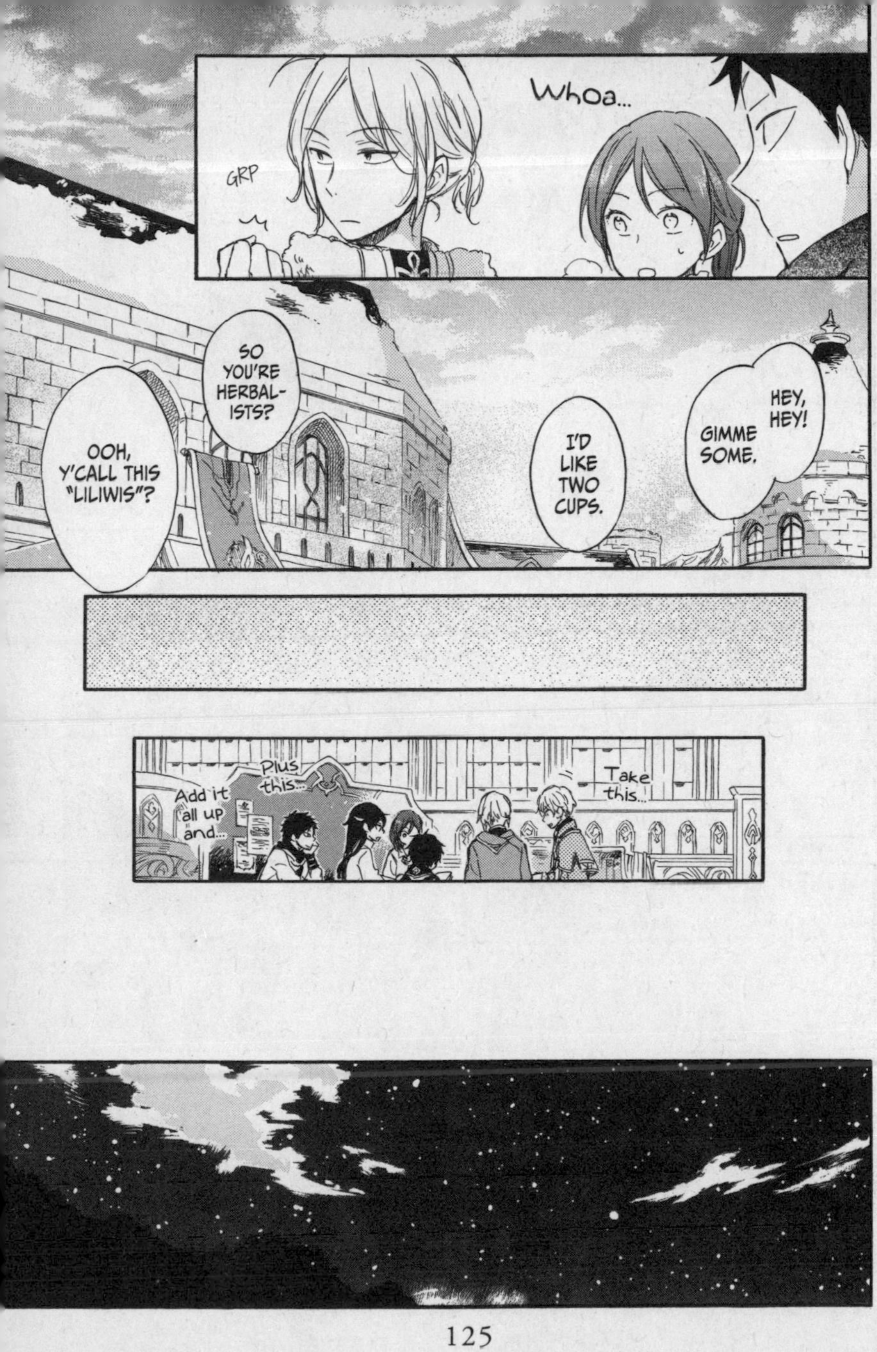
Whoa...
GRP
HEY, HEY! GIMME SOME.
I'D LIKE TWO CUPS.
SO YOU'RE HERBAL-ISTS?
OOH, Y'CALL THIS "LILIWIS"?
Take this...
Plus this...
Add it all up and...

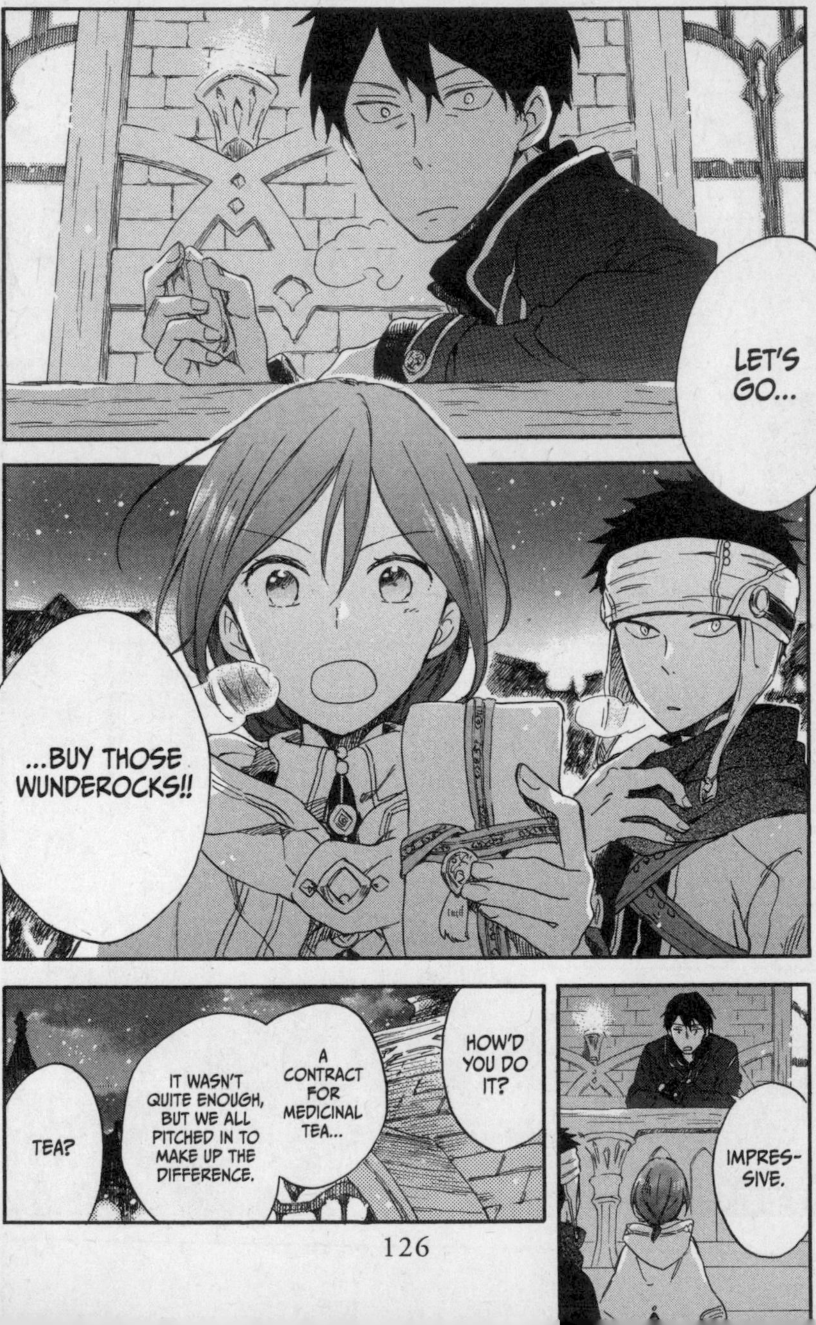
LET'S GO...
...BUY THOSE WUNDEROCKS!!
IMPRES-SIVE.
HOW'D YOU DO IT?
A CONTRACT FOR MEDICINAL TEA...
IT WASN'T QUITE ENOUGH, BUT WE ALL PITCHED IN TO MAKE UP THE DIFFERENCE.
TEA?

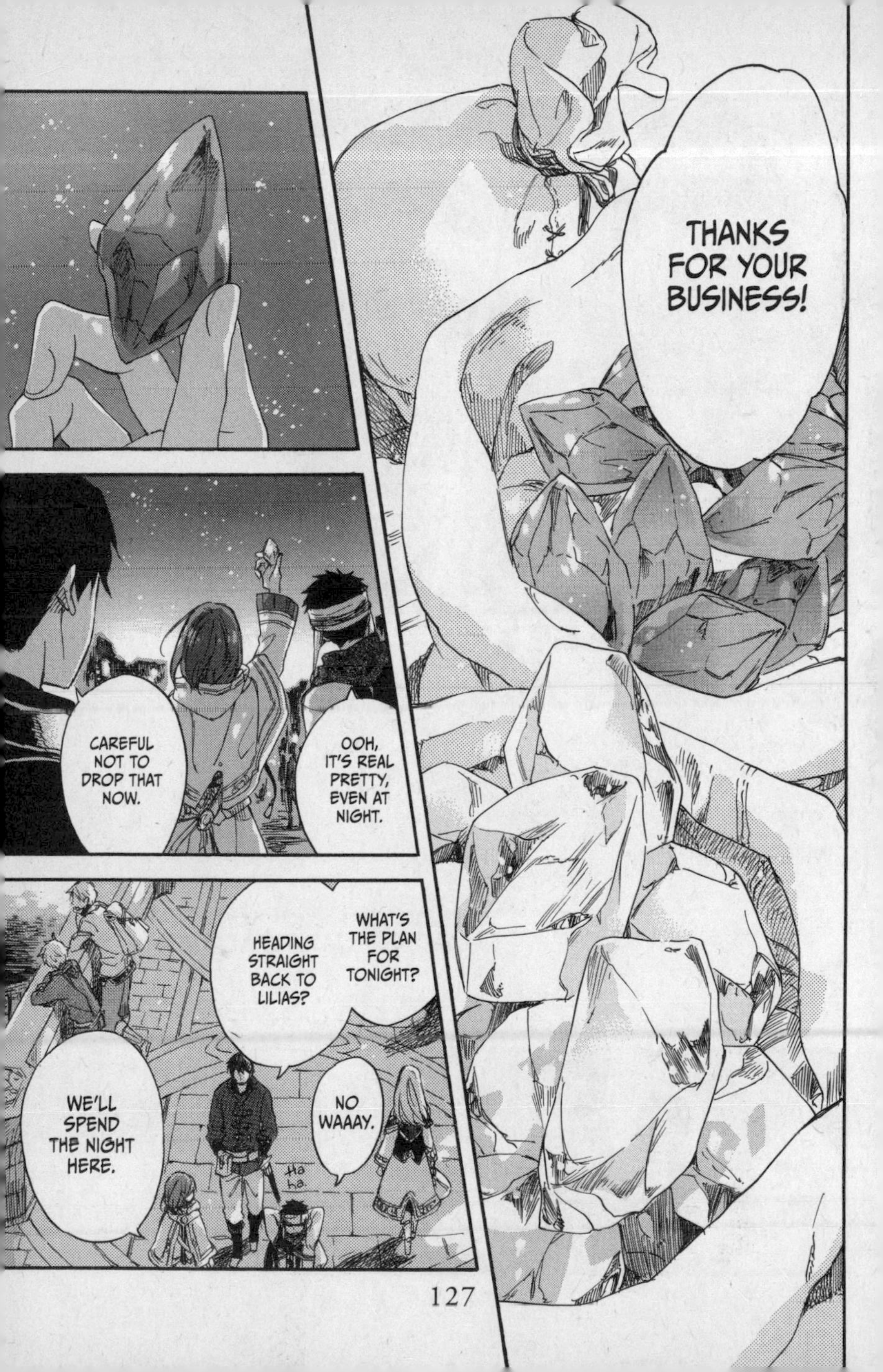
THANKS FOR YOUR BUSINESS!
OOH, IT'S REAL PRETTY, EVEN AT NIGHT.
CAREFUL NOT TO DROP THAT NOW.
WHAT'S THE PLAN FOR TONIGHT?
HEADING STRAIGHT BACK TO LILIAS?
NO WAAAY.
Ha ha.
WE'LL SPEND THE NIGHT HERE.

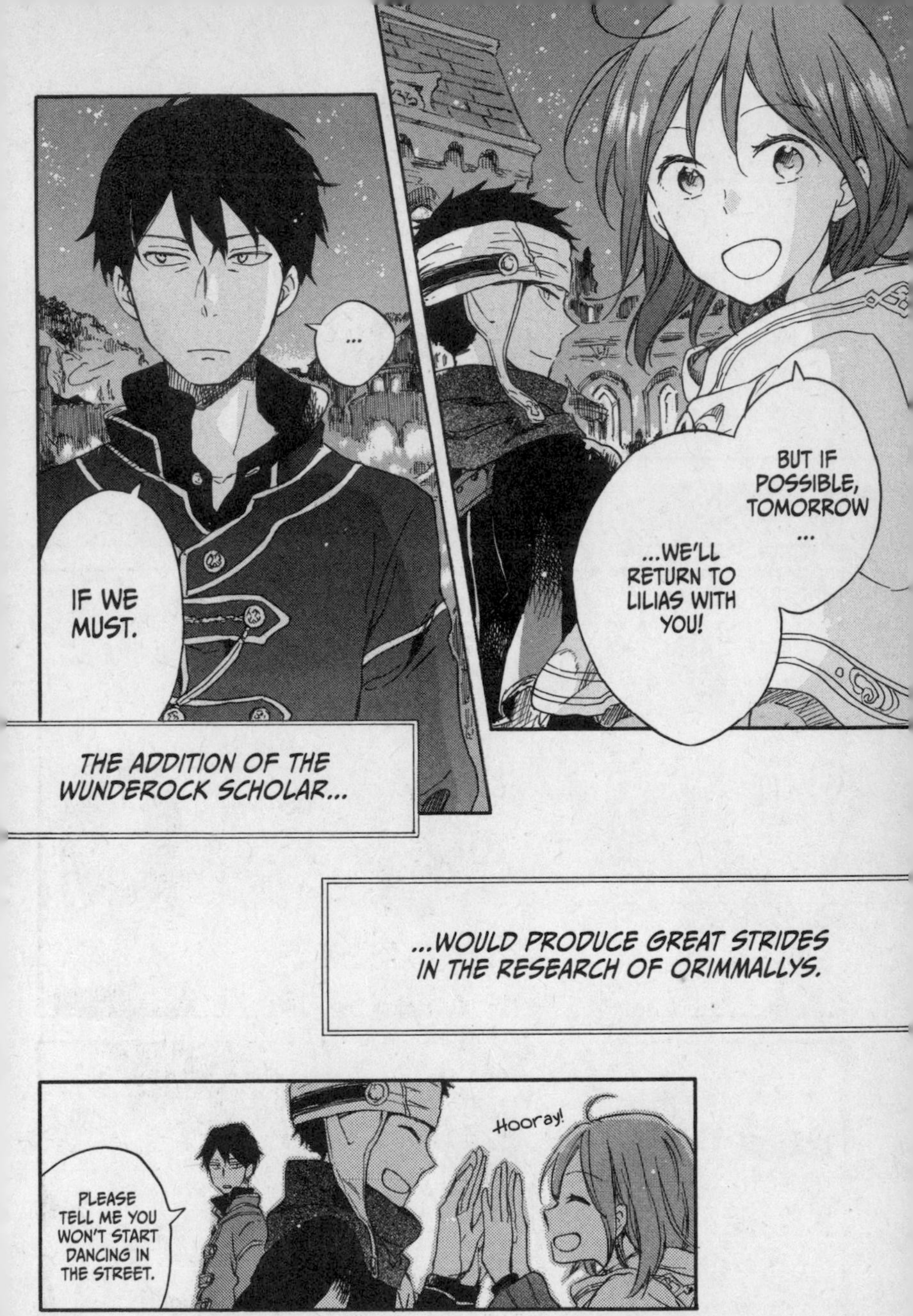

BUT IF POSSIBLE, TOMORROW ...
...WE'LL RETURN TO LILIAS WITH YOU!
...
IF WE MUST.
THE ADDITION OF THE WUNDEROCK SCHOLAR...
...WOULD PRODUCE GREAT STRIDES IN THE RESEARCH OF ORIMMALLYS.
Hooray!
PLEASE TELL ME YOU WON'T START DANCING IN THE STREET.

Chapter 70

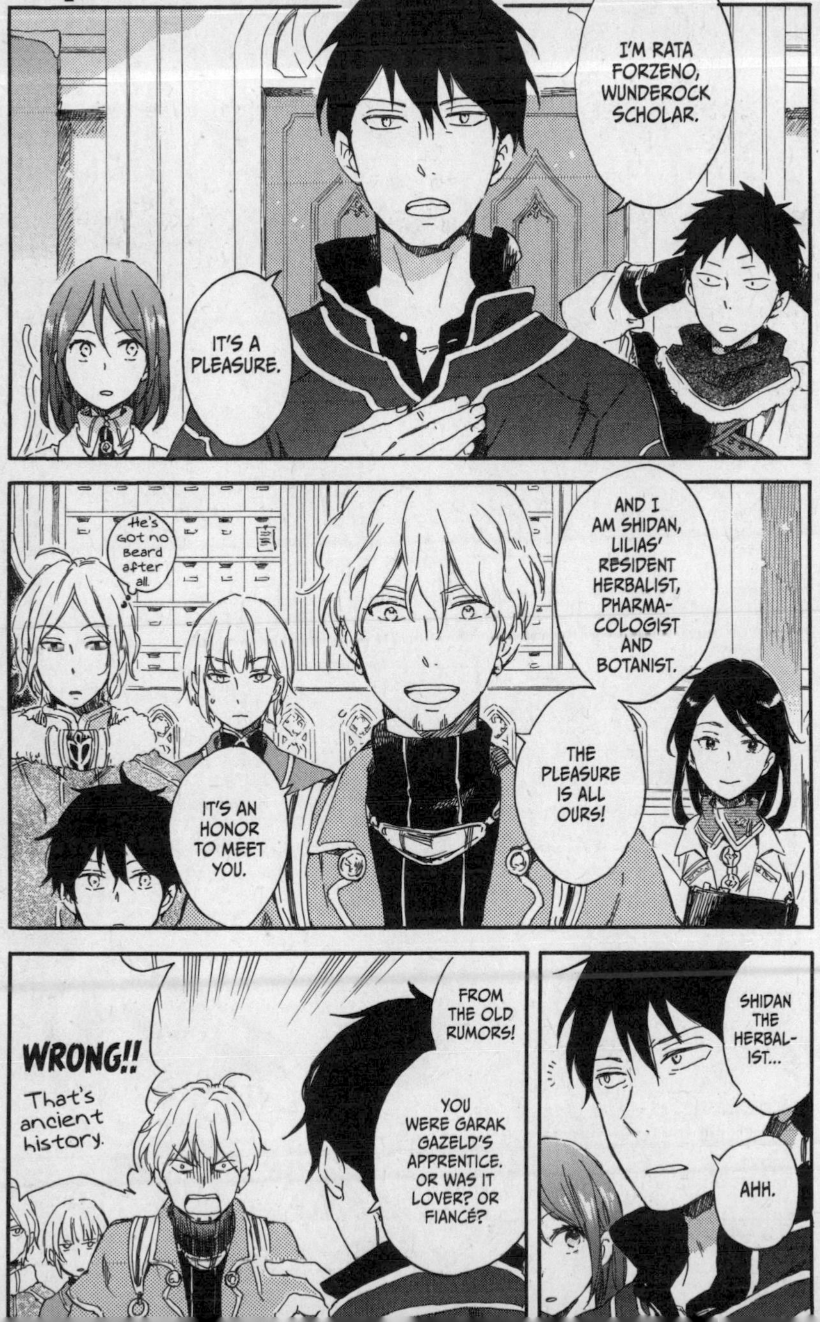

I'M RATA FORZENO, WUNDEROCK SCHOLAR.
IT'S A PLEASURE.
AND I AM SHIDAN, LILIAS' RESIDENT HERBALIST, PHARMACOLOGIST AND BOTANIST.
THE PLEASURE IS ALL OURS!
IT'S AN HONOR TO MEET YOU.
He's got no beard after all.
SHIDAN THE HERBALIST...
AHH.
FROM THE OLD RUMORS!
YOU WERE GARAK GAZELD'S APPRENTICE. OR WAS IT LOVER? OR FIANCÉ?
WRONG!!
That's ancient history.

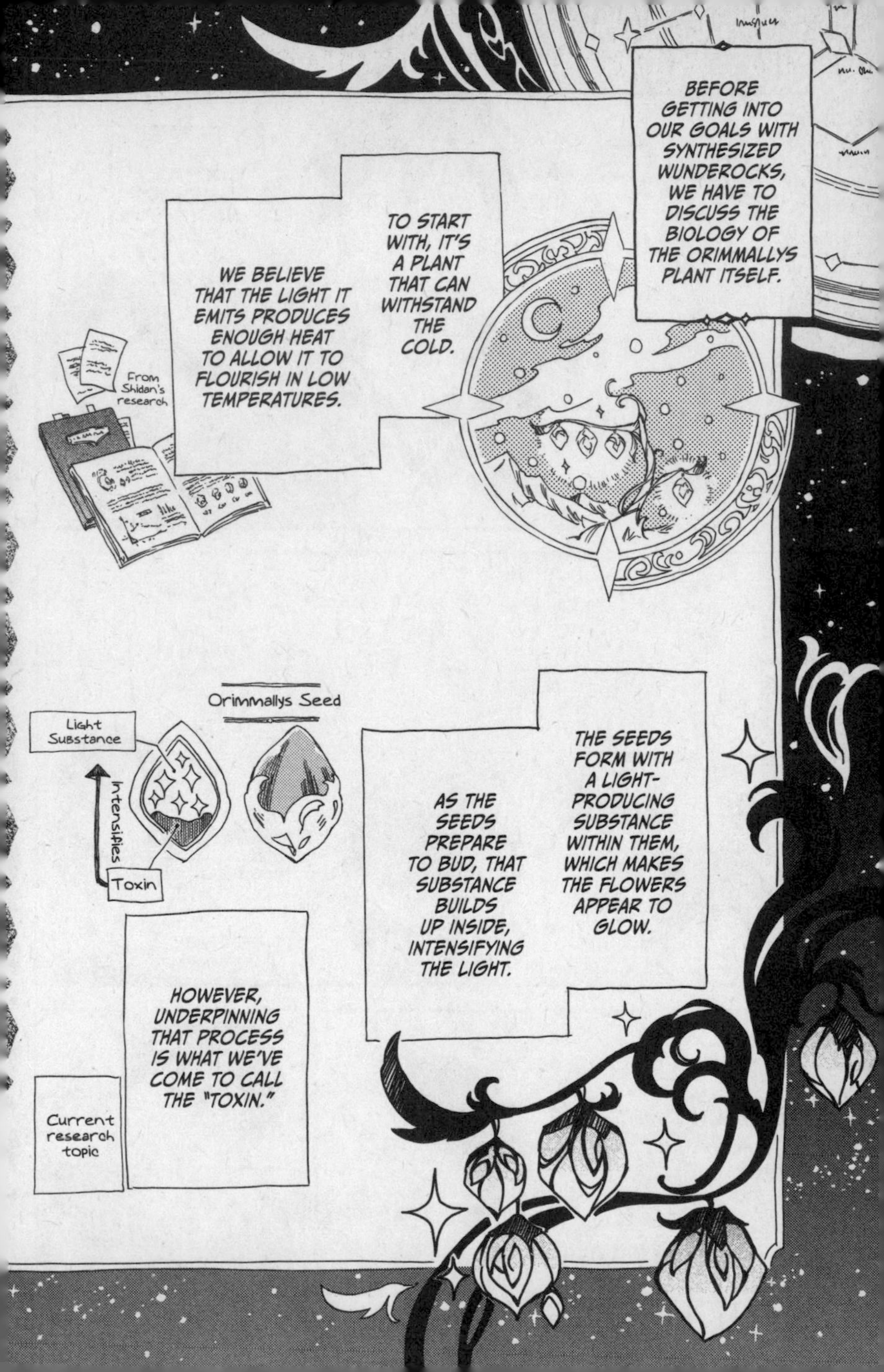
BEFORE GETTING INTO OUR GOALS WITH SYNTHESIZED WUNDEROCKS, WE HAVE TO DISCUSS THE BIOLOGY OF THE ORIMMALLYS PLANT ITSELF.
TO START WITH, IT'S A PLANT THAT CAN WITHSTAND THE COLD.
WE BELIEVE THAT THE LIGHT IT EMITS PRODUCES ENOUGH HEAT TO ALLOW IT TO FLOURISH IN LOW TEMPERATURES.
From Shidan's research
THE SEEDS FORM WITH A LIGHT-PRODUCING SUBSTANCE WITHIN THEM, WHICH MAKES THE FLOWERS APPEAR TO GLOW.
AS THE SEEDS PREPARE TO BUD, THAT SUBSTANCE BUILDS UP INSIDE, INTENSIFYING THE LIGHT.
Orimmallys Seed
Light Substance
Intensifies
Toxin
HOWEVER, UNDERPINNING THAT PROCESS IS WHAT WE'VE COME TO CALL THE "TOXIN."
Current research topic

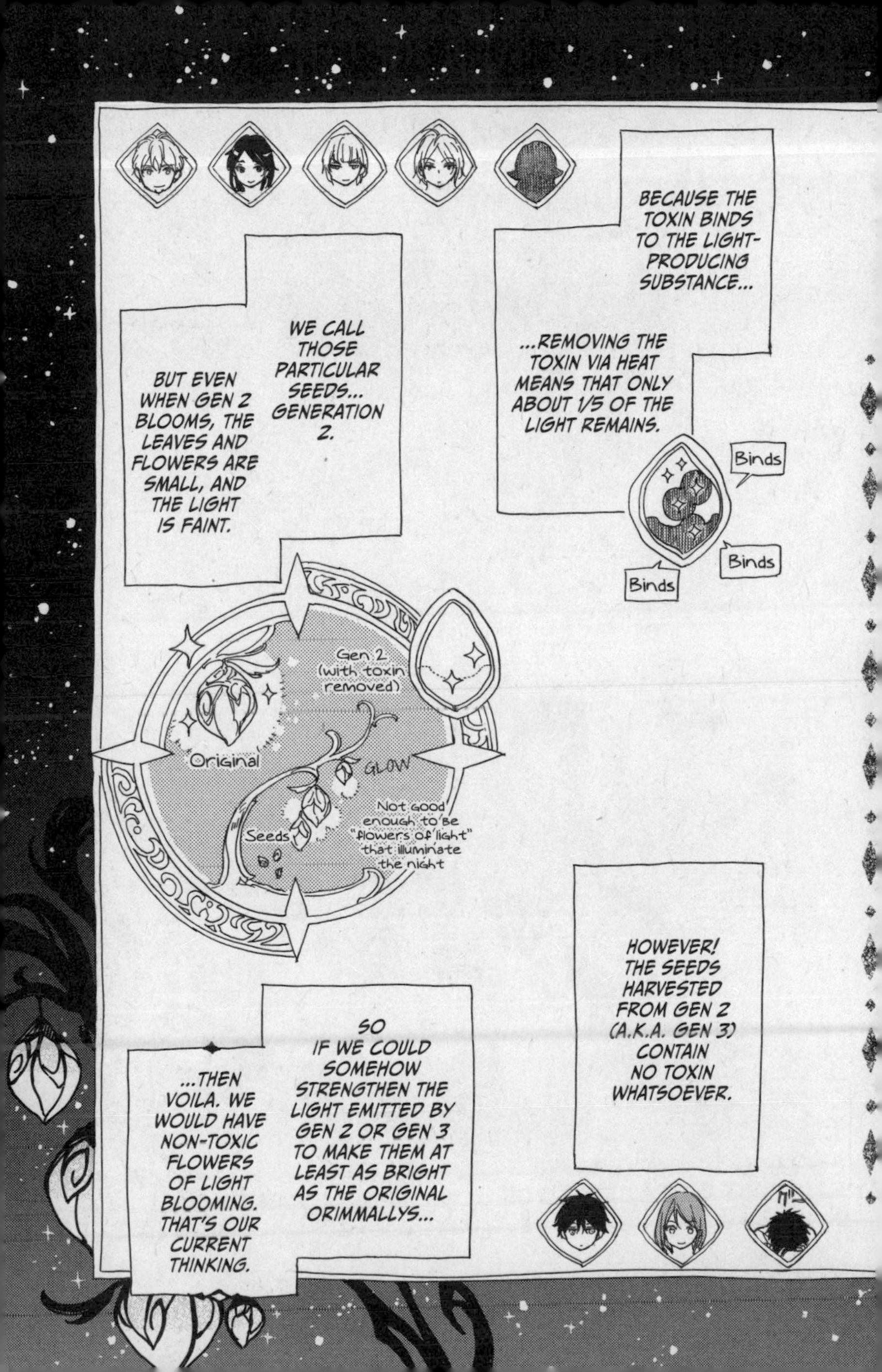

BECAUSE THE TOXIN BINDS TO THE LIGHT-PRODUCING SUBSTANCE...

...REMOVING THE TOXIN VIA HEAT MEANS THAT ONLY ABOUT 1/5 OF THE LIGHT REMAINS.

Binds

Binds

Binds

WE CALL THOSE PARTICULAR SEEDS... GENERATION 2.

BUT EVEN WHEN GEN 2 BLOOMS, THE LEAVES AND FLOWERS ARE SMALL, AND THE LIGHT IS FAINT.

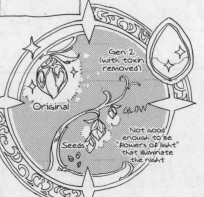

Gen 2 (with toxin removed)

"Original"

GLOW

Seeds

Not good enough to be "flowers of light" that illuminate the night

HOWEVER! THE SEEDS HARVESTED FROM GEN 2 (A.K.A. GEN 3) CONTAIN NO TOXIN WHATSOEVER.

SO IF WE COULD SOMEHOW STRENGTHEN THE LIGHT EMITTED BY GEN 2 OR GEN 3 TO MAKE THEM AT LEAST AS BRIGHT AS THE ORIGINAL ORIMMALLYS...

...THEN VOILA. WE WOULD HAVE NON-TOXIC FLOWERS OF LIGHT BLOOMING. THAT'S OUR CURRENT THINKING.

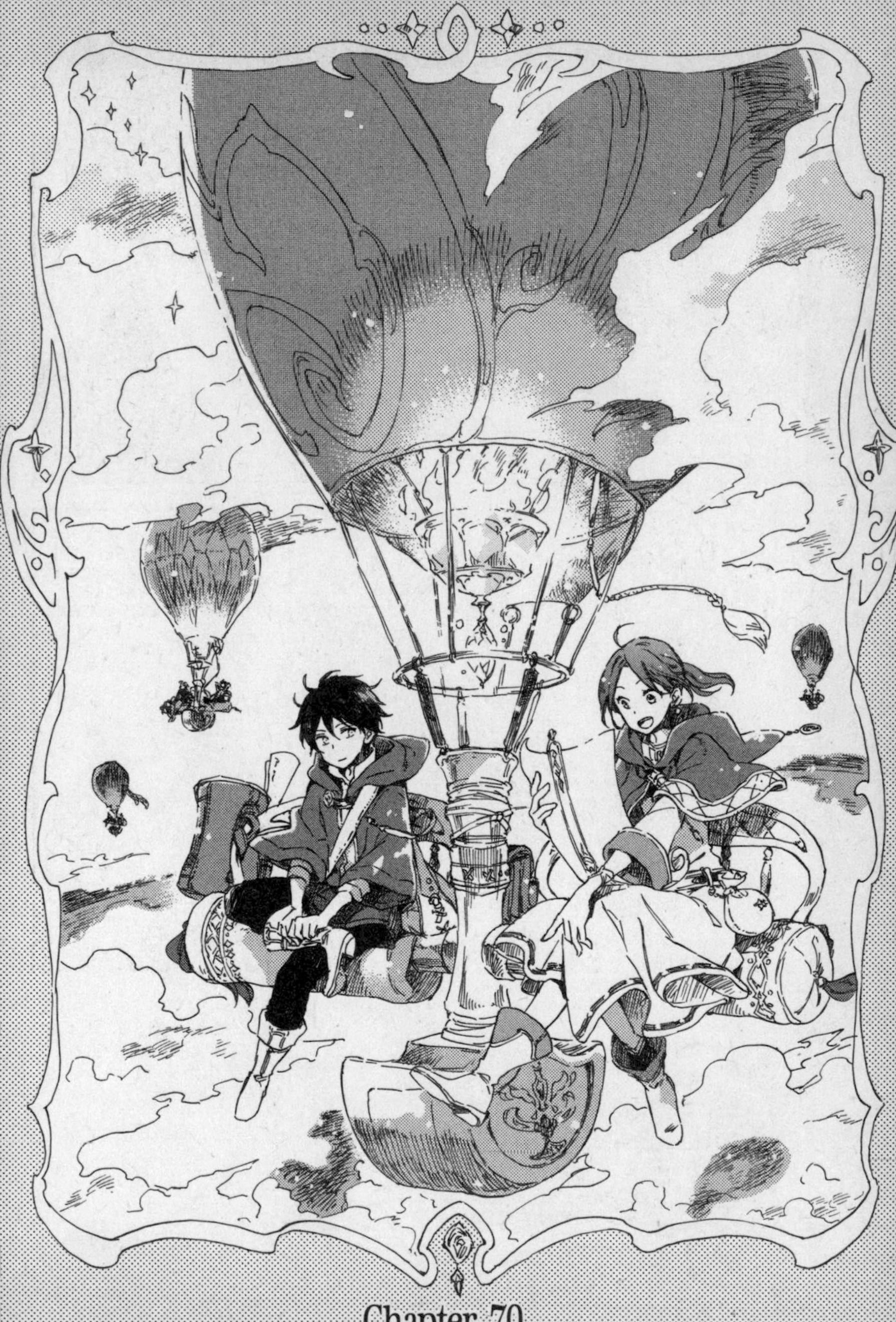

Chapter 70

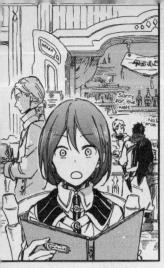

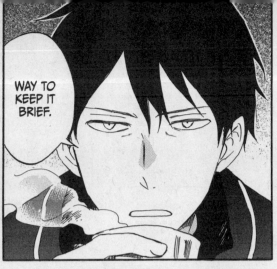

WAY TO KEEP IT BRIEF.
Sorry for the wait
No prob.
B-BUT I THOUGHT YOU'D WANT A MORE DETAILED EXPLANATION THAN THE NIGHT OF THE SOIREE...
I GOT THE GIST FROM THAT FIRST TALK WE HAD.
There's still more, actually...
No. Please, no.
WE KNOW THAT ORIMMALLYS SEEDS PRODUCE A STRONGER LIGHT WHEN EXPOSED TO A SET AMOUNT OF HEAT, SO...
...YOU'RE HOPING TO DO THAT WITH SYNTHESIZED HEAT WUNDEROCKS?
YES!
EXACTLY!

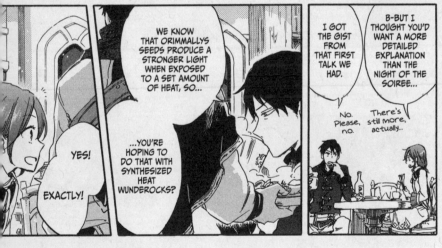

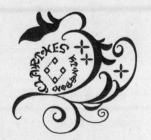

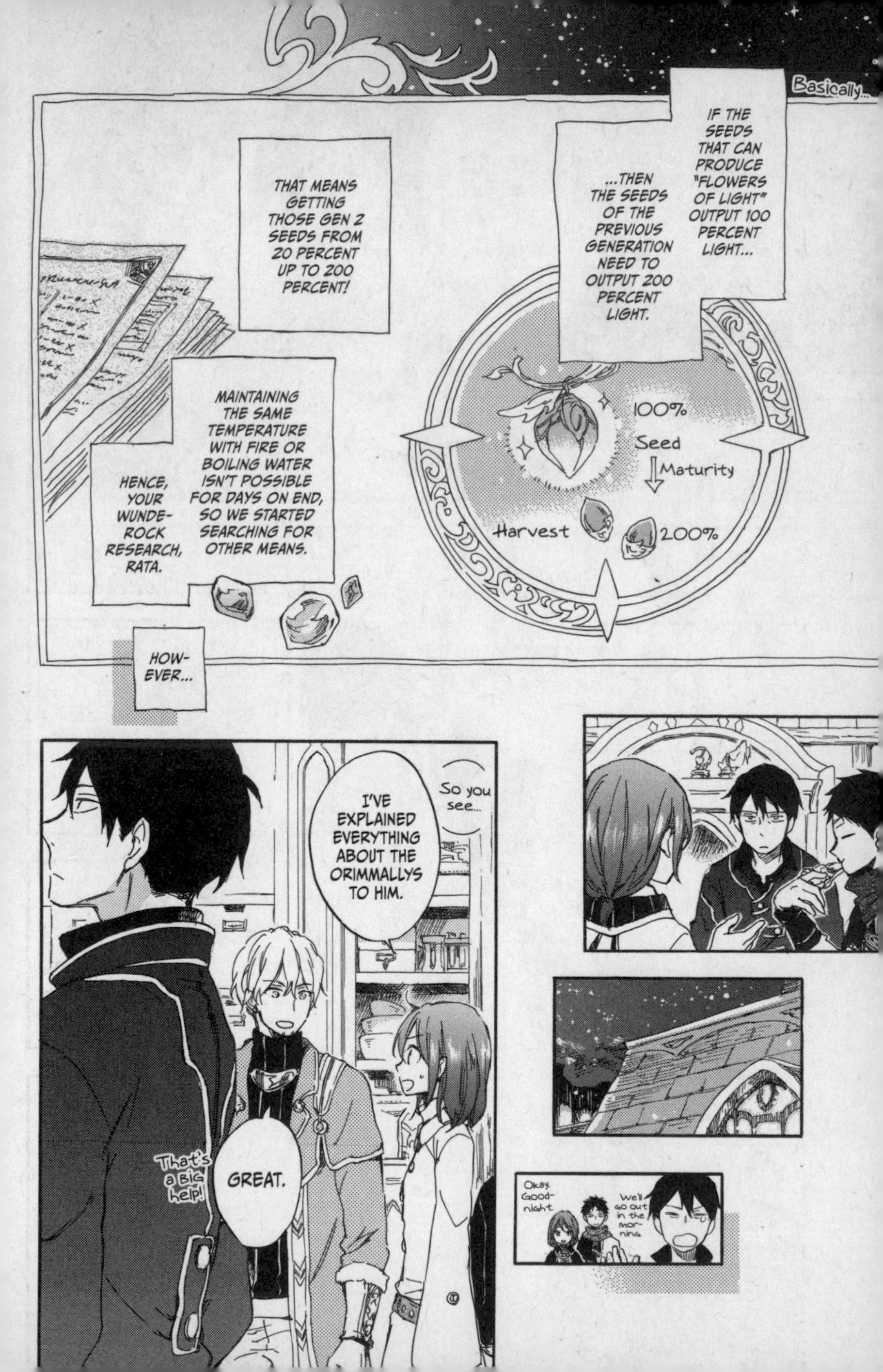
Basically...
IF THE SEEDS THAT CAN PRODUCE "FLOWERS OF LIGHT" OUTPUT 100 PERCENT LIGHT...
...THEN THE SEEDS OF THE PREVIOUS GENERATION NEED TO OUTPUT 200 PERCENT LIGHT.
THAT MEANS GETTING THOSE GEN 2 SEEDS FROM 20 PERCENT UP TO 200 PERCENT!
100%
Seed
Maturity
200%
Harvest
MAINTAINING THE SAME TEMPERATURE WITH FIRE OR BOILING WATER ISN'T POSSIBLE FOR DAYS ON END, SO WE STARTED SEARCHING FOR OTHER MEANS.
HENCE, YOUR WUNDEROCK RESEARCH, RATA.
HOW-EVER...
We'll go out in the morning.
Okay. Good-night.
So you see...
I'VE EXPLAINED EVERYTHING ABOUT THE ORIMMALLYS TO HIM.
GREAT.
That's a big help!

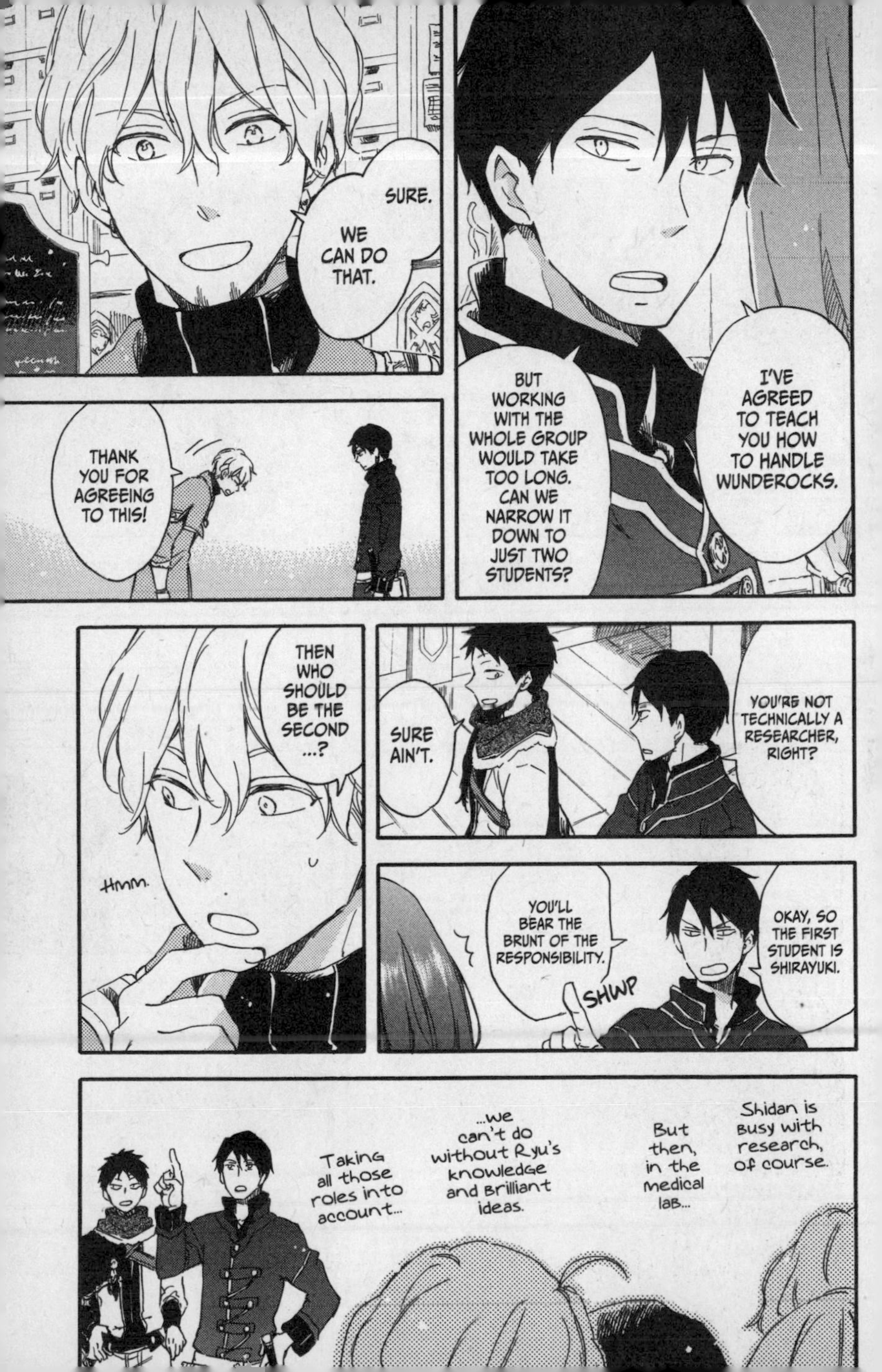
I'VE AGREED TO TEACH YOU HOW TO HANDLE WUNDEROCKS.
BUT WORKING WITH THE WHOLE GROUP WOULD TAKE TOO LONG. CAN WE NARROW IT DOWN TO JUST TWO STUDENTS?
SURE.
WE CAN DO THAT.
THANK YOU FOR AGREEING TO THIS!
YOU'RE NOT TECHNICALLY A RESEARCHER, RIGHT?
SURE AIN'T.
OKAY, SO THE FIRST STUDENT IS SHIRAYUKI.
YOU'LL BEAR THE BRUNT OF THE RESPONSIBILITY.
SHWP
THEN WHO SHOULD BE THE SECOND ...?
Hmm.
Shidan is busy with research, of course.
But then, in the medical lab...
...we can't do without Ryu's knowledge and brilliant ideas.
Taking all those roles into account...

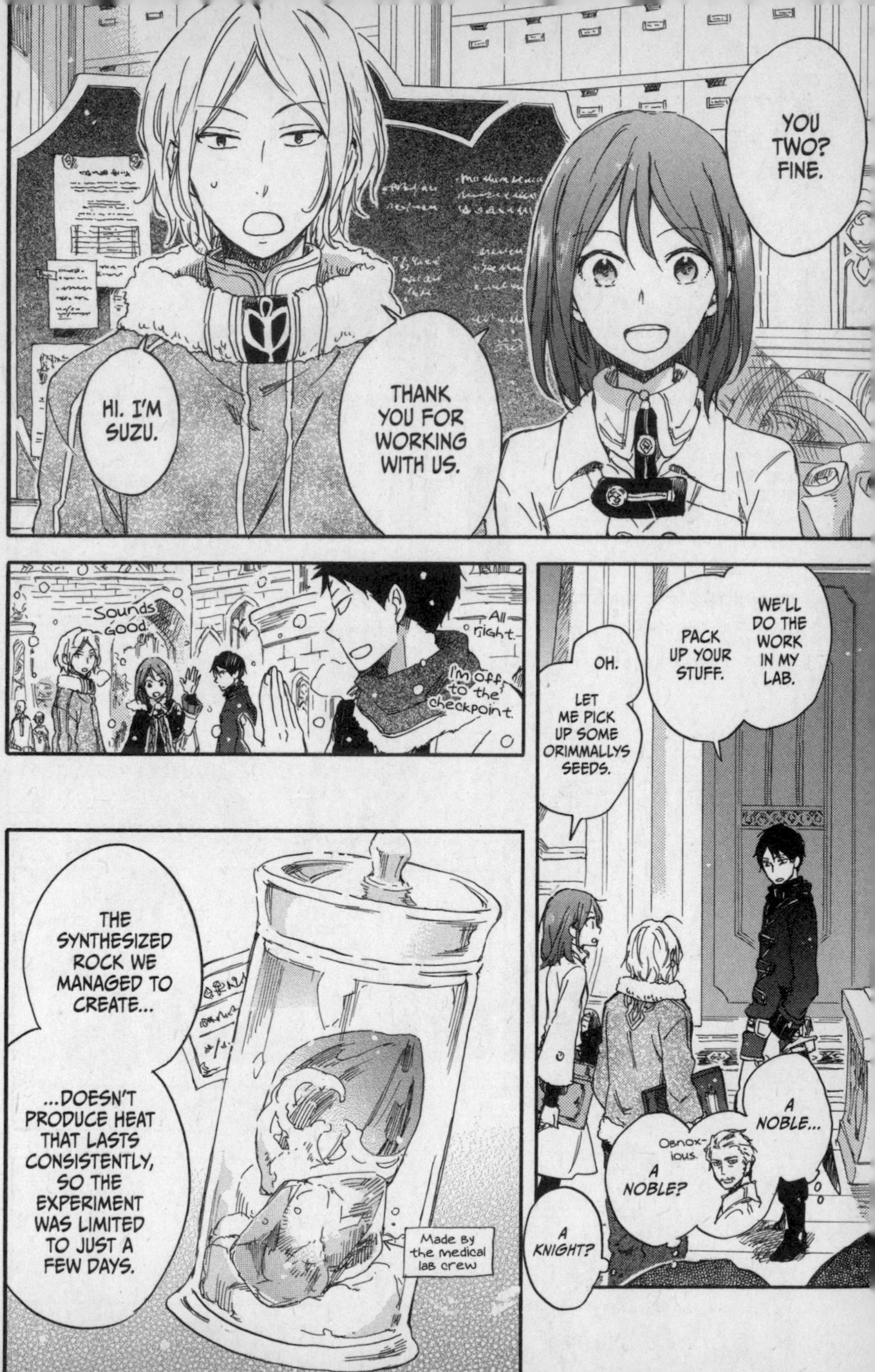
YOU TWO? FINE.
THANK YOU FOR WORKING WITH US.
HI. I'M SUZU.
WE'LL DO THE WORK IN MY LAB.
PACK UP YOUR STUFF.
OH.
LET ME PICK UP SOME ORIMMALLYS SEEDS.
A NOBLE...
Obnox-ious.
A NOBLE?
A KNIGHT?
All right.
I'm off to the checkpoint.
Sounds good.
THE SYNTHESIZED ROCK WE MANAGED TO CREATE...
...DOESN'T PRODUCE HEAT THAT LASTS CONSISTENTLY, SO THE EXPERIMENT WAS LIMITED TO JUST A FEW DAYS.
Made by the medical lab crew

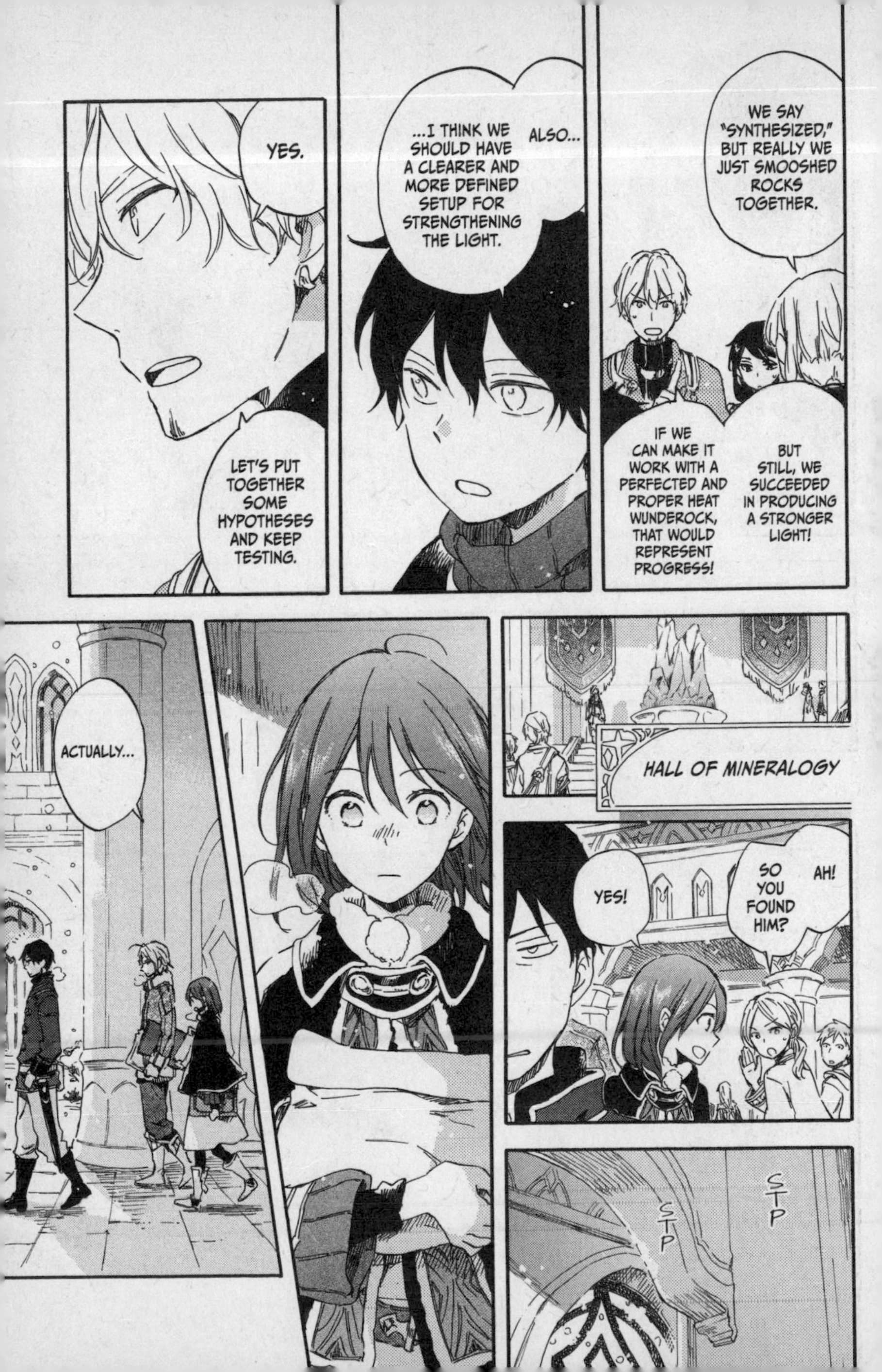
WE SAY "SYNTHESIZED," BUT REALLY WE JUST SMOOSHED ROCKS TOGETHER.
BUT STILL, WE SUCCEEDED IN PRODUCING A STRONGER LIGHT!
IF WE CAN MAKE IT WORK WITH A PERFECTED AND PROPER HEAT WUNDEROCK, THAT WOULD REPRESENT PROGRESS!
ALSO...
...I THINK WE SHOULD HAVE A CLEARER AND MORE DEFINED SETUP FOR STRENGTHENING THE LIGHT.
YES.
LET'S PUT TOGETHER SOME HYPOTHESES AND KEEP TESTING.
HALL OF MINERALOGY
AH!
SO YOU FOUND HIM?
YES!
STP
STP
ACTUALLY...

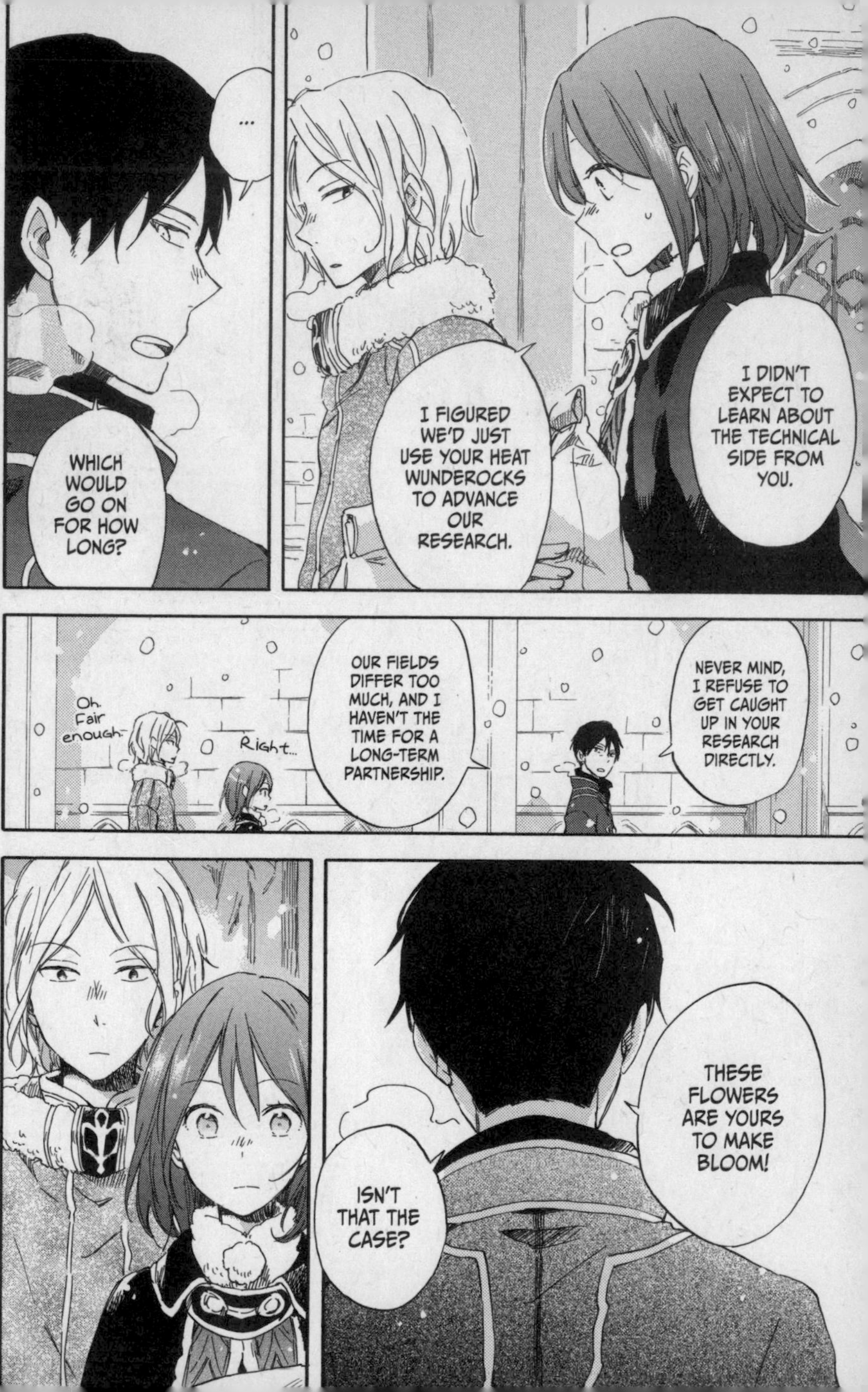
I DIDN'T EXPECT TO LEARN ABOUT THE TECHNICAL SIDE FROM YOU.
I FIGURED WE'D JUST USE YOUR HEAT WUNDEROCKS TO ADVANCE OUR RESEARCH.
...
WHICH WOULD GO ON FOR HOW LONG?
NEVER MIND, I REFUSE TO GET CAUGHT UP IN YOUR RESEARCH DIRECTLY.
OUR FIELDS DIFFER TOO MUCH, AND I HAVEN'T THE TIME FOR A LONG-TERM PARTNERSHIP.
Right...
Oh. Fair enough.
THESE FLOWERS ARE YOURS TO MAKE BLOOM!
ISN'T THAT THE CASE?

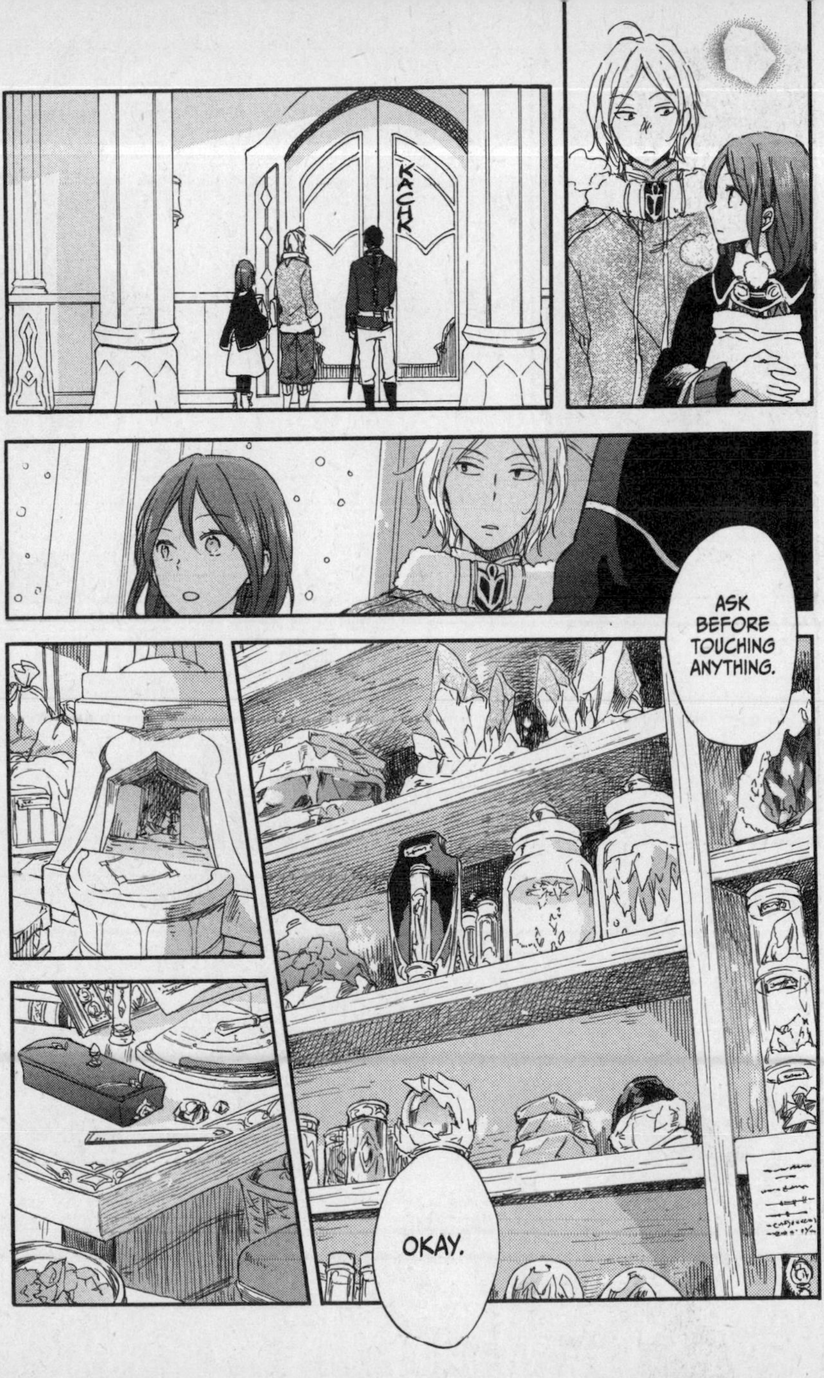
KACHK
ASK BEFORE TOUCHING ANYTHING.
OKAY.

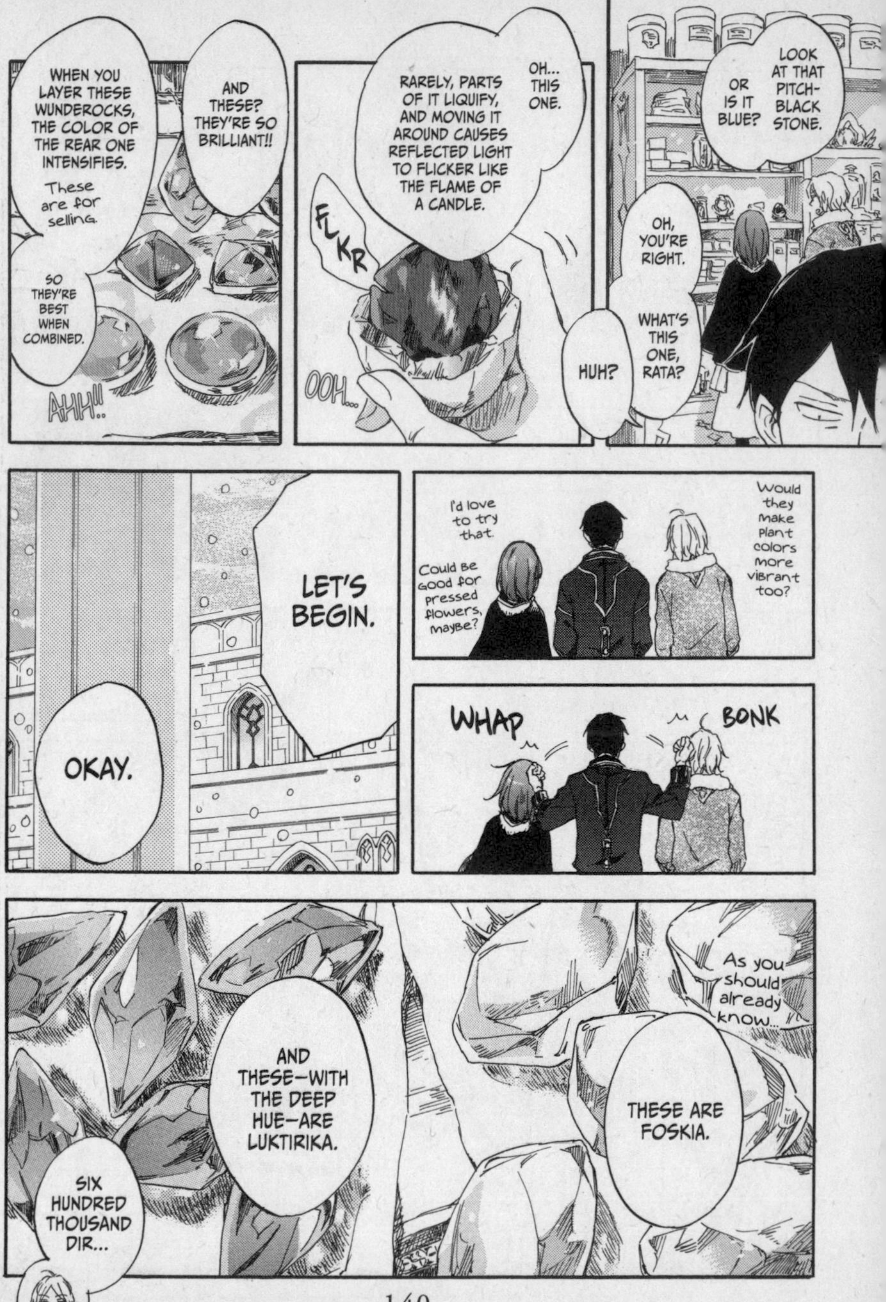
LOOK AT THAT PITCH-BLACK STONE.
OR IS IT BLUE?
OH, YOU'RE RIGHT.
WHAT'S THIS ONE, RATA?
HUH?
OH... THIS ONE.
RARELY, PARTS OF IT LIQUIFY, AND MOVING IT AROUND CAUSES REFLECTED LIGHT TO FLICKER LIKE THE FLAME OF A CANDLE.
FLKR
OOH...
AND THESE? THEY'RE SO BRILLIANT!!
WHEN YOU LAYER THESE WUNDEROCKS, THE COLOR OF THE REAR ONE INTENSIFIES.
These are for selling.
SO THEY'RE BEST WHEN COMBINED.
AHH!!
Would they make plant colors more vibrant too?
I'd love to try that.
Could be good for pressed flowers, maybe?
BONK
WHAP
LET'S BEGIN.
OKAY.
As you should already know...
THESE ARE FOSKIA.
AND THESE—WITH THE DEEP HUE—ARE LUKTIRIKA.
SIX HUNDRED THOUSAND DIR...

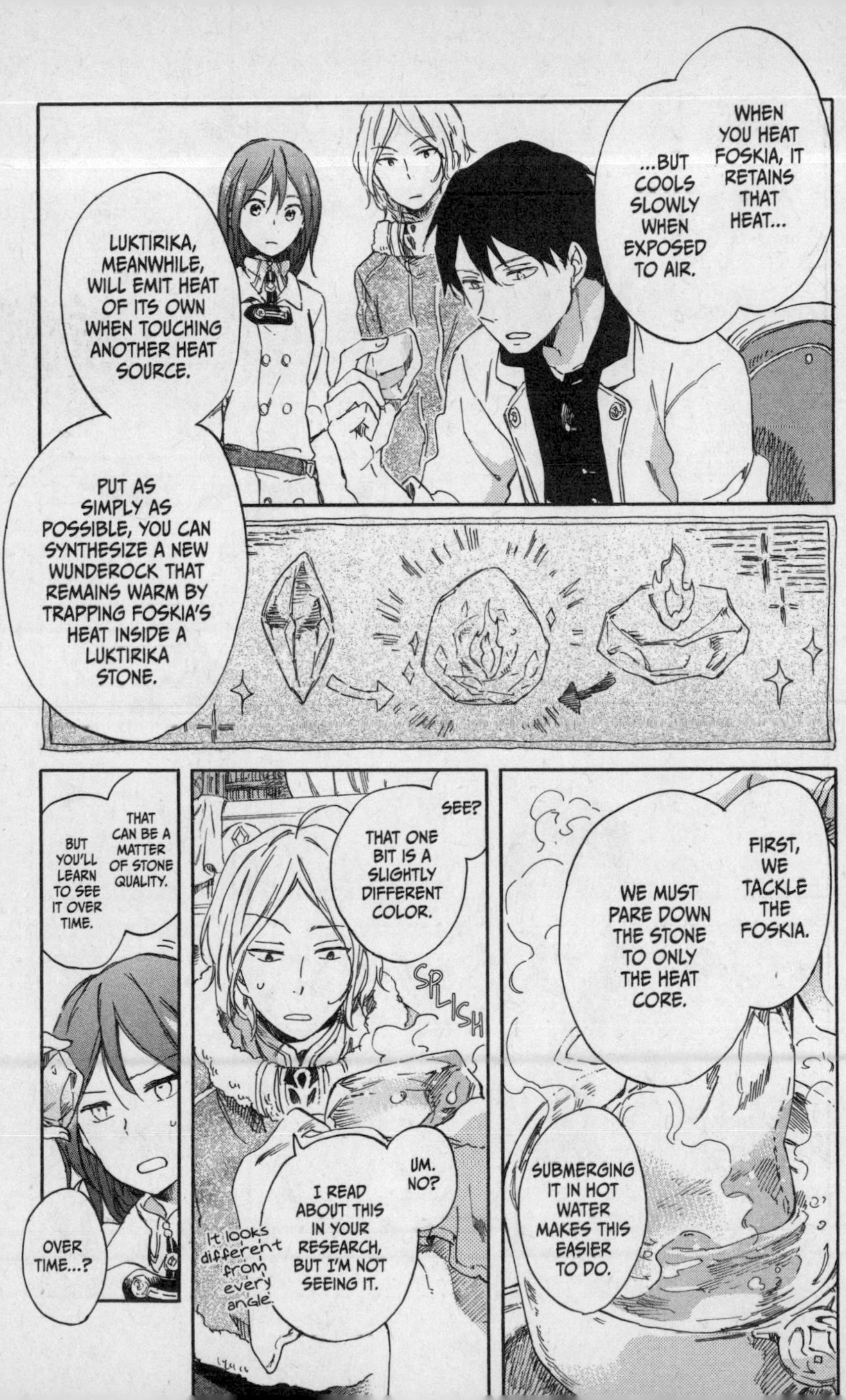
WHEN YOU HEAT FOSKIA, IT RETAINS THAT HEAT...
...BUT COOLS SLOWLY WHEN EXPOSED TO AIR.
LUKTIRIKA, MEANWHILE, WILL EMIT HEAT OF ITS OWN WHEN TOUCHING ANOTHER HEAT SOURCE.
PUT AS SIMPLY AS POSSIBLE, YOU CAN SYNTHESIZE A NEW WUNDEROCK THAT REMAINS WARM BY TRAPPING FOSKIA'S HEAT INSIDE A LUKTIRIKA STONE.
FIRST, WE TACKLE THE FOSKIA.
WE MUST PARE DOWN THE STONE TO ONLY THE HEAT CORE.
SUBMERGING IT IN HOT WATER MAKES THIS EASIER TO DO.
SEE?
THAT ONE BIT IS A SLIGHTLY DIFFERENT COLOR.
SPLISH
UM. NO?
I READ ABOUT THIS IN YOUR RESEARCH, BUT I'M NOT SEEING IT.
It looks different from every angle.
THAT CAN BE A MATTER OF STONE QUALITY.
BUT YOU'LL LEARN TO SEE IT OVER TIME.
OVER TIME...?

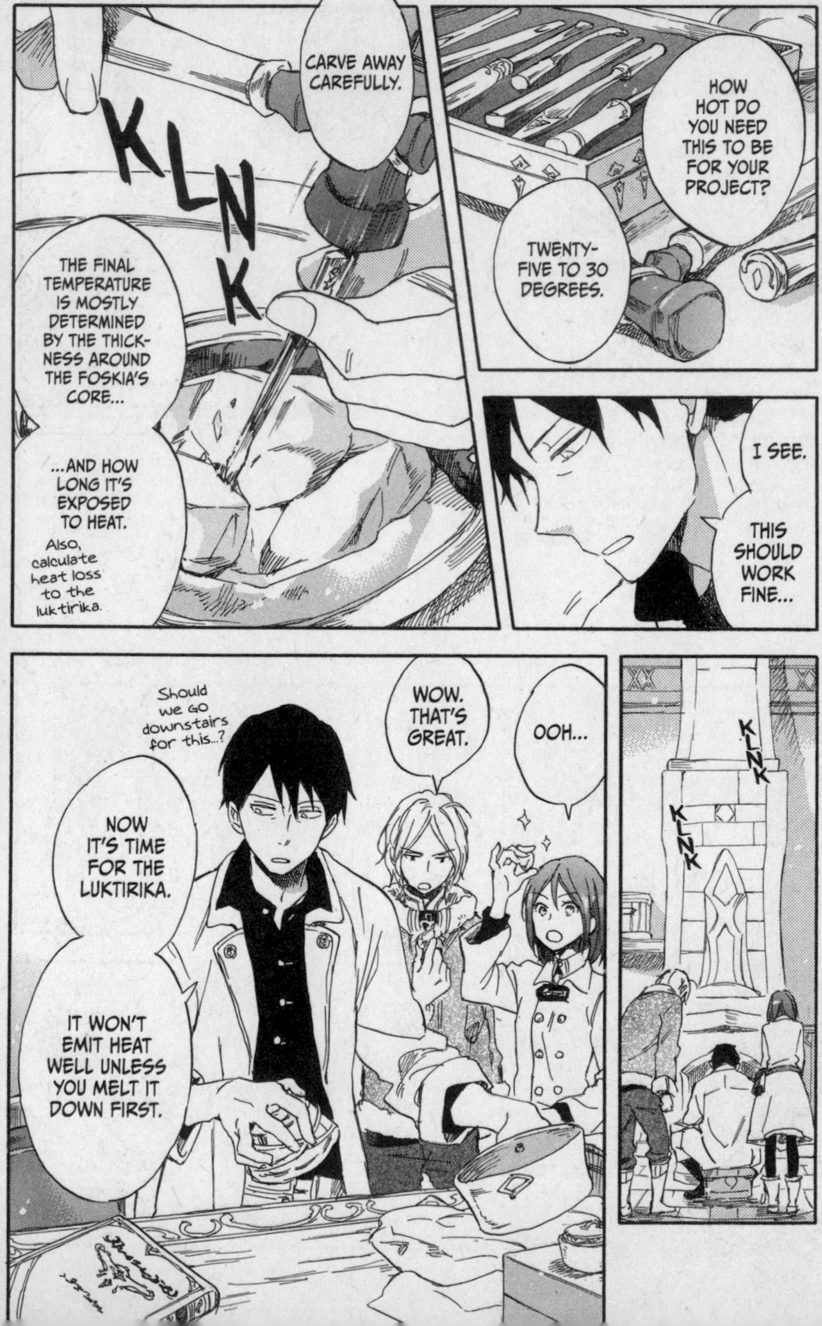
HOW HOT DO YOU NEED THIS TO BE FOR YOUR PROJECT?
TWENTY-FIVE TO 30 DEGREES.
I SEE.
THIS SHOULD WORK FINE...
CARVE AWAY CAREFULLY.
KLNK
THE FINAL TEMPERATURE IS MOSTLY DETERMINED BY THE THICKNESS AROUND THE FOSKIA'S CORE...
...AND HOW LONG IT'S EXPOSED TO HEAT.
Also, calculate heat loss to the luktirika.
KLNK
KLNK
OOH...
WOW. THAT'S GREAT.
Should we GO downstairs for this...?
NOW IT'S TIME FOR THE LUKTIRIKA.
IT WON'T EMIT HEAT WELL UNLESS YOU MELT IT DOWN FIRST.

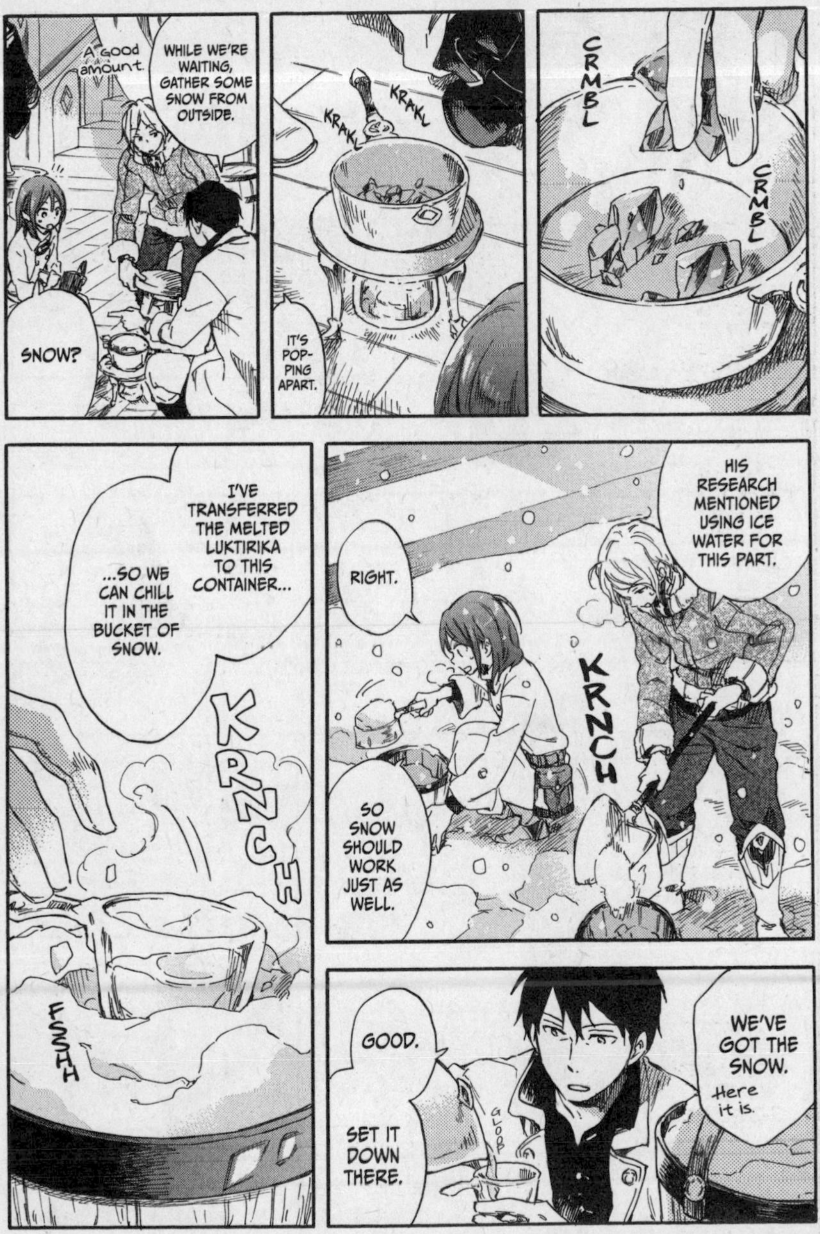
CRMBL
CRMBL
KRAKL
KRAKL
IT'S POPPING APART.
WHILE WE'RE WAITING, GATHER SOME SNOW FROM OUTSIDE.
A good amount.
SNOW?
HIS RESEARCH MENTIONED USING ICE WATER FOR THIS PART.
RIGHT.
KRNCH
SO SNOW SHOULD WORK JUST AS WELL.
WE'VE GOT THE SNOW.
Here it is.
GOOD.
GLOOB
SET IT DOWN THERE.
I'VE TRANSFERRED THE MELTED LUKTIRIKA TO THIS CONTAINER...
...SO WE CAN CHILL IT IN THE BUCKET OF SNOW.
KRNCH
FSSHH

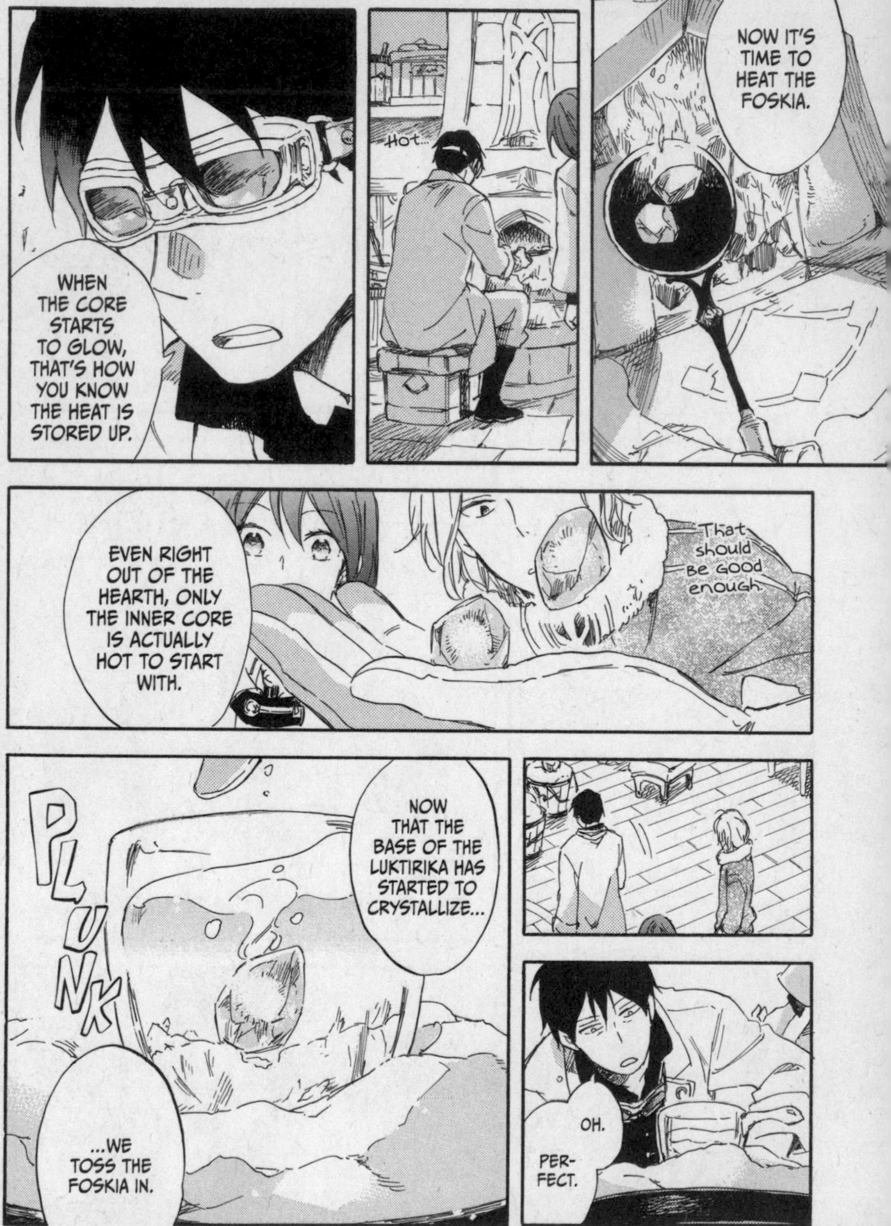
NOW IT'S TIME TO HEAT THE FOSKIA.
Hot...
WHEN THE CORE STARTS TO GLOW, THAT'S HOW YOU KNOW THE HEAT IS STORED UP.
That should be good enough.
EVEN RIGHT OUT OF THE HEARTH, ONLY THE INNER CORE IS ACTUALLY HOT TO START WITH.
OH.
PER-FECT.
NOW THAT THE BASE OF THE LUKTIRIKA HAS STARTED TO CRYSTALLIZE...
PLUNK
...WE TOSS THE FOSKIA IN.

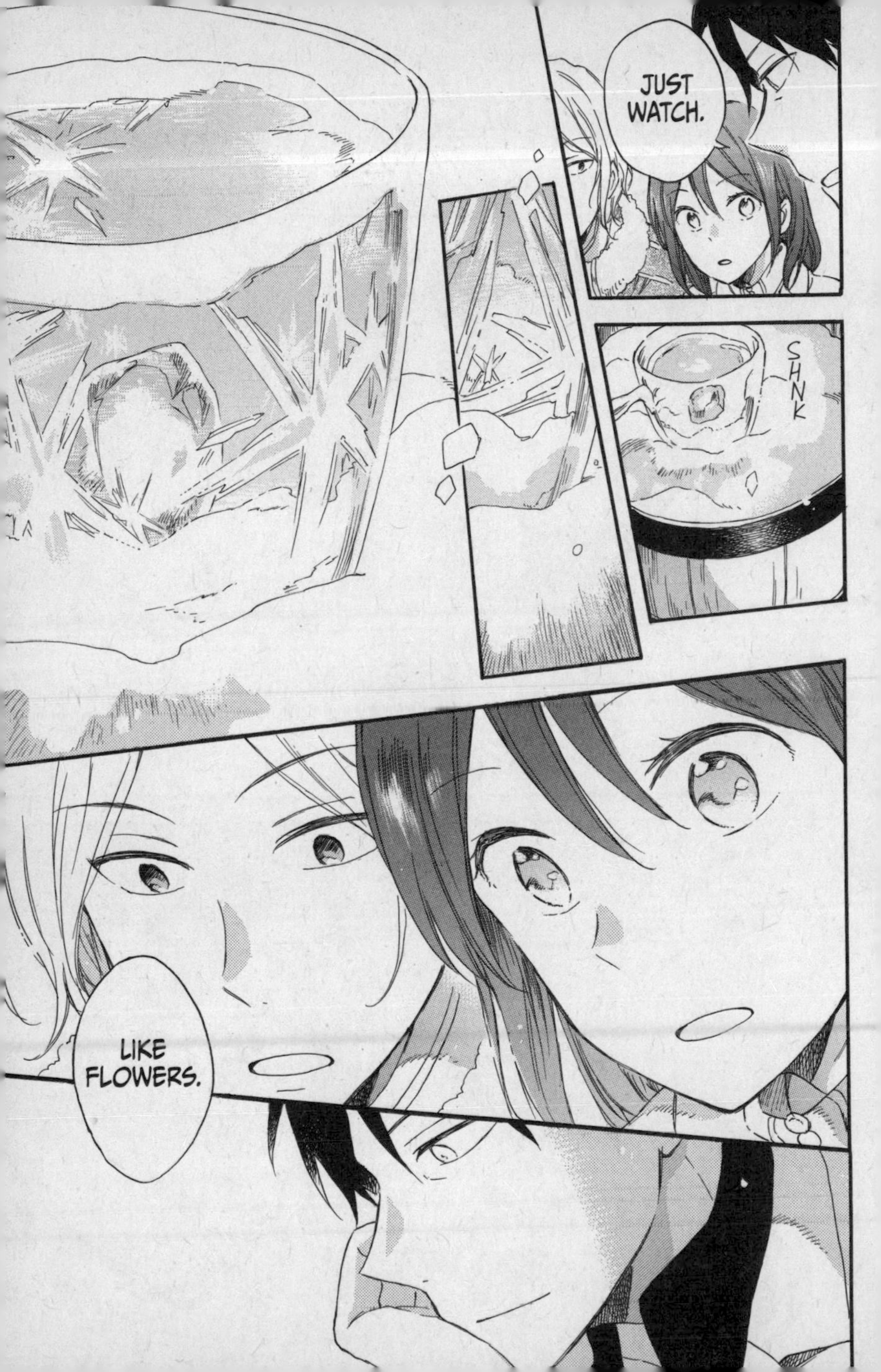
JUST WATCH.
SHNK
LIKE FLOWERS.

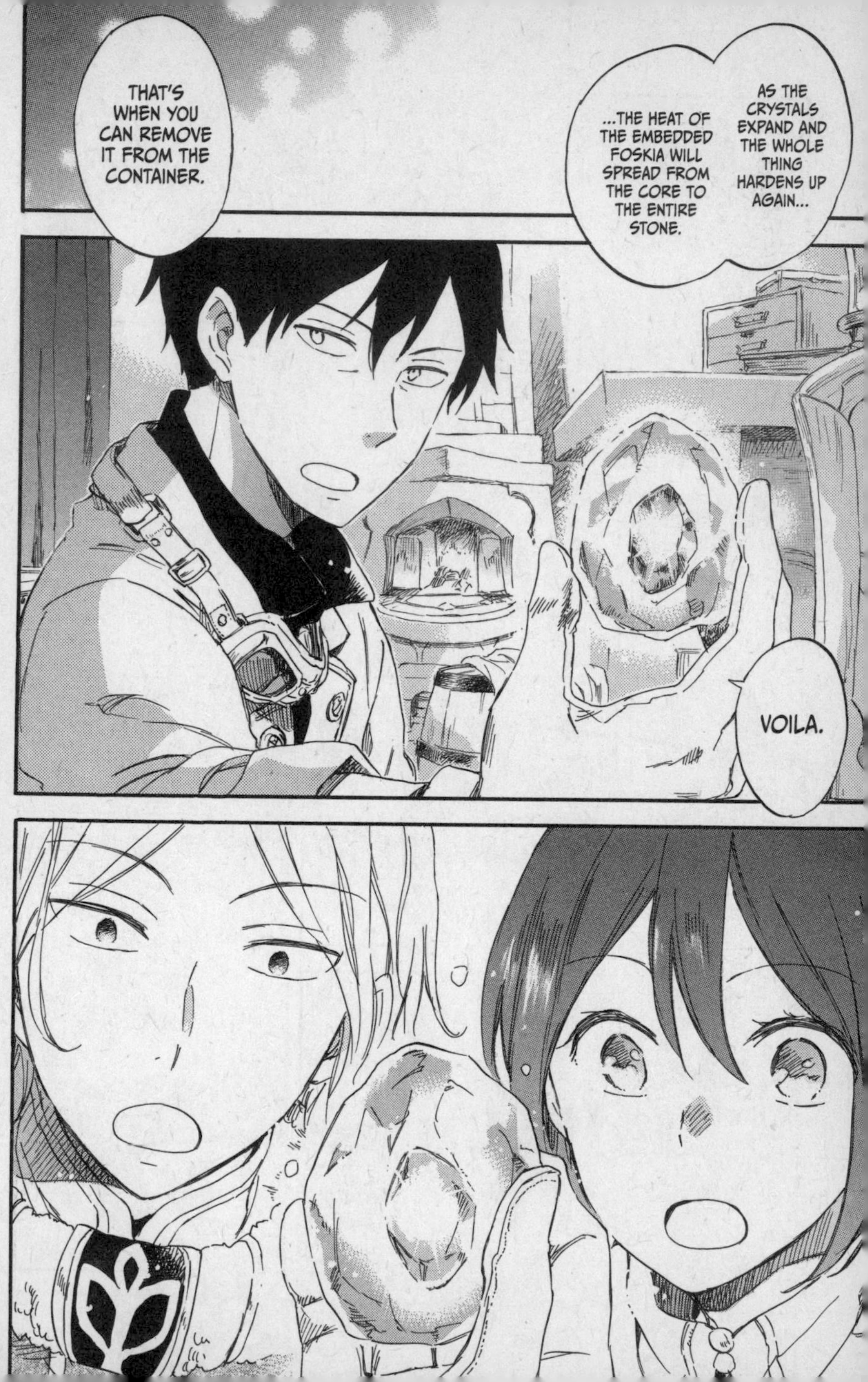
AS THE CRYSTALS EXPAND AND THE WHOLE THING HARDENS UP AGAIN...
...THE HEAT OF THE EMBEDDED FOSKIA WILL SPREAD FROM THE CORE TO THE ENTIRE STONE.
THAT'S WHEN YOU CAN REMOVE IT FROM THE CONTAINER.
VOILA.

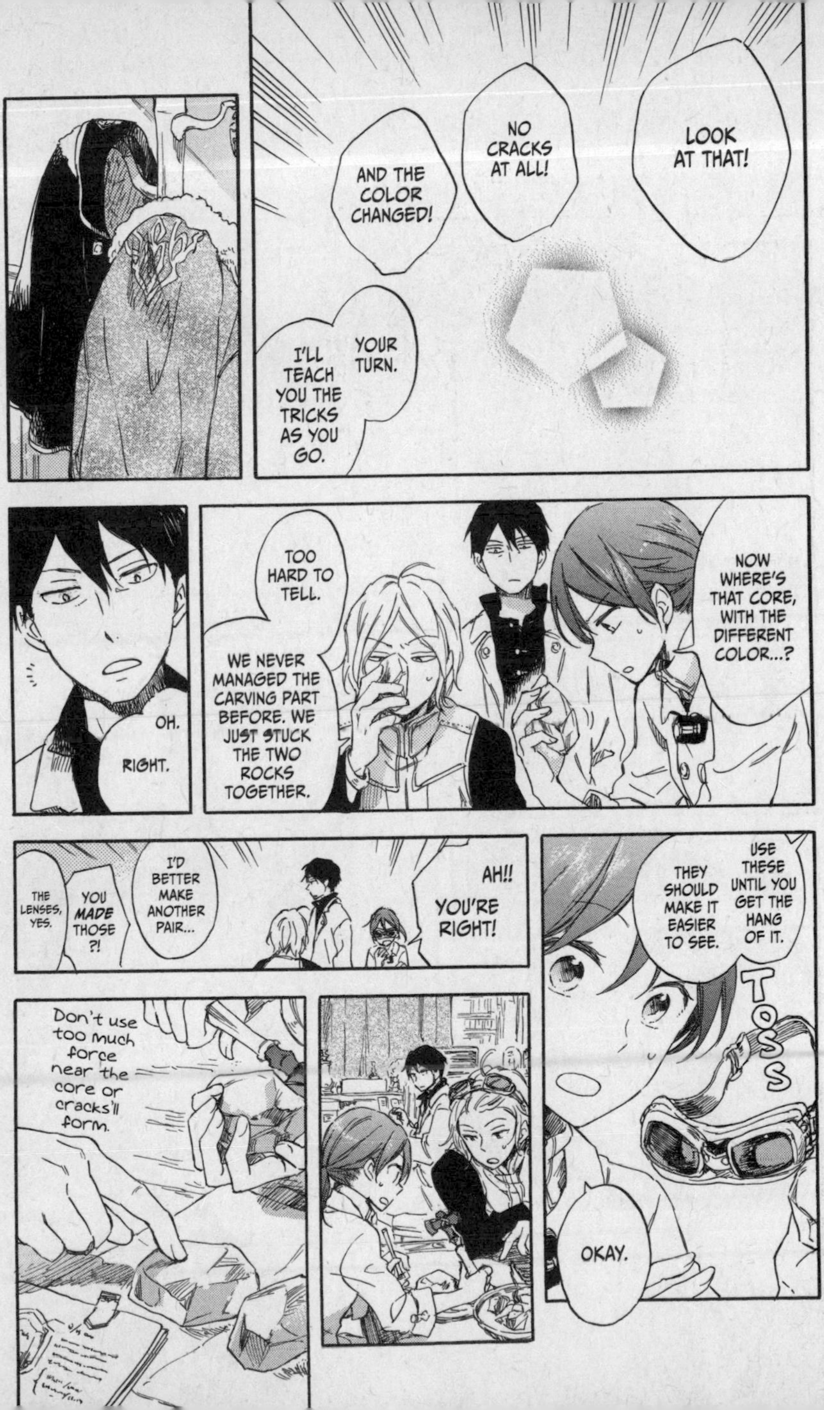
LOOK AT THAT!
NO CRACKS AT ALL!
AND THE COLOR CHANGED!
YOUR TURN.
I'LL TEACH YOU THE TRICKS AS YOU GO.
NOW WHERE'S THAT CORE, WITH THE DIFFERENT COLOR...?
TOO HARD TO TELL.
WE NEVER MANAGED THE CARVING PART BEFORE. WE JUST STUCK THE TWO ROCKS TOGETHER.
OH.
RIGHT.
USE THESE UNTIL YOU GET THE HANG OF IT.
THEY SHOULD MAKE IT EASIER TO SEE.
TOSS
OKAY.
AH!!
YOU'RE RIGHT!
I'D BETTER MAKE ANOTHER PAIR...
YOU *MADE* THOSE?!
THE LENSES, YES.
Don't use too much force near the core or cracks'll form.

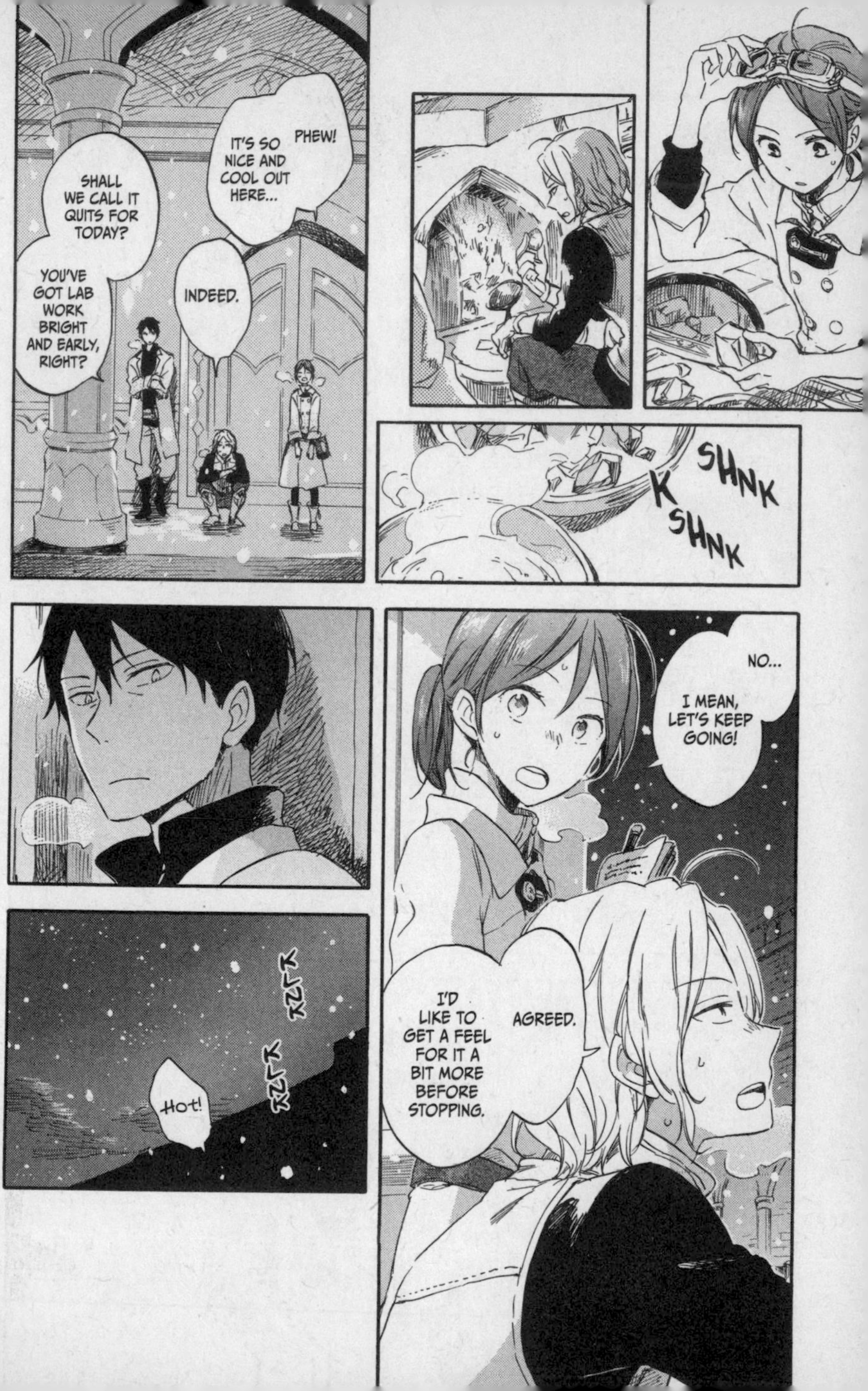
SHNK
K
SHNK
PHEW!
IT'S SO NICE AND COOL OUT HERE...
SHALL WE CALL IT QUITS FOR TODAY?
INDEED.
YOU'VE GOT LAB WORK BRIGHT AND EARLY, RIGHT?
NO...
I MEAN, LET'S KEEP GOING!
AGREED.
I'D LIKE TO GET A FEEL FOR IT A BIT MORE BEFORE STOPPING.
KRLK
KRLK
Hot!

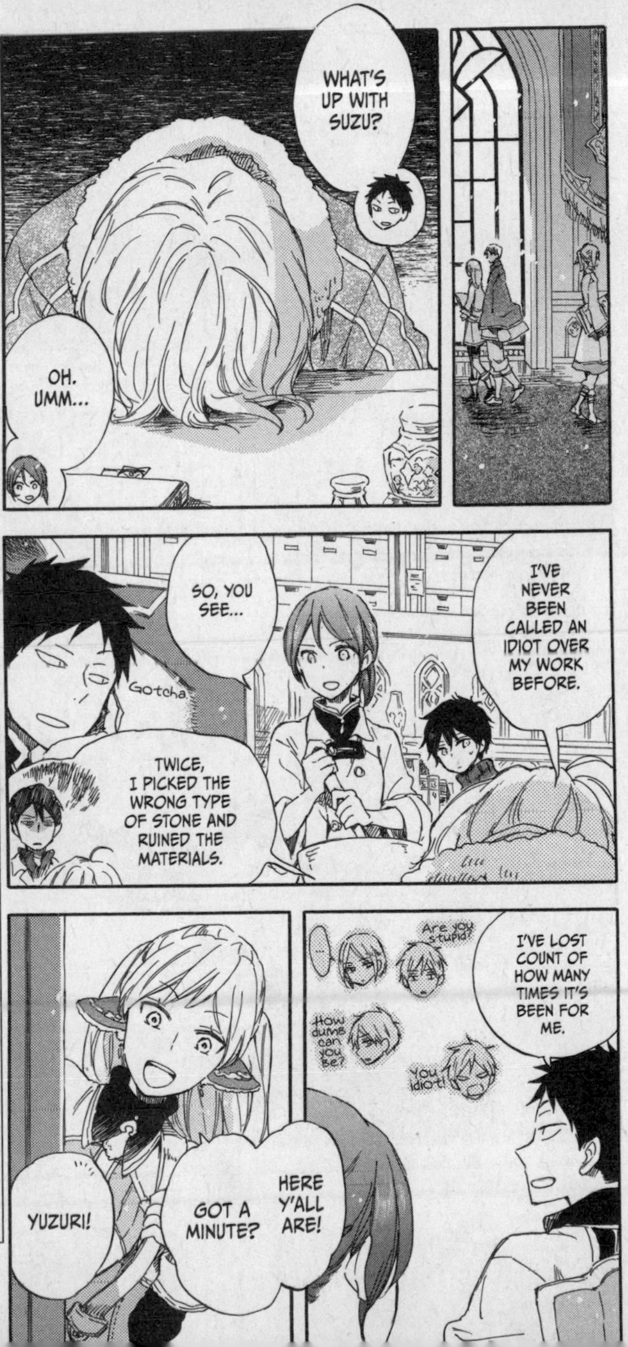
WHAT'S UP WITH SUZU?
OH. UMM...
I'VE NEVER BEEN CALLED AN IDIOT OVER MY WORK BEFORE.
SO, YOU SEE...
Gotcha.
TWICE, I PICKED THE WRONG TYPE OF STONE AND RUINED THE MATERIALS.
I'VE LOST COUNT OF HOW MANY TIMES IT'S BEEN FOR ME.
Are you stupid?
...
How dumb can you be?
You idiot!
HERE Y'ALL ARE!
GOT A MINUTE?
YUZURI!

5

CHAPTER TALK

Chapters 69, 70, 71: Orimmallys Research

Since Kirito shot up like a weed, he's wearing different outerwear than from his previous appearance.

So his outfit from that time was only shown once... You might say he's a "Kiri-total Fashionista."

I just wanted a chance to make that joke. Anyway, growth spurts are tough (on the artist who's designing the clothes)!

I originally thought the orimmallys project would be concluded within three chapters. Oh, how naïve I was...

That's why the cover art often doesn't match the book's contents.

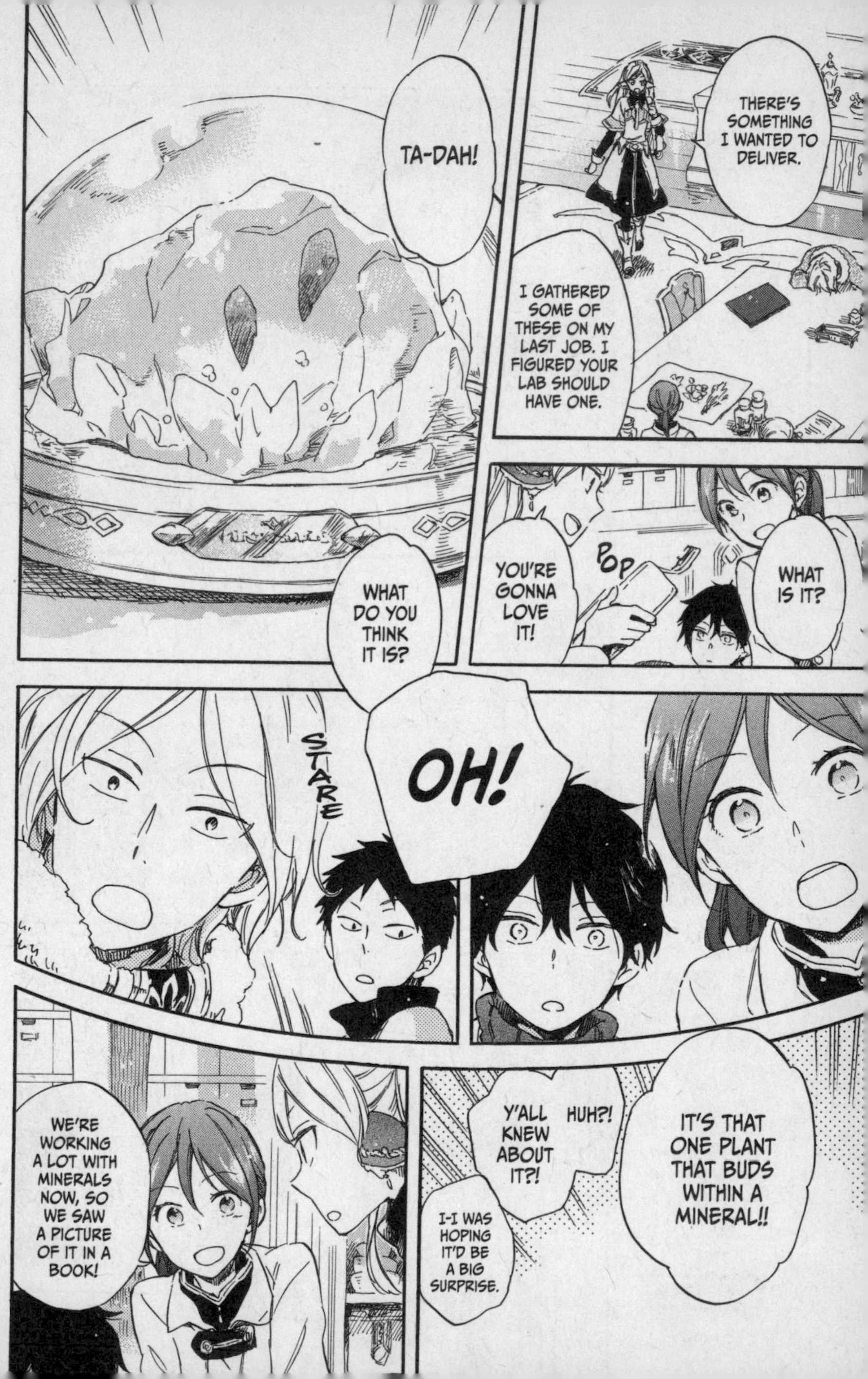
THERE'S SOMETHING I WANTED TO DELIVER.
I GATHERED SOME OF THESE ON MY LAST JOB. I FIGURED YOUR LAB SHOULD HAVE ONE.
WHAT IS IT?
POP
YOU'RE GONNA LOVE IT!
TA-DAH!
WHAT DO YOU THINK IT IS?
OH!
STARE
IT'S THAT ONE PLANT THAT BUDS WITHIN A MINERAL!!
HUH?!
Y'ALL KNEW ABOUT IT?!
I-I WAS HOPING IT'D BE A BIG SURPRISE.
WE'RE WORKING A LOT WITH MINERALS NOW, SO WE SAW A PICTURE OF IT IN A BOOK!

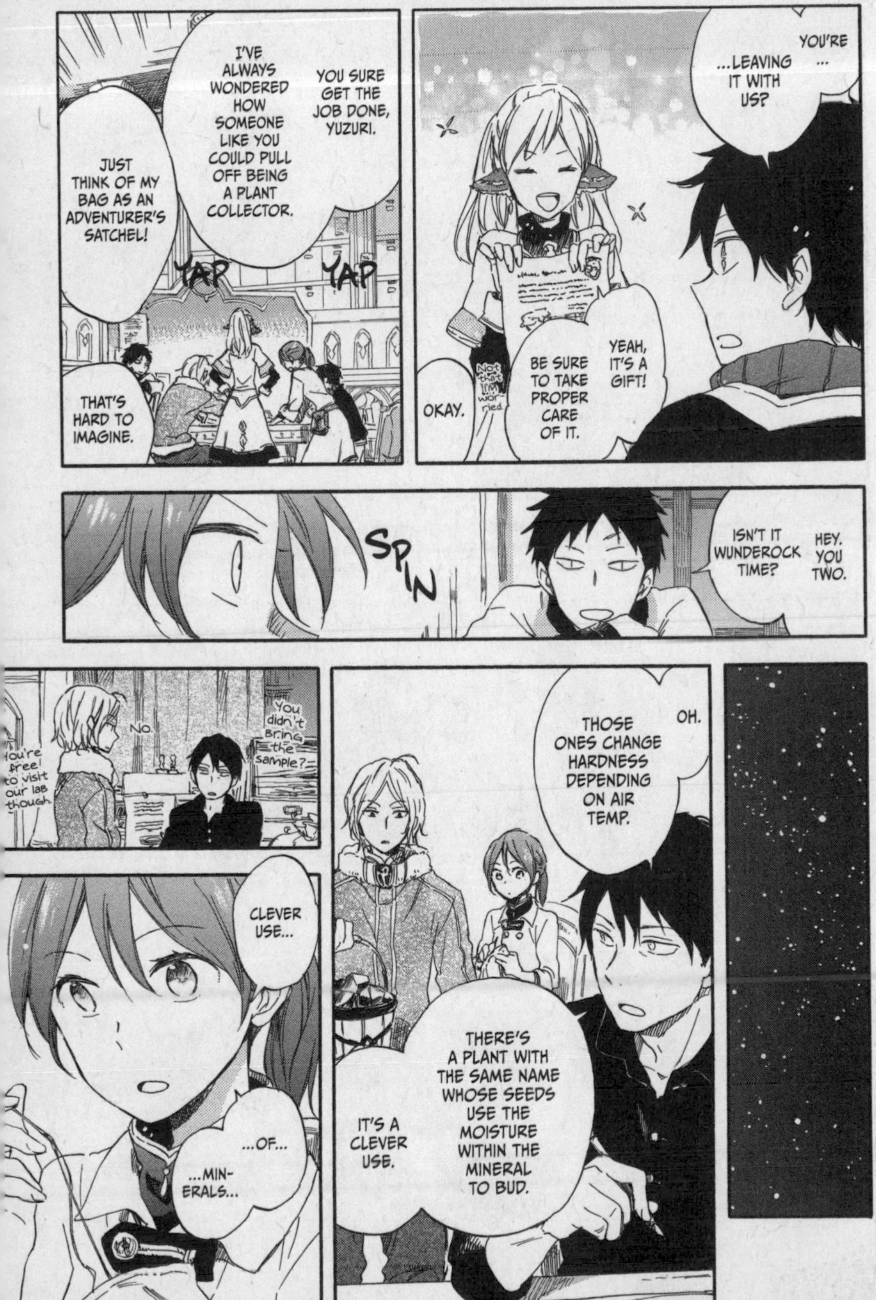
YOU'RE ...
...LEAVING IT WITH US?
YEAH, IT'S A GIFT!
BE SURE TO TAKE PROPER CARE OF IT.
Not that I'm worried
OKAY.
YOU SURE GET THE JOB DONE, YUZURI.
I'VE ALWAYS WONDERED HOW SOMEONE LIKE YOU COULD PULL OFF BEING A PLANT COLLECTOR.
JUST THINK OF MY BAG AS AN ADVENTURER'S SATCHEL!
YAP
YAP
THAT'S HARD TO IMAGINE.
HEY. YOU TWO.
ISN'T IT WUNDEROCK TIME?
SPIN
OH.
THOSE ONES CHANGE HARDNESS DEPENDING ON AIR TEMP.
THERE'S A PLANT WITH THE SAME NAME WHOSE SEEDS USE THE MOISTURE WITHIN THE MINERAL TO BUD.
IT'S A CLEVER USE.
You didn't bring the sample?
No.
You're free to visit our lab though.
CLEVER USE...
...OF...
...MIN-ERALS...

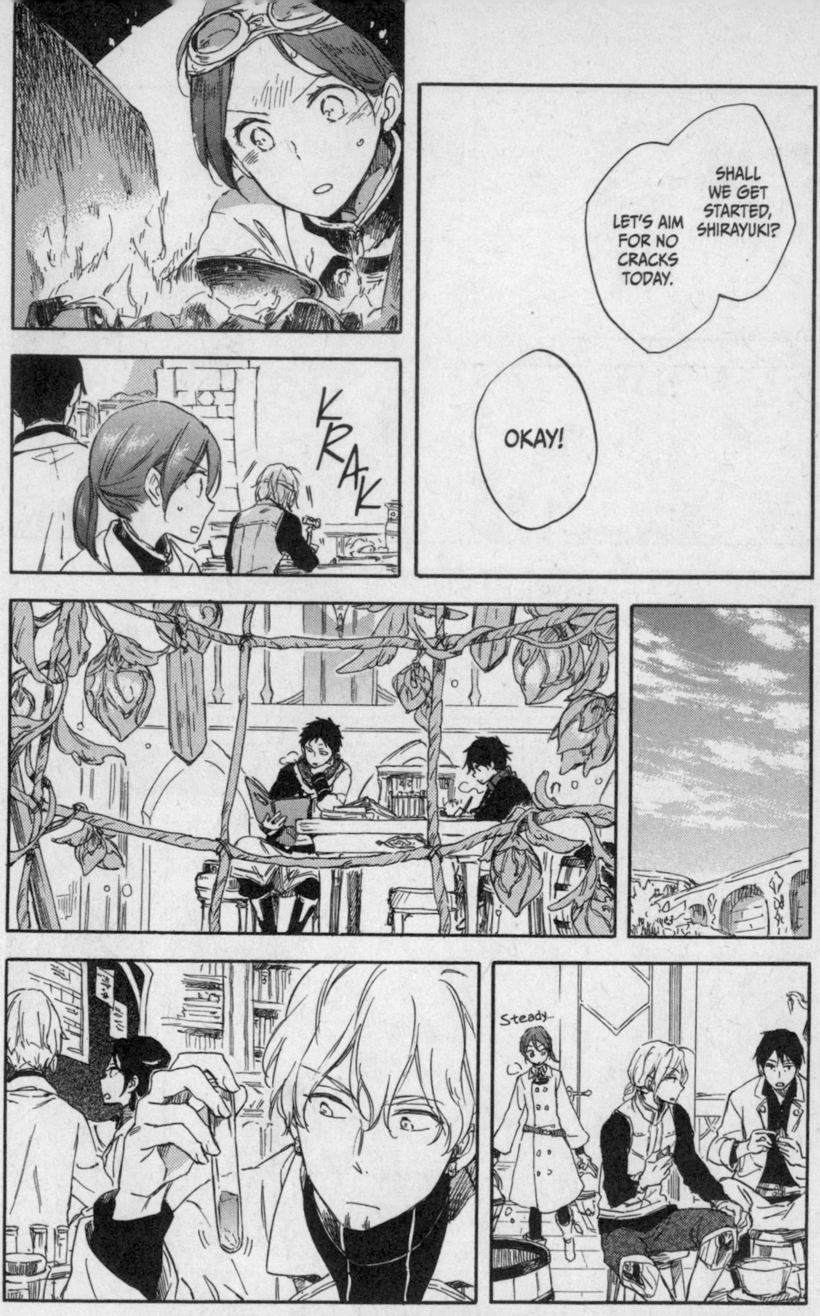
SHALL WE GET STARTED, SHIRAYUKI?
LET'S AIM FOR NO CRACKS TODAY.
OKAY!
KRAK
Steady...

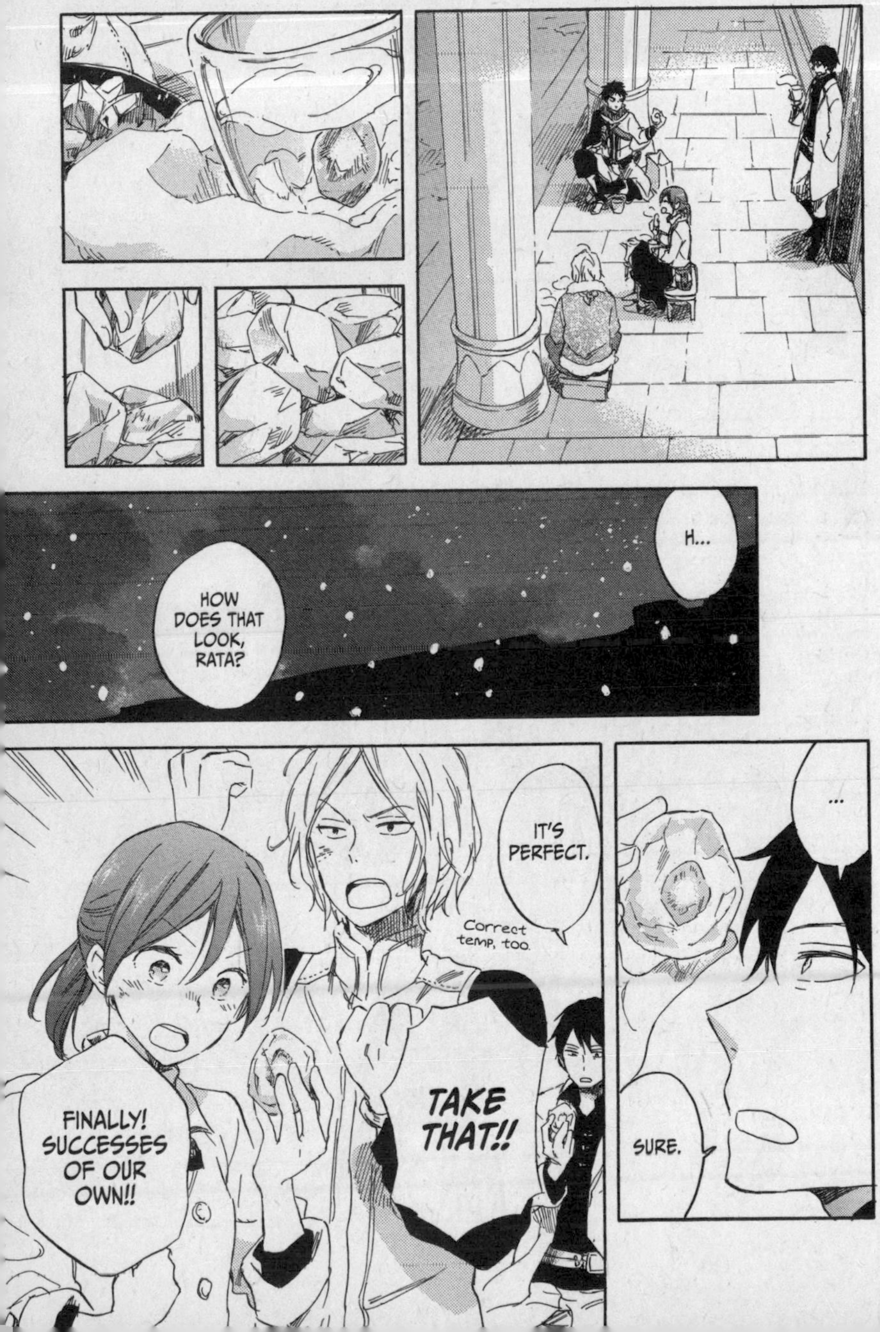
H...
HOW DOES THAT LOOK, RATA?
...
SURE.
IT'S PERFECT.
Correct temp, too.
TAKE THAT!!
FINALLY! SUCCESSES OF OUR OWN!!

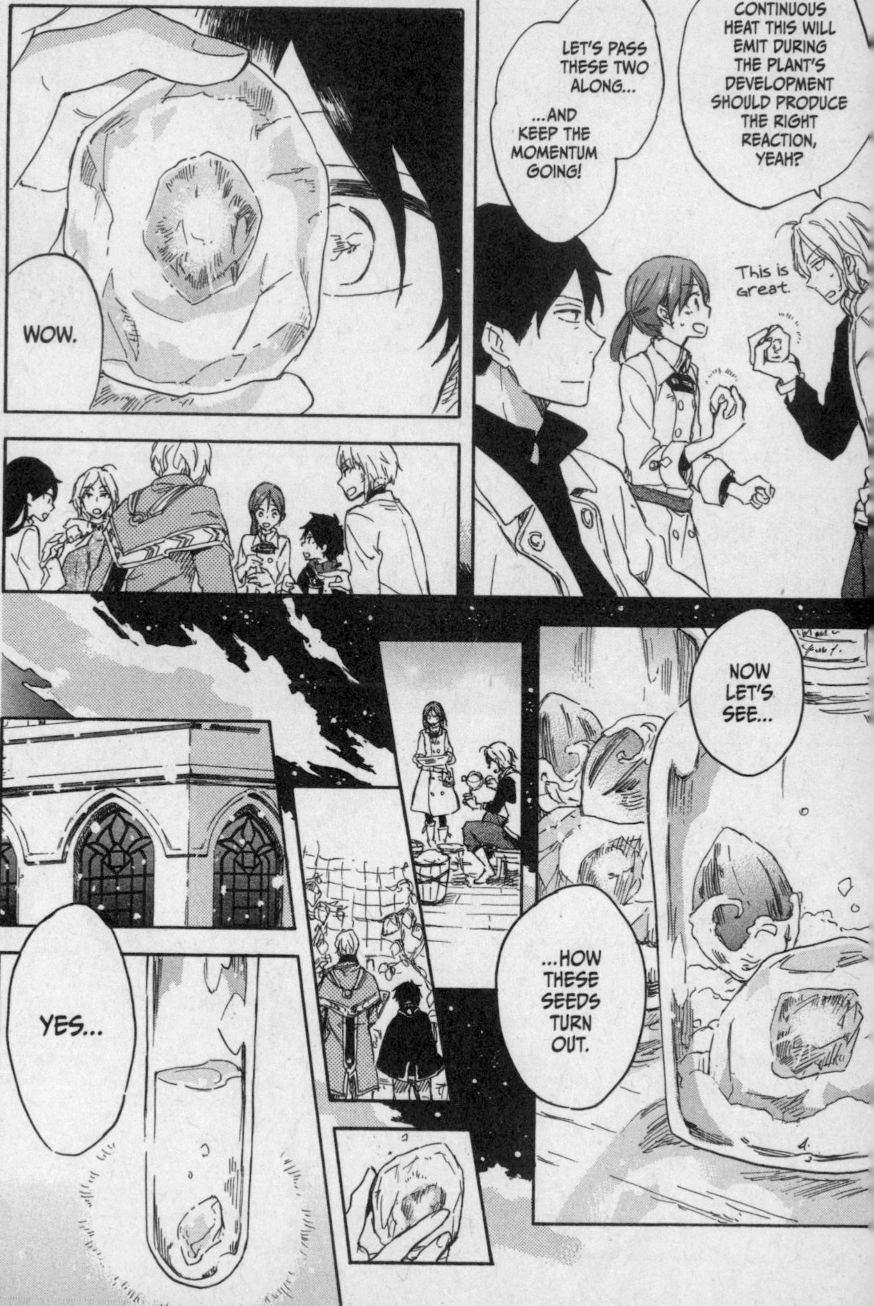
THE CONTINUOUS HEAT THIS WILL EMIT DURING THE PLANT'S DEVELOPMENT SHOULD PRODUCE THE RIGHT REACTION, YEAH?
LET'S PASS THESE TWO ALONG...
...AND KEEP THE MOMENTUM GOING!
This is great.
WOW.
NOW LET'S SEE...
...HOW THESE SEEDS TURN OUT.
YES...

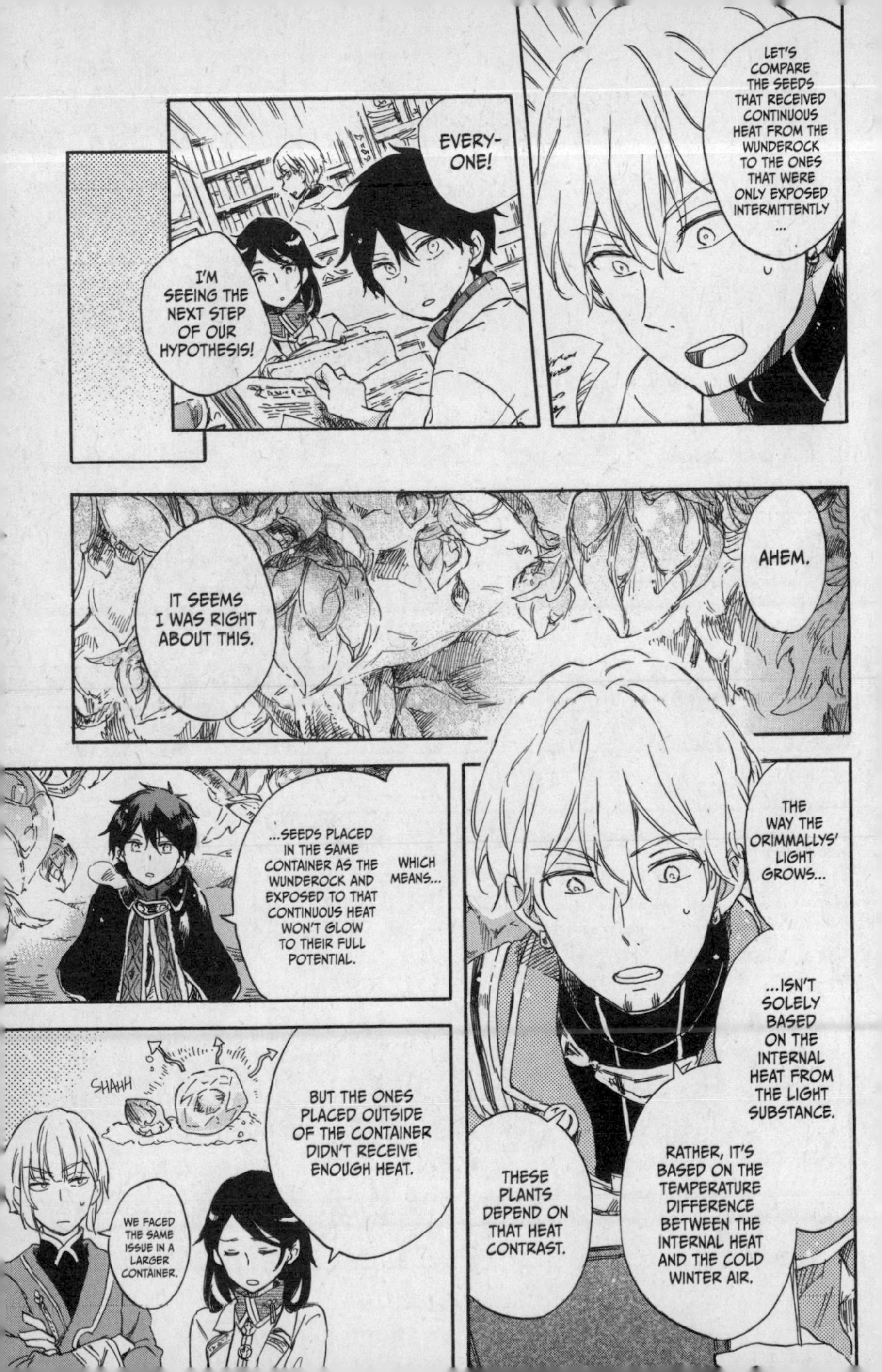
LET'S COMPARE THE SEEDS THAT RECEIVED CONTINUOUS HEAT FROM THE WUNDEROCK TO THE ONES THAT WERE ONLY EXPOSED INTERMITTENTLY ...
EVERY-ONE!
I'M SEEING THE NEXT STEP OF OUR HYPOTHESIS!
AHEM.
IT SEEMS I WAS RIGHT ABOUT THIS.
THE WAY THE ORIMMALLYS' LIGHT GROWS...
...ISN'T SOLELY BASED ON THE INTERNAL HEAT FROM THE LIGHT SUBSTANCE.
RATHER, IT'S BASED ON THE TEMPERATURE DIFFERENCE BETWEEN THE INTERNAL HEAT AND THE COLD WINTER AIR.
THESE PLANTS DEPEND ON THAT HEAT CONTRAST.
WHICH MEANS...
...SEEDS PLACED IN THE SAME CONTAINER AS THE WUNDEROCK AND EXPOSED TO THAT CONTINUOUS HEAT WON'T GLOW TO THEIR FULL POTENTIAL.
BUT THE ONES PLACED OUTSIDE OF THE CONTAINER DIDN'T RECEIVE ENOUGH HEAT.
SHAHH
WE FACED THE SAME ISSUE IN A LARGER CONTAINER.

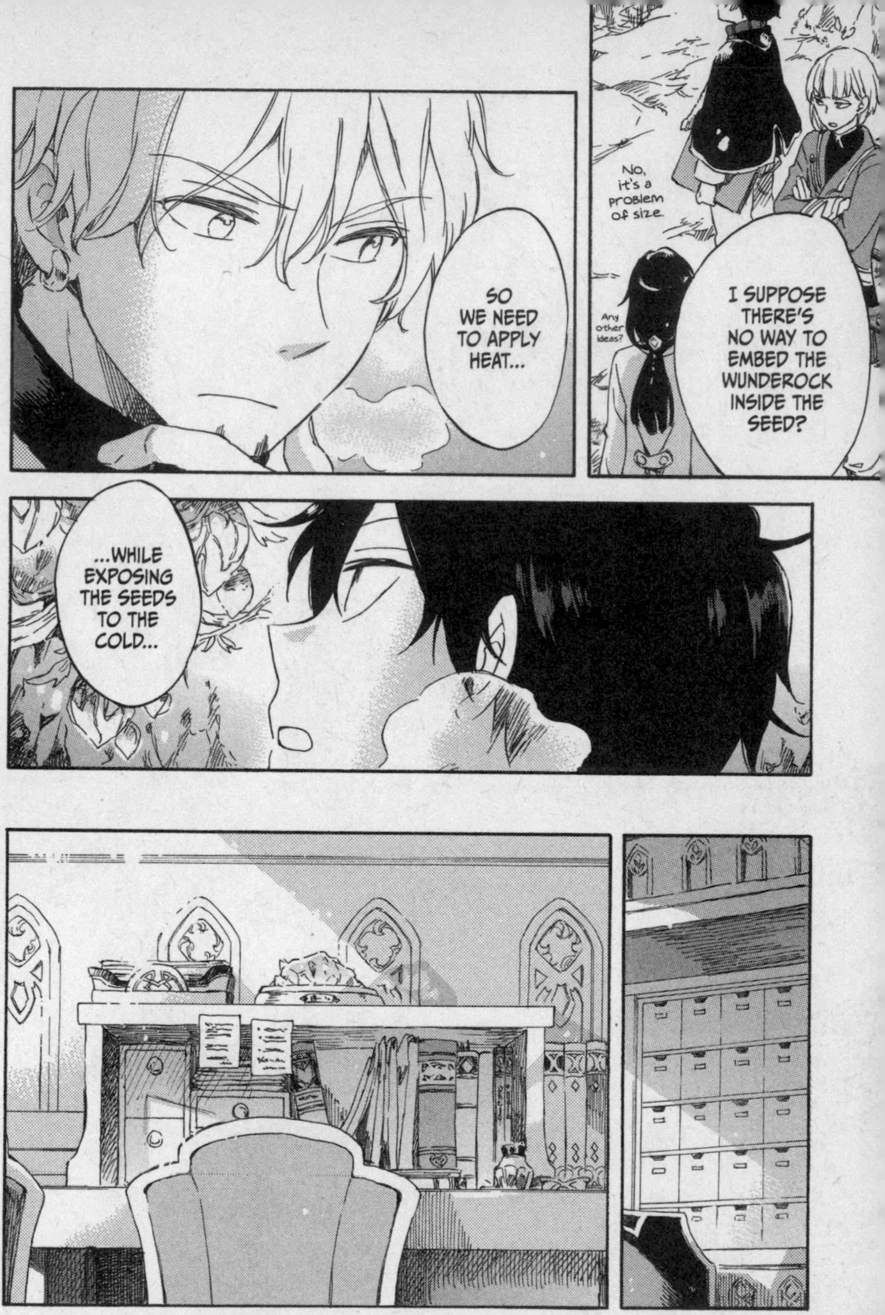
I SUPPOSE THERE'S NO WAY TO EMBED THE WUNDEROCK INSIDE THE SEED?
No, it's a problem of size.
Any other ideas?
SO WE NEED TO APPLY HEAT...
...WHILE EXPOSING THE SEEDS TO THE COLD...

Chapter 71

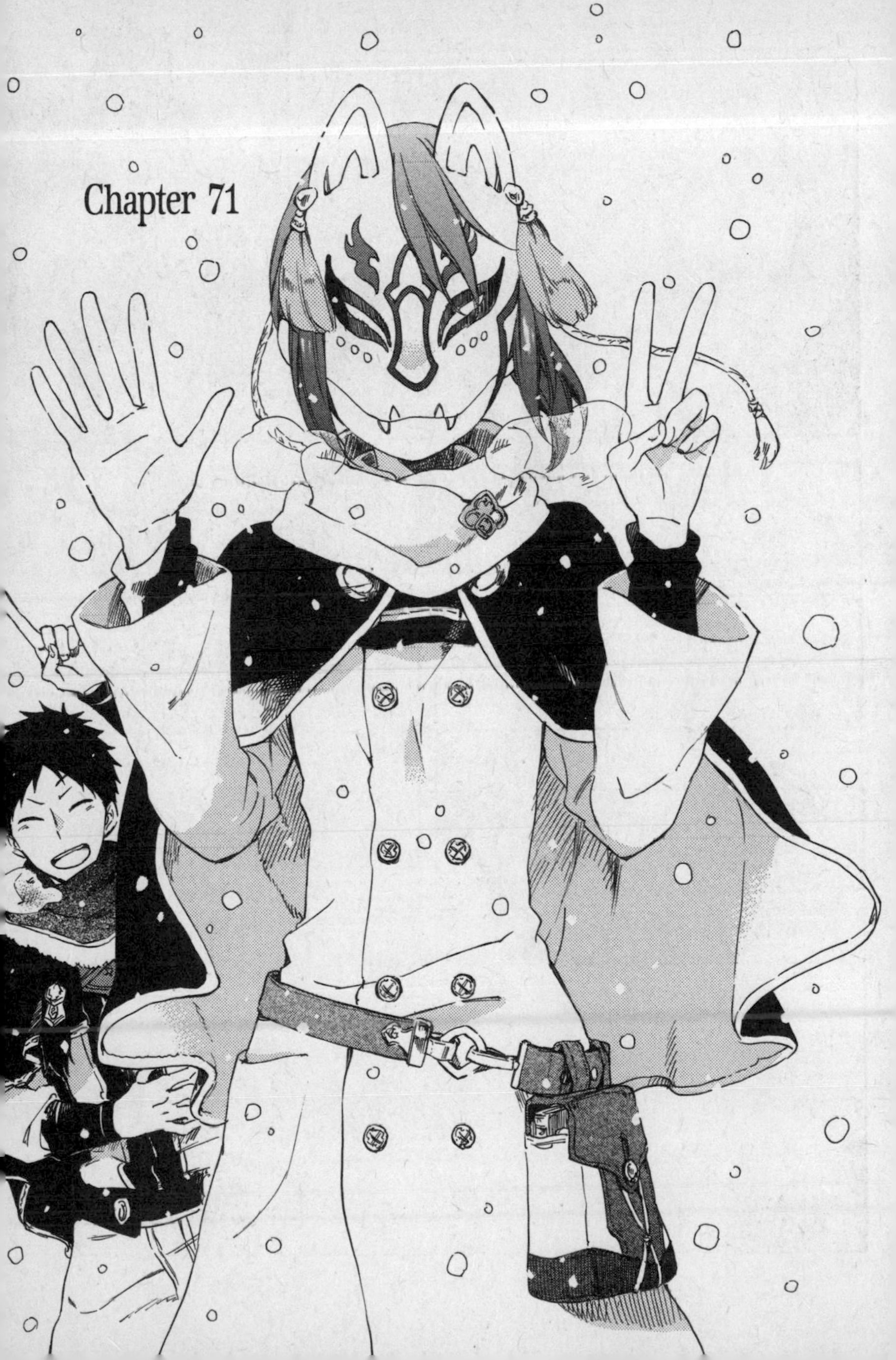

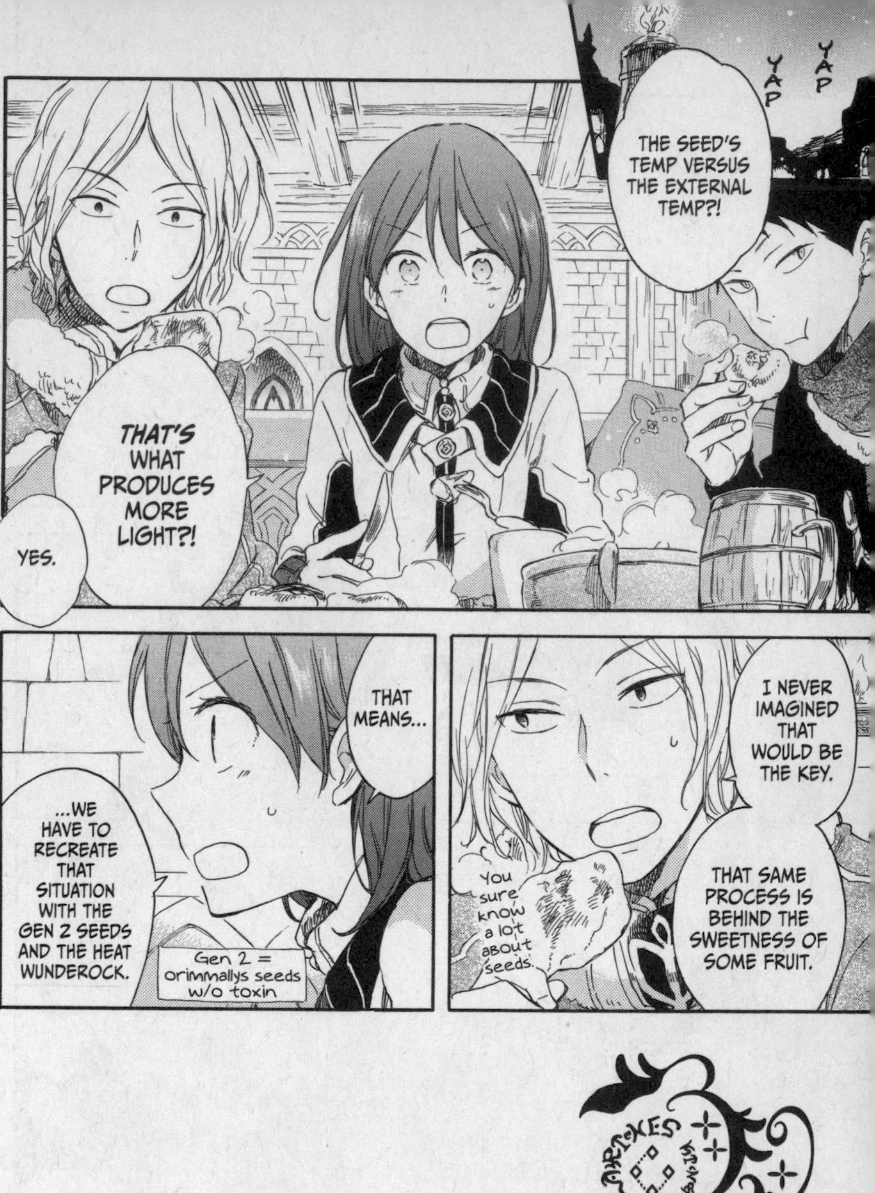
YAP YAP
THE SEED'S TEMP VERSUS THE EXTERNAL TEMP?!
THAT'S WHAT PRODUCES MORE LIGHT?!
YES.
I NEVER IMAGINED THAT WOULD BE THE KEY.
THAT SAME PROCESS IS BEHIND THE SWEETNESS OF SOME FRUIT.
You sure know a lot about seeds.
THAT MEANS...
...WE HAVE TO RECREATE THAT SITUATION WITH THE GEN 2 SEEDS AND THE HEAT WUNDEROCK.
Gen 2 = orimmallys seeds w/o toxin

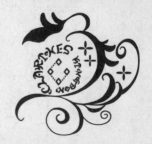

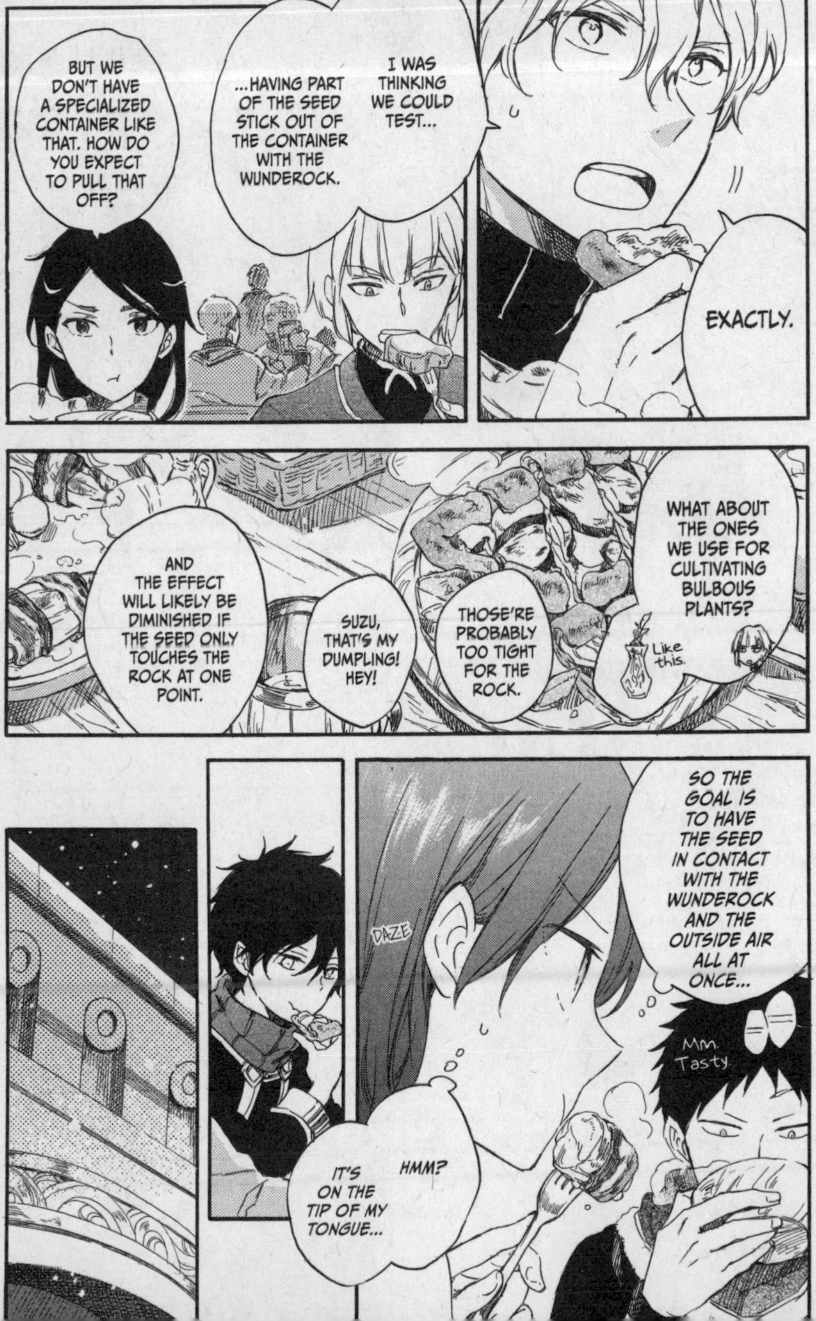
EXACTLY.
I WAS THINKING WE COULD TEST...
...HAVING PART OF THE SEED STICK OUT OF THE CONTAINER WITH THE WUNDEROCK.
BUT WE DON'T HAVE A SPECIALIZED CONTAINER LIKE THAT. HOW DO YOU EXPECT TO PULL THAT OFF?
WHAT ABOUT THE ONES WE USE FOR CULTIVATING BULBOUS PLANTS?
Like this.
THOSE'RE PROBABLY TOO TIGHT FOR THE ROCK.
SUZU, THAT'S MY DUMPLING! HEY!
AND THE EFFECT WILL LIKELY BE DIMINISHED IF THE SEED ONLY TOUCHES THE ROCK AT ONE POINT.
SO THE GOAL IS TO HAVE THE SEED IN CONTACT WITH THE WUNDEROCK AND THE OUTSIDE AIR ALL AT ONCE...
Mm. Tasty.
DAZE
HMM?
IT'S ON THE TIP OF MY TONGUE...

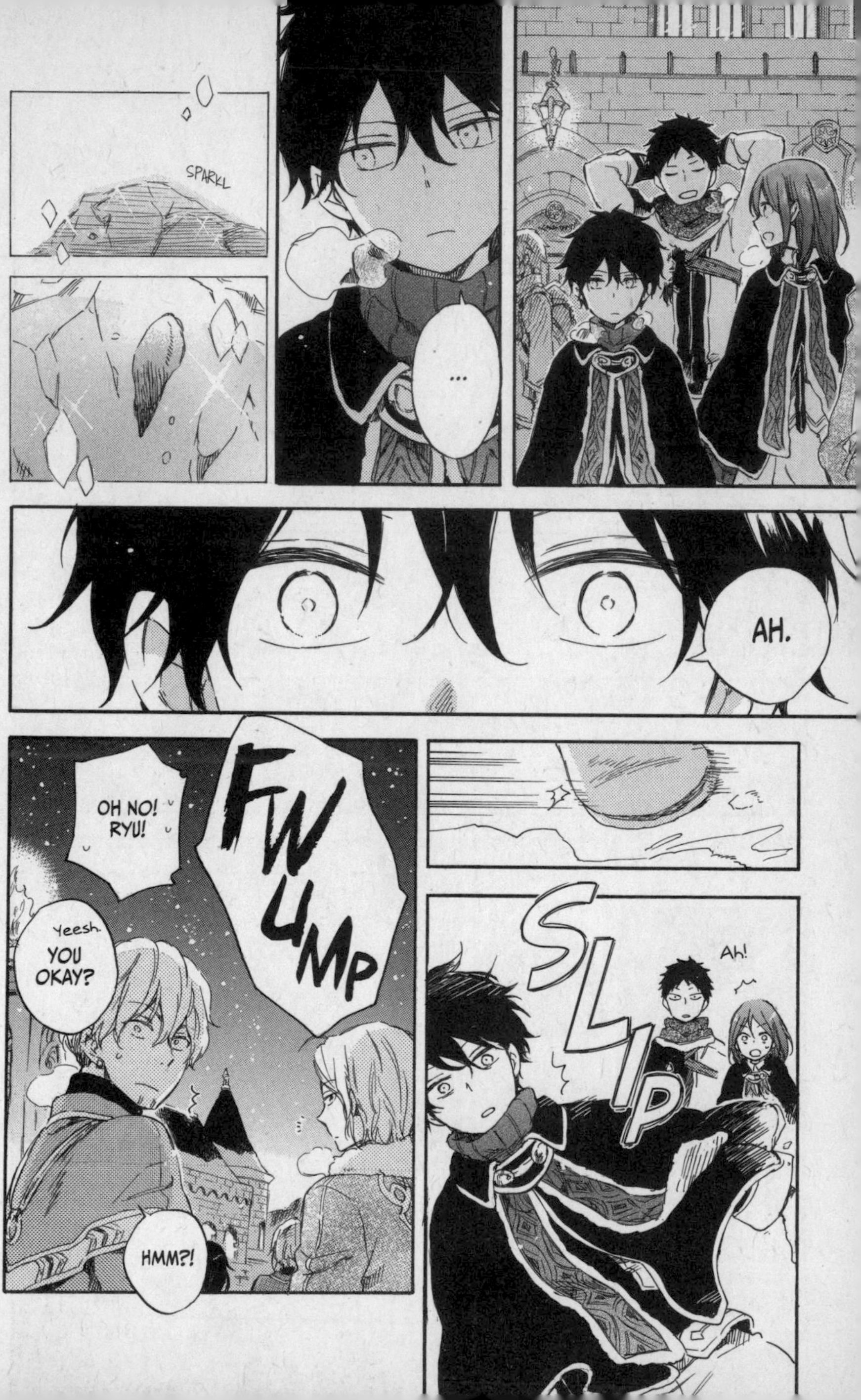
...
SPARKL
AH.
SLIP
Ah!
FWUMP
OH NO! RYU!
Yeesh. YOU OKAY?
HMM?!

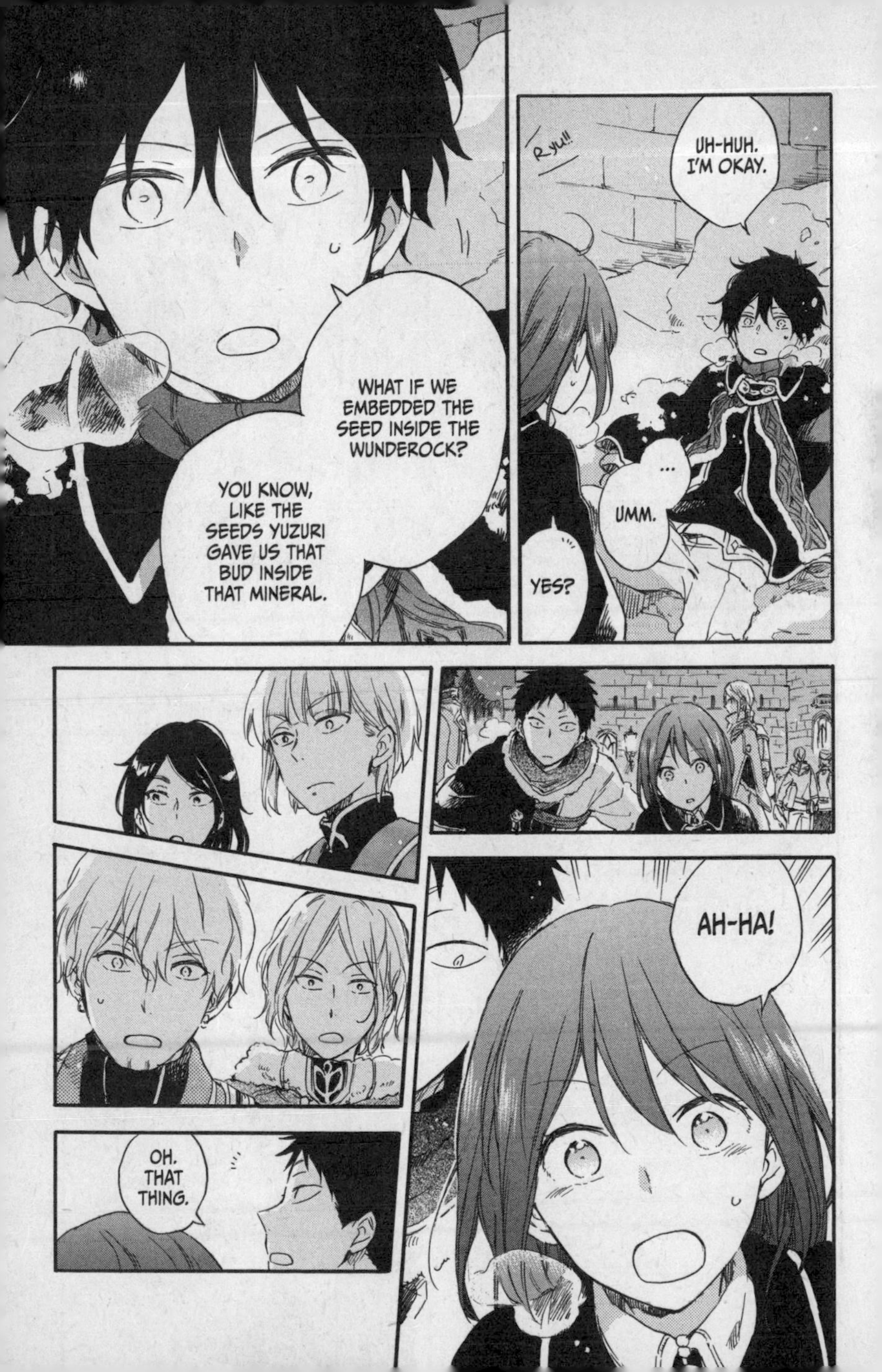
Ryu!!
UH-HUH. I'M OKAY.
...
UMM.
YES?
WHAT IF WE EMBEDDED THE SEED INSIDE THE WUNDEROCK?
YOU KNOW, LIKE THE SEEDS YUZURI GAVE US THAT BUD INSIDE THAT MINERAL.
AH-HA!
OH. THAT THING.

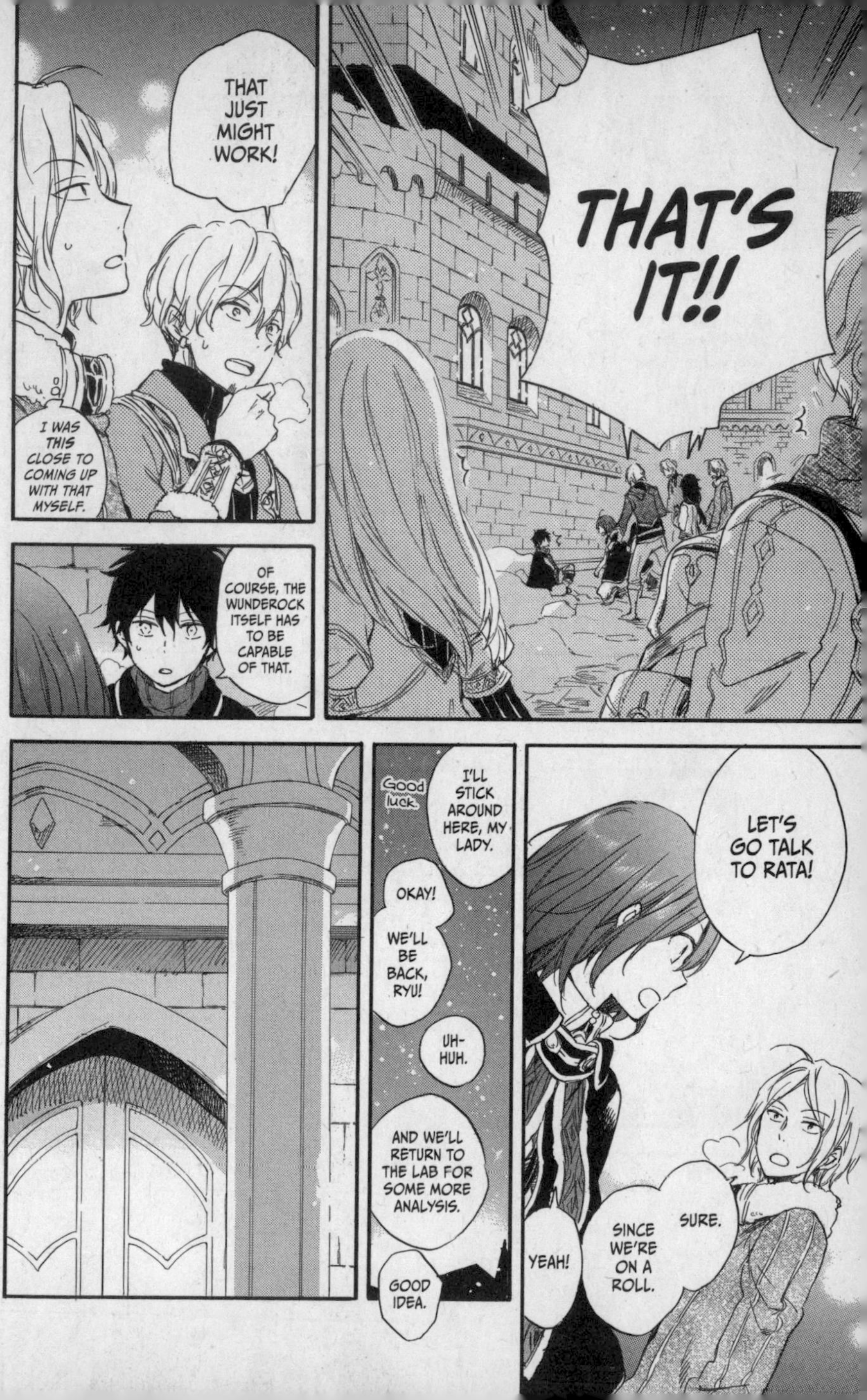
THAT'S IT!!
THAT JUST MIGHT WORK!
I WAS THIS CLOSE TO COMING UP WITH THAT MYSELF.
OF COURSE, THE WUNDEROCK ITSELF HAS TO BE CAPABLE OF THAT.
LET'S GO TALK TO RATA!
SURE.
SINCE WE'RE ON A ROLL.
YEAH!
I'LL STICK AROUND HERE, MY LADY.
Good luck.
OKAY!
WE'LL BE BACK, RYU!
UH-HUH.
AND WE'LL RETURN TO THE LAB FOR SOME MORE ANALYSIS.
GOOD IDEA.

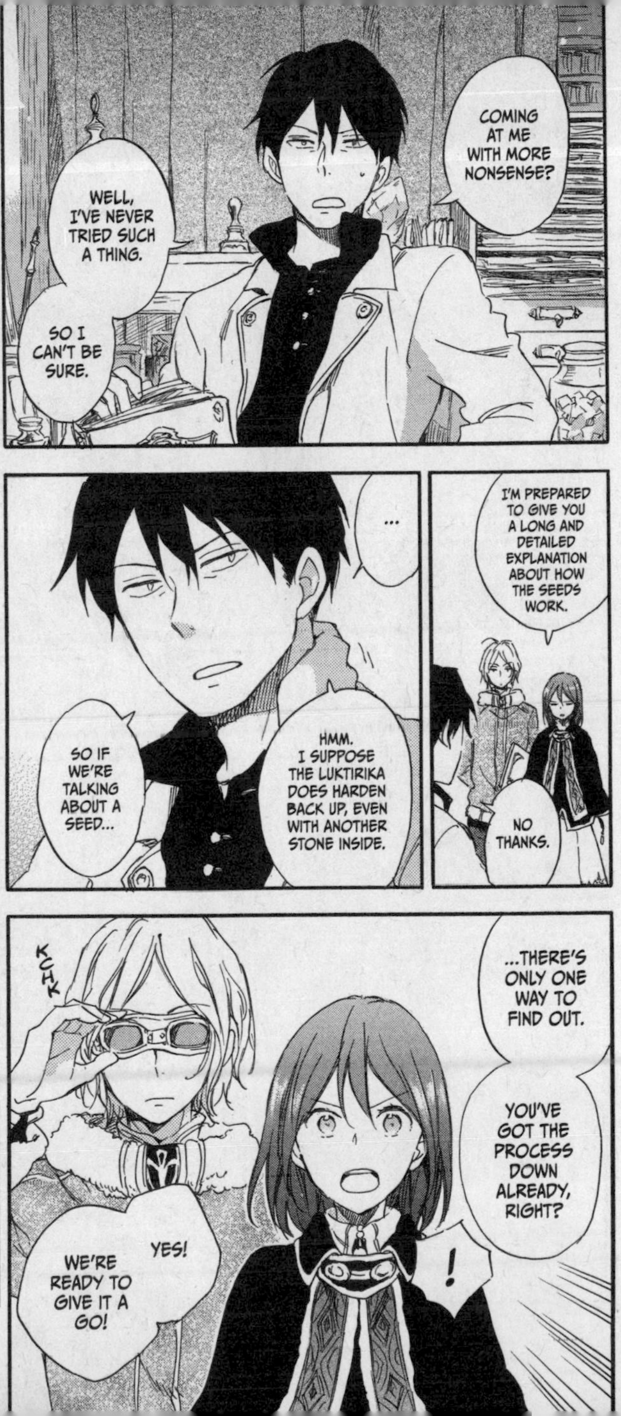
COMING AT ME WITH MORE NONSENSE?
WELL, I'VE NEVER TRIED SUCH A THING.
SO I CAN'T BE SURE.
I'M PREPARED TO GIVE YOU A LONG AND DETAILED EXPLANATION ABOUT HOW THE SEEDS WORK.
NO THANKS.
...
HMM. I SUPPOSE THE LUKTIRIKA DOES HARDEN BACK UP, EVEN WITH ANOTHER STONE INSIDE.
SO IF WE'RE TALKING ABOUT A SEED...
...THERE'S ONLY ONE WAY TO FIND OUT.
YOU'VE GOT THE PROCESS DOWN ALREADY, RIGHT?
!
KCHK
YES!
WE'RE READY TO GIVE IT A GO!

6

FINAL SIDEBAR

I contemplated writing a story here about how in the autumn of 2015 I went for a drive with a friend where we ended up taste testing a bunch of *kurikinton* (mashed sweet potatoes with sweet chestnuts) and buying lots of dried persimmons.

But then my sister suggested having a character from the story do a little wrap-up here instead.

So take it away, Marquis Haruka!

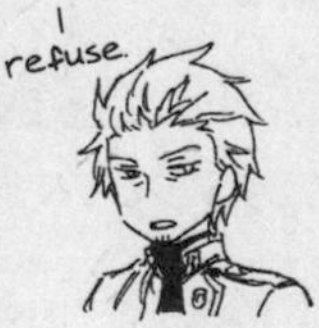
I refuse.

'Kay. See you at the end of the book!

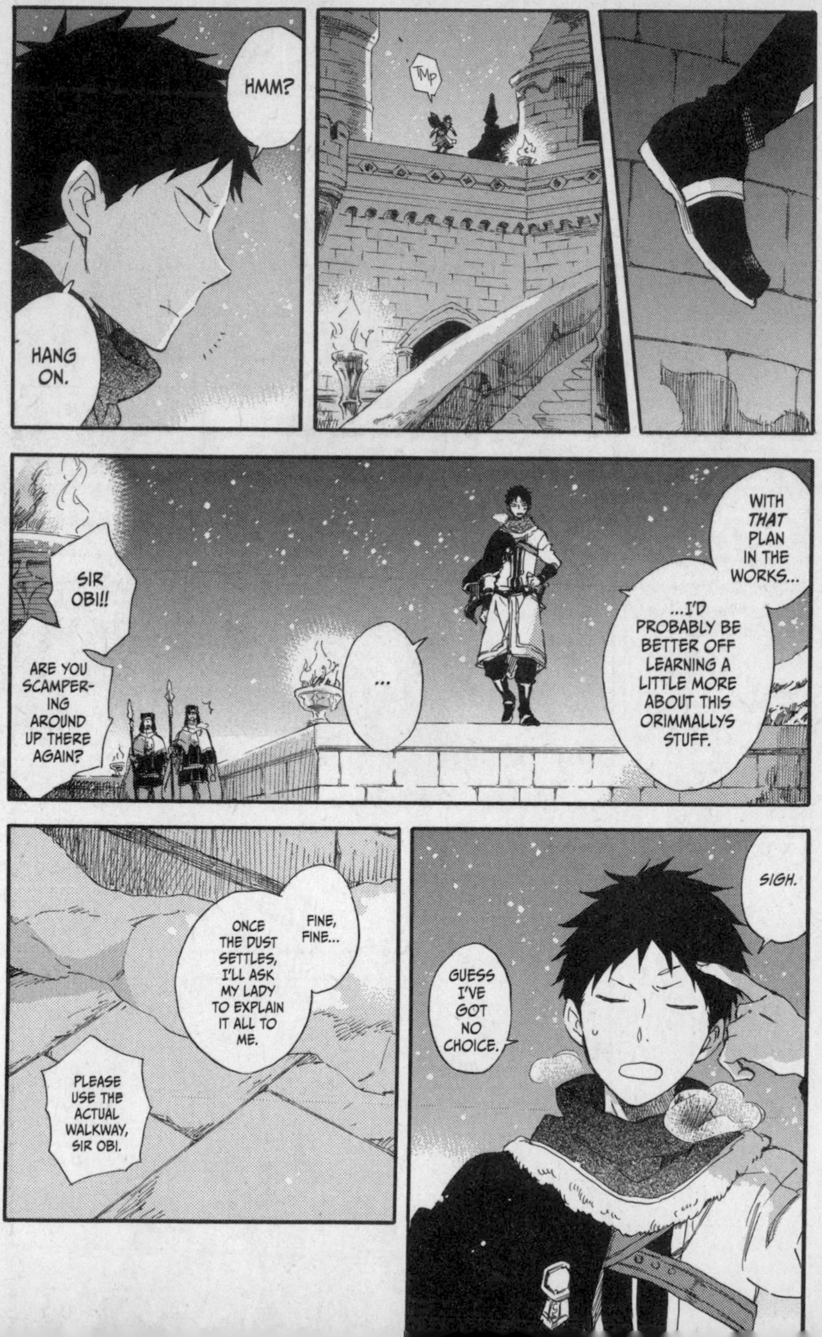
TMP
HMM?
HANG ON.
WITH *THAT* PLAN IN THE WORKS...
...I'D PROBABLY BE BETTER OFF LEARNING A LITTLE MORE ABOUT THIS ORIMMALLYS STUFF.
...
SIR OBI!!
ARE YOU SCAMPERING AROUND UP THERE AGAIN?
SIGH.
GUESS I'VE GOT NO CHOICE.
FINE, FINE...
ONCE THE DUST SETTLES, I'LL ASK MY LADY TO EXPLAIN IT ALL TO ME.
PLEASE USE THE ACTUAL WALKWAY, SIR OBI.

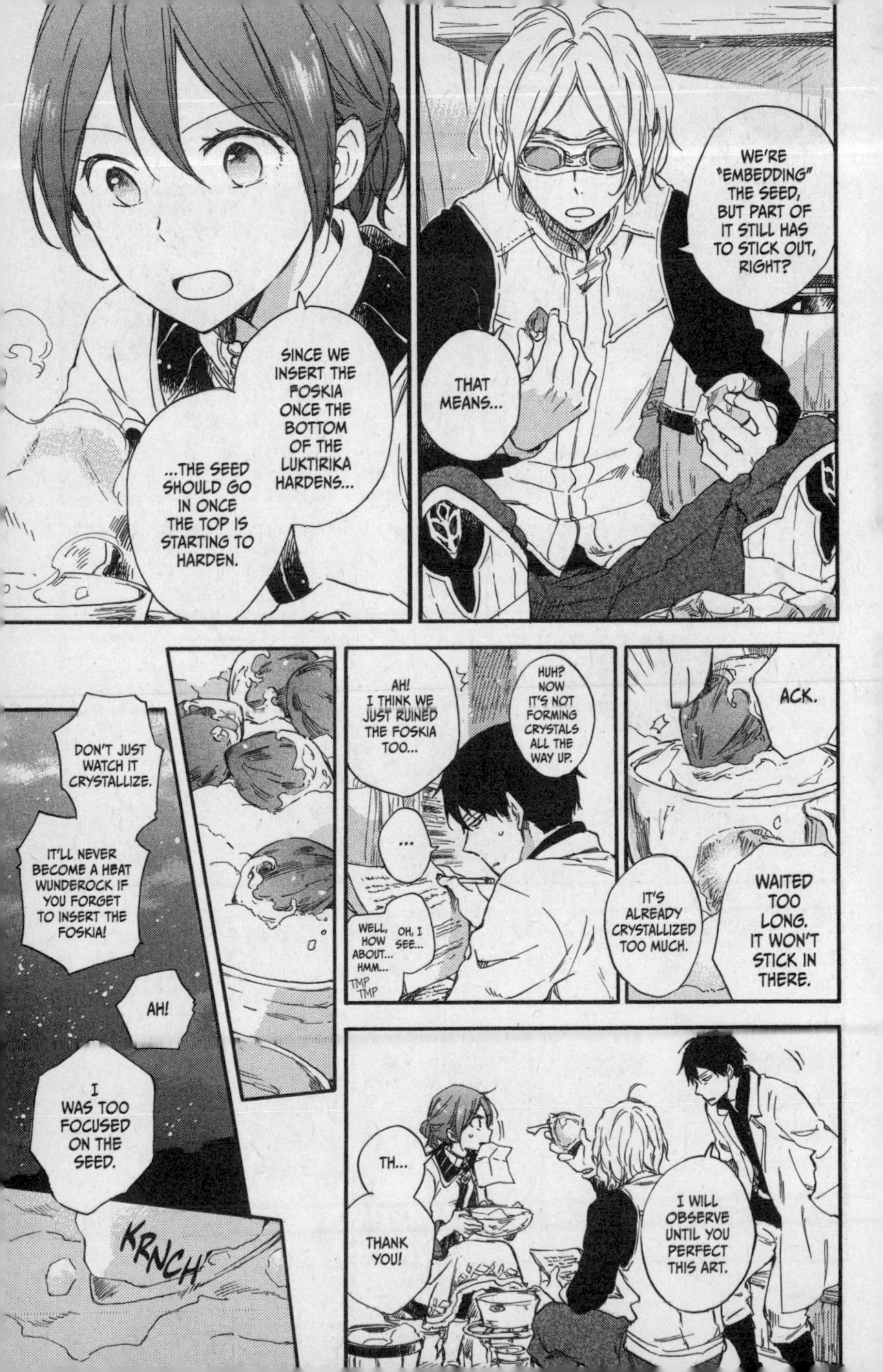
WE'RE "EMBEDDING" THE SEED, BUT PART OF IT STILL HAS TO STICK OUT, RIGHT?
THAT MEANS...
SINCE WE INSERT THE FOSKIA ONCE THE BOTTOM OF THE LUKTIRIKA HARDENS...
...THE SEED SHOULD GO IN ONCE THE TOP IS STARTING TO HARDEN.
ACK.
WAITED TOO LONG. IT WON'T STICK IN THERE.
IT'S ALREADY CRYSTALLIZED TOO MUCH.
HUH? NOW IT'S NOT FORMING CRYSTALS ALL THE WAY UP.
AH! I THINK WE JUST RUINED THE FOSKIA TOO...
...
OH, I SEE...
WELL, HOW ABOUT... HMM...
TMP TMP
I WILL OBSERVE UNTIL YOU PERFECT THIS ART.
TH...
THANK YOU!
DON'T JUST WATCH IT CRYSTALLIZE.
IT'LL NEVER BECOME A HEAT WUNDEROCK IF YOU FORGET TO INSERT THE FOSKIA!
AH!
I WAS TOO FOCUSED ON THE SEED.
KRNCH

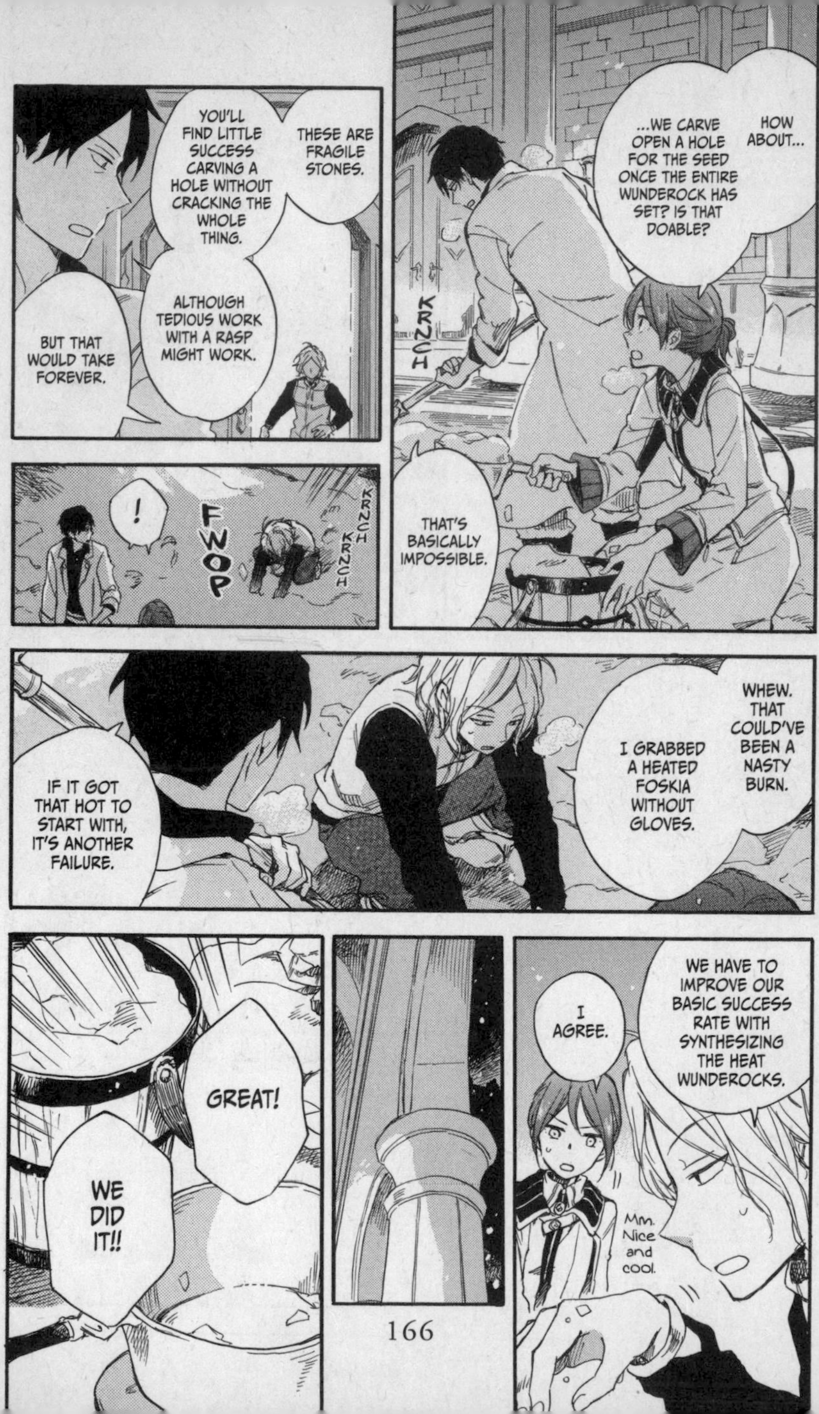
HOW ABOUT...
...WE CARVE OPEN A HOLE FOR THE SEED ONCE THE ENTIRE WUNDEROCK HAS SET? IS THAT DOABLE?
KRNCH
THAT'S BASICALLY IMPOSSIBLE.
THESE ARE FRAGILE STONES.
YOU'LL FIND LITTLE SUCCESS CARVING A HOLE WITHOUT CRACKING THE WHOLE THING.
ALTHOUGH TEDIOUS WORK WITH A RASP MIGHT WORK.
BUT THAT WOULD TAKE FOREVER.
KRNCH
KRNCH
FWOP
!
WHEW. THAT COULD'VE BEEN A NASTY BURN.
I GRABBED A HEATED FOSKIA WITHOUT GLOVES.
IF IT GOT THAT HOT TO START WITH, IT'S ANOTHER FAILURE.
WE HAVE TO IMPROVE OUR BASIC SUCCESS RATE WITH SYNTHESIZING THE HEAT WUNDEROCKS.
I AGREE.
Mm. Nice and cool.
GREAT!
WE DID IT!!

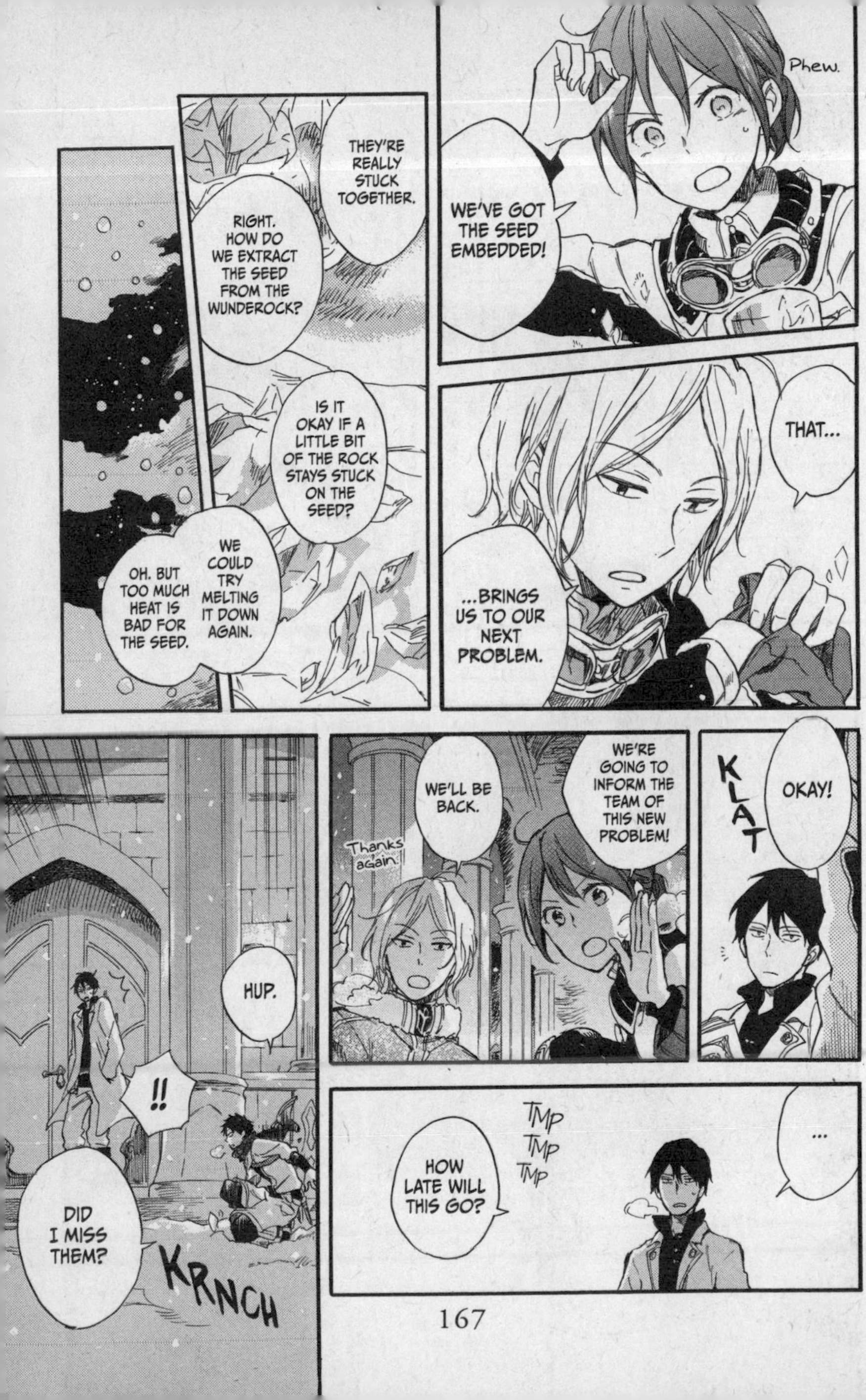
Phew.
WE'VE GOT THE SEED EMBEDDED!
THAT...
...BRINGS US TO OUR NEXT PROBLEM.
THEY'RE REALLY STUCK TOGETHER.
RIGHT. HOW DO WE EXTRACT THE SEED FROM THE WUNDEROCK?
IS IT OKAY IF A LITTLE BIT OF THE ROCK STAYS STUCK ON THE SEED?
WE COULD TRY MELTING IT DOWN AGAIN.
OH. BUT TOO MUCH HEAT IS BAD FOR THE SEED.
OKAY!
KLAT
WE'RE GOING TO INFORM THE TEAM OF THIS NEW PROBLEM!
WE'LL BE BACK.
Thanks again.
...
TMP TMP TMP
HOW LATE WILL THIS GO?
HUP.
!!
DID I MISS THEM?
KRNCH

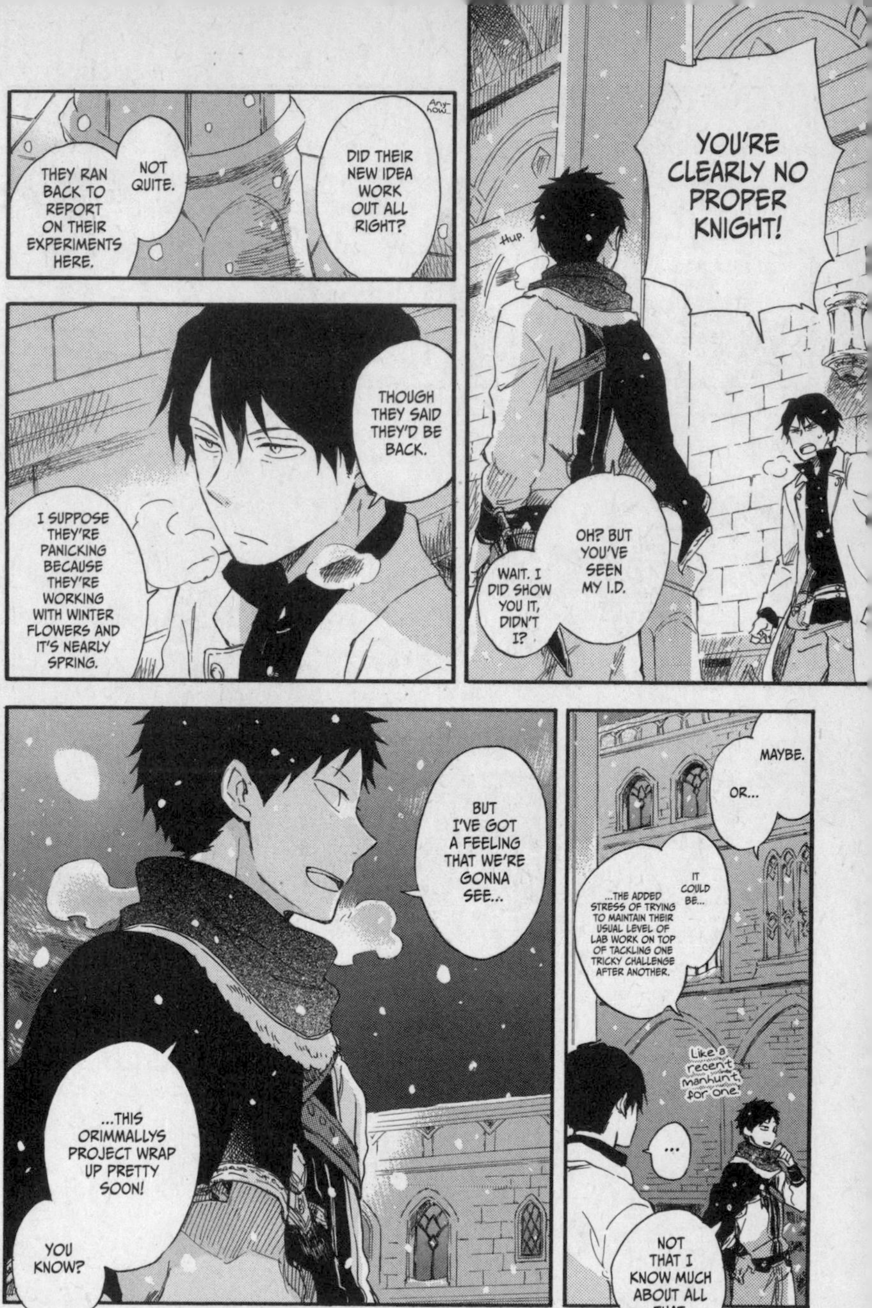
YOU'RE CLEARLY NO PROPER KNIGHT!
Hup.
OH? BUT YOU'VE SEEN MY I.D.
WAIT. I DID SHOW YOU IT, DIDN'T I?
Any how...
DID THEIR NEW IDEA WORK OUT ALL RIGHT?
NOT QUITE.
THEY RAN BACK TO REPORT ON THEIR EXPERIMENTS HERE.
THOUGH THEY SAID THEY'D BE BACK.
I SUPPOSE THEY'RE PANICKING BECAUSE THEY'RE WORKING WITH WINTER FLOWERS AND IT'S NEARLY SPRING.
MAYBE.
OR...
IT COULD BE...
...THE ADDED STRESS OF TRYING TO MAINTAIN THEIR USUAL LEVEL OF LAB WORK ON TOP OF TACKLING ONE TRICKY CHALLENGE AFTER ANOTHER.
Like a recent manhunt, for one.
...
NOT THAT I KNOW MUCH ABOUT ALL THAT.
BUT I'VE GOT A FEELING THAT WE'RE GONNA SEE...
...THIS ORIMMALLYS PROJECT WRAP UP PRETTY SOON!
YOU KNOW?

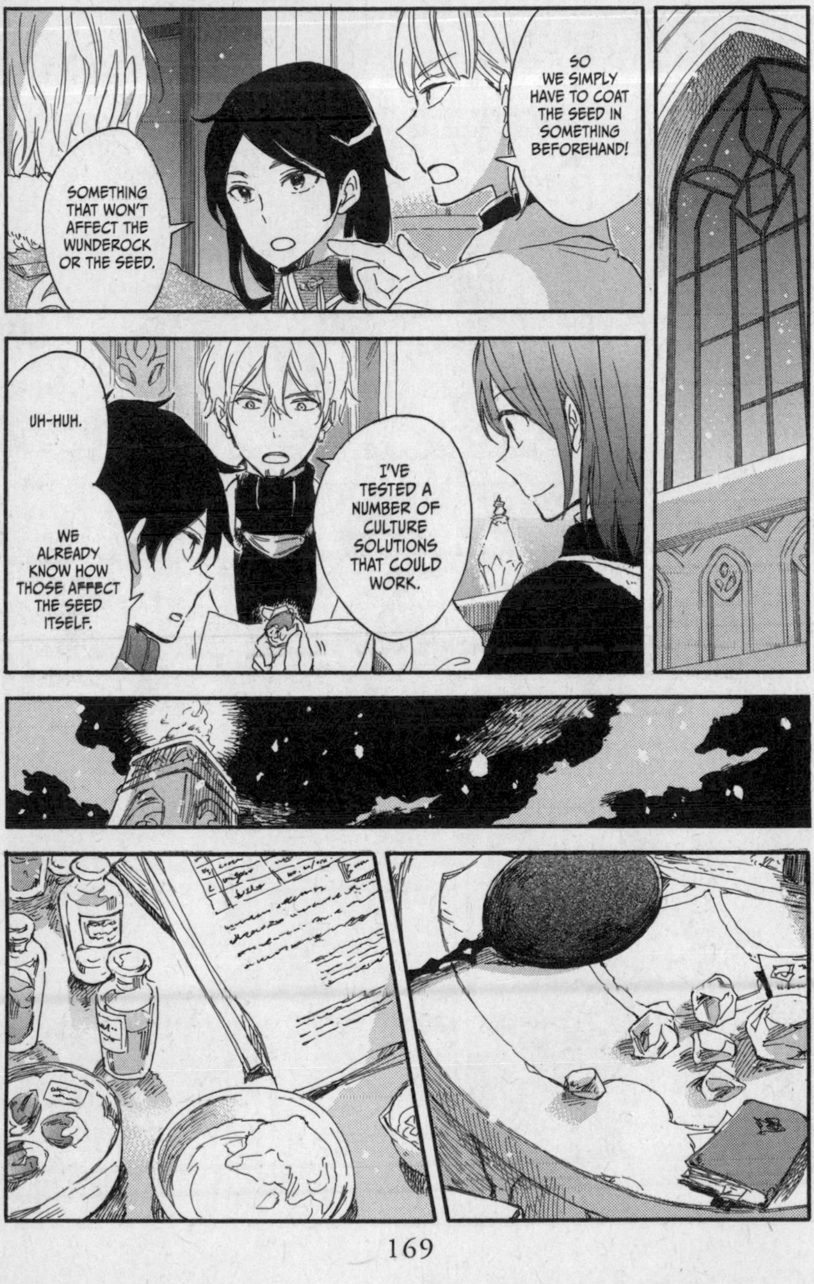
SO WE SIMPLY HAVE TO COAT THE SEED IN SOMETHING BEFOREHAND!
SOMETHING THAT WON'T AFFECT THE WUNDEROCK OR THE SEED.
I'VE TESTED A NUMBER OF CULTURE SOLUTIONS THAT COULD WORK.
UH-HUH.
WE ALREADY KNOW HOW THOSE AFFECT THE SEED ITSELF.

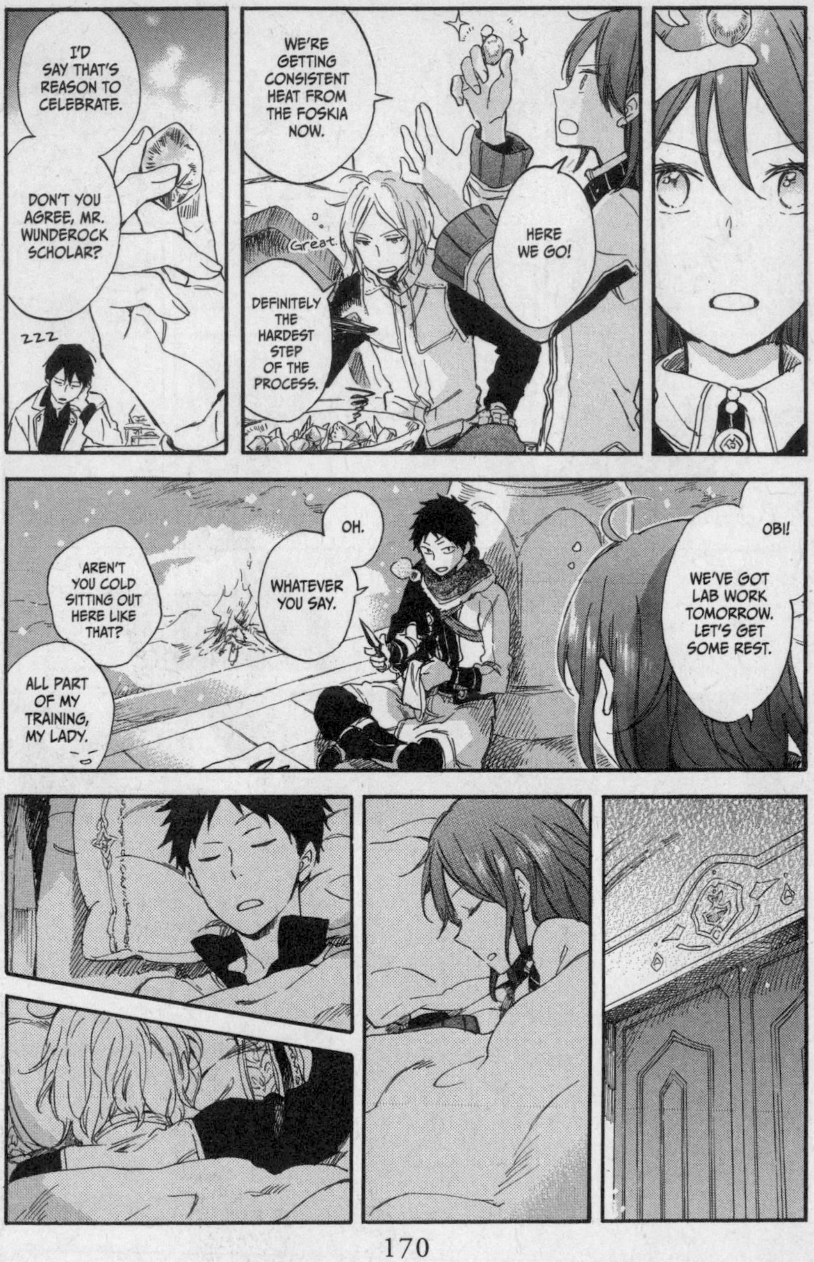
WE'RE GETTING CONSISTENT HEAT FROM THE FOSKIA NOW.
HERE WE GO!
Great.
DEFINITELY THE HARDEST STEP OF THE PROCESS.
I'D SAY THAT'S REASON TO CELEBRATE.
DON'T YOU AGREE, MR. WUNDEROCK SCHOLAR?
ZZZ
OBI!
WE'VE GOT LAB WORK TOMORROW. LET'S GET SOME REST.
OH.
WHATEVER YOU SAY.
AREN'T YOU COLD SITTING OUT HERE LIKE THAT?
ALL PART OF MY TRAINING, MY LADY.

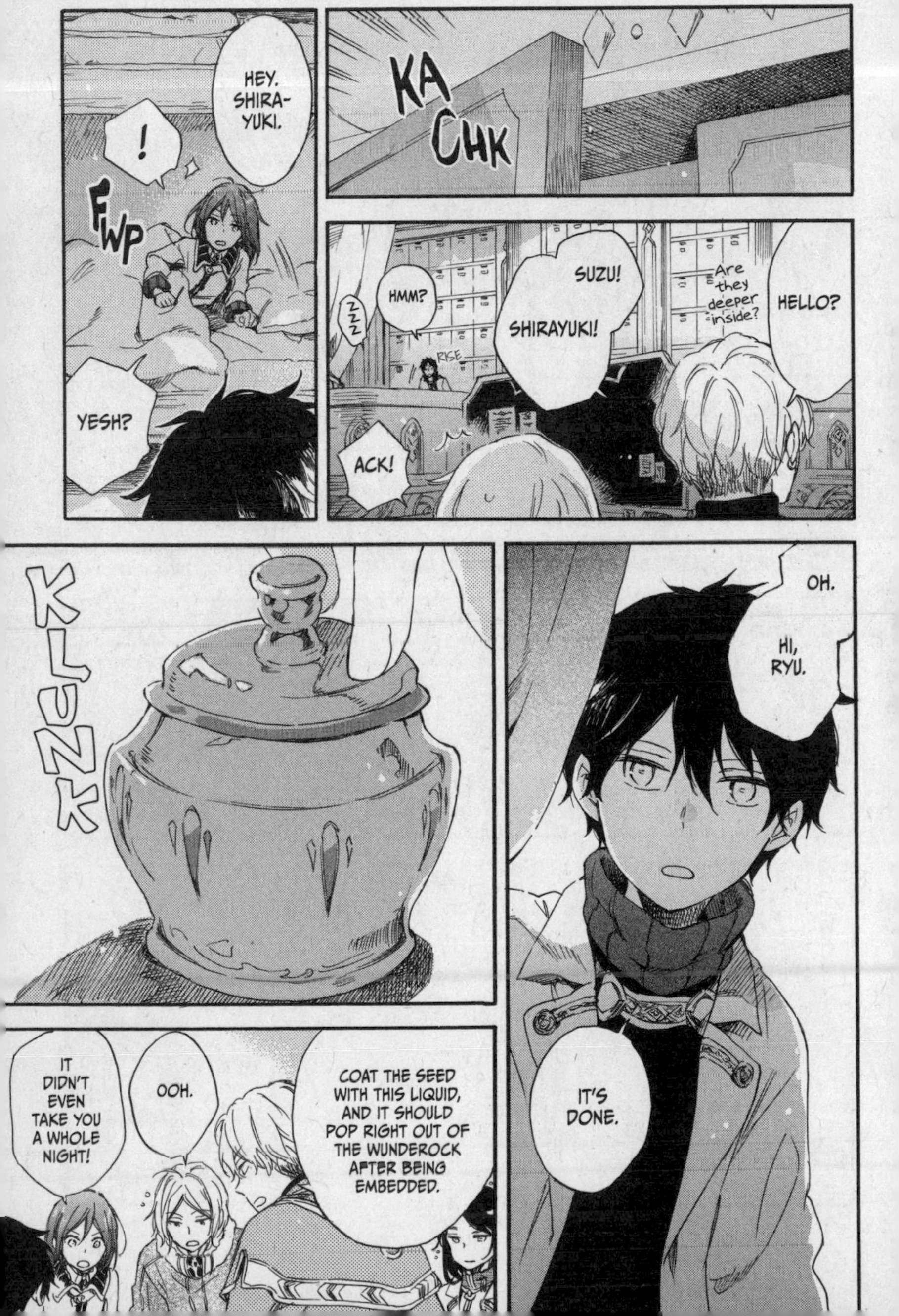
KA CHK
HELLO?
Are they deeper inside?
SUZU!
SHIRAYUKI!
HMM?
ZZZ
RISE
ACK!
HEY. SHIRA-YUKI.
!
FWP
YESH?
OH.
HI, RYU.
IT'S DONE.
KLUNK
COAT THE SEED WITH THIS LIQUID, AND IT SHOULD POP RIGHT OUT OF THE WUNDEROCK AFTER BEING EMBEDDED.
OOH.
IT DIDN'T EVEN TAKE YOU A WHOLE NIGHT!

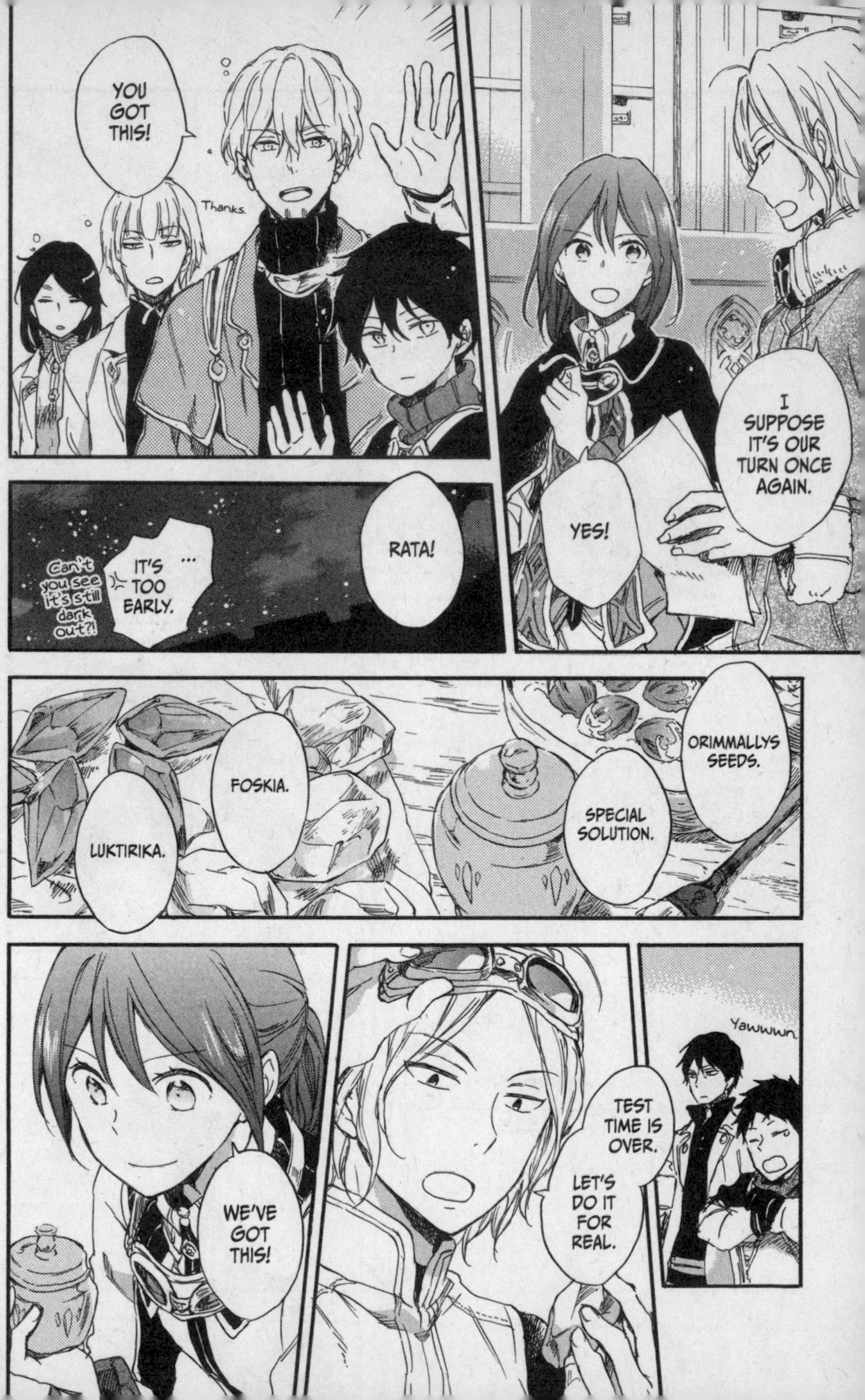
I SUPPOSE IT'S OUR TURN ONCE AGAIN.
YES!
YOU GOT THIS!
Thanks.
RATA!
IT'S TOO EARLY. ...
Can't you see it's still dark out?!
ORIMMALLYS SEEDS.
SPECIAL SOLUTION.
FOSKIA.
LUKTIRIKA.
Yawwwn.
TEST TIME IS OVER.
LET'S DO IT FOR REAL.
WE'VE GOT THIS!

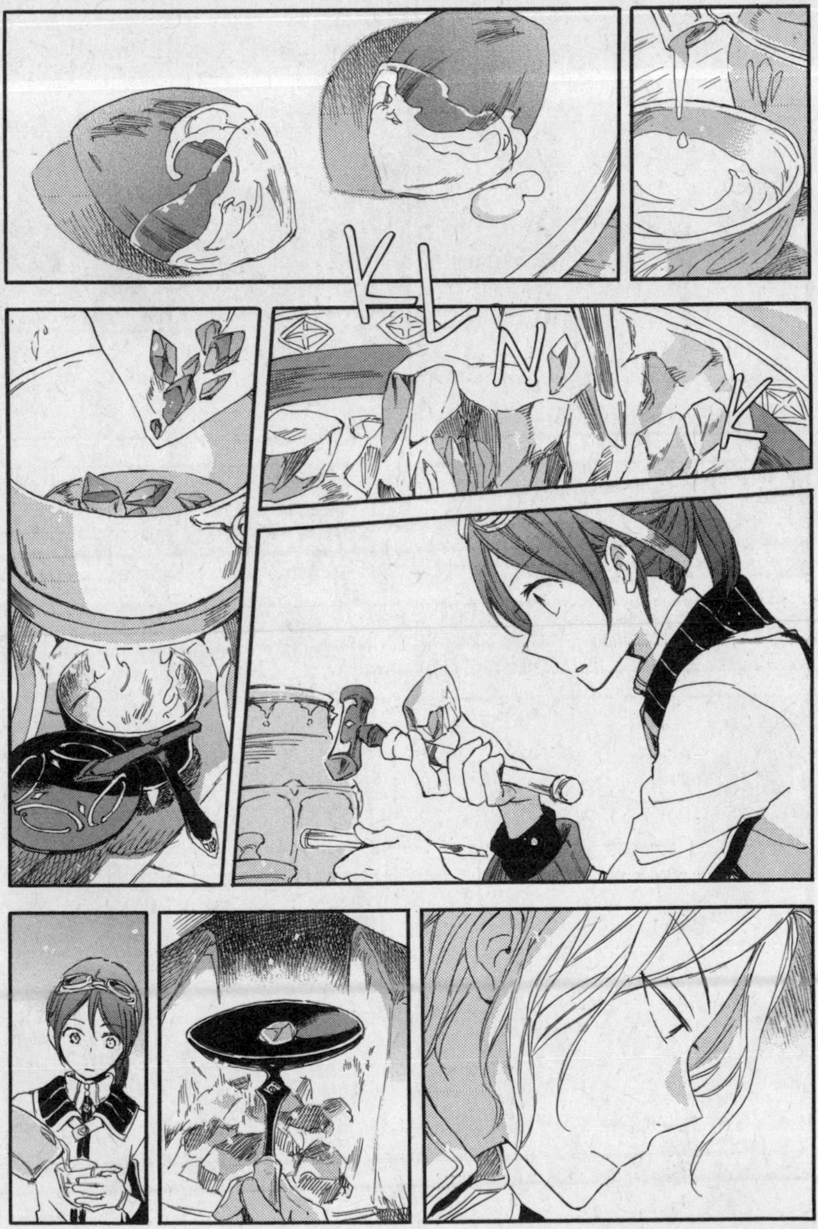
KLNK

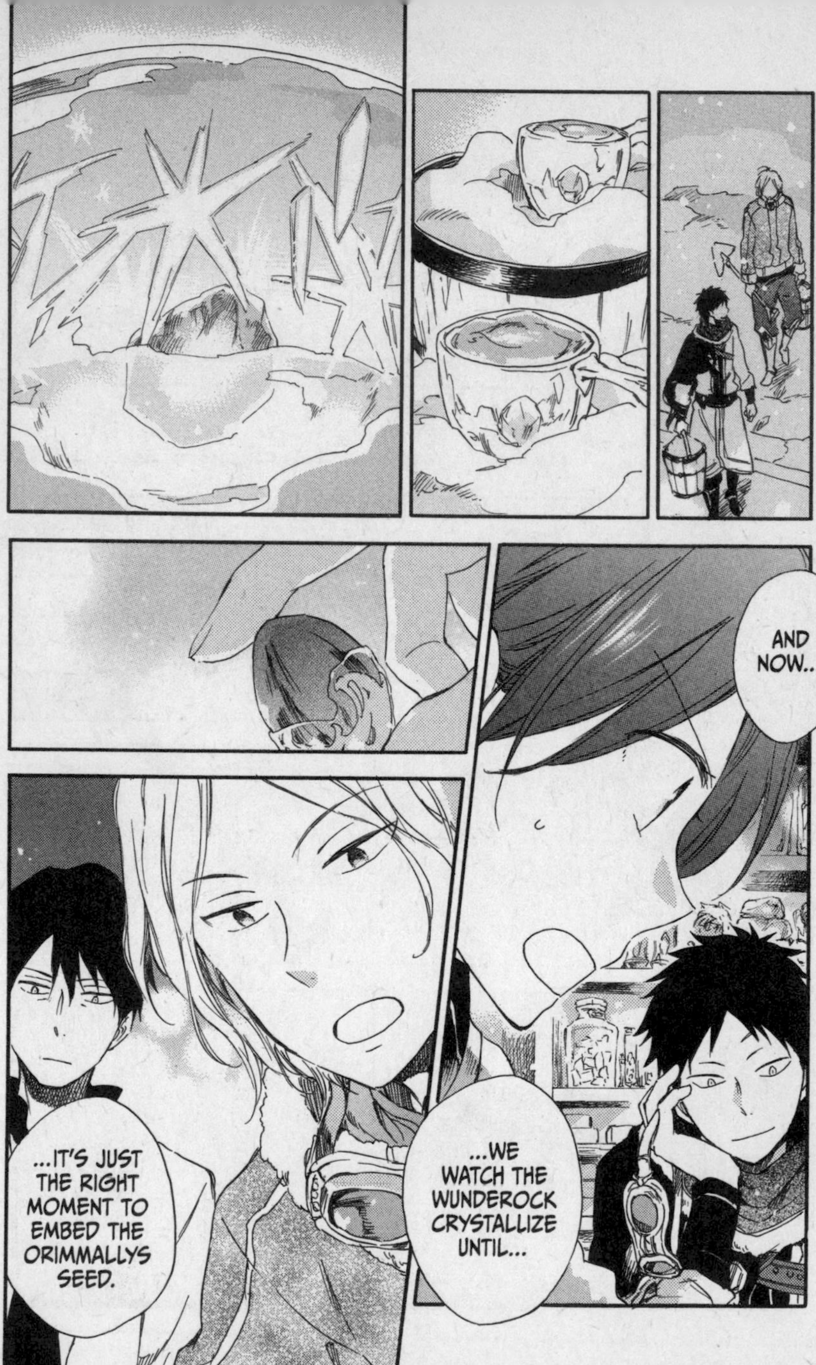
AND NOW...
...WE WATCH THE WUNDEROCK CRYSTALLIZE UNTIL...
...IT'S JUST THE RIGHT MOMENT TO EMBED THE ORIMMALLYS SEED.

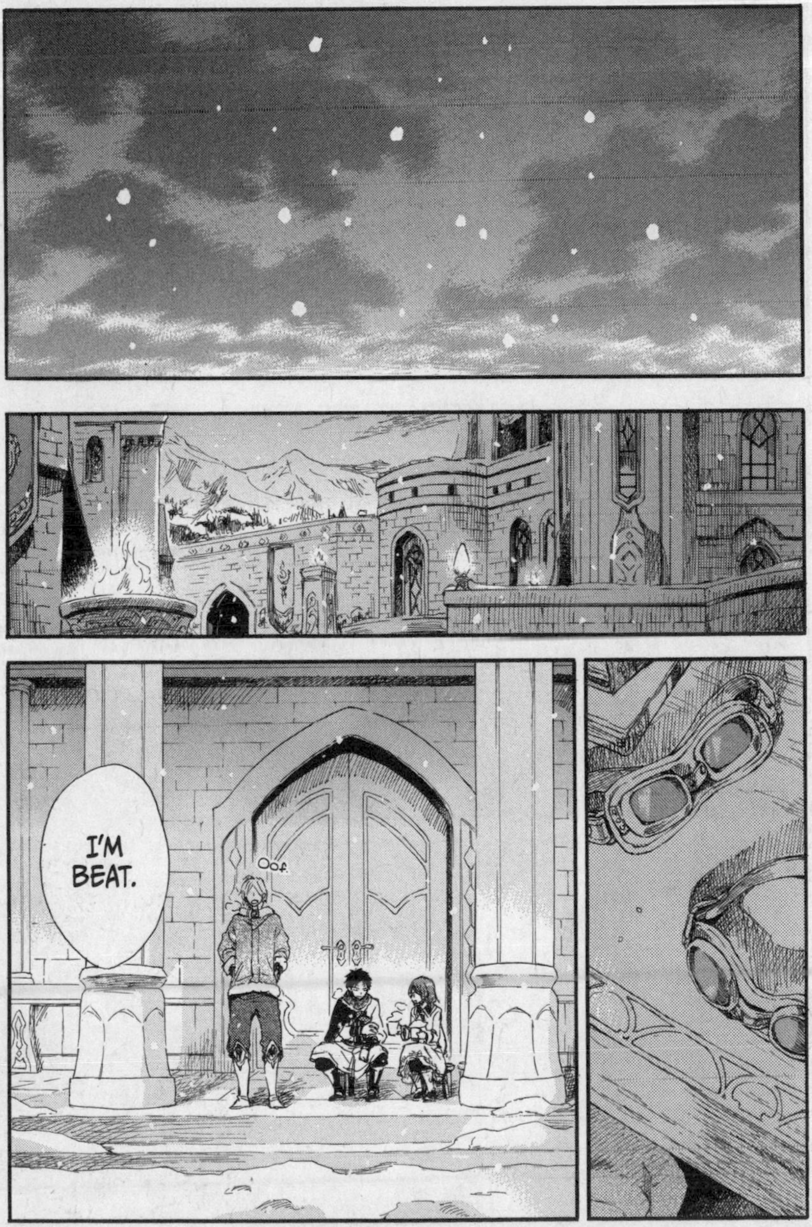
Oof.
I'M BEAT.

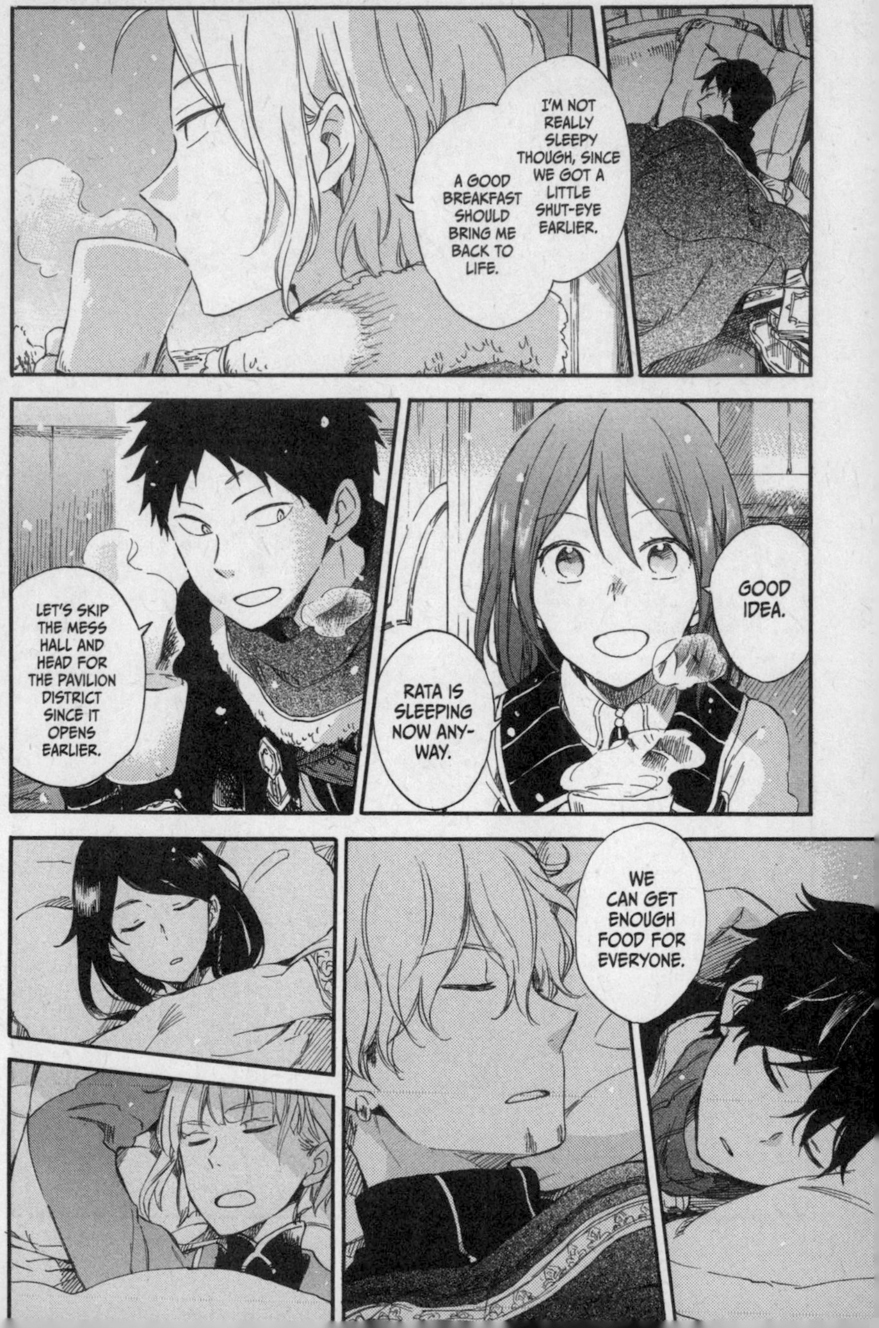
I'M NOT REALLY SLEEPY THOUGH, SINCE WE GOT A LITTLE SHUT-EYE EARLIER.
A GOOD BREAKFAST SHOULD BRING ME BACK TO LIFE.
GOOD IDEA.
RATA IS SLEEPING NOW ANY-WAY.
LET'S SKIP THE MESS HALL AND HEAD FOR THE PAVILION DISTRICT SINCE IT OPENS EARLIER.
WE CAN GET ENOUGH FOOD FOR EVERYONE.

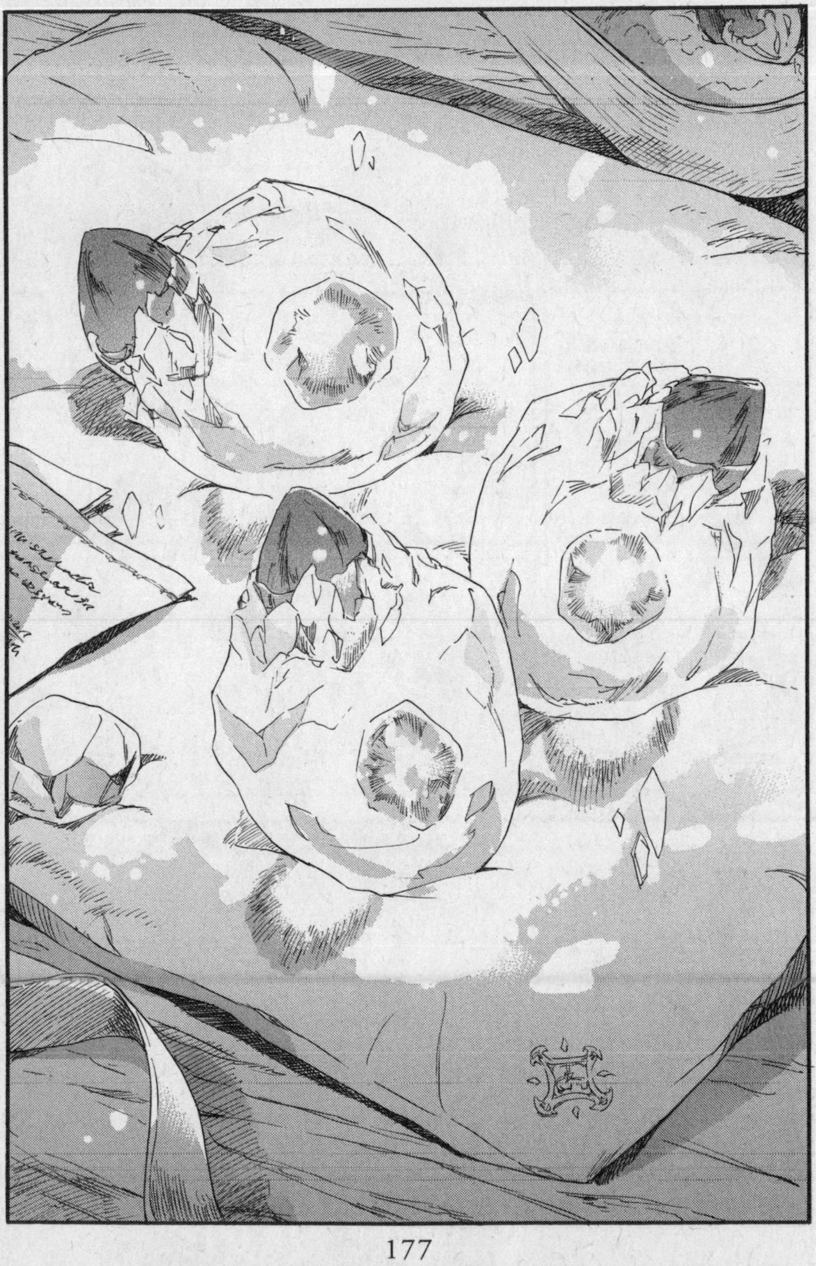

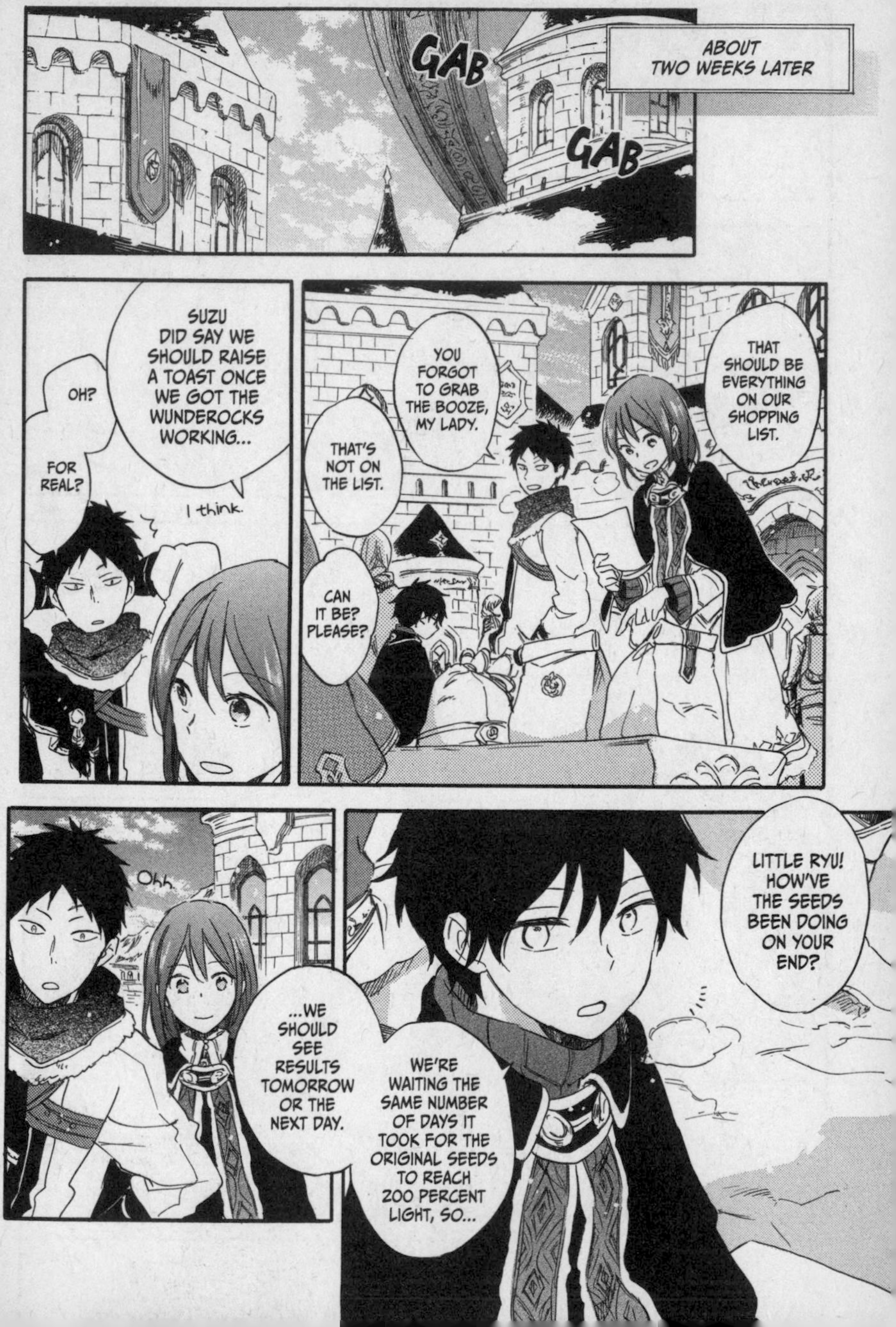
ABOUT TWO WEEKS LATER
GAB
GAB
THAT SHOULD BE EVERYTHING ON OUR SHOPPING LIST.
YOU FORGOT TO GRAB THE BOOZE, MY LADY.
THAT'S NOT ON THE LIST.
CAN IT BE? PLEASE?
SUZU DID SAY WE SHOULD RAISE A TOAST ONCE WE GOT THE WUNDEROCKS WORKING...
OH?
FOR REAL?
I think.
LITTLE RYU! HOW'VE THE SEEDS BEEN DOING ON YOUR END?
WE'RE WAITING THE SAME NUMBER OF DAYS IT TOOK FOR THE ORIGINAL SEEDS TO REACH 200 PERCENT LIGHT, SO...
...WE SHOULD SEE RESULTS TOMORROW OR THE NEXT DAY.
Ohh.

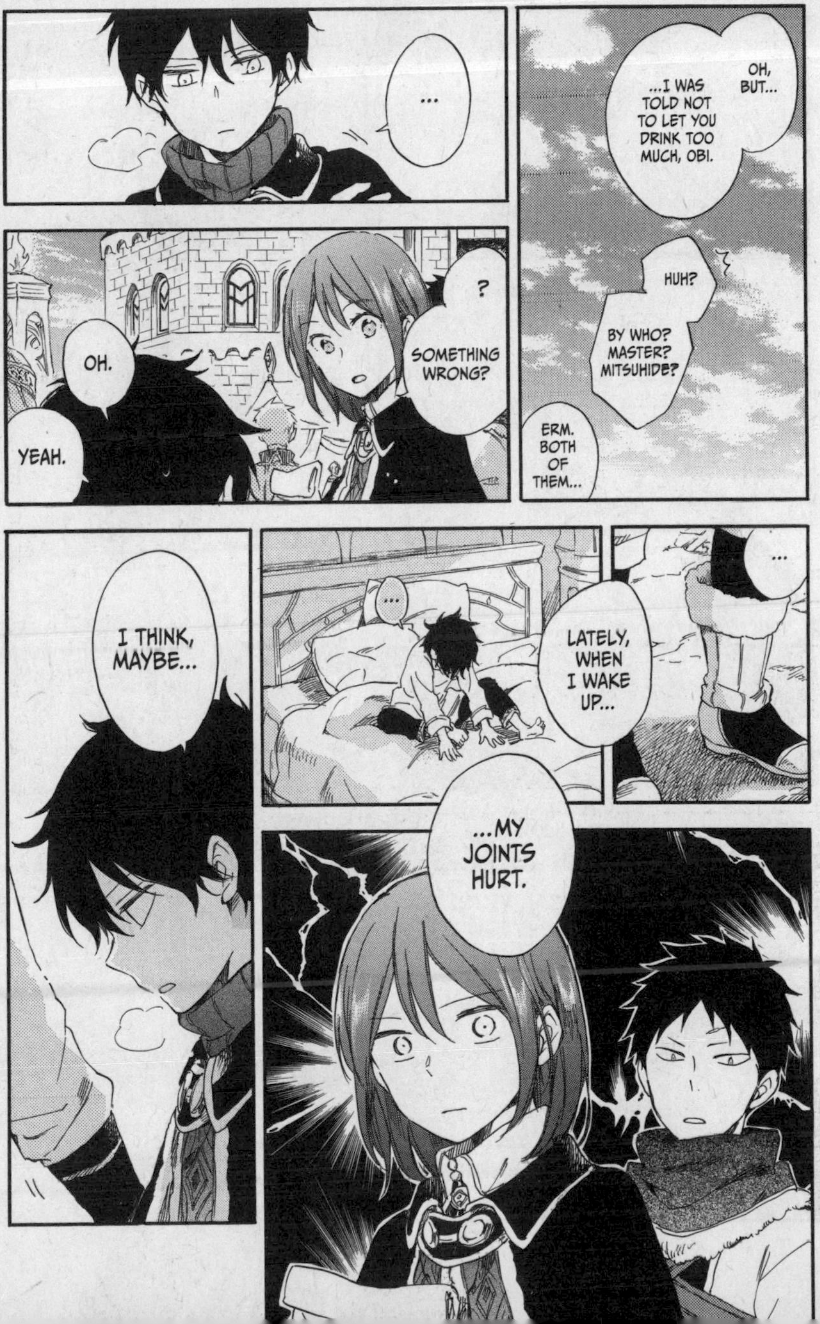
OH, BUT...
...I WAS TOLD NOT TO LET YOU DRINK TOO MUCH, OBI.
HUH?
BY WHO? MASTER? MITSUHIDE?
ERM. BOTH OF THEM...
...
?
SOMETHING WRONG?
OH.
YEAH.
...
LATELY, WHEN I WAKE UP...
...
...MY JOINTS HURT.
I THINK, MAYBE...

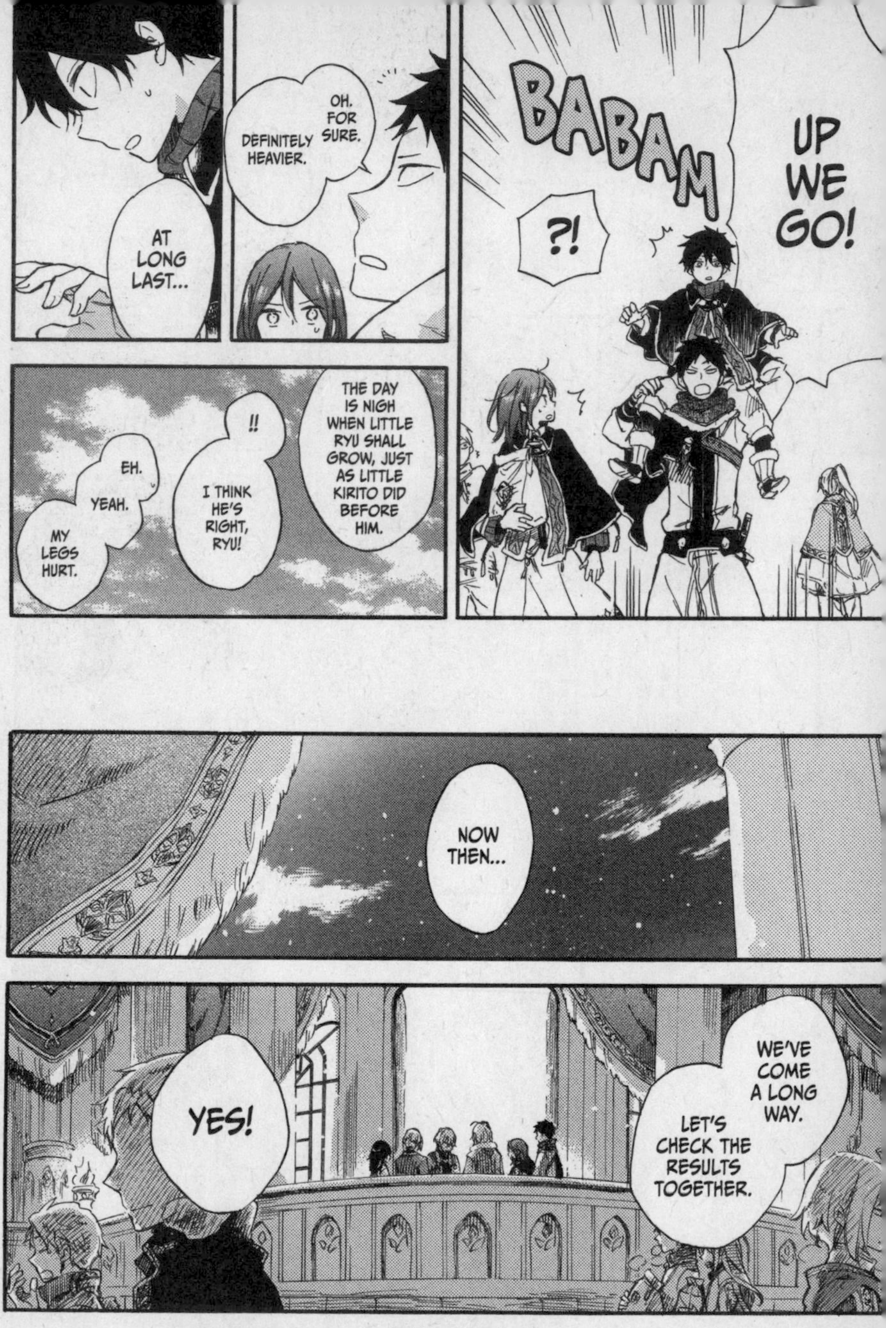

UP WE GO!
BABAM
?!
OH. FOR SURE.
DEFINITELY HEAVIER.
AT LONG LAST...
THE DAY IS NIGH WHEN LITTLE RYU SHALL GROW, JUST AS LITTLE KIRITO DID BEFORE HIM.
!!
I THINK HE'S RIGHT, RYU!
EH.
YEAH.
MY LEGS HURT.
NOW THEN...
WE'VE COME A LONG WAY.
LET'S CHECK THE RESULTS TOGETHER.
YES!

GULP

WE EXTRACTED THE LIGHT SUBSTANCE FROM SEEDS EMBEDDED IN THE HEAT WUNDEROCK.

IF THE REACTION IS JUST AS STRONG AS THE ORIGINAL ORIMMALLYS SEED'S EXTRACT, THEN...

KLUNK

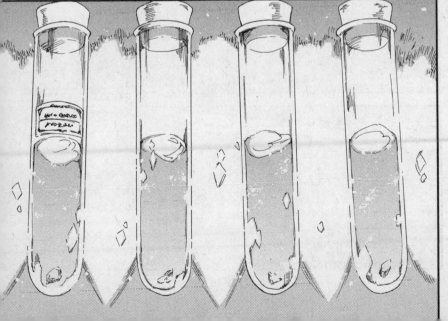

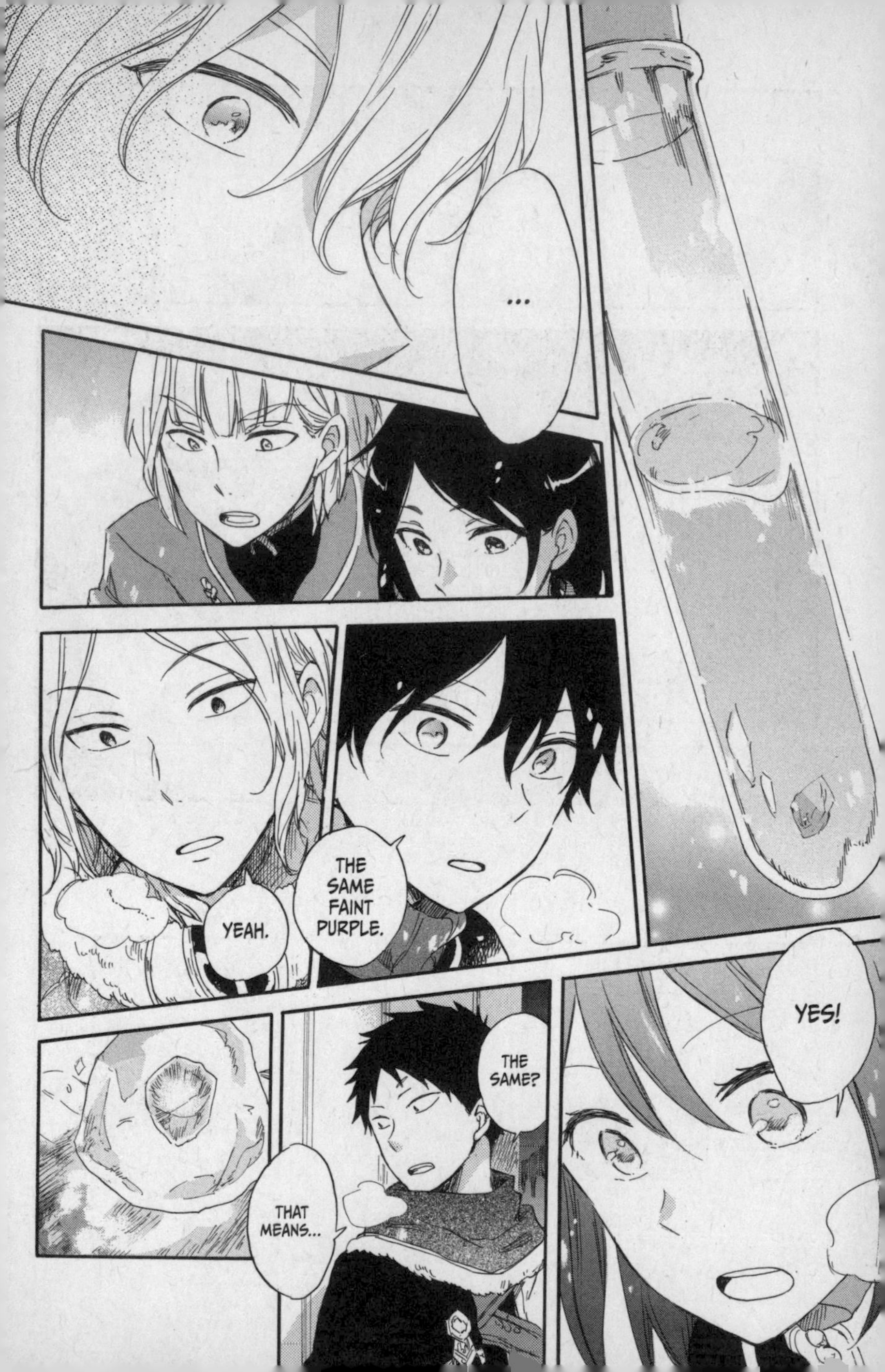
...
THE SAME FAINT PURPLE.
YEAH.
YES!
THE SAME?
THAT MEANS...

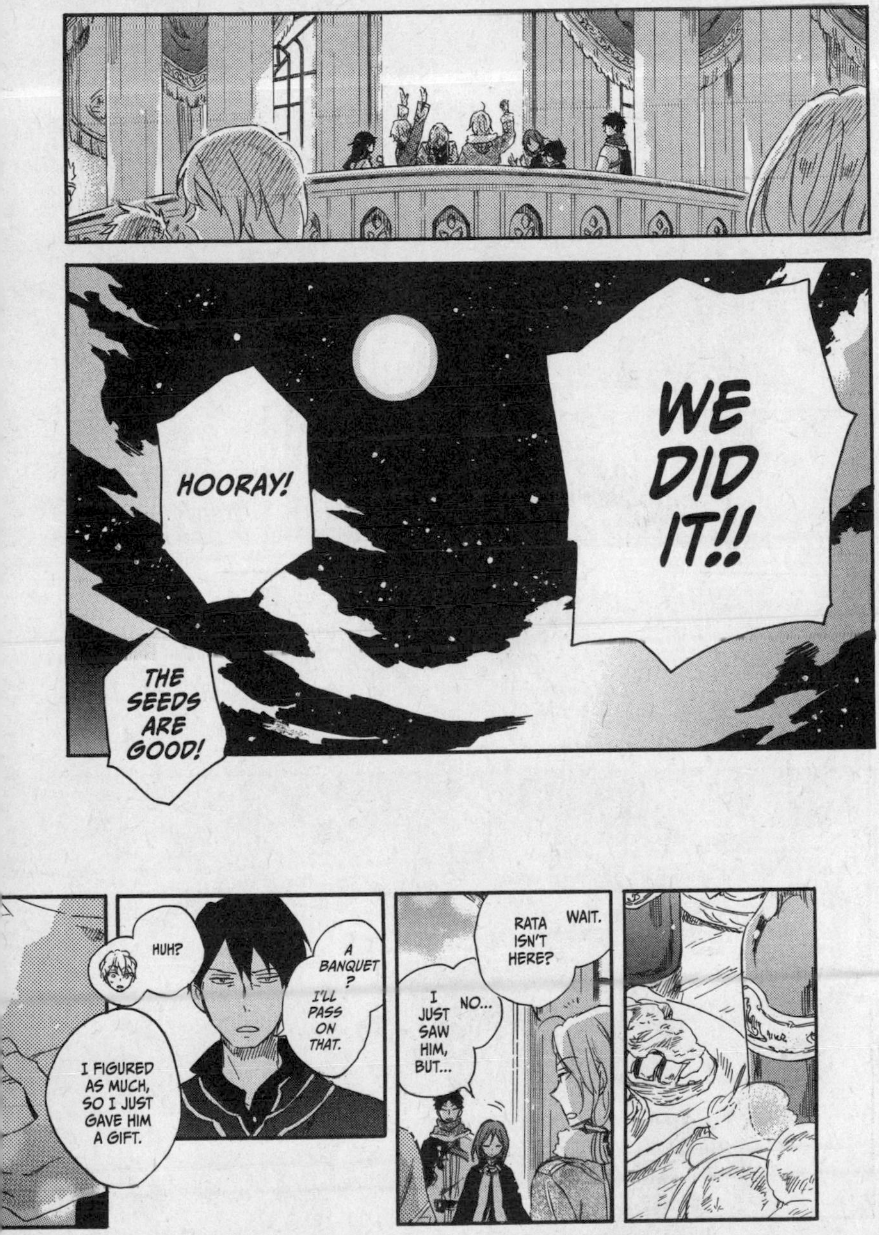
WE DID IT!!
HOORAY!
THE SEEDS ARE GOOD!
WAIT.
RATA ISN'T HERE?
NO...
I JUST SAW HIM, BUT...
A BANQUET? I'LL PASS ON THAT.
HUH?
I FIGURED AS MUCH, SO I JUST GAVE HIM A GIFT.

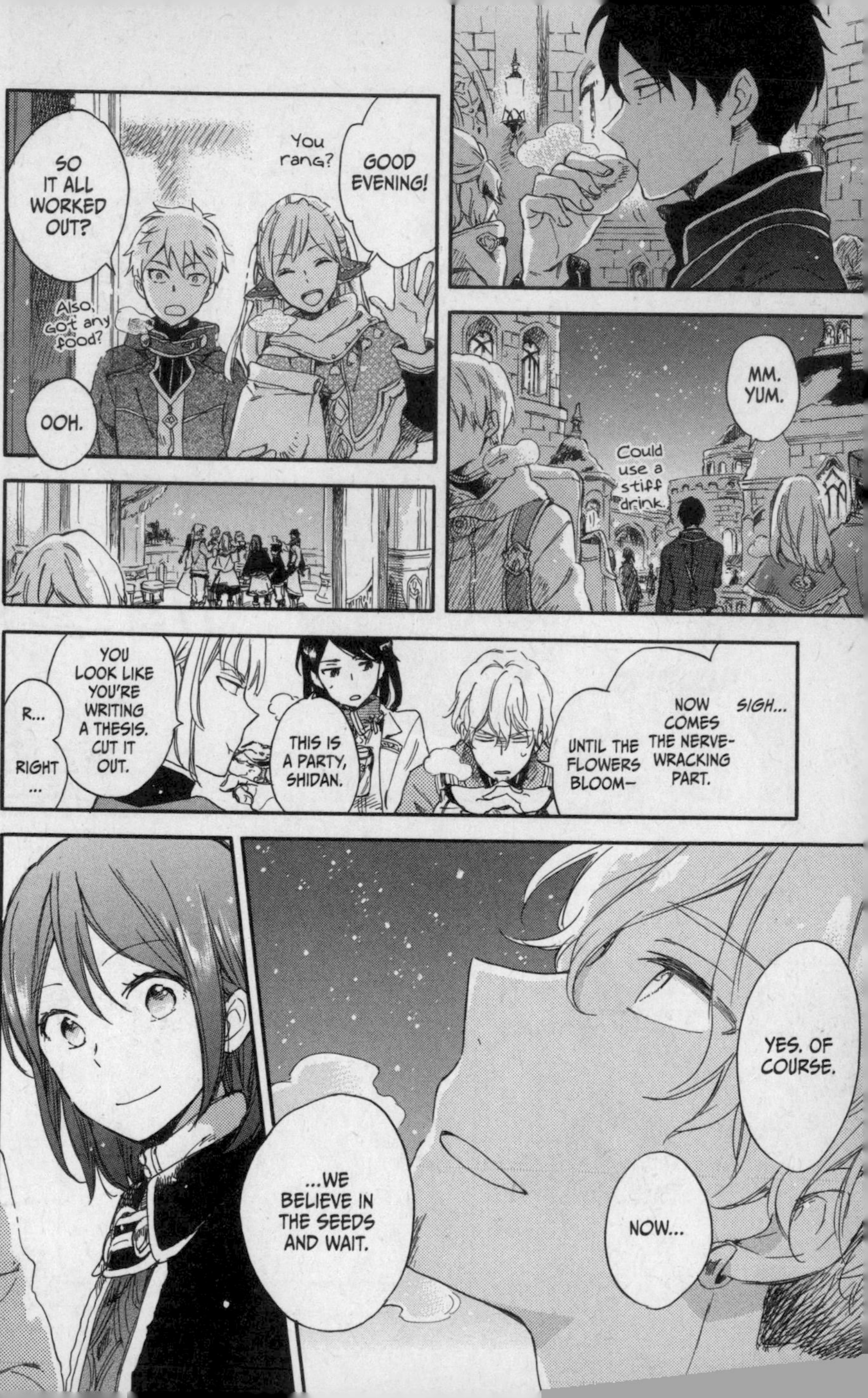
GOOD EVENING!
You rang?
SO IT ALL WORKED OUT?
Also, Got any food?
OOH.
MM. YUM.
Could use a stiff drink.
SIGH...
NOW COMES THE NERVE-WRACKING PART.
UNTIL THE FLOWERS BLOOM—
THIS IS A PARTY, SHIDAN.
YOU LOOK LIKE YOU'RE WRITING A THESIS. CUT IT OUT.
R... RIGHT...
YES. OF COURSE.
NOW...
...WE BELIEVE IN THE SEEDS AND WAIT.

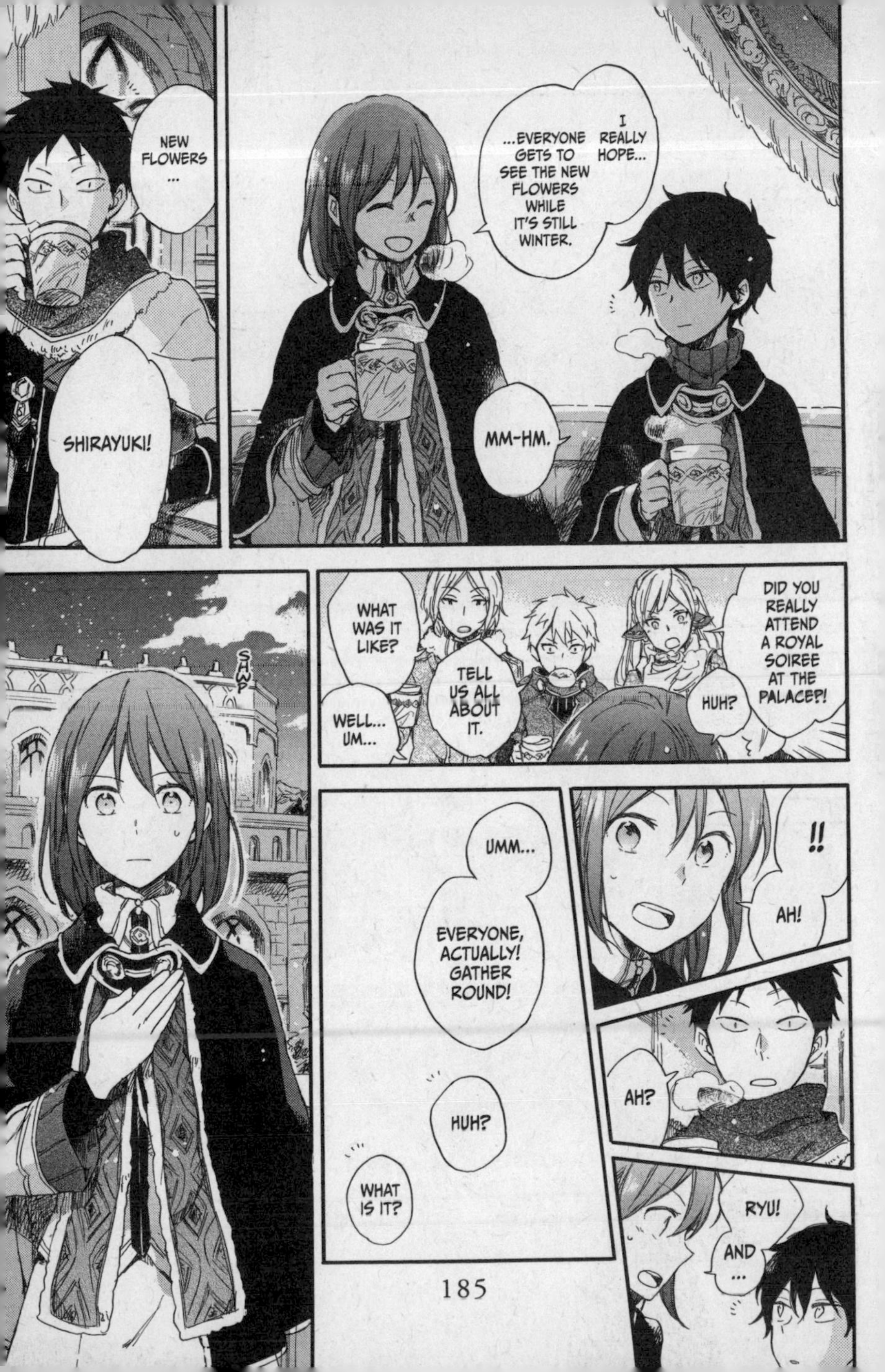
I REALLY HOPE...
...EVERYONE GETS TO SEE THE NEW FLOWERS WHILE IT'S STILL WINTER.
MM-HM.
NEW FLOWERS ...
SHIRAYUKI!
DID YOU REALLY ATTEND A ROYAL SOIREE AT THE PALACE?!
HUH?
WHAT WAS IT LIKE?
TELL US ALL ABOUT IT.
WELL... UM...
!!
AH!
AH?
RYU!
AND ...
UMM...
EVERYONE, ACTUALLY! GATHER ROUND!
HUH?
WHAT IS IT?
SHWP

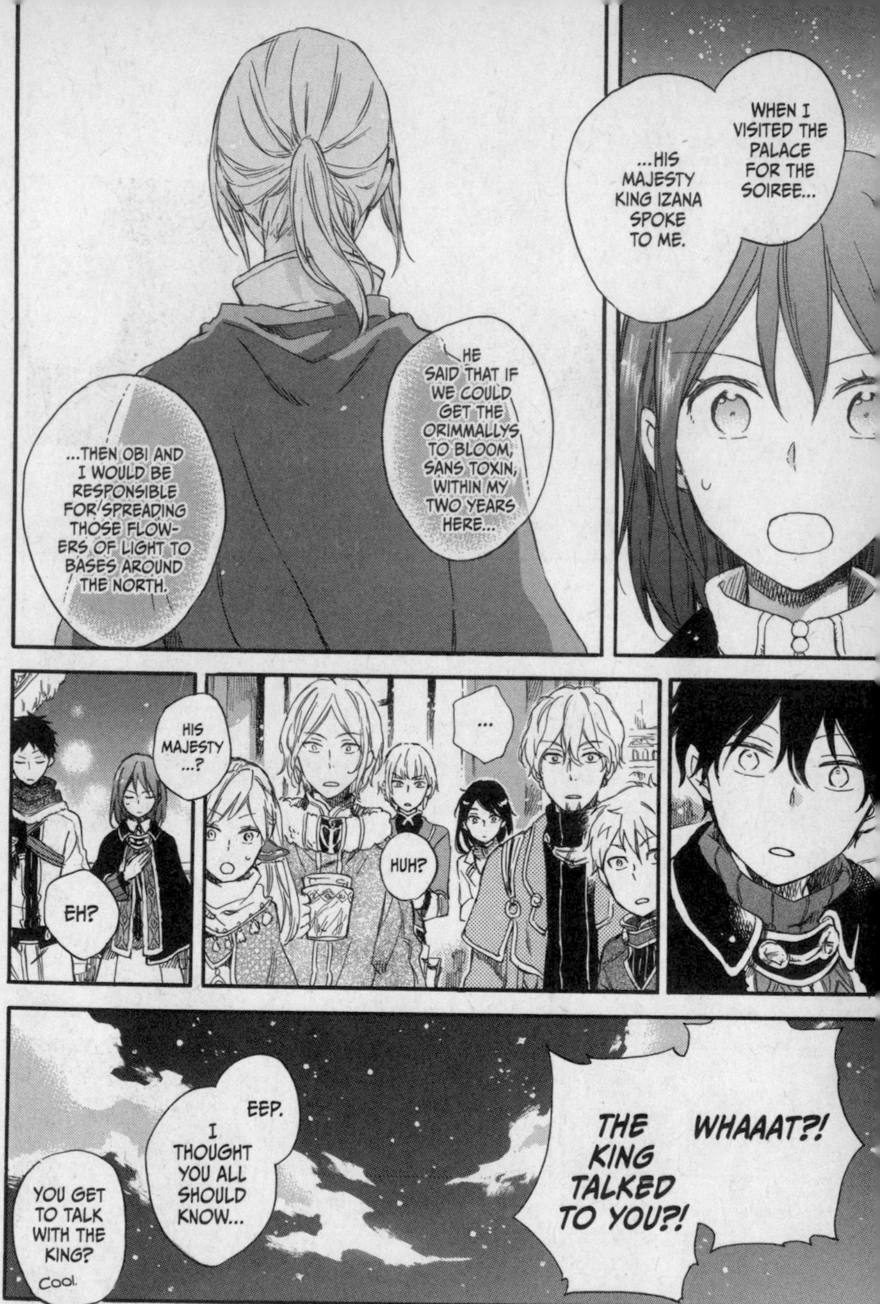
WHEN I VISITED THE PALACE FOR THE SOIREE...
...HIS MAJESTY KING IZANA SPOKE TO ME.
HE SAID THAT IF WE COULD GET THE ORIMMALLYS TO BLOOM, SANS TOXIN, WITHIN MY TWO YEARS HERE...
...THEN OBI AND I WOULD BE RESPONSIBLE FOR SPREADING THOSE FLOWERS OF LIGHT TO BASES AROUND THE NORTH.
...
HIS MAJESTY ...?
HUH?
EH?
WHAAAT?!
THE KING TALKED TO YOU?!
EEP. I THOUGHT YOU ALL SHOULD KNOW...
YOU GET TO TALK WITH THE KING?
Cool.

Snow White with the Red Hair

Vol. 15: End

Palace Gang 1

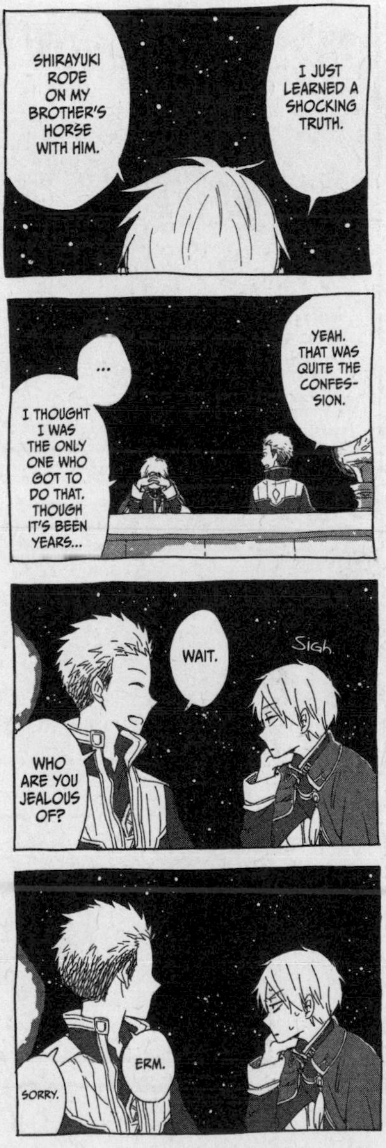
I JUST LEARNED A SHOCKING TRUTH.
SHIRAYUKI RODE ON MY BROTHER'S HORSE WITH HIM.
YEAH. THAT WAS QUITE THE CONFESSION.
...
I THOUGHT I WAS THE ONLY ONE WHO GOT TO DO THAT. THOUGH IT'S BEEN YEARS...
Sigh.
WAIT.
WHO ARE YOU JEALOUS OF?
ERM.
SORRY.

Palace Gang 2

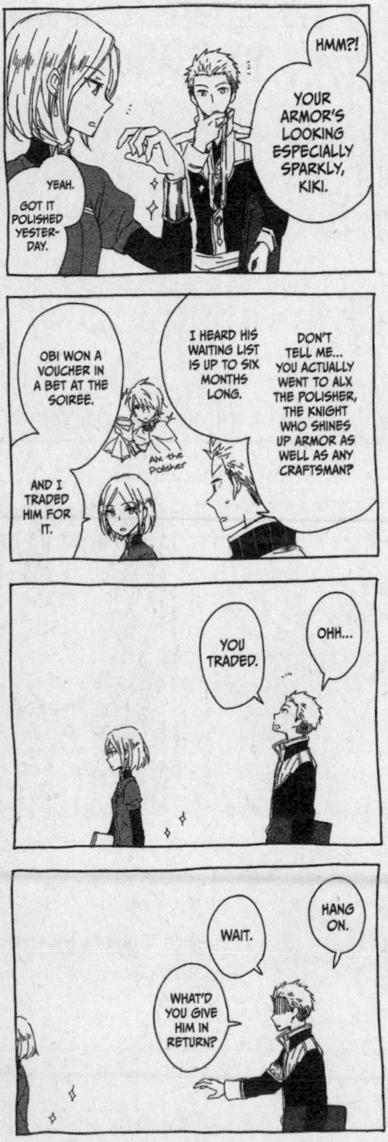
HMM?!
YOUR ARMOR'S LOOKING ESPECIALLY SPARKLY, KIKI.
YEAH. GOT IT POLISHED YESTERDAY.
DON'T TELL ME... YOU ACTUALLY WENT TO ALX THE POLISHER, THE KNIGHT WHO SHINES UP ARMOR AS WELL AS ANY CRAFTSMAN?
I HEARD HIS WAITING LIST IS UP TO SIX MONTHS LONG.
OBI WON A VOUCHER IN A BET AT THE SOIREE.
Alx the Polisher
AND I TRADED HIM FOR IT.
OHH...
YOU TRADED.
HANG ON.
WAIT.
WHAT'D YOU GIVE HIM IN RETURN?

SEASON 2 OF THE SNOW WHITE WITH THE RED HAIR ANIME IS STARTING!!

✦ Starts airing 1/11/16

✦ Official anime site:
http://clarines-kingdom.com

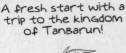

A fresh start with a trip to the kingdom of Tanbarun!

Big
✦ Thanks ✦
To:

-Ide-sama, Iwakiri-sama

-Noro-sama

-Yamashita-sama

-The editorial staff at LaLa

-Everyone in Publishing/Sales

-All the anime staff and cast

-My mother, father and sister

-All the readers out there!

December 2015
Sorata Akiduki

Sorata Akiduki was born on March 21 and is an accomplished shojo manga author. She made her debut in January 2002 with a one-shot titled "Utopia." Her previous works include *Vahlia no Hanamuko* (Vahlia's Bridegroom), *Seishun Kouryakubon* (Youth Strategy Guide) and *Natsu Yasumi Zero Zero Nichime* (00 Days of Summer Vacation). *Snow White with the Red Hair* began serialization in August 2006 in *LaLa DX* in Japan and has since moved to *LaLa*.

Snow White
with the Red Hair

15

SHOJO BEAT EDITION

STORY AND ART BY
Sorata Akiduki

TRANSLATION **Caleb Cook**
TOUCH-UP ART & LETTERING **Brandon Bovia**
DESIGN **Alice Lewis**
EDITOR **Karla Clark**

Akagami no Shirayukihime by Sorata Akiduki
© Sorata Akiduki 2016
All rights reserved.
First published in Japan in 2016 by HAKUSENSHA, Inc., Tokyo.
English language translation rights arranged with HAKUSENSHA, Inc., Tokyo.

The stories, characters and incidents mentioned
in this publication are entirely fictional.

Printed in Canada

Published by VIZ Media, LLC
P.O. Box 77010
San Francisco, CA 94107

10 9 8 7 6 5 4 3 2 1
First printing, September 2021

viz.com

shojobeat.com

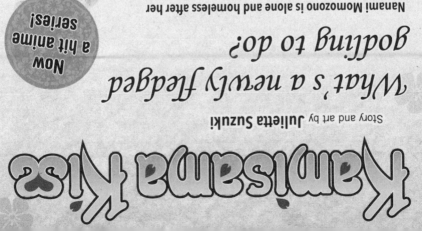

YOU'RE READING
THE WRONG WAY!

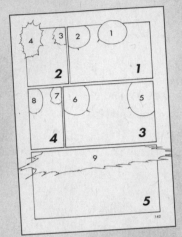

Snow White with the Red Hair reads from right to left, starting in the upper-right corner. Japanese is read from right to left, meaning that action, sound effects and word-balloon order are completely reversed from English order.

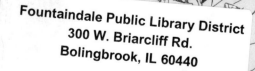